Rust Programming Cookbook

Explore the latest features of Rust 2018 for building fast and secure apps

Claus Matzinger

BIRMINGHAM - MUMBAI

Rust Programming Cookbook

Copyright © 2019 Packt Publishing

Commissioning Editor: Pavan Ramchandani
Acquisition Editor: Denim Pinto
Content Development Editor: Pathikrit Roy
Senior Editor: Storm Mann
Technical Editor: Gaurav Gala
Copy Editor: Safis Editing
Project Coordinator: Prajakta Naik
Proofreader: Safis Editing
Indexer: Pratik Shirodkar
Production Designer: Jyoti Chauhan

First published: October 2019

Production reference: 1181019

Published by Packt Publishing Ltd.
Livery Place
35 Livery Street
Birmingham
B3 2PB, UK.

ISBN 978-1-78953-066-7

www.packt.com

A book like this can only stand on the shoulders of giants – those in the Rust community and those in my life. To the community, thank you for maintaining Rust, the packages, and a great spirit; to my wife, Christine, thank you for your support, all the feedback, and for being so much more than my friend.

– Claus Matzinger

`Packt.com`

Subscribe to our online digital library for full access to over 7,000 books and videos, as well as industry leading tools to help you plan your personal development and advance your career. For more information, please visit our website.

Why subscribe?

- Spend less time learning and more time coding with practical eBooks and Videos from over 4,000 industry professionals

- Improve your learning with Skill Plans built especially for you

- Get a free eBook or video every month

- Fully searchable for easy access to vital information

- Copy and paste, print, and bookmark content

Did you know that Packt offers eBook versions of every book published, with PDF and ePub files available? You can upgrade to the eBook version at `www.packt.com` and as a print book customer, you are entitled to a discount on the eBook copy. Get in touch with us at `customercare@packtpub.com` for more details.

At `www.packt.com`, you can also read a collection of free technical articles, sign up for a range of free newsletters, and receive exclusive discounts and offers on Packt books and eBooks.

Claus and I share a common history in the Rust project. We are both members of the Rust community, and we are both Rust teachers – Claus as a book writer, and I as a trainer. We spent hours and hours thinking about where Rust can be useful and how to motivate people to apply the language to their problem domain.

Rust is a surprisingly flexible language with huge potential in all domains. From server-side distributed systems down to tiny embedded devices, Rust can be your language of choice. This can be great, but also daunting. To a beginner or even to those switching domains, this can make the language harder to approach. Cookbooks are one way to deal with this problem. They give you a small glimpse into a number of different domains and somewhere to start. These examples are not meant to be used as-is. They are a starting point to iterate away from.

Rust is, in all its perceived complexity, a language based on a strong core principle: keeping reasoning local. You don't need much context to read a Rust function. This makes small examples, like the ones in this book, the perfect starting point: whether you are using them as a reference for learning or as a basis to steadily iterate towards the solution to your problem.

To write cookbooks, you need a tinkerer that wants to play across multiple domains. Claus is such a tinkerer while also being excellent at explaining! Finding the "motivating example" is his core skill. Every time we speak, there is something new he has tinkered with. Not only that, he'll tell you the why, the how, and the what of the bit he played with along with what the bit embodies. The examples in this book are well-researched and reasoned. This gives them longevity, even if minutiae might change.

Cookbooks differ from the usual introduction book in that they don't pick a path or a story through their subject. They invite the reader to look around, find something of interest, and play with it. They are perfect for cross-reading and browsing. The metaphor of the cookbook is a strong one.

Programming language cookbooks are not for the restaurant kitchen. Restaurant kitchens need to ensure that every meal is of the same high quality, which is why they cook exactly by numbers. This book is for the home kitchen: you use an example once, to figure out how it works. Then you modify it or combine it with others. Sometimes, the result is pleasing, sometimes not. But you will have learned in the process. This exploration style of learning is strong and pleasing. A good cookbook sparks this process and the one in your hands is no exception.

Florian Gilcher
Managing Director at Ferrous Systems

Contributors

About the author

Claus Matzinger is a software engineer with a very diverse background. After working in a small company maintaining code for embedded devices, he joined a large corporation to work on legacy Smalltalk applications. This led to a great interest in programming languages early on, and Claus became the CTO for a health games start-up based on Scala technology. Since then, Claus' roles have shifted toward customer-facing roles in the IoT database technology start-up, Crate IO (creators of CrateDB), and, most recently, Microsoft. There, he hosts a podcast, writes code together with customers, and blogs about the solutions arising from these engagements. For more than 5 years, Claus has been implementing software to help customers innovate, achieve, and maintain success.

About the reviewer

Pradeep R is a software professional and technology enthusiast from Gigamon who is passionate about network programming and security. He has extensive experience in working on leading enterprise network switching, routing, and security solutions, as well as working on next-generation network pervasive visibility solutions to improve network analysis and security.

His areas of interest span over different programming languages and he extensively works with C, C++, Python, and Rust. In his spare time, he works on building competence in emerging technologies and reviews books related to software programming, the most recent being *Rust Cookbook* and *Rust Networking Basics*.

I would like to thank Vigneshwer Dhinakaran, my brother, who has shown me that boundaries exist only in our minds and that they are meant to be breached. I would also like to acknowledge, with gratitude, members of my family: my mother, Vasanthi; my grandma, Sulochana; and my sister, Deepika, for their constant encouragement and support.

Packt is searching for authors like you

If you're interested in becoming an author for Packt, please visit `authors.packtpub.com` and apply today. We have worked with thousands of developers and tech professionals, just like you, to help them share their insight with the global tech community. You can make a general application, apply for a specific hot topic that we are recruiting an author for, or submit your own idea.

Table of Contents

Preface

Several years ago, I set out learning a new programming language every year – as many programmers do. There are many paradigms, rules, and insights to be gained from knowing another programming language, and then I found Rust. Rust turned out to be too much fun to write to simply move on, and after the steep learning curve, it became even more fun. So, there I had it: having learned a total of two additional (TypeScript and Rust) languages, I stuck to Rust. Why? Let's find out.

Rust is a systems programming language that provides memory safety by default without a garbage collector, which impacts its runtime behavior. Regardless of this fact, Rust is a very versatile language that can be used across various domains, be it web programming, game engines, or web clients. Moreover, it challenges conventional thinking about scopes and memory allocation, making you a better programmer in any language, be it C#, Java, or Python. The latest push on the part of companies such as Amazon, Microsoft, and Google shows that the ecosystem has now evolved to a point where things are stabilizing enough for enterprise usage – a great sign for a future Rust professional.

In this book, we have compiled the most useful experiments with sensible use cases to make you productive fast. We have tried to cover a wide range of applications and hope you find useful concepts as well as solutions that are directly applicable to your daily development work.

Who this book is for

This book is not your typical book to learn a programming language. Instead of diving deep into concepts, we want to show a range of possible projects, solutions, and applications that provide further links to concepts and other resources. Thus, we think this book is for anyone looking to get into practical applications quickly – regardless of their Rust experience. However, programming fundamentals (in any language) are required – they are the fundamental base your Rust skills will rest on.

What this book covers

Chapter 1, *Starting off with Rust*, covers how to set up Rust toolchains on your computer and the fundamental constructs of the language. These range from writing tests and benchmarks to language constructs such as loops, `if` expressions, traits, and structs.

Chapter 2, *Going Further with Advanced Rust*, answers questions about more in-depth features of the language as well as patterns for creating meaningful programs. Topics include borrowing and ownership in complex scenarios, the Option type, pattern matching, generics, explicit lifetimes, and enums.

Chapter 3, *Managing Projects with Cargo*, uses the cargo tool to manage additional crates, extensions, projects, and tests. You will find recipes that empower you to work on larger projects and solve challenges faced in managing them.

Chapter 4, *Fearless Concurrency*, goes into some best practices and recipes to build safe, fast programs. In addition to this, popular libraries such as Rayon are presented as we demonstrate that Rust is a great language for doing all kinds of concurrent tasks.

Chapter 5, *Handling Errors and Other Results*, explains how Rust uses the Result type and panics to perform error handling, integrating most failure cases into a regular workflow that needs to be treated. This chapter shows applicable patterns and best practices around avoiding unexpected crashes and unnecessary complexity.

Chapter 6, *Expressing Yourself with Macros*, explains how Rust's unique macro system extends the functionality of programs before compilation—in a type safe way. These macros can be implemented for many possible custom scenarios, and many crates use this ability. This chapter is all about creating useful macros to make your life easier and your programs safer.

Chapter 7, *Integrating Rust with Other Languages,* uses and works with different binary units and languages from within Rust in order to port legacy software or benefit from better SDKs. This is realized mostly through the **Foreign Function Interface (FFI)**, which enables quick and easy integration with other native binaries. On top of that, it is possible to publish to npm (the Node.js package repository) from Rust using WebAssembly. These and other things are discussed in this chapter.

Chapter 8, *Safe Programming for the Web*, uses a state-of-the-art web framework to show the fundamentals of web programming – actix-web, which showcases an actor-based approach to handling requests, in productive use at Microsoft.

Chapter 9, *Systems Programming Made Easy*, explains how Rust is a great choice for running workloads on small devices with limited resources. In particular, the lack of a garbage collector and the resulting predictable runtime makes it a great fit for running sensor data collectors. Creating such a loop together with the required driver to read data is what we cover in this chapter.

`Chapter 10`, *Getting Practical with Rust*, covers practical considerations in Rust programming, such as parsing command-line arguments, working with neural networks (machine learning with PyTorch's C++ API), searching, regular expressions, web requests, and much more.

To get the most out of this book

We consider a few things in terms of programming fundamentals and we assume that you are familiar with these concepts already. Here is a list of terms you should be able to explain in a programming context:

- Types and enums
- Control statements and execution flow
- Program architectures and patterns
- Streams and iterators
- Linking
- Generics

Equipped with this knowledge, you can dive in with an editor of your choice (we recommend Visual Studio Code (`https://code.visualstudio.com`), together with the official Rust extension (`https://marketplace.visualstudio.com/items?itemName=rust-lang.rust`)). While Rust is a cross-platform programming language, some recipes are significantly easier on Linux or macOS. Windows users are encouraged to use the Windows Subsystem for Linux (`https://docs.microsoft.com/en-us/windows/wsl/install-win10`) for a better experience.

Download the example code files

You can download the example code files for this book from your account at `www.packt.com`. If you purchased this book elsewhere, you can visit `www.packtpub.com/support` and register to have the files emailed directly to you.

You can download the code files by following these steps:

1. Log in or register at `www.packt.com`.
2. Select the **Support** tab.
3. Click on **Code Downloads**.
4. Enter the name of the book in the **Search** box and follow the onscreen instructions.

Once the file is downloaded, please make sure that you unzip or extract the folder using the latest version of:

- WinRAR/7-Zip for Windows
- Zipeg/iZip/UnRarX for Mac
- 7-Zip/PeaZip for Linux

The code bundle for the book is also hosted on GitHub at `https://github.com/PacktPublishing/Rust-Programming-Cookbook`. In case there's an update to the code, it will be updated on the existing GitHub repository.

We also have other code bundles from our rich catalog of books and videos available at `https://github.com/PacktPublishing/`. Check them out!

Download the color images

We also provide a PDF file that has color images of the screenshots/diagrams used in this book. You can download it here: `https://static.packt-cdn.com/downloads/9781789530667_ColorImages.pdf`.

Code in Action

Visit the following link to check out videos of the code being run: `http://bit.ly/2oMSy1J`

Conventions used

There are a number of text conventions used throughout this book.

`CodeInText`: Indicates code words in text, database table names, folder names, filenames, file extensions, pathnames, dummy URLs, user input, and Twitter handles. Here is an example: "Mount the downloaded `WebStorm-10*.dmg` disk image file as another disk in your system."

A block of code is set as follows:

```
macro_rules! strange_patterns {
    (The pattern must match precisely) => { "Text" };
    (42) => { "Numeric" };
    (;<=,<=;) => { "Alpha" };
}
```

When we wish to draw your attention to a particular part of a code block, the relevant lines or items are set in bold:

```
#[test]
#[should_panic]
fn test_failing_make_fn() {
    make_fn!(fail, {assert!(false)});
    fail();
 }
```

Any command-line input or output is written as follows:

```
$ cargo run
```

Bold: Indicates a new term, an important word, or words that you see on screen. For example, words in menus or dialog boxes appear in the text like this. Here is an example: "Select **System info** from the **Administration** panel."

Warnings or important notes appear like this.

Tips and tricks appear like this.

Sections

In this book, you will find several headings that appear frequently (*Getting ready*, *How to do it...*, *How it works...*, *There's more...*, and *See also*).

To give clear instructions on how to complete a recipe, use these sections as follows:

Getting ready

This section tells you what to expect in the recipe and describes how to set up any software or any preliminary settings required for the recipe.

How to do it...

This section contains the steps required to follow the recipe.

How it works...

This section usually consists of a detailed explanation of what happened in the previous section.

There's more...

This section consists of additional information about the recipe in order to make you more knowledgeable about the recipe.

See also

This section provides helpful links to other useful information for the recipe.

Get in touch

Feedback from our readers is always welcome.

General feedback: If you have questions about any aspect of this book, mention the book title in the subject of your message and email us at customercare@packtpub.com.

Errata: Although we have taken every care to ensure the accuracy of our content, mistakes do happen. If you have found a mistake in this book, we would be grateful if you would report this to us. Please visit www.packtpub.com/support/errata, selecting your book, clicking on the Errata Submission Form link, and entering the details.

Piracy: If you come across any illegal copies of our works in any form on the internet, we would be grateful if you would provide us with the location address or website name. Please contact us at copyright@packt.com with a link to the material.

If you are interested in becoming an author: If there is a topic that you have expertise in, and you are interested in either writing or contributing to a book, please visit authors.packtpub.com.

Reviews

Please leave a review. Once you have read and used this book, why not leave a review on the site that you purchased it from? Potential readers can then see and use your unbiased opinion to make purchase decisions, we at Packt can understand what you think about our products, and our authors can see your feedback on their book. Thank you!

For more information about Packt, please visit `packt.com`.

Starting Off with Rust 1

The Rust ecosystem has grown considerably over the last year, and the 2018 edition, in particular, brought a significant push toward stabilization. The tooling is developing and important libraries are maturing to a point where many bigger companies use Rust in production.

One of the features of Rust is a steep learning curve—which is mostly due to a fundamental change in how to think about memory allocation. It is not uncommon for experienced programmers in other languages (such as C#) to feel overwhelmed with the way things are done in Rust. In this chapter, we will try to overcome this and lower the bar to get started!

In this chapter, we will cover the following recipes:

- Getting everything ready
- Working with the command line I/O
- Creating and using data types
- Controlling execution flow
- Splitting your code with crates and modules
- Writing tests and benchmarks
- Documenting your code
- Testing your documentation
- Sharing code among types
- Sequence types in Rust
- Debugging Rust

Setting up your environment

Since the programming language comes with a variety of toolchains, tools, linkers, and compiler versions, choosing the best-fitting variation is not easy. Additionally, Rust works on all major operating systems—which adds another variable.

However, installing Rust has become a trivial task when using `rustup` (`https://rustup.rs/`). On the website, a helpful script (or installer on Windows) that takes care of retrieving and installing the required components can be downloaded. The same tool lets you switch between and update (and uninstall) these components as well. This is the recommended way.

 Choosing to use the **Microsoft Visual Studio Compiler** (**MSVC**) together with Rust requires that you install additional software such as the Visual C++ runtime and compiler tools.

To write code, an editor is also required. Since Visual Studio Code sports some Rust parts, it is a great choice together with the Rust extension. It's an open source editor developed by Microsoft and is well received across the world and the Rust community. In this recipe, we will install the following components:

- Visual Studio Code (`https://code.visualstudio.com/`)
- `rustup` (`https://rustup.rs`)
- `rustc` (and the rest of the compiler toolchains)
- `cargo`
- **RLS** (short for **Rust Language Server**—this is for autocompletion)
- Rust language support for Visual Studio Code

Getting ready

On a computer running either macOS, Linux, or Windows, only a web browser and internet connection are required. Bear in mind that the Windows installation works a little bit different from the ***nix** systems (Linux and macOS), which use scripts.

How to do it...

Each of the parts requires us to navigate to their respective websites, download the installer, and follow their instructions:

1. Open the browser and navigate to `https://rustup.rs` and `https://code.visualstudio.com/`.
2. Choose the installers fit for your operating system.
3. After downloading, run the installers and follow their instructions, choosing the `stable` branches.
4. Once successfully installed, we'll go deeper into each installation.

Now, let's go behind the scenes to understand the installation better

Managing the Rust installation with rustup.rs

To test whether the installation of the Rust toolchain with `rustup` was successful, the `rustc` command is available to run in Terminal (or PowerShell on Windows):

```
$ rustc --version
rustc 1.33.0 (2aa4c46cf 2019-02-28)
```

Note that you will have a later version when you are running this. It doesn't matter if you stick to the 2018 edition for your code.

 Rust requires a native linker to be available on your system. On Linux or Unix systems (such as macOS), Rust calls `cc` for linking, whereas on Windows, the linker of choice is Microsoft Visual Studio's linker, which depends on having Microsoft Visual C++ Build Tools installed. While it's possible to use an open source toolchain on Windows as well, this exercise is left for more advanced users.

Even with the 2018 edition, some useful features are still only available on `nightly`. To install the nightly edition of `rustc`, perform these steps:

1. Run `rustup install nightly` (use `nightly-msvc` on Windows if you are not using the GNU toolchain) in a Terminal or PowerShell window.
2. After the command finishes, the default toolchain (used in `cargo`) can be switched using `rustup default nightly`.

Installing Visual Studio Code and extensions

In its vanilla version, Visual Studio Code comes with syntax highlighting for many languages. However, for autocompletion or/and checking syntax, an extension is required. The Rust project supplies this extension:

1. Open Visual Studio Code.
2. Use *Ctrl + P* (*cmd + P* on macOS) to open the command-line interface, then type `ext install rust-lang.rust` to install the extension. The process should look like this:

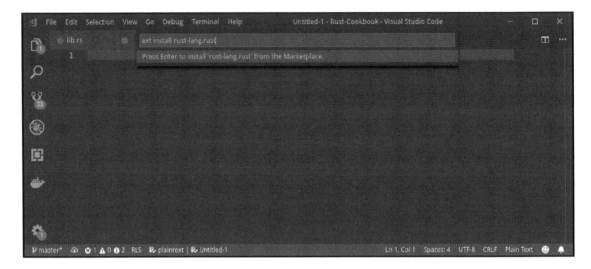

The extension uses RLS to do static code analysis and provide completion and syntax checking. The extension *should* install the RLS component automatically, but sometimes it will fail to do this. One solution is to add the following configuration to Visual Studio Code's `settings.json` file (use *Ctrl + P/cmd + P* to find it):

```
{
    "rust-client.channel":"stable"
}
```

Alternatively, `rustup` will also install RLS with the `rustup component add rls` command.

Troubleshooting

Occasionally, updating the tools will lead to errors that files are missing or cannot be overwritten. This can be for a wide range of reasons, but a full reset of the installations can help. On Linux or macOS systems, the following command takes care of deleting anything `rustup` installed:

```
$ rm -Rf ~/.rustup
```

Windows's PowerShell now supports many Linux-like commands:

```
PS> rm ~/.rustup
```

This leads to the same result. After deleting the current installation, install `rustup` from scratch—this should install the latest version.

Now, let's go behind the scenes to understand the code better.

How it works...

The shell script, `rustup.sh`, is a great way to install Rust and it is the primary way to install Rust and other components today. In fact, it is common to use the script also in CI systems to install the compiler and other tools.

`rustup` is an open source project maintained by the Rust project and can be found on GitHub: `https://github.com/rust-lang/rustup.rs`.

We've successfully learned how to set up our environment. Now let's move on to the next recipe.

Working with the command line I/O

The traditional way of communicating with the user on the command line is using standard streams. Rust includes helpful macros to deal with these simple cases. In this recipe, we will explore the basic workings of the classic `Hello World` program.

How to do it...

In just five steps, we will explore command line I/O and formatting:

1. Open a Terminal window (PowerShell on Windows) and run the `cargo new hello-world` command, which creates a new Rust project in a `hello-world` folder.

2. Once created, change into the directory with `cd hello-world` and open `src/main.rs` with a Visual Studio Code. The default code generated by `cargo` looks like this:

```
fn main() {
    println!("Hello, world!");
}
```

3. Let's expand it! These are variations on the preceding traditional `print` statement, showing some formatting options, parameters, and writing on streams, among other things. Let's start with some common prints (and imports):

```
use std::io::{self, Write};
use std::f64;

fn main() {
    println!("Let's print some lines:");
    println!();
    println!("Hello, world!");
    println!("{}, {}!", "Hello", "world");
    print!("Hello, ");
    println!("world!");
```

However, we can do much more complex argument combinations:

```
println!("Arguments can be referred to by their position: {0},
{1}! and {1}, {0}! are built from the same arguments", "Hello",
"world");

println!("Furthermore the arguments can be named: \"{greeting},
{object}!\"", greeting = "Hello", object = "World");

println!("Number formatting: Pi is {0:.3} or {0:.0} for short",
f64::consts::PI);

println!("... and there is more: {0:>0width$}={0:>width$}=
{0:#x}", 1535, width = 5);

let _ = write!(&mut io::stdout(), "Underneath, it's all writing
```

```
        to a stream...");
        println!();

        println!("Write something!");
        let mut input = String::new();
        if let Ok(n) = io::stdin().read_line(&mut input) {
            println!("You wrote: {} ({} bytes) ", input, n);
        }
        else {
            eprintln!("There was an error :(");
        }
    }
}
```

This should provide several variations of reading and writing to the console.

4. Go back to Terminal and navigate to the directory where `Cargo.toml` is located.

5. Use `cargo run` to see the snippet's output:

```
$ cargo run
   Compiling hello-world v0.1.0 (/tmp/hello-world)
    Finished dev [unoptimized + debuginfo] target(s) in 0.37s
     Running 'target/debug/hello-world'
Let's print some lines:

Hello, world!
Hello, world!
Hello, world!
Arguments can be referred to by their position: Hello, world! and
world, Hello! are built from the same arguments
Furthermore the arguments can be named: "Hello, World!"
Number formatting: Pi is 3.142 or 3 for short
... and there is more: 01535= 1535=0x5ff
Underneath, it's all writing to a stream...
Write something!
Hello, world!
You wrote: Hello, world!
  (14 bytes)
```

Each line in the output represents a way to print text to the console! We recommend playing with the variations and seeing how it changes the result. On a side note, `rustc` will check for the correct number of arguments in any `println!()` or `format!()` call.

Now, let's go behind the scenes to understand the code better.

How it works...

Let's go through the code to understand the execution flow.

cargo is described in depth in Chapter 2, *Managing Projects with Cargo*, in this book.

The initial snippet is generated when cargo new hello-world is executed in *step 1*. As a project of type binary, a main function is required and rustc will be looking for it. Upon calling cargo run, cargo orchestrates compilation (with rustc) and linking (msvc on Windows, cc on *nix) and runs the resultant binary via its entry point: the main function (*step 5*).

In the function we create in *step 3*, we write a series of print!/println!/eprintln! statements, which are Rust macros. These macros facilitate the writing to the standard output or standard error channels of a command-line application and include additional arguments. In fact, if arguments are missing, the compiler won't compile the program.

Rust's macros work directly on the syntax tree of the language, providing type safety and the ability to check the parameters and arguments. Therefore, they can be seen as a function call with a few special abilities—but more on that in Chapter 6, *Expressing Yourself with Macros*.

The various arguments and the template string are combined using formatters, a powerful way to add real variables to the output without the need of concatenations or similar workarounds. This will reduce the number of allocations, considerably improving performance and memory efficiency. There is a wide range of how to format data types; to understand it more deeply, check out Rust's excellent documentation (https://doc.rust-lang.org/std/fmt/).

The last step then shows the output that the various combinations produced.

We've successfully learned to work with the command line I/O. Now, let's move on to the next recipe.

Creating and using data types

Rust features all of the basic types: signed and unsigned integers up to 64 bits in width; floating-point types up to 64 bits; character types; and Booleans. Of course, any program will need more complex data structures to remain readable.

 If you are unfamiliar with unit tests in Rust (or in general), we suggest going through the *Writing tests and benchmarks* recipe here in this chapter first.

In this recipe, we'll look at good basic practices to create and use data types.

How to do it...

Let's use Rust's unit tests as a playground for some data type experiments:

1. Create a new project using `cargo new data-types -- lib` and use an editor to open the `projects` directory.
2. Open `src/lib.rs` in your favorite text editor (Visual Studio Code).
3. In there, you will find a small snippet to run a test:

```
#[cfg(test)]
mod tests {
    #[test]
    fn it_works() {
        assert_eq!(2 + 2, 4);
    }
}
```

4. Let's replace the default test to play with various standard data types. This test uses a few ways to work with data types and their math functions, as well as mutability and overflows:

```
#[test]
fn basic_math_stuff() {
    assert_eq!(2 + 2, 4);

    assert_eq!(3.14 + 22.86, 26_f32);

    assert_eq!(2_i32.pow(2), 4);
    assert_eq!(4_f32.sqrt(), 2_f32);

    let a: u64 = 32;
```

```
        let b: u64 = 64;

        // Risky, this could overflow
        assert_eq!(b - a, 32);
        assert_eq!(a.overflowing_sub(b), (18446744073709551584,
        true));
        let mut c = 100;
        c += 1;
        assert_eq!(c, 101);
    }
```

5. Having the basic numeric types covered, let's check a major limitation: overflows! Rust panics when an overflow occurs, so we are going to expect that with the #[should_panic] attribute (the test will actually fail if it doesn't panic):

```
#[test]
#[should_panic]
fn attempt_overflows() {
    let a = 10_u32;
    let b = 11_u32;

    // This will panic since the result is going to be an
    // unsigned type which cannot handle negative numbers
    // Note: _ means ignore the result
    let _ = a - b;
}
```

6. Next, let's create a custom type as well. Rust's types are structs and they add no overhead in memory. The type features a new() (constructor by convention) and a sum() function, both of which we'll call in a test function:

```
// Rust allows another macro type: derive. It allows to "auto-
implement"
// supported traits. Clone, Debug, Copy are typically handy to
derive.
#[derive(Clone, Debug, Copy)]
struct MyCustomStruct {
    a: i32,
    b: u32,
    pub c: f32
}

// A typical Rust struct has an impl block for behavior
impl MyCustomStruct {
    // The new function is static function, and by convention a
    // constructor
```

```
pub fn new(a: i32, b: u32, c: f32) -> MyCustomStruct {
    MyCustomStruct {
        a: a, b: b, c: c
    }
}

// Instance functions feature a "self" reference as the first
// parameter
// This self reference can be mutable or owned, just like other
// variables
pub fn sum(&self) -> f32 {
    self.a as f32 + self.b as f32 + self.c
}
}
```

7. To see the new `struct` function in action, let's add a test to do some and clone memory tricks with types (note: pay attention to the asserts):

```
use super::MyCustomStruct;

#[test]
fn test_custom_struct() {
    assert_eq!(mem::size_of::<MyCustomStruct>(),
        mem::size_of::<i32>() + mem::size_of::<u32>() +
        mem::size_of::<f32>());

    let m = MyCustomStruct::new(1, 2, 3_f32);
    assert_eq!(m.a, 1);
    assert_eq!(m.b, 2);
    assert_eq!(m.c, 3_f32);

    assert_eq!(m.sum(), 6_f32);
    let m2 = m.clone();
    assert_eq!(format!("{:?}", m2), "MyCustomStruct { a: 1, b:
     2,
    c: 3.0 }");
    let mut m3 = m;
    m3.a = 100;

    assert_eq!(m2.a, 1);
    assert_eq!(m.a, 1);
    assert_eq!(m3.a, 100);
}
```

8. Lastly, let's see whether all of that works. Run `cargo test` in the `data-types` directory and you should see the following output:

```
$ cargo test
Compiling data-types v0.1.0 (Rust-Cookbook/Chapter01/data-types)
warning: method is never used: `new`
  --> src/lib.rs:13:5
   |
13 | pub fn new(a: i32, b: u32, c: f32) -> MyCustomStruct {
   | ^^^^^^^^^^^^^^^^^^^^^^^^^^^^^^^^^^^^^^^^^^^^^^^^^^^^^^
   |
   = note: #[warn(dead_code)] on by default

warning: method is never used: `sum`
  --> src/lib.rs:19:5
   |
19 | pub fn sum(&self) -> f32 {
   | ^^^^^^^^^^^^^^^^^^^^^^^^

    Finished dev [unoptimized + debuginfo] target(s) in 0.50s
     Running target/debug/deps/data_types-33e3290928407ff5

running 3 tests
test tests::basic_math_stuff ... ok
test tests::attempt_overflows ... ok
test tests::test_custom_struct ... ok

test result: ok. 3 passed; 0 failed; 0 ignored; 0 measured; 0
filtered out

   Doc-tests data-types

running 0 tests

test result: ok. 0 passed; 0 failed; 0 ignored; 0 measured; 0
filtered out
```

Now, let's go behind the scenes to understand the code better.

How it works...

This recipe played with several concepts, so let's unpack them here. After setting up a library to work with unit tests as our playground in *step 1* to *step 3*, we create a first test to work on some built-in data types to go through the basics in *step 4* and *step 5*. Since Rust is particularly picky about type conversions, the test applies some math functions on the outcomes and inputs of different types.

For experienced programmers, there is nothing new here, except for the fact that there is an `overflow_sub()` type operation that allows for overflowing operations. Other than that, Rust might be a bit more verbose thanks to the (intentional) lack of implicit casting. In *step 5*, we intentionally provoke an overflow, which leads to a runtime panic (and is the test result we are looking for).

As shown in *step 5*, Rust offers `struct` as the foundation for complex types, which can have attached implementation blocks as well as derived (`#[derive(Clone, Copy, Debug)]`) implementations (such as the `Debug` and `Copy` traits). In *step 6*, we go through using the type and its implications:

- No overhead on custom types: `struct` has exactly the size that the sum of its properties has
- Some operations implicitly invoke a trait implementation—such as the assignment operator or the `Copy` trait (which is essentially a shallow copy)
- Changing property values requires the mutability of the entire `struct` function

There are a few aspects that work like that because the default allocation strategy is to prefer the stack whenever possible (or if nothing else is mentioned). Therefore, a shallow copy of the data performs a copy of the actual data as opposed to a reference to it, which is what happens with heap allocations. In this case, Rust forces an explicit call to `clone()` so the data behind the reference is copied as well.

We've successfully learned how to create and use data types. Now, let's move on to the next recipe.

Controlling execution flow

In Rust, controlling the execution flow of a program goes beyond simple `if` and `while` statements. We will see how to do that in this recipe.

How to do it...

For this recipe, the steps are as follows:

1. Create a new project using `cargo new execution-flow -- lib` and open the project in an editor.

2. Basic conditionals such as `if` statements work just like in any other language, so let's start with those and replace the default `mod tests { ... }` statement in the file:

```
#[cfg(test)]
mod tests {
    #[test]
    fn conditionals() {
        let i = 20;
        // Rust's if statement does not require parenthesis
        if i < 2 {
            assert!(i < 2);
        } else if i > 2 {
            assert!(i > 2);
        } else {
            assert_eq!(i, 2);
        }
    }
}
```

3. Conditionals in Rust can do much more! Here is an additional test to show what they can do—add it before the last closing parenthesis:

```
#[test]
fn more_conditionals() {
    let my_option = Some(10);

    // If let statements can do simple pattern matching
    if let Some(unpacked) = my_option {
        assert_eq!(unpacked, 10);
    }

    let mut other_option = Some(2);
    // there is also while let, which does the same thing
    while let Some(unpacked) = other_option {

        // if can also return values in assignments
        other_option = if unpacked > 0 {
            Some(unpacked - 1)
        } else {
            None
```

```
        }
    }
    assert_eq!(other_option, None)
}
```

4. A conditional isn't the only statement that can be used to change the flow of execution. There is, of course, also the loop and its variations. Let's add another test for those as well, starting with a few basics:

```
#[test]
fn loops() {

    let mut i = 42;
    let mut broke = false;
    // a basic loop with control statements
    loop {
        i -= 1;
        if i < 2 {
            broke = true;
            break;
        } else if i > 2 {
            continue;
        }
    }
    assert!(broke);

    // loops and other constructs can be named for better
    readability ...
    'outer: loop {
        'inner: loop {
            break 'inner; // ... and specifically jumped out of
        }
        break 'outer;
    }
```

5. Next, we will add more code to the test to see that loops are regular statements that can return values and that ranges can be used in `for` loops as well:

```
    let mut iterations: u32 = 0;

    let total_squared = loop {
        iterations += 1;

        if iterations >= 10 {
            break iterations.pow(2);
        }
    };
    assert_eq!(total_squared, 100);
```

```
        for i in 0..10 {
            assert!(i >= 0 && i < 10)
        }

        for v in vec![1, 1, 1, 1].iter() {
            assert_eq!(v, &1);
        }
    }
```

6. With these three tests prepared, let's run `cargo test` to see them working:

```
$ cargo test
   Compiling execution-flow v0.1.0 (Rust-
Cookbook/Chapter01/execution-flow)
warning: value assigned to `broke` is never read
  --> src/lib.rs:20:17
   |
20 | let mut broke = false;
   | ^^^^^
   |
   = note: #[warn(unused_assignments)] on by default
   = help: maybe it is overwritten before being read?

    Finished dev [unoptimized + debuginfo] target(s) in 0.89s
      Running target/debug/deps/execution_flow-5a5ee2c7dd27585c

running 3 tests
test tests::conditionals ... ok
test tests::loops ... ok
test tests::more_conditionals ... ok

test result: ok. 3 passed; 0 failed; 0 ignored; 0 measured; 0
filtered out
```

Now, let's go behind the scenes to understand the code better.

How it works...

Although not vastly different from many languages' control statements, the basic constructs in Rust can change the way you think about variable assignments. It certainly transformed our mental models to be more data-focused. This means that instead of thinking *if this condition is reached, assign this other value to a variable*, a reversed *assign this other value to a variable if this condition is reached*—or shorter *transform this variable if this condition applies*—may take over.

This is the functional stream in the Rust programming language and it lends itself well to shortening and focusing the important parts of a piece of code. Similar implications can be made from the loop constructs since everything is a scope and has a return value. Using these capabilities will make every program a lot more readable and shorter, especially if it's just simple operations.

We've successfully learned how to control execution flow. Now, let's move on to the next recipe.

Splitting your code with crates and modules

Rust knows two types of code units: crates and modules. A crate is an external library, complete with its own `Cargo.toml` configuration file, dependencies, tests, and code. Modules, on the other hand, split the crate into logical parts that are only visible to the user if they import specific functions. Since the 2018 edition of Rust, the difference in using these structural encapsulations has been minimized.

Getting ready

This time, we are going to create two projects: one that offers some type of function and another one to use it. Therefore, use `cargo` to create both projects: `cargo new rust-pilib --lib` and `cargo new pi-estimator`. The second command creates a binary executable so we can run the compilation result, while the former is a library (crate).

This recipe is going to create a small program that prints out estimations of pi (π) and rounds them to two decimal places. It's nothing fancy and easy for anyone to understand.

Naming crates is hard. The main repository (`https://crates.io/`) is very permissive and has already seen name squatting (where people reserve names with the intent to sell them—think of names such as *YouTube* or *Facebook*, which would make nice API client names for these companies), and many crates are re-implementations of C libraries or wrap them. A good practice is to call the repository or directory `rust-mycoolCwrapper` and use `mycoolCwrapper` to name the crate itself. This way, only issues specific to your crate come in while the name is easy to guess in people's dependencies!

How to do it...

In just a few steps, we will be working with different modules:

1. First, we are going to implement the `rust-pilib` crate. As a simple example, it estimates the constant pi using the Monte Carlo method. This method is somewhat similar to throwing darts at a dartboard and counting the hits. Read more on Wikipedia (`https://en.wikipedia.org/wiki/Monte_Carlo_method`). Add to the `tests` submodule this snippet:

```
use rand::prelude::*;

pub fn monte_carlo_pi(iterations: usize) -> f32 {
    let mut inside_circle = 0;
    for _ in 0..iterations {

        // generate two random coordinates between 0 and 1
        let x: f32 = random::<f32>();
        let y: f32 = random::<f32>();
        // calculate the circular distance from 0, 0
        if x.powi(2) + y.powi(2) <= 1_f32 {
            // if it's within the circle, increase the count
            inside_circle += 1;
        }
    }
    // return the ratio of 4 times the hits to the total
    iterations
    (4_f32 * inside_circle as f32) / iterations as f32
}
```

2. Additionally, the Monte Carlo method uses a random number generator. Since Rust doesn't come with one in its standard library, an external crate is required! Modify `Cargo.toml` of the `rust-pilib` project to add the dependency:

```
[dependencies]
rand = "^0.5"
```

3. As good engineers, we are also going to add tests to our new library. Replace the original `test` module with the following tests to approximate `pi` using the Monte Carlo method:

```
#[cfg(test)]
mod tests {
    // import the parent crate's functions
    use super::*;
```

```
fn is_reasonably_pi(pi: f32) -> bool {
    pi >= 3_f32 && pi <= 4.5_f32
}

#[test]
fn test_monte_carlo_pi_1() {
    let pi = monte_carlo_pi(1);
    assert!(pi == 0_f32 || pi == 4_f32);
}

#[test]
fn test_monte_carlo_pi_500() {
    let pi = monte_carlo_pi(500);
    assert!(is_reasonably_pi(pi));
}
```

We can even go beyond 500 iterations:

```
#[test]
fn test_monte_carlo_pi_1000() {
    let pi = monte_carlo_pi(1000);
    assert!(is_reasonably_pi(pi));
}

#[test]
fn test_monte_carlo_pi_5000() {
    let pi = monte_carlo_pi(5000);
    assert!(is_reasonably_pi(pi));
}
}
```

4. Next, let's run the tests so we are certain of the quality of our product. Run `cargo test` in the root of the `rust-pilib` project. The output should be somewhat like this:

```
$ cargo test
   Compiling libc v0.2.50
   Compiling rand_core v0.4.0
   Compiling rand_core v0.3.1
   Compiling rand v0.5.6
   Compiling rust-pilib v0.1.0 (Rust-Cookbook/Chapter01/rust-pilib)
    Finished dev [unoptimized + debuginfo] target(s) in 3.78s
     Running target/debug/deps/rust_pilib-d47d917c08b39638

running 4 tests
test tests::test_monte_carlo_pi_1 ... ok
test tests::test_monte_carlo_pi_500 ... ok
test tests::test_monte_carlo_pi_1000 ... ok
```

```
test tests::test_monte_carlo_pi_5000 ... ok

test result: ok. 4 passed; 0 failed; 0 ignored; 0 measured; 0
filtered out

    Doc-tests rust-pilib

running 0 tests

test result: ok. 0 passed; 0 failed; 0 ignored; 0 measured; 0
filtered out
```

5. Now we want to offer the crate's feature(s) to the user, which is why we created a second project for the user to execute. Here, we declare to use the other library as an external crate first. Add the following to Cargo.toml in the pi-estimator project:

```
[dependencies]
rust-pilib = { path = '../rust-pilib', version = '*'}
```

6. Then, let's take a look at the src/main.rs file. Rust looks there to find a main function to run and, by default, it simply prints Hello, World! to standard output. Let's replace that with a function call:

```rust
// import from the module above
use printer::pretty_print_pi_approx;


fn main() {
    pretty_print_pi_approx(100_000);
}
```

7. Now, where does this new function live? It has its own module:

```rust
// Rust will also accept if you implement it right away
mod printer {
    // import a function from an external crate (no more extern
    declaration required!)
    use rust_pilib::monte_carlo_pi;

    // internal crates can always be imported using the crate
    // prefix
    use crate::rounding::round;

    pub fn pretty_print_pi_approx(iterations: usize) {
        let pi = monte_carlo_pi(iterations);
        let places: usize = 2;
```

```
        println!("Pi is ~ {} and rounded to {} places {}", pi,
        places, round(pi, places));
    }
}
```

8. This module was implemented inline, which is common for tests—but works almost like it was its own file. Looking at the use statements, we are still missing a module, however: rounding. Create a file in the same directory as main.rs and name it rounding.rs. Add this public function and its test to the file:

```
pub fn round(nr: f32, places: usize) -> f32 {
    let multiplier = 10_f32.powi(places as i32);
    (nr * multiplier + 0.5).floor() / multiplier
}


#[cfg(test)]
mod tests {
    use super::round;

    #[test]
    fn round_positive() {
        assert_eq!(round(3.123456, 2), 3.12);
        assert_eq!(round(3.123456, 4), 3.1235);
        assert_eq!(round(3.999999, 2), 4.0);
        assert_eq!(round(3.0, 2), 3.0);
        assert_eq!(round(9.99999, 2), 10.0);
        assert_eq!(round(0_f32, 2), 0_f32);
    }

    #[test]
    fn round_negative() {
        assert_eq!(round(-3.123456, 2), -3.12);
        assert_eq!(round(-3.123456, 4), -3.1235);
        assert_eq!(round(-3.999999, 2), -4.0);
        assert_eq!(round(-3.0, 2), -3.0);
        assert_eq!(round(-9.99999, 2), -10.0);
    }
}
```

9. So far, the module is ignored by the compiler since it was never declared. Let's do just that and add two lines at the top of main.rs:

```
// declare the module by its file name
mod rounding;
```

10. Lastly, we want to see whether everything worked. cd into the root directory of the pi-estimator project and run cargo run. The output should look similar to this (note that the library crate and dependencies are actually built with pi-estimator):

```
$ cargo run
    Compiling libc v0.2.50
    Compiling rand_core v0.4.0
    Compiling rand_core v0.3.1
    Compiling rand v0.5.6
    Compiling rust-pilib v0.1.0 (Rust-Cookbook/Chapter01/rust-pilib)
    Compiling pi-estimator v0.1.0 (Rust-Cookbook/Chapter01/pi-
estimator)
     Finished dev [unoptimized + debuginfo] target(s) in 4.17s
      Running `target/debug/pi-estimator`
     Pi is ~ 3.13848 and rounded to 2 places 3.14
```

11. Library crates are not the only ones to have tests. Run cargo test to execute the tests in the new pi-estimator project:

```
$ cargo test
    Compiling pi-estimator v0.1.0 (Rust-Cookbook/Chapter01/pi-
estimator)
     Finished dev [unoptimized + debuginfo] target(s) in 0.42s
      Running target/debug/deps/pi_estimator-1c0d8d523fadde02

running 2 tests
test rounding::tests::round_negative ... ok
test rounding::tests::round_positive ... ok

test result: ok. 2 passed; 0 failed; 0 ignored; 0 measured; 0
filtered out
```

Now, let's go behind the scenes to understand the code better.

How it works...

In this recipe, we explored the relationship between crates and modules. Rust supports several ways of encapsulating code into units, and the 2018 edition has made it a lot easier to do. Seasoned Rust programmers will miss the extern crate declaration(s) at the top of the files, which is nowadays only necessary in special cases. Instead, the crate's contents can be used right away in a use statement.

In this way, the line between modules and crates is now blurred. However, modules are much simpler to create since they are part of the project and only need to be declared in the root module to be compiled. This declaration is done using the `mod` statement, which also supports implementation in its body—something that is used a lot in testing. Regardless of the implementation's location, using an external or internal function requires a `use` statement, often prefixed with `crate::` to hint toward its location.

Alternatively to simple files, a module can also be a directory that contains at least a `mod.rs` file. This way, large code bases can nest and structure their traits and structs accordingly.

A note on function visibility: Rust's default parameter is module visibility. Hence, a function declared and implemented in a module can only be seen from within that module. Contrary to that, the `pub` modifier exports the function to outside users. The same goes for properties and functions attached to a struct.

We've successfully learned how to split our code with crates and modules. Now, let's move on to the next recipe.

Writing tests and benchmarks

When we start developing, tests take a backseat more often than not. There are several reasons why this might be necessary at the time, but the inability to set up a testing framework and surroundings is not one of them. Unlike many languages, Rust supports testing right out of the box. This recipe covers how to use these tools.

Although we mostly talk about unit testing here, that is, tests on a function/`struct` level, the tools remain the same for integration tests.

Getting ready

Again, this recipe is best worked on in its own project space. Use `cargo new testing --lib` to create the project. Inside the project directory, create another folder and call it `tests`.

Additionally, the benchmarks feature is still only available on the `nightly` branch of Rust. It is required to install the `nightly` build of Rust: `rustup install nightly`.

How to do it...

Follow these steps to learn more about creating a test suite for your Rust projects:

1. Once created, a library project already contains a very simple test (probably to encourage you to write more). The `cfg(test)` and `test` attributes tell `cargo` (the test runner) how to deal with the module:

```
#[cfg(test)]
mod tests {
    #[test]
    fn it_works() {
        assert_eq!(2 + 2, 4);
    }
}
```

2. Before we add further tests, let's add a subject that needs testing. In this case, let's use something interesting: a singly linked list from our other book (*Hands-On Data Structures and Algorithms with Rust*) made generic. It consists of three parts. First is a node type:

```
#[derive(Clone)]
struct Node<T> where T: Sized + Clone {
    value: T,
    next: Link<T>,
}

impl<T> Node<T> where T: Sized + Clone {
    fn new(value: T) -> Rc<RefCell<Node<T>>> {
        Rc::new(RefCell::new(Node {
            value: value,
            next: None,
        }))
    }
}
```

Second, we have a `Link` type to make writing easier:

```
type Link<T> = Option<Rc<RefCell<Node<T>>>>;
```

The last type is the list complete with functions to add and remove nodes. First, we have the type definition:

```
#[derive(Clone)]
pub struct List<T> where T: Sized + Clone {
    head: Link<T>,
    tail: Link<T>,
    pub length: usize,
}
```

In the `impl` block, we can then specify the operations for the type:

```
impl<T> List<T> where T: Sized + Clone {
    pub fn new_empty() -> List<T> {
        List { head: None, tail: None, length: 0 }
    }

    pub fn append(&mut self, value: T) {
        let new = Node::new(value);
        match self.tail.take() {
            Some(old) => old.borrow_mut().next = Some(new.clone()),
            None => self.head = Some(new.clone())
        };
        self.length += 1;
        self.tail = Some(new);
    }

    pub fn pop(&mut self) -> Option<T> {
        self.head.take().map(|head| {
            if let Some(next) = head.borrow_mut().next.take() {
                self.head = Some(next);
            } else {
                self.tail.take();
            }
            self.length -= 1;
            Rc::try_unwrap(head)
                .ok()
                .expect("Something is terribly wrong")
                .into_inner()
                .value
        })
    }
}
```

3. With the list ready to be tested, let's add some tests for each function, starting with a benchmark:

```rust
#[cfg(test)]
mod tests {
    use super::*;
    extern crate test;
    use test::Bencher;

    #[bench]
    fn bench_list_append(b: &mut Bencher) {
        let mut list = List::new_empty();
        b.iter(|| {
            list.append(10);
        });
    }
}
```

Add some more tests for basic list functionality inside the `test` module:

```rust
#[test]
fn test_list_new_empty() {
    let mut list: List<i32> = List::new_empty();
    assert_eq!(list.length, 0);
    assert_eq!(list.pop(), None);
}

#[test]
fn test_list_append() {
    let mut list = List::new_empty();
    list.append(1);
    list.append(1);
    list.append(1);
    list.append(1);
    list.append(1);
    assert_eq!(list.length, 5);
}


#[test]
fn test_list_pop() {
    let mut list = List::new_empty();
    list.append(1);
    list.append(1);
    list.append(1);
    list.append(1);
    list.append(1);
    assert_eq!(list.length, 5);
    assert_eq!(list.pop(), Some(1));
```

```
            assert_eq!(list.pop(), Some(1));
            assert_eq!(list.pop(), Some(1));
            assert_eq!(list.pop(), Some(1));
            assert_eq!(list.pop(), Some(1));
            assert_eq!(list.length, 0);
            assert_eq!(list.pop(), None);
        }
    }
```

4. It's also a good idea to have an integration test that tests the library from end to end. For that, Rust offers a special folder in the project called `tests`, which can house additional tests that treat the library as a black box. Create and open the `tests/list_integration.rs` file to add a test that inserts 10,000 items into our list:

```
use testing::List;

#[test]
fn test_list_insert_10k_items() {
    let mut list = List::new_empty();
    for _ in 0..10_000 {
        list.append(100);
    }
    assert_eq!(list.length, 10_000);
}
```

5. Great, now each function has one test. Try it out by running `cargo +nightly test` in the `testing/` root directory. The result should look like this:

```
$ cargo test
    Compiling testing v0.1.0 (Rust-Cookbook/Chapter01/testing)
    Finished dev [unoptimized + debuginfo] target(s) in 0.93s
     Running target/debug/deps/testing-a0355a7fb781369f

running 4 tests
test tests::test_list_new_empty ... ok
test tests::test_list_pop ... ok
test tests::test_list_append ... ok
test tests::bench_list_append ... ok

test result: ok. 4 passed; 0 failed; 0 ignored; 0 measured; 0
filtered out

     Running target/debug/deps/list_integration-77544dc154f309b3

running 1 test
test test_list_insert_10k_items ... ok
```

```
test result: ok. 1 passed; 0 failed; 0 ignored; 0 measured; 0
filtered out

    Doc-tests testing

running 0 tests

test result: ok. 0 passed; 0 failed; 0 ignored; 0 measured; 0
filtered out
```

6. To run the benchmark, issue `cargo +nightly bench`:

```
cargo +nightly bench
    Compiling testing v0.1.0 (Rust-Cookbook/Chapter01/testing)
     Finished release [optimized] target(s) in 0.81s
      Running target/release/deps/testing-246b46f1969c54dd

running 4 tests
test tests::test_list_append ... ignored
test tests::test_list_new_empty ... ignored
test tests::test_list_pop ... ignored
test tests::bench_list_append ... bench: 78 ns/iter (+/- 238)

test result: ok. 0 passed; 0 failed; 3 ignored; 1 measured; 0
filtered out
```

Now, let's go behind the scenes to understand the code better.

How it works...

Testing frameworks are a third-party library in many programming languages although well-tested code should be the default! By providing a (tiny) testing framework along with a test runner and even a small benchmarking framework (only on `nightly` as of this writing), the barrier for testing your Rust code is significantly lower. Although there are still some missing features (for example, mocking), the community is working on providing many of these things via external crates.

After setting everything up in *step 1*, *step 2* creates a singly linked list as the test subject. A singly linked list is a series of the same node types, connected with some sort of pointer. In this recipe, we decided to use the interior mutability pattern, which allows for borrowing mutably at runtime to modify the node it points to. The attached operations (`append()` and `pop()`) make use of this pattern. *Step 3* then creates the tests that we can use to verify that our code does what we think it should. These tests cover the basic workings of the list: create an empty list, append a few items, and remove them again using `pop`.

Tests can be failed using a variety of `assert!` macros. They cover equals (`assert_eq!`), not equals (`assert_ne!`), Boolean conditions (`assert!`), and non-release mode compilation only (`debug_assert!`). With these available and attributes such as `#[should_panic]`, there is no case that cannot be covered. Additionally, this great Rust book offers an interesting read as well: `https://doc.rust-lang.org/book/ch11-01-writing-tests.html`.

Step 4 adds a special integration test in a separate file. This restricts programmers to think like the user of the crate, without access to internal modules and functions that can be available in the nested `tests` module. As a simple test, we insert 10,000 items into the list to see whether it can handle the volume.

 The `+nightly` parameter instructs `cargo` to use the `nightly` toolchain for this command.

Only in *step 5* are we ready to run the benchmarks using `cargo +nightly test`, but tests are not automatically benchmarked. On top of that, benchmarks (`cargo +nightly bench`) compile the code using `--release` flags, thereby adding several optimizations that could lead to different outcomes from `cargo +nightly test` (including a headache for debugging those).

Step 6 shows the output of the benchmarking harness with nanosecond precision for each loop execution (and the standard deviation). Whenever doing any kind of performance optimization, have a benchmark ready to show that it actually worked!

Other nice things that the Rust documentation tool adds to testing are `doctests`. These are snippets that are compiled and executed as well as rendered as documentation. We were so delighted, we gave it its own recipe! So, let's move on to the next recipe.

Documenting your code

Documentation is an important part of software engineering. Instead of simply writing up some functions and chaining them together on a hunch, we like to promote writing reusable and readable code. Part of this is also writing sensible documentation—which, in ideal cases, can be rendered into other formats such as HTML or PDF. As many languages do by default, Rust provides a tool and language support as well: `rustdoc`.

Getting ready

Failing our high standards of software engineering, we did not document the code from the last recipe! To change that, let's load a project with code to be documented (such as the previous recipe, *Writing tests and benchmarks*) into an editor.

How to do it...

Compile your code comments to a shiny HTML in just a few steps:

1. Rust's docstrings (strings that explicitly are documentation to be rendered) are denoted by `///` (instead of the regular `//`). Within these sections, markdown—a shorthand language for HTML—can be used to create full documentation. Let's add the following before the `List<T>` declaration:

```
///
/// A singly-linked list, with nodes allocated on the heap using
///`Rc`s and `RefCell`s. Here's an image illustrating a linked
list:
///
///
/// ![](https://upload.wikimedia.org/wikipedia/commons/6/6d/Singly-
///linked-list.svg)
///
/// *Found on https://en.wikipedia.org/wiki/Linked_list*
///
/// # Usage
///
/// ```
/// let list = List::new_empty();
/// ```
///
#[derive(Clone)]
pub struct List<T> where T: Sized + Clone {
[...]
```

2. This makes the code a lot more verbose, but is this worth it? Let's see with `cargo doc`, a subcommand that runs `rustdoc` on the code and outputs HTML in the `target/doc` directory of the project. When opened in a browser, the `target/doc/testing/index.html` page shows the following (and more):

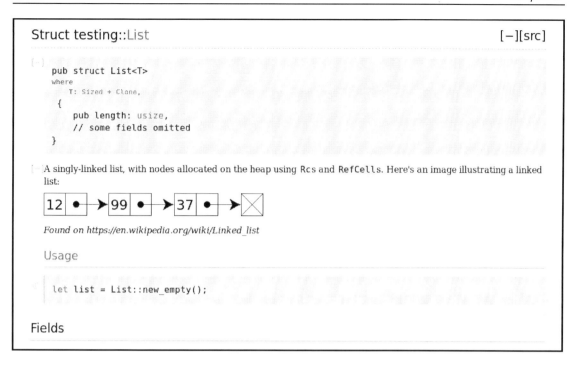

Struct testing::List   [−][src]

```
pub struct List<T>
where
    T: Sized + Clone,
{
    pub length: usize,
    // some fields omitted
}
```

A singly-linked list, with nodes allocated on the heap using `Rc`s and `RefCell`s. Here's an image illustrating a linked list:

| 12 | • | → | 99 | • | → | 37 | • | → | ⊠ |

Found on https://en.wikipedia.org/wiki/Linked_list

Usage

```
let list = List::new_empty();
```

Fields

Replace `testing` with the name of your project!

3. Great, let's add more documentation in the code. There are even special sections that are recognized by the compiler (by convention):

```
///
/// Appends a node to the list at the end.
///
///
/// # Panics
///
/// This never panics (probably).
///
/// # Safety
///
/// No unsafe code was used.
///
/// # Example
///
/// ```
```

```
/// use testing::List;
///
/// let mut list = List::new_empty();
/// list.append(10);
/// ```
///
pub fn append(&mut self, value: T) {
[...]
```

4. The `///` comments add documentation for expressions that follow it. This is going to be a problem for modules: should we put the documentation outside of the current module? No. Not only will this make the maintainers confused, but it also has a limit. Let's use `//!` to document the module from within:

```
//!
//! A simple singly-linked list for the Rust-Cookbook by Packt
//! Publishing.
//!
//! Recipes covered in this module:
//! - Documenting your code
//! - Testing your documentation
//! - Writing tests and benchmarks
//!
```

5. A quick `cargo doc` run reveals whether it worked:

Crate testing [−][src]

[−]A simple singly-linked list for the Rust-Cookbook by Packt Publishing.

Recipes covered in this module:

- Documenting your code
- Testing your documentation
- Writing tests and benchmarks

Structs

List   A singly-linked list, with nodes allocated on the heap using Rcs and RefCells. Here's an image illustrating a linked list:

---

6. While there is some benefit in having similar-looking documentation in any Rust project, corporate marketing often likes to have things such as logos or a custom favicon to stand out. `rustdoc` supports that with attributes on the module level—they can be added right below the module documentation (note: this is the logo of my Rust blog, `https://blog.x5ff.xyz`):

```
#![doc(html_logo_url = "https://blog.x5ff.xyz/img/main/logo.png")]
```

7. To see whether it worked, let's run `cargo doc` again:

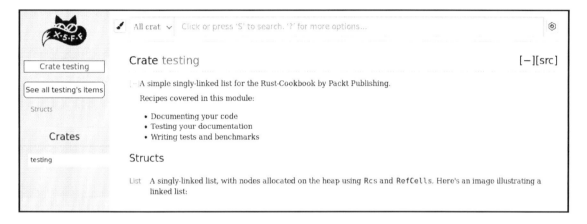

Now, let's go behind the scenes to understand the code better.

How it works...

Markdown is a great language that allows for creating formatted documentation quickly. However, feature support is typically tricky, so check out Rust's RFC for supported formatting (`https://github.com/rust-lang/rfcs/blob/master/text/0505-api-comment-conventions.md`) to find out whether some more advanced statements can be used. In general, writing documentation is dreaded by most developers, which is why it's very important to make it as simple and effortless as possible. The `///` pattern is quite common and has been expanded in Rust so that the documentation can apply to the code that follows (`///`) or that contains it (`//!`). Examples can be seen in *step 1* and *step 4*.

The approach the Rust project chose allows for a few lines explaining the (`public`) function, and then the `rustdoc` compiler (invoked in *step 2* with `cargo doc`) does the rest: exposing public members, cross-linking, listing all of the available types and modules, and much more. While the output is fully customizable (*step 6*), the default is already visually quite appealing (we think).

 By default, `cargo doc` builds the documentation for the entire project—including dependencies.

Special sections (*step 3*) add another dimension to the documentation output: they allow for IDEs or editors to make some sense of the provided information and highlight, for example, that (and when) a function may panic. The examples section in your newly generated documentation will even compile and run code in the form of `doctests` (see the *Testing your documentation* recipe) so you will be notified when your examples become invalid.

The `rustdoc` output is also independent of a web server, which means that it can be used wherever static hosting is supported. In fact, the Rust project builds and serves every crate's documentation that is hosted on `https://crates.io`, on `https://docs.rs`.

Now that we can create documentation successfully, we should move on to the next recipe.

Testing your documentation

Out-of-date documentation and examples that aren't working as promised are an unfortunate truth of many technologies. However, these examples can be valuable (black box) regression tests to make sure that we didn't break anything while improving the code, so how can they be used as such? Rust's documentation strings (`///`) can include executable code snippets—and they can be seen all over the place on `https://www.rust-lang.org/learn`!

Getting ready

We'll continue to improve the linked list from a previous recipe but focus some more on the documentation. However, the added code will work in any project, so pick one that you want to add documentation to and open it in your favorite editor.

How to do it...

Here are the steps for this recipe:

1. Find a function or `struct` (or module) to add a documentation string, for
   example, the `new_empty()` function of `List<T>`:

   ```
   ///
   /// Creates a new empty list.
   ///
   ///
   pub fn new_empty() -> List<T> {
       ...
   ```

2. Use the special (H1) section `# Example` to provide a cue for the compiler to run
   any snippet contained in that section:

   ```
   ///
   /// Creates a new empty list.
   ///
   ///
   /// # Example
   ```

3. Now let's add a code example. Since `doctests` are considered black box tests,
   we import the `struct` (only if it's public, of course) and show what we want to
   show:

   ```
   ///
   /// Creates a new empty list.
   ///
   ///
   /// # Example
   ///
   /// ```
   /// use testing::List;
   ///
   /// let mut list: List<i32> = List::new_empty();
   /// ```
   ///
   ```

4. With that ready, let's see whether the tests work: run `cargo +nightly test` in
   the project's root directory. You can see that we cheated a little bit and added
   tests to the other functions as well:

   ```
   $ cargo +nightly test
       Compiling testing v0.1.0 (Rust-Cookbook/Chapter01/testing)
        Finished dev [unoptimized + debuginfo] target(s) in 0.86s
   ```

```
        Running target/debug/deps/testing-a0355a7fb781369f

running 6 tests
[...]
   Doc-tests testing

running 4 tests
test src/lib.rs - List (line 44) ... ok
test src/lib.rs - List<T>::new_empty (line 70) ... ok
test src/lib.rs - List<T>::append (line 94) ... ok
test src/lib.rs - List<T>::pop (line 121) ... ok

test result: ok. 4 passed; 0 failed; 0 ignored; 0 measured; 0
filtered out
```

5. The code obviously has been augmented with several examples that have been run in this case—is that always what we want? Sometimes, it's all about the output, and adding all of the required imports for the test to successfully run is a pain. Hence, there are options to add to the *fenced* area (``` inside the fence ```), and `ignore` will neither compile nor run the code:

```
///
/// A singly-linked list, with nodes allocated on the heap using
`Rc`s and `RefCell`s. Here's an image illustrating a linked list:
///
///
///
![](https://upload.wikimedia.org/wikipedia/commons/6/6d/Singly-link
ed-list.svg)
///
/// *Found on https://en.wikipedia.org/wiki/Linked_list*
///
/// # Example
///
/// ```ignore
///
/// let list = List::new_empty();
/// ```
///
#[derive(Clone)]
pub struct List<T> where T: Sized + Clone {
[...]
```

6. By running `cargo test` again, we see the changes reflected in the output:

```
$ cargo test
[...]
   Doc-tests testing

running 4 tests
test src/lib.rs - List (line 46) ... ignored
test src/lib.rs - List<T>::append (line 94) ... ok
test src/lib.rs - List<T>::new_empty (line 70) ... ok
test src/lib.rs - List<T>::pop (line 121) ... ok

test result: ok. 3 passed; 0 failed; 1 ignored; 0 measured; 0
filtered out
```

7. Let's check the HTML output as well: run `cargo doc` to generate a `target/doc/` directory containing all of the CSS/HTML/JavaScript/... required to show the documentation in a local browser. Open `target/doc/testing/index.html` with your favorite browser:

```
pub fn new_empty() -> List<T>                                    [src]

Creates a new empty list.

Example
─────────────────────────────────────────────────────────

use testing::List;

let list: List<i32> = List::new_empty();
```

 Note: Replace `testing` with the name of your project.

8. Let's remove the ugly `use` statement at the top of the snippet. At that point, it doubles the lines displayed without adding anything—and `rustdoc` provides a simple way to do that, too. Add # in front of the offending line:

```
///
/// Creates a new empty list.
///
///
```

```
/// # Example
///
/// ```
/// # use testing::List;
/// let list: List<i32> = List::new_empty();
/// ```
///
pub fn new_empty() -> List<T> {
    [...]
```

9. Lastly, there are additional ways to configure the testing behavior of `doctests`. In this case, let's change warnings to errors by *denying* the warning while ignoring (allowing) unused variables:

```
#![doc(html_logo_url = "https://blog.x5ff.xyz/img/main/logo.png",
    test(no_crate_inject, attr(allow(unused_variables),
    deny(warnings))))]
```

10. One last time, let's check whether the output is what we expect and run `cargo doc`:

```
[-] pub fn new_empty() -> List<T>                                        [src]

Creates a new empty list.

Example

    let list: List<i32> = List::new_empty();
```

Now, let's see whether we can find out more about how the code works.

How it works...

Rust's documentation is very versatile and allows for variations on `doctests` that would not be possible to cover in a single recipe. However, the documentation of these tools is also excellent, so, for more details, check out `https://doc.rust-lang.org/rustdoc/documentation-tests.html`.

What we covered in this recipe is a great way to document `structs` and functions in your code by adding examples that will be compiled and run on every test run. Not only will these be helpful for your readers and regression testing, but they also require you to think about how the code works as a black box. These tests are executed whenever code (`` ` `` `` ` `` in a fence `` ` `` `` ` ``) is encountered in the `Example` section of the documentation. In *step 2* and *step 3*, we create these examples and see the result in *step 4* and *step 10*.

If you are now wondering how some documentation can show a fraction of the code required while it is supposed to be run, *step 8* shows the resolution to this riddle: # can hide individual lines while executing them. However, sometimes the code is not executed at all, as *step 5* shows. We can declare a section as `ignore` and this code won't be run (without any visual indication in the output).

Furthermore, these tests can fail just like any other test by panicking (which can be allowed as well) or falling through an `assert!` macro. All in all, by hiding away boilerplate or other non-essential code, the reader can focus on the important bits, while the test still covers everything.

We've successfully tested our documentation—we can sleep easy and move on to the next recipe.

Sharing code among types

An unusual feature of the Rust programming language is the decision to use traits over interfaces. The latter is very common across modern object-oriented languages and unifies the API of a class (or similar) to the caller, making it possible to switch the entire implementation without the caller's knowledge. In Rust, the separation is a bit different: traits are more akin to abstract classes since they provide the API aspect as well as default implementations. `struct` can implement various traits, thereby offering the same behavior with other structs that implement the same traits.

How to do it...

Let's go through the following steps:

1. Use `cargo` to create a new project, `cargo new traits --lib`, or clone it from this book's GitHub repository (`https://github.com/PacktPublishing/Rust-Programming-Cookbook`). Use Visual Studio Code and Terminal to open the project's directory.

2. Implement a simple configuration management service. To do that, we need some structs to work with:

   ```
   use std::io::{Read, Write};

   ///
   /// Configuration for our application
   ///
   pub struct Config {
       values: Vec<(String, String)>
   }

   ///
   /// A service for managing a configuration
   ///
   pub struct KeyValueConfigService {}
   ```

   Additionally, some constructors make them easier to use:

   ```
   // Impls

   impl Config {
       pub fn new(values: Vec<(String, String)>) -> Config {
           Config { values: values }
       }
   }

   impl KeyValueConfigService {
       pub fn new() -> KeyValueConfigService {
           KeyValueConfigService { }
       }
   }
   ```

3. To use a unified interface with other potential implementations, we have some traits to share the interface:

   ```
   ///
   /// Provides a get() function to return values associated with
   /// the specified key.
   ```

```
///
pub trait ValueGetter {
    fn get(&self, s: &str) -> Option<String>;
}

///
/// Write a config
///
pub trait ConfigWriter {
    fn write(&self, config: Config, to: &mut impl Write) ->
std::io::Result<()>;
}

///
/// Read a config
///
pub trait ConfigReader {
    fn read(&self, from: &mut impl Read) ->
std::io::Result<Config>;
}
```

4. Rust demands its own implementation block for each trait:

```
impl ConfigWriter for KeyValueConfigService {
    fn write(&self, config: Config, mut to: &mut impl Write) ->
std::io::Result<()> {
        for v in config.values {
            writeln!(&mut to, "{0}={1}", v.0, v.1)?;
        }
        Ok(())
    }
}

impl ConfigReader for KeyValueConfigService {
    fn read(&self, from: &mut impl Read) -> std::io::Result<Config>
{
        let mut buffer = String::new();
        from.read_to_string(&mut buffer)?;

        // chain iterators together and collect the results
        let values: Vec<(String, String)> = buffer
            .split_terminator("\n") // split
            .map(|line| line.trim()) // remove whitespace
            .filter(|line| { // filter invalid lines
                let pos = line.find("=")
                    .unwrap_or(0);
                pos > 0 && pos < line.len() - 1
            })
```

```
                    .map(|line| { // create a tuple from a line
                        let parts = line.split("=")
                                        .collect::<Vec<&str>>();
                        (parts[0].to_string(), parts[1].to_string())
                    })
                    .collect(); // transform it into a vector
            Ok(Config::new(values))
        }
    }

    impl ValueGetter for Config {
        fn get(&self, s: &str) -> Option<String> {
            self.values.iter()
                .find_map(|tuple| if &tuple.0 == s {
                        Some(tuple.1.clone())
                    } else {
                        None
                })
        }
    }
```

5. Next, we need some tests to show it in action. To cover some basics, let's add best-case unit tests:

```
#[cfg(test)]
mod tests {
    use super::*;
    use std::io::Cursor;

    #[test]
    fn config_get_value() {
        let config = Config::new(vec![("hello".to_string(),
        "world".to_string())]);
        assert_eq!(config.get("hello"), Some("world".to_string()));
        assert_eq!(config.get("HELLO"), None);
    }


    #[test]
    fn keyvalueconfigservice_write_config() {
        let config = Config::new(vec![("hello".to_string(),
        "world".to_string())]);

        let service = KeyValueConfigService::new();
        let mut target = vec![];
        assert!(service.write(config, &mut target).is_ok());

        assert_eq!(String::from_utf8(target).unwrap(),
```

```
            "hello=world\n".to_string());
    }

    #[test]
    fn keyvalueconfigservice_read_config() {

        let service = KeyValueConfigService::new();
        let readable = &format!("{}\n{}", "hello=world",
        "a=b").into_bytes();
        let config = service.read(&mut Cursor::new(readable))
            .expect("Couldn't read from the vector");

        assert_eq!(config.values, vec![
                ("hello".to_string(), "world".to_string()),
                ("a".to_string(), "b".to_string())]);
    }
}
```

6. Lastly, we run `cargo test` and see that everything works out:

```
$ cargo test
   Compiling traits v0.1.0 (Rust-Cookbook/Chapter01/traits)
    Finished dev [unoptimized + debuginfo] target(s) in 0.92s
     Running target/debug/deps/traits-e1d367b025654a89

running 3 tests
test tests::config_get_value ... ok
test tests::keyvalueconfigservice_write_config ... ok
test tests::keyvalueconfigservice_read_config ... ok

test result: ok. 3 passed; 0 failed; 0 ignored; 0 measured; 0
filtered out

   Doc-tests traits

running 0 tests

test result: ok. 0 passed; 0 failed; 0 ignored; 0 measured; 0
filtered out
```

Now, let's go behind the scenes to understand the code better.

How it works...

Using traits instead of interfaces and other object-oriented constructs has many implications for the general architecture. In fact, common architectural thinking will likely lead to more complex and verbose code that may perform worse on top of that! Let's examine popular object-oriented principles from the Gang of Four's book, *Design Patterns* (1994):

- **Program to an interface not to an implementation**: This principle requires some thinking in Rust. With the 2018 edition, functions can accept an `impl MyTrait` parameter, where earlier versions had to use `Box<MyTrait>` or `o: T` and later `where T: MyTrait`, all of which have their own issues. It's a trade-off for every project: either less complex abstractions with the concrete type or more generics and other complexity for cleaner encapsulation.
- **Favor object composition over class inheritance**: While this only applies to some extent (there is no inheritance in Rust), object composition is still something that seems like a good idea. Add trait type properties to your struct instead of the actual type. However, unless it's a boxed trait (that is, slower dynamic dispatch), there is no way for the compiler to know exactly the size it should reserve—a type instance could have 10 times the size of the trait from other things. Therefore, a reference is required. Unfortunately, though, that introduces explicit lifetimes—making the code a lot more verbose and complex to handle.

Rust clearly favors splitting off behavior from data, where the former goes into a trait and the latter remains with the original struct. In this recipe, `KeyValueConfigService` did not have to manage any data—its task was to read and write `Config` instances.

After creating these structs in *step 2*, we created the behavior traits in *step 3*. There, we split the tasks off into two individual traits to keep them small and manageable. Anything can implement these traits and thereby acquire the capabilities of writing or reading config files or retrieving a specific value by its key.

We kept the functions on the trait generic as well to allow for easy unit testing (we can use `Vec<T>` instead of faking files). Using Rust's `impl` trait feature, we only care about the fact that `std::io::Read` and `std::io::Write` have been implemented by whatever is passed in.

Step 4 implements the traits in an individual `impl` block for the structs. The `ConfigReader` strategy is naive: split into lines, split those lines at the first = character, and declare the left- and right-hand parts key and value respectively. The `ValueGetter` implementation then walks through the key-value pairs to find the requested key. We preferred `Vec` with `String` tuples here for simplicity, for example, `HashMap` can improve performance substantially.

The tests implemented in *step 5* provide an overview of how the system works and how we seamlessly use the types by the traits they implement. `Vec` doubles as a read/write stream, no type-casting required. To make sure the tests actually run through, we run `cargo test` in *step 6*.

After this lesson on structuring code, let's move on to the next recipe.

Sequence types in Rust

Sequences are supported in many forms in Rust. The regular array is strictly implemented: it has to be defined at compile time (using literals) and be of a single data type, and cannot change in size. Tuples can have members of different types, but cannot change in size either. `Vec<T>` is a generic sequence type (of whatever you define as type `T`) that provides dynamic resizing—but `T` can only be of a single type. All in all, each of them has its purpose and, in this recipe, we will explore each.

How to do it...

The steps for this recipe are as follows:

1. Use `cargo` to create a new project, `cargo new sequences --lib`, or clone it from this book's GitHub repository (`https://github.com/PacktPublishing/Rust-Programming-Cookbook`). Use Visual Studio Code and Terminal to open the project's directory.
2. With the test module ready, let's start with arrays. Arrays in Rust have a familiar syntax but they follow a stricter definition. We can try out various abilities of the Rust array in a test:

```
#[test]
fn exploring_arrays() {
    let mut arr: [usize; 3] = [0; 3];
    assert_eq!(arr, [0, 0, 0]);
```

```
        let arr2: [usize; 5] = [1,2,3,4,5];
        assert_eq!(arr2, [1,2,3,4,5]);

        arr[0] = 1;
        assert_eq!(arr, [1, 0, 0]);
        assert_eq!(arr[0], 1);
        assert_eq!(mem::size_of_val(&arr), mem::size_of::<usize>()
          * 3);
    }
```

3. Users of more recent programming languages and data science/math environments will also be familiar with the tuple, a fixed-size variable type collection. Add a test for working with tuples:

```
    struct Point(f32, f32);

    #[test]
    fn exploring_tuples() {
        let mut my_tuple: (i32, usize, f32) = (10, 0, -3.42);

        assert_eq!(my_tuple.0, 10);
        assert_eq!(my_tuple.1, 0);
        assert_eq!(my_tuple.2, -3.42);

        my_tuple.0 = 100;
        assert_eq!(my_tuple.0, 100);

        let (_val1, _val2, _val3) = my_tuple;

        let point = Point(1.2, 2.1);
        assert_eq!(point.0, 1.2);
        assert_eq!(point.1, 2.1);
    }
```

4. As the last collection, the vector is the basis for all of the other quick and expandable data types. Create the following test with several assertions that show how to use the vec! macro and the vector's memory usage:

```
    use std::mem;

    #[test]
    fn exploring_vec() {
        assert_eq!(vec![0; 3], [0, 0, 0]);
        let mut v: Vec<i32> = vec![];

        assert_eq!(mem::size_of::<Vec<i32>>(),
          mem::size_of::<usize>
          () * 3);
```

```
    assert_eq!(mem::size_of_val(&*v), 0);

    v.push(10);

    assert_eq!(mem::size_of::<Vec<i32>>(),
     mem::size_of::<i32>() * 6);
```

The remainder of the test shows how to modify and read the vector:

```
    assert_eq!(v[0], 10);
    v.insert(0, 11);
    v.push(12);
    assert_eq!(v, [11, 10, 12]);
    assert!(!v.is_empty());

    assert_eq!(v.swap_remove(0), 11);
    assert_eq!(v, [12, 10]);

    assert_eq!(v.pop(), Some(10));
    assert_eq!(v, [12]);

    assert_eq!(v.remove(0), 12);
    v.shrink_to_fit();
    assert_eq!(mem::size_of_val(&*v), 0);
  }
```

5. Run `cargo test` to see the working tests run:

```
$ cargo test
   Compiling sequences v0.1.0 (Rust-Cookbook/Chapter01/sequences)
    Finished dev [unoptimized + debuginfo] target(s) in 1.28s
     Running target/debug/deps/sequences-f931e7184f2b4f3d

running 3 tests
test tests::exploring_arrays ... ok
test tests::exploring_tuples ... ok
test tests::exploring_vec ... ok

test result: ok. 3 passed; 0 failed; 0 ignored; 0 measured; 0
filtered out

   Doc-tests sequences

running 0 tests

test result: ok. 0 passed; 0 failed; 0 ignored; 0 measured; 0
filtered out
```

Now, let's go behind the scenes to understand the code better.

How it works...

Sequence types are compound types that allocate a continuous part of the memory for faster and easier access. `Vec<T>` creates a simple, heap-allocated version of an array that grows (and shrinks) dynamically (*step 4*).

The original array (*step 2*) allocates memory on the stack and has to have a known size at compile time, which is a significant factor in using it. Both can be iterated and viewed using slices (`https://doc.rust-lang.org/book/ch04-03-slices.html`).

Tuples (*step 3*) are a different beast since they don't lend themselves to slices and are more a group of variables that have a semantic relationship—like a point in a two-dimensional space. Another use case is to return more than one variable to the caller of a function without the use of an additional struct or misusing a collection type.

Sequences in Rust are special because of the low overhead they produce. The size of `Vec<T>` is a pointer to an `n * size of T` memory on the heap, along with the size of the allocated memory, and how much of that is used. For arrays, the capacity is the current size (which the compiler can fill in during compilation), and tuples are more or less syntactic sugar on top of three distinct variables. Each of the three types provides convenience functions to change the contents—and, in the case of `Vec<T>`, the size of the collection. We recommend taking a close look at the tests and their comments to find out more about each type.

We have covered the basics of sequences in Rust, so let's move on to the next recipe.

Debugging Rust

Debugging has been a notoriously difficult topic in Rust, but still, it pales in comparison to Visual Studio debugging or IntelliJ IDEA's (`https://www.jetbrains.com/idea/`) capabilities in the Java world. However, debugging capabilities go beyond simple `println!` statements nowadays.

Getting ready

Debugging Rust is available via an additional extension in Visual Studio Code. Install it by running `ext install vadimcn.vscode-lldb` in the command window
(*Ctrl + P/cmd + P*).

On Windows, debugging is limited thanks to its incomplete LLVM support. However, the extension will prompt you to automatically install several things. Additionally, install **Python 3.6** and add it to `%PATH%`. With these dependencies installed, it worked well for us (in March 2019).

Read more at `https://github.com/vadimcn/vscode-lldb/wiki/Setup`.

How to do it...

Execute the following steps for this recipe:

1. Create a new binary project to debug: `cargo new debug-me`. Open this project in Visual Studio Code with the new extension loaded.

2. Before anything can happen, Visual Studio Code needs a launch configuration to recognize Rust's LLVM output. First, let's create this launch configuration; for that, add a `.vscode` directory containing a `launch.json` file to the project directory. This can be autogenerated, so make sure that `launch.json` contains the following:

```
{
    "version": "0.2.0",
    "configurations": [
        {
            "type": "lldb",
            "request": "launch",
            "name": "Debug executable 'debug-me'",
            "cargo": {
                "args": [
                    "build",
                    "--bin=debug-me",
                    "--package=debug-me"
                ],
                "filter": {
                    "kind": "bin"
                }
            },
            "args": [],
```

```
                    "cwd": "${workspaceFolder}"
            },
            {
                "type": "lldb",
                "request": "launch",
                "name": "Debug unit tests in executable 'debug-me'",
                "cargo": {
                    "args": [
                        "test",
                        "--no-run",
                        "--bin=debug-me",
                        "--package=debug-me"
                    ],
                    "filter": {
                        "kind": "bin"
                    }
                },
                "args": [],
                "cwd": "${workspaceFolder}"
            }
        ]
    }
```

3. Now, let's open src/main.rs and add some code to debug:

```
struct MyStruct {
    prop: usize,
}

struct Point(f32, f32);

fn main() {
    let a = 42;
    let b = vec![0, 0, 0, 100];
    let c = [1, 2, 3, 4, 5];
    let d = 0x5ff;
    let e = MyStruct { prop: 10 };
    let p = Point(3.14, 3.14);

    println!("Hello, world!");
}
```

4. Save and add a breakpoint in VS Code's user interface. Click left of the line numbers and a red dot should appear there. This is a breakpoint:

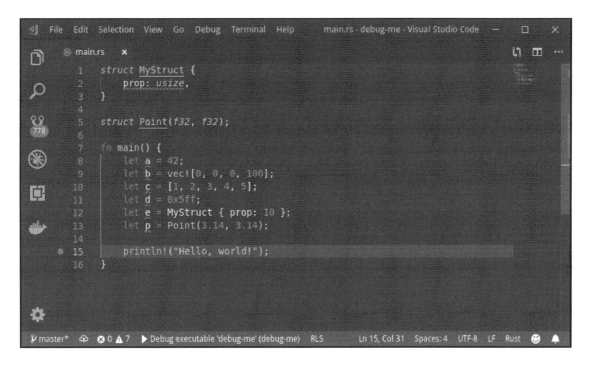

5. Having set a breakpoint, we expect the program to pause there and give us some insights into the current memory layout, that is, the state of any variables at that particular point in time. Run the debug launch configuration with *F5* (or **Debug | Start Debugging**). The window configuration should change slightly and a panel on the left-hand side of the window shows local variables (among other things):

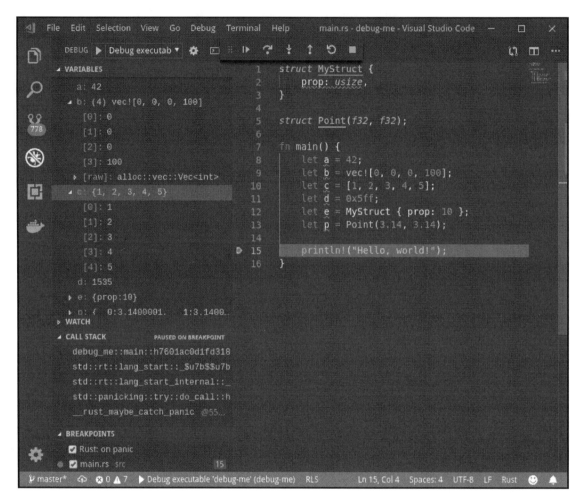

6. Using the small control panel on top, you can then control the execution flow and watch the stack and memory on the left change accordingly. Note also the difference between an array and a (heap-allocated) vector!

Now, let's go behind the scenes to understand the code better.

How it works...

Rust is built on the LLVM compiler toolkit that comes with a range of features out of the box. When a Rust program compiles, it only gets translated into an intermediate language, from which the LLVM compiler creates native bytecode.

This is also the reason why debugging can work in this case—it builds on the LLVM debug symbols. While it clearly lacks the convenience of modern IDEs, it's a large step forward and allows users to inspect types. Future development of the tools will hopefully improve this situation as well; for now, the general debugger, GDB (`https://www.gnu.org/software/gdb/`), handles most of the cases where debug symbols are compiled into the program. The configuration for connecting the debugger with the code in the IDE can be found in *step 2* and, by setting the breakpoint in *step 4*, it can track the relationship between lines of code and output. With the default setting to compile to debug, the debugger can then stop at this exact point. While it's not perfect (on the UX side), its capabilities are amazing.

Even this simple connection to a (UX-wise) very basic debugger can have great benefits for developers and represents a huge step up from `println!()` statements to inspect the current value of a variable.

We hope that you can use the debugger's capabilities in the remainder of this book. With this knowledge, you can now move on to the next chapter.

Going Further with Advanced Rust

2

There are no doubts as to the difficulties that the Rust language poses to the avid learner. However, if you are reading this, you have gone further than most and invested the time needed to improve. The language and the way it forces you to think about memory is going to introduce new concepts into your programming habits. Rust does not necessarily provide new tools to accomplish things, but the borrowing and ownership rules help us to concern ourselves more with scopes, lifetimes, and freeing memory appropriately, regardless of the language. Hence, let's go deeper into more advanced concepts in Rust in order to complete our understanding of the language – when, why, and how to apply concepts such as the following:

- Creating meaningful numbers with enums
- There is no null
- Complex conditions with pattern matching
- Implementing custom iterators
- Filtering and transforming sequences efficiently
- Reading memory the unsafe way
- Shared ownership
- Shared mutable ownership
- References with explicit lifetimes

- Enforcing behavior with trait bounds
- Working with generic data types

Creating meaningful numbers with enums

Enums, short for enumerations, are well-known programming constructs that many languages feature. These special cases of types allow a number to be mapped to a name. This can be used to tie constants together under a single name and lets us declare values as variants. For example, we could have pi, as well as Euler's number, as variants of an enum, MathConstants. Rust is no different, but it can go a lot further. Instead of simply relying on *naming numbers*, Rust allows enums the same flexibility as other Rust types have. Let's see what this means in practice.

How to do it...

Follow these steps to explore enums:

1. Create a new project with `cargo new enums --lib` and open this folder in Visual Studio Code, or any IDE of your choosing.
2. Open `src/lib.rs` and declare an enum containing some data:

```
use std::io;

pub enum ApplicationError {
    Code { full: usize, short: u16 },
    Message(String),
    IOWrapper(io::Error),
    Unknown
}
```

3. In addition to the declaration, we also implement a simple function:

```
impl ApplicationError {

    pub fn print_kind(&self, mut to: &mut impl io::Write) ->
    io::Result<()> {
        let kind = match self {
            ApplicationError::Code { full: _, short: _ } => "Code",
            ApplicationError::Unknown => "Unknown",
            ApplicationError::IOWrapper(_) => "IOWrapper",
            ApplicationError::Message(_) => "Message"
        };
```

```
        write!(&mut to, "{}", kind)?;
        Ok(())
    }
}
```

4. Now, we also need to do something with the enum, so let's implement a dummy function called `do_work`:

```
pub fn do_work(choice: i32) -> Result<(), ApplicationError> {
    if choice < -100 {
            Err(ApplicationError::IOWrapper(io::Error::
                from(io::ErrorKind::Other
    )))
        } else if choice == 42 {
            Err(ApplicationError::Code { full: choice as usize, short:
            (choice % u16::max_value() as i32) as u16 } )
        } else if choice > 42 {
            Err(ApplicationError::Message(
                format!("{} lead to a terrible error", choice)
            ))
        } else {
            Err(ApplicationError::Unknown)
        }
}
```

5. Nothing is true until it's tested! Now, add a number of tests that show the powerful matching of enums, starting with the `do_work()` function:

```
#[cfg(test)]
mod tests {
    use super::{ApplicationError, do_work};
    use std::io;

    #[test]
    fn test_do_work() {
        let choice = 10;
        if let Err(error) = do_work(choice) {
            match error {
                ApplicationError::Code { full: code, short: _ } =>
                assert_eq!(choice as usize, code),
                // the following arm matches both variants (OR)
                ApplicationError::Unknown |
                ApplicationError::IOWrapper(_) => assert!(choice <
                42),
                ApplicationError::Message(msg) =>
                assert_eq!(format!
                ("{} lead to a terrible error", choice), msg)
            }
```

```
            }
        }
```

For the `get_kind()` function, we also require a test:

```
#[test]
fn test_application_error_get_kind() {
    let mut target = vec![];
    let _ = ApplicationError::Code { full: 100, short: 100
    }.print_kind(&mut target);
    assert_eq!(String::from_utf8(target).unwrap(),
    "Code".to_string());
    let mut target = vec![];
    let _ = ApplicationError::Message("0".to_string()).
    print_kind(&mut target);
    assert_eq!(String::from_utf8(target).unwrap(),
    "Message".to_string());
    let mut target = vec![];
    let _ = ApplicationError::Unknown.print_kind(&mut target);
    assert_eq!(String::from_utf8(target).unwrap(),
    "Unknown".to_string());
    let mut target = vec![];
    let error = io::Error::from(io::ErrorKind::WriteZero);
    let _ = ApplicationError::IOWrapper(error).print_kind(&mut
    target);
    assert_eq!(String::from_utf8(target).unwrap(),
    "IOWrapper".to_string());

}
}
```

6. In a call to `cargo test` in the root directory of the project, we can observe the output:

```
$ cargo test
    Compiling enums v0.1.0 (Rust-Cookbook/Chapter02/enums)
     Finished dev [unoptimized + debuginfo] target(s) in 0.61s
      Running target/debug/deps/enums-af52cbd5cd8d54cb

running 2 tests
test tests::test_do_work ... ok
test tests::test_application_error_get_kind ... ok

test result: ok. 2 passed; 0 failed; 0 ignored; 0 measured; 0
filtered out

    Doc-tests enums
```

```
running 0 tests

test result: ok. 0 passed; 0 failed; 0 ignored; 0 measured; 0
filtered out
```

Now, let's see how enums work under the hood.

How it works...

Enums in Rust encapsulate choices—just as in any language. However, they behave similarly to regular structures in a lot of ways:

- They can have `impl` blocks for traits and functions.
- Unnamed and named properties can carry different values.

These aspects make them really great candidates for choices of all kinds, be it configuration values, flags, constants, or wrapping errors, as we did in *Step 2*. Typical enums in other languages map a name to a numerical value of your choice, but Rust goes one step further. Instead of just numerical values, Rust's enum can have any value and even named properties. Take a look at the definition in *Step 2*:

```
pub enum ApplicationError {
    Code { full: usize, short: u16 },
    Message(String),
    IOWrapper(io::Error),
    Unknown
}
```

`ApplicationError::Code` features two properties, one called `full` and one called `short`—assignable just like any other `struct` instance. The second and third variations, `Message` and `IOWrapper`, encapsulate another type instance entirely, one a `String`, and the other an `std::io::Error`, similar to tuples.

The additional ability to work in match clauses makes these constructs very useful, especially for large code bases where readability is important—an example of which can be found in *Step 3*, where we implement a function at the enum's type. This function maps explicit enum instances to strings for easier printing.

Step 4 implements a helper function that provides us with different kinds of errors and values to work with, something that we require in *Step 5*, where we create two extensive tests of these functions. There, we use the `match` clause (which will also be discussed in a later recipe in this chapter) to extract values from the errors and match on multiple enum variants in a single arm. Additionally, we created a test to show that the `print_kind()` function works by using a `Vec` as a stream (thanks to it implementing the `Write` trait).

We've successfully learned how to create meaningful numbers with enums. Now, let's move on to the next recipe.

There is no null

Functional languages typically don't have a concept of **null** for the simple reason that it's always a special case. If you strictly follow functional principles, each input must have a workable output—but what is null? Is it an error? Or within normal operating parameters, but a negative result?

As a legacy feature, null has been around since C/C++, when a pointer could actually point to the (invalid) address, 0. However, many new languages try to move away from that. Rust does not have null, and no return value as a normal case with the `Option` type. The case of error is covered by the `Result` type, to which we dedicated an entire chapter, `Chapter 5`, *Handling Errors and Other Results*.

How to do it...

Since we are exploring a built-in library feature, we'll create several tests that cover everything:

1. Create a new project using `cargo new not-null --lib` and open the project folder using Visual Studio code.
2. To start off, let's see what `unwrap()` does and replace the default test in `src/lib.rs` with the following code:

```
#[test]
#[should_panic]
fn option_unwrap() {
    // Options to unwrap Options
    assert_eq!(Some(10).unwrap(), 10);
    assert_eq!(None.unwrap_or(10), 10);
    assert_eq!(None.unwrap_or_else(|| 5 * 2), 10);
```

```
        Option::<i32>::None.unwrap();
        Option::<i32>::None.expect("Better say something when
        panicking");
}
```

3. `Option` also wraps values well, and it's sometimes complicated (or simply verbose) to get them out. Here are a number of ways of getting the value out:

```
#[test]
fn option_working_with_values() {
    let mut o = Some(42);

    let nr = o.take();
    assert!(o.is_none());
    assert_eq!(nr, Some(42));

    let mut o = Some(42);
    assert_eq!(o.replace(1535), Some(42));
    assert_eq!(o, Some(1535));

    let o = Some(1535);
    assert_eq!(o.map(|v| format!("{:#x}", v)),
    Some("0x5ff".to_owned()));

    let o = Some(1535);
    match o.ok_or("Nope") {
        Ok(nr) => assert_eq!(nr, 1535),
        Err(_) => assert!(false)
    }
}
```

4. Due to their functional origins, where it's often not important whether one works on a single value or a collection, `Option` also behaves like a collection in some ways:

```
#[test]
fn option_sequentials() {
    let a = Some(42);
    let b = Some(1535);
    // boolean logic with options. Note the returned values
    assert_eq!(a.and(b), Some(1535));
    assert_eq!(a.and(Option::<i32>::None), None);
    assert_eq!(a.or(None), Some(42));
    assert_eq!(a.or(b), Some(42));
    assert_eq!(None.or(a), Some(42));
    let new_a = a.and_then(|v| Some(v + 100))
                 .filter(|&v| v != 42);
```

```
    assert_eq!(new_a, Some(142));
    let mut a_iter = new_a.iter();
    assert_eq!(a_iter.next(), Some(&142));
    assert_eq!(a_iter.next(), None);
}
```

5. Lastly, using the `match` clause on `Option` is very popular and often necessary:

```
#[test]
fn option_pattern_matching() {

    // Some trivial pattern matching since this is common
    match Some(100) {
        Some(v) => assert_eq!(v, 100),
        None => assert!(false)
    };

    if let Some(v) = Some(42) {
        assert_eq!(v, 42);
    }
    else {
        assert!(false);
    }
}
```

6. To see it all working, we should also run `cargo test`:

```
$ cargo test
   Compiling not-null v0.1.0 (Rust-Cookbook/Chapter02/not-null)
    Finished dev [unoptimized + debuginfo] target(s) in 0.58s
     Running target/debug/deps/not_null-ed3a746487e7e3fc

running 4 tests
test tests::option_pattern_matching ... ok
test tests::option_sequentials ... ok
test tests::option_unwrap ... ok
test tests::option_working_with_values ... ok

test result: ok. 4 passed; 0 failed; 0 ignored; 0 measured; 0
filtered out

    Doc-tests not-null

running 0 tests

test result: ok. 0 passed; 0 failed; 0 ignored; 0 measured; 0
filtered out
```

Now, let's go behind the scenes to understand the code better.

How it works...

Options are, to our initial surprise, an enum. While this almost guarantees great match compatibility, enums behave a lot like structs in the remaining aspects. In *Step 2*, we see that it's not just a regular enum, but also a typed enum—which forces us to add a type declaration to None as well. *Step 2* also shows ways how to get values out of the Option type, with and without panicking. unwrap() is a popular choice, but it comes with some variations that don't halt the thread if None is encountered.

unwrap() is always a dangerous thing, and should only be used in non-production code. It panics, which can bring the entire program to a sudden, unexpected halt, and doesn't even leave you with a proper error message. If stopping the program is the desired outcome, expect() is a better choice since it lets you add a simple message. This is why we added the #[should_panic] attribute to the unit test, so that we can prove to you that it actually panics (or otherwise the test fails).

Step 3 shows some non-intrusive ways to *unwrap* the value of Option. Especially since unwrap() returns the owned value while destroying Option itself, other ways can be more useful if Option remains part of a data structure and only temporarily holds a value. take() was designed for these situations that replace the value with None, similar to replace(), which does the same for the replacement value. Furthermore, there is map(), which lets you work directly with the value (if present) and ignore the usual if-then or match constructs, which add a lot of code verbosity (refer to *step 5*).

Step 4 features an interesting tidbit in the middle: Options can be used like Booleans to perform logic operations, similar to Python, where AND/OR operations return a particular operand (https://docs.python.org/3/reference/expressions.html#boolean-operations) in either case. Last but not least, Options can also be treated like collections using an iterator.

Rust's options are very versatile and, by looking at the documents (https://doc.rust-lang.org/std/option/index.html), you can find out many different ways to transform values on the fly without tedious guard clauses with if, let, and match.

Now that we have successfully learned that there is no null in Rust, let's move on to the next recipe.

Complex conditions with pattern matching

As shown in the previous recipe, pattern matching is very useful with enums. However, there is more! Pattern matching is a construct that originates in functional languages and curtails much of the choice between conditional branches and the assignment of properties in struct that commonly follows. These steps are taken at once, reducing the amount of code on the screen and creating something akin to a higher-order switch-case statement.

How to do it...

Just a few steps need to be followed in order to learn more about pattern matching:

1. Create a new binary project using cargo new pattern-matching. This time, we'll run an actual executable! Again, open the project using Visual Studio Code or another editor.

2. Let's check out literal matching. Just like a switch-case statement in other languages, each matching arm can match to literals as well:

```
fn literal_match(choice: usize) -> String {
    match choice {
        0 | 1 => "zero or one".to_owned(),
        2 ... 9 => "two to nine".to_owned(),
        10 => "ten".to_owned(),
        _ => "anything else".to_owned()
    }
}
```

3. However, pattern matching is way more powerful than that. For example, tuple elements can be extracted and selectively matched:

```
fn tuple_match(choices: (i32, i32, i32, i32)) -> String {
    match choices {
        (_, second, _, fourth) => format!("Numbers at positions 1
        and 3 are {} and {} respectively", second, fourth)
    }
}
```

4. **Destructuring** (moving properties out of a `struct` into their own variables) is a powerful feature in conjunction with structs and enums. First, this facilitates the assigning of multiple variables in a single matching arm to values that are assigned to properties at the incoming struct instance. Now, let's define a few structs and enums:

```
enum Background {
    Color(u8, u8, u8),
    Image(&'static str),
}

enum UserType {
    Casual,
    Power
}

struct MyApp {
    theme: Background,
    user_type: UserType,
    secret_user_id: usize
}
```

Then, the individual properties can be matched in a destructuring match. Enums work just as well—however, be sure to cover all possible variations; the compiler will notice (or use the special _ to match all). Matching is also done from top to bottom, so whichever rule applies first will be executed. The following snippet matches variations of the structs we just defined. It matches and assigns variables if a particular user type and theme is detected:

```
fn destructuring_match(app: MyApp) -> String {
    match app {
        MyApp { user_type: UserType::Power,
                secret_user_id: uid,
                theme: Background::Color(b1, b2, b3) } =>
            format!("A power user with id >{}< and color background
            (#{:02x}{:02x}{:02x})", uid, b1, b2, b3),
        MyApp { user_type: UserType::Power,
                secret_user_id: uid,
                theme: Background::Image(path) } =>
            format!("A power user with id >{}< and image background
            (path: {})", uid, path),
        MyApp { user_type: _, secret_user_id: uid, .. } => format!
        ("A regular user with id >{}<, individual backgrounds not
        supported", uid),
    }
}
```

5. On top of the powerful regular matching, a guard can also enforce certain conditions. Similar to destructuring, we can add more constraints:

```
fn guarded_match(app: MyApp) -> String {
    match app {
        MyApp { secret_user_id: uid, .. } if uid <= 100 => "You are
        an early bird!".to_owned(),
        MyApp { .. } => "Thank you for also joining".to_owned()
    }
}
```

6. So far, borrowing and ownership has not been a significant concern. However, the match clauses so far have all taken ownership and transferred it to the scope of the matching arm (anything after =>), which, unless you return it, means that the outside scope cannot do any other work with it. To remedy that, references can be matched as well:

```
fn reference_match(m: &Option<&str>) -> String {
    match m {
        Some(ref s) => s.to_string(),
        _ => "Nothing".to_string()
    }
}
```

7. In order to go full circle, we have not yet matched a particular type of literal: the string literal. Due to their heap allocation, they are fundamentally different from types such as i32 or usize. Syntactically, however, they don't look different from any other form of matching:

```
fn literal_str_match(choice: &str) -> String {
    match choice {
        " 🏋 " => "Power lifting".to_owned(),
        " ⚽ " => "Football".to_owned(),
        " 🥋 " => "BJJ".to_owned(),
        _ => "Competitive BBQ".to_owned()
    }
}
```

8. Now, let's tie it all together and build a main function that calls the various functions with the right parameters. Let's begin by printing a few simpler matches:

```
pub fn main() {
    let opt = Some(42);
    match opt {
        Some(nr) => println!("Got {}", nr),
```

```
        _ => println!("Found None")
    }
    println!();
    println!("Literal match for 0: {}", literal_match(0));
    println!("Literal match for 10: {}", literal_match(10));
    println!("Literal match for 100: {}", literal_match(100));

    println!();
    println!("Literal match for 0: {}", tuple_match((0, 10, 0,
    100)));
    println!();
    let mystr = Some("Hello");
    println!("Matching on a reference: {}",
    reference_match(&mystr));
    println!("It's still owned here: {:?}", mystr);
```

Next, we can also print the destructured matches:

```
    println!();
    let power = MyApp {
        secret_user_id: 99,
        theme: Background::Color(255, 255, 0),
        user_type: UserType::Power
    };
    println!("Destructuring a power user: {}",
    destructuring_match(power));
    let casual = MyApp {
        secret_user_id: 10,
        theme: Background::Image("my/fav/image.png"),
        user_type: UserType::Casual
    };
    println!("Destructuring a casual user: {}",
    destructuring_match(casual));

    let power2 = MyApp {
        secret_user_id: 150,
        theme: Background::Image("a/great/landscape.png"),
        user_type: UserType::Power
    };
    println!("Destructuring another power user: {}",
    destructuring_match(power2));
```

And lastly, let's see about guards and literal string matches on UTF symbols:

```
    println!();
    let early = MyApp {
        secret_user_id: 4,
        theme: Background::Color(255, 255, 0),
```

```
            user_type: UserType::Power
        };
        println!("Guarded matching (early): {}", guarded_match(early));

        let not_so_early = MyApp {
            secret_user_id: 1003942,
            theme: Background::Color(255, 255, 0),
            user_type: UserType::Power
        };
        println!("Guarded matching (late): {}",
        guarded_match(not_so_early));
        println!();

        println!("Literal match for 🏆: {}", literal_str_match("🏆"));
        println!("Literal match for 🏅: {}", literal_str_match("🏅"));
        println!("Literal match for 🏐: {}", literal_str_match("🏐"));
        println!("Literal match for 🏔: {}", literal_str_match("🏔"));
    }
```

9. The last step again involves running the program. Since this is not a library project, the results will be printed on the command line. Feel free to change any of the variables in the `main` function to see how it affects the output. Here's what the output *should* be:

```
$ cargo run
   Compiling pattern-matching v0.1.0 (Rust-
   Cookbook/Chapter02/pattern-matching)
    Finished dev [unoptimized + debuginfo] target(s) in 0.43s
     Running `target/debug/pattern-matching`
Got 42

Literal match for 0: zero or one
Literal match for 10: ten
Literal match for 100: anything else

Literal match for 0: Numbers at positions 1 and 3 are 10 and 100
respectively

Matching on a reference: Hello
It's still owned here: Some("Hello")

Destructuring a power user: A power user with id >99< and color
background (#ffff00)
Destructuring a casual user: A regular user with id >10<,
individual backgrounds not supported
Destructuring another power user: A power user with id >150< and
image background (path: a/great/landscape.png)
```

```
Guarded matching (early): You are an early bird!
Guarded matching (late): Thank you for also joining

Literal match for 🥋 : BJJ
Literal match for 🏉 : Football
Literal match for 🏋 : Power lifting
Literal match for 🍖 : Competitive BBQ
```

Now, let's take a peek behind the scenes to understand the code better.

How it works...

Ever since we came across pattern matching in the Scala programming language, we fell in love with its simplicity. As a major pillar of functional programming, the technique provides a quick way to transform values in various ways without sacrificing Rust's type safety.

The literal matches in *Steps* 2 and 7 are a great way to save on if-else chains. However, the most common matching is probably done to unpack Result or Option types for extracting the encapsulated values. While multiple matches are only possible using the | symbol , there are special operators to match to particular variations: ... denotes a range, while .. means to skip the remaining members of a struct. _ is almost always a wildcard for ignoring a particular thing and, as a match clause, it is a catch-all and should be placed last. In *Step 3*, we did a lot of unpacking of tuples; we skipped some of the matches using an _ in place of a variable name.

In a similar fashion, *Step 4* sets up and uses Rust's mechanism to match properties inside types when using the match clause (also called destructuring). This feature supports nesting and lets us pick values and sub-structs out of a complex struct instance. Neat!

However, it is often not done with matching on the type and then working with the unpacked values only in the match arm. Instead, having the match conditions lined up is a much better way to deal with allowed values within types. Rust's match clause supports guards for exactly that reason. *Step 5* shows what they are capable of.

Steps 8 and 9 both then show the use of the previously implemented match functions. We highly recommend going through some experiments yourself and seeing what changes. The typed matching allows for complex architectures without verbose safeguards or workarounds, which is exactly what we want!

We've successfully learned about complex conditions with pattern matching. Now, let's move on to the next recipe.

Implementing custom iterators

The true power of a great language is the way in which it lets the programmer integrate with types in the standard library and around the general ecosystem. One way to do this is the iterator pattern: defined by the Gang of Four in their book *Design Patterns* (Addison-Wesley Professional, 1994), an iterator is an encapsulation of a pointer moving through a collection. Rust provides a range of implementations on top of the `Iterator` trait. Let's see how we can leverage that power with only a few lines of code.

Getting ready

We will build an iterator for the linked list we built in an earlier recipe. We recommend either using the `Chapter01/testing` project or walking with us through construction of the iterator. In case you are too busy for that, the full solution can be found in `Chapter02/custom-iterators`. These paths refer to the GitHub repository for this book at `https://github.com/PacktPublishing/Rust-Programming-Cookbook`.

How to do it...

Iterators are typically their own structs and, since there can be different types (for example, for returning references instead of owned values), they are a good choice architecturally as well:

1. Let's create the struct for the iterator of `List<T>`:

```
pub struct ConsumingListIterator<T>
where
    T: Clone + Sized,
{
    list: List<T>,
}

impl<T> ConsumingListIterator<T>
where
    T: Clone + Sized,
{
    fn new(list: List<T>) -> ConsumingListIterator<T> {
        ConsumingListIterator { list: list }
    }
}
```

2. So far, this is only a regular `struct` that lacks everything an iterator should have. Their defining nature is a `next()` function that advances the internal pointer and returns the value that it just moved off of. In typical Rust fashion, the returned value is wrapped in an `Option` that becomes `None` once the collection runs out of items. Let's implement the `Iterator` trait to get all of these features:

```
impl<T> Iterator for ConsumingListIterator<T>
where
    T: Clone + Sized,
{
    type Item = T;

    fn next(&mut self) -> Option<T> {
        self.list.pop_front()
    }
}
```

3. Right now, we could instantiate `ConsumingListIterator` and pass our own `List` instance to it and it would work well. However, that is far from a seamless integration! The Rust standard library offers an additional trait to implement `IntoIterator`. By implementing this trait's functions, even a `for` loop knows what to do, and it looks just like any other collection and is easily interchangeable:

```
impl<T> IntoIterator for List<T>
where
    T: Clone + Sized,
{
    type Item = T;
    type IntoIter = ConsumingListIterator<Self::Item>;

    fn into_iter(self) -> Self::IntoIter {
        ConsumingListIterator::new(self)
    }
}
```

4. Lastly, we need to write a test to prove that everything is working. Let's add this to the existing test suite:

```
fn new_list(n: usize, value: Option<usize>) -> List<usize>{
    let mut list = List::new_empty();
    for i in 1..=n {
        if let Some(v) = value {
            list.append(v);
        } else {
            list.append(i);
```

```
            }
        }
        return list;
    }

    #[test]
    fn test_list_iterator() {
        let list = new_list(4, None);
        assert_eq!(list.length, 4);

        let mut iter = list.into_iter();
        assert_eq!(iter.next(), Some(1));
        assert_eq!(iter.next(), Some(2));
        assert_eq!(iter.next(), Some(3));
        assert_eq!(iter.next(), Some(4));
        assert_eq!(iter.next(), None);

        let list = new_list(4, Some(1));
        assert_eq!(list.length, 4);

        for item in list {
            assert_eq!(item, 1);
        }

        let list = new_list(4, Some(1));
        assert_eq!(list.length, 4);
        assert_eq!(list.into_iter().fold(0, |s, e| s + e), 4);
    }
```

5. Running the tests will show how well this integration works. The `cargo test` command's output demonstrates this:

```
$ cargo test
    Finished dev [unoptimized + debuginfo] target(s) in 0.02s
     Running target/debug/deps/custom_iterators-77e564edad00bd16

running 7 tests
test tests::bench_list_append ... ok
test tests::test_list_append ... ok
test tests::test_list_new_empty ... ok
test tests::test_list_split ... ok
test tests::test_list_iterator ... ok
test tests::test_list_split_panics ... ok
test tests::test_list_pop_front ... ok

test result: ok. 7 passed; 0 failed; 0 ignored; 0 measured; 0
filtered out
```

```
Doc-tests custom-iterators

running 5 tests
test src/lib.rs - List (line 52) ... ignored
test src/lib.rs - List<T>::append (line 107) ... ok
test src/lib.rs - List<T>::new_empty (line 80) ... ok
test src/lib.rs - List<T>::pop_front (line 134) ... ok
test src/lib.rs - List<T>::split (line 173) ... ok

test result: ok. 4 passed; 0 failed; 1 ignored; 0 measured; 0
filtered out
```

The next section is going to dive deeper into what's happening behind the scenes!

How it works...

Iterators are a great way of providing advanced capabilities to custom data structures. With their simple, unified interface, collection types can be switched out easily as well and programmers don't have to get used to new APIs for every data structure.

By implementing the `Iterator` trait in *Steps 1* and *2*, it becomes easy to provide exactly the desired access level to a collection's elements. In the case of this recipe (and similar to `Vec<T>`), it will consume the list entirely and remove the items one by one, starting at the front.

In *Step 3*, we implement `IntoIterator`, a trait that makes this construct available to the `for` loop and other users who call `into_iter()`. Not every collection implements this trait to provide multiple different iterators; for example, the second iterator of `Vec<T>` is reference-based, and only accessible via an `iter()` function on the type. By the way, a reference is a data type, just like the actual instance, so it's all about the type definition in this case. These definitions are made inside the trait implementation with the `type Item` declaration (so-called **associated types**: `https://doc.rust-lang.org/rust-by-example/ generics/assoc_items/types.html`). These types are called associated types, and can be referenced using `Self::Item`—just like generics, but without the added syntax verbosity.

With these interfaces, you can get access to a large library of functions that only assume a working iterator to be present! Check out *Steps 4* and *5* to see the implementation and outcome of using the iterator on a newly created list type.

We've successfully learned how to implement custom iterators. Now, let's move on to the next recipe.

Filtering and transforming sequences efficiently

While in the previous recipe we discussed implementing a custom iterator, it's now time to make use of the functions they provide. Iterators can transform, filter, reduce, or simply convert the underlying elements in a single go, thereby making it a very efficient endeavor.

Getting ready

First, create a new project using `cargo new iteration --lib` and add the following to the newly created `Cargo.toml` file in the project's directory:

```
[dev-dependencies]
rand = "^0.5"
```

This adds a dependency to the `rand` (`https://github.com/rust-random/rand`) crate to the project, which will be installed upon running `cargo test` the first time. Open the entire project (or the `src/lib.rs` file) in Visual Studio Code.

How to do it...

In four easy steps, we'll be able to filter and transform collections in Rust:

1. In order to use an iterator, you have to retrieve it first! Let's do that and implement a test that quickly shows how an iterator works on a regular Rust Vec<T>:

```
#[test]
fn getting_the_iterator() {
    let v = vec![10, 10, 10];
    let mut iter = v.iter();
    assert_eq!(iter.next(), Some(&10));
    assert_eq!(iter.next(), Some(&10));
    assert_eq!(iter.next(), Some(&10));
    assert_eq!(iter.next(), None);

    for i in v {
        assert_eq!(i, 10);
    }
}
```

2. With one test added, let's explore the notion of iterator functions further. They are compose able and let you perform multiple steps in a single iteration (think of adding more things to a single `for` loop). Additionally, the outcome's type can be completely different from what you started with! Here is another test to add to the project that performs some data transformations:

```
fn count_files(path: &String) -> usize {
    path.len()
}

#[test]
fn data_transformations() {
    let v = vec![10, 10, 10];
    let hexed = v.iter().map(|i| format!("{:x}", i));
    assert_eq!(
        hexed.collect::<Vec<String>>(),
        vec!["a".to_string(), "a".to_string(), "a".to_string()]
    );
    assert_eq!(v.iter().fold(0, |p, c| p + c), 30);
    let dirs = vec![
        "/home/alice".to_string(),
        "/home/bob".to_string(),
        "/home/carl".to_string(),
        "/home/debra".to_string(),
    ];

    let file_counter = dirs.iter().map(count_files);

    let dir_file_counts: Vec<(&String, usize)> =
    dirs.iter().zip(file_counter).collect();

    assert_eq!(
        dir_file_counts,
        vec![
            (&"/home/alice".to_string(), 11),
            (&"/home/bob".to_string(), 9),
            (&"/home/carl".to_string(), 10),
            (&"/home/debra".to_string(), 11)
        ]
    )
}
```

3. As the final step, let's also look at some filtering and splitting. These have proven to be the most useful in our personal experience—it removes a lot of code verbosity. Here is some code:

```rust
#[test]
fn data_filtering() {
    let data = vec![1, 2, 3, 4, 5, 6, 7, 8];
    assert!(data.iter().filter(|&n| n % 2 == 0).all(|&n| n % 2
        == 0));

    assert_eq!(data.iter().find(|&&n| n == 5), Some(&5));
    assert_eq!(data.iter().find(|&&n| n == 0), None);
    assert_eq!(data.iter().position(|&n| n == 5), Some(4));

    assert_eq!(data.iter().skip(1).next(), Some(&2));
    let mut data_iter = data.iter().take(2);
    assert_eq!(data_iter.next(), Some(&1));
    assert_eq!(data_iter.next(), Some(&2));
    assert_eq!(data_iter.next(), None);

    let (validation, train): (Vec<i32>, Vec<i32>) = data
        .iter()
        .partition(|&_| (rand::random::<f32>() % 1.0) > 0.8);

    assert!(train.len() > validation.len());
}
```

4. As always, we want to see the examples working! Run `cargo test` to do just that:

```
$ cargo test
    Compiling libc v0.2.50
    Compiling rand_core v0.4.0
    Compiling iteration v0.1.0 (Rust-Cookbook/Chapter02/iteration)
    Compiling rand_core v0.3.1
    Compiling rand v0.5.6
     Finished dev [unoptimized + debuginfo] target(s) in 5.44s
      Running target/debug/deps/iteration-a23e5d58a97c9435

running 3 tests
test tests::data_transformations ... ok
test tests::getting_the_iterator ... ok
test tests::data_filtering ... ok

test result: ok. 3 passed; 0 failed; 0 ignored; 0 measured; 0
filtered out
```

```
     Doc-tests iteration

running 0 tests

test result: ok. 0 passed; 0 failed; 0 ignored; 0 measured; 0
filtered out
```

Do you want to know more? Let's see how it works.

How it works...

Rust's iterators are heavily inspired by functional programming languages, which makes them very handy to use. As an iterator, every operation is applied sequentially one element at a time, but only as far as the iterator is moved forward. There are several types of operations shown in this recipe. The most important ones are as follows:

- `map()` operations execute a value or type transformation, and they are very common and easy to use.
- `filter()`, in the same way as many similar operations, executes a predicate (a function with a Boolean return value) in order to determine whether an element is to be included in the output. Examples are `find()`, `take_while()`, `skip_while()`, and `any()`.
- Aggregation functions such as `fold()`, `sum()`, `min()`, and `max()` are used to reduce the entire iterator's contents into a single object. That could be a number (`sum()`) or a hash map (for example, by using `fold()`).
- `chain()`, `zip()`, `fuse()`, and many more combine iterators so that they can be iterated over in a single loop. Typically, we use these if multiple run-throughs are otherwise required.

This more functional style of programming not only reduces the amount of code that has to be written, but also acts as a universal vocabulary: instead of reading through the entire `for` loop that pushes items into a previously defined list if a condition applies, a function call to `filter()` tells the reader what to expect. *Steps 2* and *3* show different function invocations to transform (*Step 2*) or filter (*Step 3*) collections based on various use cases.

Additionally, iterators can be chained together, so a call to
`iterator.filter().map().fold()` is not unusual and typically quicker to reason about than a loop that does the same thing. As the last step, most iterators are collected into their target collection or variable type. `collect()` evaluates the entire chain, which means that its execution is costly. Since the entire topic is very specific to the tasks at hand, check out the code we wrote and the outcomes/invocations to get the most out of it. *Step 4* only shows running the tests, but the real story is inside the code.

Done! We've successfully learned how to filter and transform sequences efficiently. Move on to the next recipe to learn more!

Reading memory the unsafe way

`unsafe` is a concept in Rust where some compiler safety mechanisms are turned off. These **superpowers** bring Rust closer to C's abilities to manipulate (almost) arbitrary parts of the memory. `unsafe` itself qualifies a scope (or function) to be able to use these four superpowers (from `https://doc.rust-lang.org/book/ch19-01-unsafe-rust.html`):

- Dereference a raw pointer.
- Call an `unsafe` function or method.
- Access or modify a mutable static variable.
- Implement an unsafe trait.

In most projects, `unsafe` is only required for using the **FFI** (short for **Foreign Function Interface**) because it's outside of the borrow checker's reach. Regardless, in this recipe, we are going to explore some unsafe ways to read memory.

How to do it...

In just a few steps, we are `unsafe`:

1. Create a new library project using `cargo new unsafe-ways --lib`. Open the project using Visual Studio Code or another editor.
2. Open `src/libr.rs` to add the following function before the test module:

```
#![allow(dead_code)]
use std::slice;

fn split_into_equal_parts<T>(slice: &mut [T], parts: usize) ->
Vec<&mut [T]> {
```

```
let len = slice.len();
assert!(parts <= len);
let step = len / parts;
unsafe {
    let ptr = slice.as_mut_ptr();

    (0..step + 1)
        .map(|i| {
            let offset = (i * step) as isize;
            let a = ptr.offset(offset);
            slice::from_raw_parts_mut(a, step)
        })
        .collect()
    }
}
```

3. With that ready, we now have to add some tests inside `mod tests {}`:

```
#[cfg(test)]
mod tests {
    use super::*;
    #[test]
    fn test_split_into_equal_parts() {
        let mut v = vec![1, 2, 3, 4, 5, 6];
        assert_eq!(
            split_into_equal_parts(&mut v, 3),
            &[&[1, 2], &[3, 4], &[5, 6]]
        );
    }
}
```

4. Recalling the `unsafe` superpowers, we could try and change the way we are reading memory. Let's add this test to see how it works:

```
#[test]
fn test_str_to_bytes_horribly_unsafe() {
    let bytes = unsafe { std::mem::transmute::<&str, &[u8]>("Going
                off the menu") };
    assert_eq!(
        bytes,
        &[
            71, 111, 105, 110, 103, 32, 111, 102, 102, 32, 116,
            104, 101, 32, 109, 101, 110, 117
        ]
    );
}
```

5. The last step is to see the positive test results after running `cargo test`:

```
$ cargo test
    Compiling unsafe-ways v0.1.0 (Rust-Cookbook/Chapter02/unsafe-
ways)
     Finished dev [unoptimized + debuginfo] target(s) in 0.41s
      Running target/debug/deps/unsafe_ways-e7a1d3ffcc456d53

running 2 tests
test tests::test_str_to_bytes_horribly_unsafe ... ok
test tests::test_split_into_equal_parts ... ok

test result: ok. 2 passed; 0 failed; 0 ignored; 0 measured; 0
filtered out

    Doc-tests unsafe-ways

running 0 tests

test result: ok. 0 passed; 0 failed; 0 ignored; 0 measured; 0
filtered out
```

Safety is an important concept in Rust, so let's find out what we trade off by using `unsafe`.

How it works...

While `unsafe` is one way to enable easier solutions to sometimes tricky situations, this book (`https://rust-unofficial.github.io/too-many-lists/index.html`) describes the limitations of safe programming perfectly with something as simple as a linked list.

Rust is a safe programming language, which means that the compiler makes sure that all the memory is accounted for. Thus, it is impossible for programs to obtain multiple mutable references to the same memory address, use memory after it has been freed, or incorrect type safety, among other things. This lets Rust avoid undefined behavior. For some limited use cases, however, these constraints prohibit valid use cases, which is why `unsafe` loosens some of these guarantees to accommodate some of the things only C would allow.

After setting up the project in *Step 1*, we are adding the first function in *Step 2*. Its purpose is similar to `chunks()` (`https://doc.rust-lang.org/std/primitive.slice.html#method.chunks_mut`), but instead of an iterator, we are returning the entire collection right away, which is OK as an example, but should be thought about when implementing it for production use. Our function splits a provided (mutable) slice into a `parts` number of chunks of equal size and returns mutable references to them. Since the input is also a mutable reference to the entire part of the memory, we will have `parts + 1` number of mutable references to the same memory area; clearly, a violation of safe Rust! On top of that, this function allows going beyond the allocated memory with the `ptr.offset()` call (which does pointer arithmetic).

In the test created in *Step 3*, we show that it compiles and executes without any major problems. *Step 4* provides another example for unsafe code: changing the data type without casting. The `transmute` (`https://doc.rust-lang.org/std/mem/fn.transmute.html`) function can easily change the data type of a variable with all the consequences that come with that. Had we changed the type to something else, such as `u64`, we would end up with a totally different result and read memory that does not belong to the program. In *Step 5*, we run the whole test suite.

`unsafe` Rust can be interesting to get that last bit of performance out of a data structure, do some magic bin-packing, or to implement `Send` and `Sync` (`https://doc.rust-lang.org/std/mem/fn.transmute.html`). Whatever you intend to do with `unsafe`, check out the nomicon (`https://doc.rust-lang.org/nightly/nomicon/`) to delve deeper into the depths.

Equipped with that knowledge, let's move on to the next recipe.

Shared ownership

Ownership and borrowing are fundamental concepts in Rust; they are the reason no runtime garbage collection is required. As a quick primer: how do they work? In short: scopes. Rust (and many other languages) use (nested) scopes to determine the validity of a variable, so it cannot be used outside of the scope (like a function). In Rust, these scopes *own* their variables, so they will be gone after the scope finishes. In order for the program to *move* around values, it can transfer ownership to a nested scope or return it to the parent scope.

For temporary transfers (and multiple viewers), Rust has **borrowing,** which creates a reference back to the owned value. However, these references are less powerful, and sometimes more complex to maintain (for example, can the reference outlive the original value?), and they are probably the reason why the compiler complains.

In this recipe, we are getting around this problem by sharing ownership using a reference counter that only drops the variable after the counter reaches zero.

Getting ready

Using `new sharing-ownership --lib`, create a new library project and open the directory in your favorite editor. We will also use the `nightly` compiler for benchmarks, so running `rustup default nightly` is highly recommended.

To enable benchmarks, add `#![feature(test)]` to the top of the `lib.rs` file.

How to do it...

Understanding shared ownership only requires eight steps:

1. In the fairly young ecosystem that is Rust, APIs and function signatures are not always the most efficient, especially when they require somewhat advanced knowledge of memory layout. So, consider a simple `length` function (add it to the `mod tests` scope):

```
///
/// A length function that takes ownership of the input
/// variable
///
fn length(s: String) -> usize {
    s.len()
}
```

While unnecessary, the function requires that you pass your owned variable to the scope.

2. Luckily, the `clone()` function is ready for you if you still need ownership after the function call. This is similar to a loop, by the way, where ownership is moved in the first iteration, which means it is **gone** by the second iteration—leading to a compiler error. Let's add a simple test to illustrate these moves:

```
#[test]
fn cloning() {
    let s = "abcdef".to_owned();
    assert_eq!(length(s), 6);
    // s is now "gone", we can't use it anymore
    // therefore we can't use it in a loop either!
    // ... unless we clone s - at a cost! (see benchmark)
    let s = "abcdef".to_owned();

    for _ in 0..10 {
        // clone is typically an expensive deep copy
        assert_eq!(length(s.clone()), 6);
    }
}
```

3. This works, but creates a lot of clones of a string, only then to drop it shortly after. This leads to wasting resources and, with large enough strings, slows down the program. To establish a baseline, let's check this by adding a benchmark:

```
extern crate test;
use std::rc::Rc;
use test::{black_box, Bencher};

#[bench]
fn bench_string_clone(b: &mut Bencher) {
    let s: String = (0..100_000).map(|_| 'a').collect();
    b.iter(|| {
        black_box(length(s.clone()));
    });
}
```

4. Some APIs require ownership of the input variables without a semantic meaning. For example, the `length` function from *Step 1* pretends to require variable ownership, but unless mutability is also necessary, Rust's `std::rc::Rc` (short for **Reference Counted**) type is a great choice for avoiding heavyweight cloning or taking away ownership from the calling scope. Let's try it out by creating a better `length` function:

```
///
/// The same length function, taking ownership of a Rc
///
```

```
        fn rc_length(s: Rc<String>) -> usize {
            s.len() // calls to the wrapped object require no additions
        }
```

5. We can now continue to use the owned type after passing it into the function:

```
  #[test]
 fn refcounting() {
     let s = Rc::new("abcdef".to_owned());
     // we can clone Rc (reference counters) with low cost
     assert_eq!(rc_length(s.clone()), 6);

     for _ in 0..10 {
         // clone is typically an expensive deep copy
         assert_eq!(rc_length(s.clone()), 6);
     }
 }
```

6. After we have created a baseline benchmark, we certainly want to know how well the Rc version fares:

```
        #[bench]
        fn bench_string_rc(b: &mut Bencher) {
            let s: String = (0..100_000).map(|_| 'a').collect();
            let rc_s = Rc::new(s);
            b.iter(|| {
                black_box(rc_length(rc_s.clone()));
            });
        }
```

7. First, we should check whether the implementations are correct by running cargo test:

```
$ cargo test
    Compiling sharing-ownership v0.1.0 (Rust-
    Cookbook/Chapter02/sharing-ownership)
     Finished dev [unoptimized + debuginfo] target(s) in 0.81s
      Running target/debug/deps/sharing_ownership-f029377019c63d62

running 4 tests
test tests::cloning ... ok
test tests::refcounting ... ok
test tests::bench_string_rc ... ok
test tests::bench_string_clone ... ok

test result: ok. 4 passed; 0 failed; 0 ignored; 0 measured; 0
filtered out
```

```
       Doc-tests sharing-ownership

running 0 tests

test result: ok. 0 passed; 0 failed; 0 ignored; 0 measured; 0
filtered out
```

8. Now, we can check which variation is faster, and what the differences are:

```
$ cargo bench
    Compiling sharing-ownership v0.1.0 (Rust-
    Cookbook/Chapter02/sharing-ownership)
     Finished release [optimized] target(s) in 0.54s
       Running target/release/deps/sharing_ownership-68bc8eb23caa9948

running 4 tests
test tests::cloning ... ignored
test tests::refcounting ... ignored
test tests::bench_string_clone ... bench: 2,703 ns/iter (+/- 289)
test tests::bench_string_rc ... bench: 1 ns/iter (+/- 0)

test result: ok. 0 passed; 0 failed; 2 ignored; 2 measured; 0
filtered out
```

After we have explored shared ownership with Rc, let's go behind the scenes to understand them better.

How it works...

The impressive benchmark results are no accident: Rc objects are smart pointers to locations on the heap, and while we still call clone to do a *deep copy*, Rc only duplicates a pointer and increments the number of references to it. While the actual example function is kept simple so that we don't have to worry about it, it does have all the properties of complex functions we often encounter. We define the first version, which only works with owned memory (the input parameter is not a reference), in *Step 1*. *Steps 2* and *3* show the consequences of the API chosen in *Step 1*: we need to call the clone function if we want to keep (a copy of) the data we pass in.

In *Steps 4* to *6*, we do the equivalent with a Rust construct called Rc. Having ownership of one of those means that you own the pointer location, but not the actual value, which makes the entire construct very lightweight. In fact, allocating the memory for the original value once and pointing to it from multiple locations is a common way to improve performance in applications that require a lot of moving around of a string. This is a result that can be observed in *Steps 7* and *8*, where we execute tests and benchmarks.

One caveat remains. Rc constructs do not allow for mutable ownership, something that we'll solve in the next recipe.

Shared mutable ownership

Sharing ownership is great for read-only data. However, mutability is sometimes required, and Rust provides a great way to achieve this. If you recall the rules of ownership and borrowing, if there is a mutable reference, it has to be the only reference to avoid anomalies.

This is typically where the borrow checker comes in: at compile time, it makes sure that the condition holds true. This is where Rust introduces the pattern of interior mutability. By wrapping the data into a RefCell or Cell-type object, immutable and mutable access can be handed out dynamically. Let's see how this works in practice.

Getting ready

Create a new library project using cargo new --lib mut-shared-ownership and open src/lib.rs in your favorite editor. To enable benchmarks, please switch to nightly Rust using rustup default nightly, and add #![feature(test)] (which facilitates the use of the types required for benchmark-type tests) at the top of the lib.rs file.

How to do it...

Let's create a test to establish the best way to share mutable ownership in just a few steps:

1. Let's create a couple of new functions inside the testing module:

```
use std::cell::{Cell, RefCell};
use std::borrow::Cow;
use std::ptr::eq;

fn min_sum_cow(min: i32, v: &mut Cow<[i32]>) {
    let sum: i32 = v.iter().sum();
    if sum < min {
        v.to_mut().push(min - sum);
    }
}

fn min_sum_refcell(min: i32, v: &RefCell<Vec<i32>>) {
    let sum: i32 = v.borrow().iter().sum();
```

```
        if sum < min {
            v.borrow_mut().push(min - sum);
        }
    }

    fn min_sum_cell(min: i32, v: &Cell<Vec<i32>>) {
        let mut vec = v.take();
        let sum: i32 = vec.iter().sum();
        if sum < min {
            vec.push(min - sum);
        }
        v.set(vec);
    }
```

2. These functions dynamically (based on incoming data) mutate a list of integers to fit a particular condition (such as the sum needs to be at least *X*) and rely on three ways of sharing mutable ownership. Let's explore how these behave on the outside! Cell objects (and RefCell objects) are simply wrappers that either return a reference or ownership of a value:

```
#[test]
fn about_cells() {
    // we allocate memory and use a RefCell to dynamically
    // manage ownership
    let ref_cell = RefCell::new(vec![10, 20, 30]);

    // mutable borrows are fine,
    min_sum_refcell(70, &ref_cell);

    // they are equal!
    assert!(ref_cell.borrow().eq(&vec![10, 20, 30, 10]));

    // cells are a bit different
    let cell = Cell::from(vec![10, 20, 30]);

    // pass the immutable cell into the function
    min_sum_cell(70, &cell);

    // unwrap
    let v = cell.into_inner();

    // check the contents, and they changed!
    assert_eq!(v, vec![10, 20, 30, 10]);
}
```

3. Since this seems very familiar to other programming languages, where references can be passed around freely, we should also know the caveats. One important aspect is that these `Cell` threads panic if the borrow check fails, which brings the current thread at least to a sudden halt. In a few lines of code, this is what this looks like:

```
#[test]
#[should_panic]
fn failing_cells() {
    let ref_cell = RefCell::new(vec![10, 20, 30]);

    // multiple borrows are fine
    let _v = ref_cell.borrow();
    min_sum_refcell(60, &ref_cell);

    // ... until they are mutable borrows
    min_sum_refcell(70, &ref_cell); // panics!
}
```

4. Intuitively, these cells should add runtime overhead and thereby be slower than a regular – precompiled – borrow check. In order to confirm this, let's add a benchmark:

```
extern crate test;
use test::{ Bencher};

#[bench]
fn bench_regular_push(b: &mut Bencher) {
    let mut v = vec![];
    b.iter(|| {
        for _ in 0..1_000 {
            v.push(10);
        }
    });
}

#[bench]
fn bench_refcell_push(b: &mut Bencher) {
    let v = RefCell::new(vec![]);
    b.iter(|| {
        for _ in 0..1_000 {
            v.borrow_mut().push(10);
        }
    });
}

#[bench]
```

```
fn bench_cell_push(b: &mut Bencher) {
    let v = Cell::new(vec![]);
    b.iter(|| {
        for _ in 0..1_000 {
            let mut vec = v.take();
            vec.push(10);
            v.set(vec);
        }
    });
}
```

5. However, we did not address the dangers of unforeseen panics in Cell, which might be prohibitive in complex applications. This is where Cow comes in. Cow is a **Copy-on-Write** type that replaces the value it wraps by lazily cloning if mutable access is requested. By using this struct, we can be certain to avoid panics with this code:

```
#[test]
fn handling_cows() {
    let v = vec![10, 20, 30];

    let mut cow = Cow::from(&v);
    assert!(eq(&v[..], &*cow));

    min_sum_cow(70, &mut cow);

    assert_eq!(v, vec![10, 20, 30]);
    assert_eq!(cow, vec![10, 20, 30, 10]);
    assert!(!eq(&v[..], &*cow));

    let v2 = cow.into_owned();

    let mut cow2 = Cow::from(&v2);
    min_sum_cow(70, &mut cow2);

    assert_eq!(cow2, v2);
    assert!(eq(&v2[..], &*cow2));
}
```

6. Lastly, let's verify that the tests and benchmarks are successful by running cargo test:

```
$ cargo test
    Compiling mut-sharing-ownership v0.1.0 (Rust-
Cookbook/Chapter02/mut-sharing-ownership)
    Finished dev [unoptimized + debuginfo] target(s) in 0.81s
     Running target/debug/deps/mut_sharing_ownership-
```

```
d086077040f0bd34

running 6 tests
test tests::about_cells ... ok
test tests::bench_cell_push ... ok
test tests::bench_refcell_push ... ok
test tests::failing_cells ... ok
test tests::handling_cows ... ok
test tests::bench_regular_push ... ok

test result: ok. 6 passed; 0 failed; 0 ignored; 0 measured; 0
filtered out

    Doc-tests mut-sharing-ownership

running 0 tests

test result: ok. 0 passed; 0 failed; 0 ignored; 0 measured; 0
filtered out
```

7. Let's see the benchmark timings in the output of `cargo bench`:

   $ cargo bench
   ```
       Finished release [optimized] target(s) in 0.02s
        Running target/release/deps/mut_sharing_ownership-
       61f1f68a32def1a8

   running 6 tests
   test tests::about_cells ... ignored
   test tests::failing_cells ... ignored
   test tests::handling_cows ... ignored
   test tests::bench_cell_push ... bench: 10,352 ns/iter (+/- 595)
   test tests::bench_refcell_push ... bench: 3,141 ns/iter (+/- 6,389)
   test tests::bench_regular_push ... bench: 3,341 ns/iter (+/- 124)

   test result: ok. 0 passed; 0 failed; 3 ignored; 3 measured; 0
   filtered out
   ```

Sharing memory in various ways is complex, so let's dive deeper into how they work.

How it works...

This recipe is set up like a large benchmark or testing scheme: in *Step 1*, we define the functions to be tested, each with different input parameters, but the same behavior; it fills Vec up to a minimum sum. These parameters reflect different ways of sharing ownership, including RefCell, Cell, and Cow.

Steps 2 and *3* create tests that work exclusively on the different ways adopted by RefCell and Cell of handling and failing these values. *Step 5* does something similar to the Cow type; all are great opportunities to test out your own theories as well!

In *Steps 4* and *6*, we are creating and running benchmarks and tests on the functions we created in this recipe. The results are surprising. In fact, we tried different computers and versions and arrived at the same conclusion: RefCell is almost as fast as the regular way of retrieving a mutable reference (the runtime behavior results in a higher variance). The Cell parameter's slowdown is also expected; they move the entire data in and out at every iteration—and this is what we can also expect from Cow, so feel free to try it out yourself.

Both Cell objects and RefCell objects move the data onto the heap memory and use references (pointers) to get to these values, often requiring an extra jump. However, they offer a similar way of moving object references around with the comfort of C#, Java, or other such languages.

We hope you have successfully learned about shared mutable ownership. Now, let's move on to the next recipe.

Referencing with explicit lifetimes

Lifetimes are common in many languages and typically decide whether a variable is available outside the scope. In Rust, the situation is a bit more complicated thanks to the borrowing and ownership model that extensively uses lifetimes and scopes to automatically manage memory. Instead of reserving memory and cloning stuff into it, we developers want to avoid the inefficiencies and potential slowdowns this causes with references. However, this leads down a tricky path because, as the original value goes out of scope, what happens to the reference?

Since the compiler cannot infer this information from code, you have to help it and annotate the code so it can go and check for proper usage. Let's see what this looks like.

How to do it...

Lifetimes can be explored in a few steps:

1. Create a new project using `cargo new lifetimes --lib` and open it in your favorite editor.

2. Let's start with a simple function that takes in a reference that might not outlive the function! Let's make sure that the function and the input parameter are on the same lifetime:

```
// declaring a lifetime is optional here, since the compiler
automates this


///
/// Compute the arithmetic mean
///
pub fn mean<'a>(numbers: &'a [f32]) -> Option<f32> {
    if numbers.len() > 0 {
        let sum: f32 = numbers.iter().sum();
        Some(sum / numbers.len() as f32)
    } else {
        None
    }
}
```

3. Where the lifetime declaration is required is in structs. Therefore, we define the base `struct` first. It comes with a lifetime annotation for the type it contains:

```
///
/// Our almost generic statistics toolkit
///
pub struct StatisticsToolkit<'a> {
    base: &'a [f64],
}
```

4. What follows is the implementation, which continues the lifetime specifications.
   First, we implement the constructor (`new()`):

```
impl<'a> StatisticsToolkit<'a> {

    pub fn new(base: &'a [f64]) ->
     Option<StatisticsToolkit> {
        if base.len() < 3 {
            None
        } else {
            Some(StatisticsToolkit { base: base })
        }
    }
```

Then, we want to implement the variance calculation along with the standard deviation and the mean:

```
    pub fn var(&self) -> f64 {
        let mean = self.mean();

        let ssq: f64 = self.base.iter().map(|i| (i -
        mean).powi(2)).sum();
        return ssq / self.base.len() as f64;
    }

    pub fn std(&self) -> f64 {
        self.var().sqrt()
    }

    pub fn mean(&self) -> f64 {
        let sum: f64 = self.base.iter().sum();

        sum / self.base.len() as f64
    }
```

As a final operation, we add the median calculation:

```
    pub fn median(&self) -> f64 {
        let mut clone = self.base.to_vec();

        // .sort() is not implemented for floats
        clone.sort_by(|a, b| a.partial_cmp(b).unwrap());

        let m = clone.len() / 2;
        if clone.len() % 2 == 0 {
            clone[m]
        } else {
            (clone[m] + clone[m - 1]) / 2.0
```

```
                }
            }
        }
```

5. And that's it! Some tests are required so that we can be certain everything works as expected. Let's start with a few helper functions and a test for calculating the mean:

```
#[cfg(test)]
mod tests {

    use super::*;

    ///
    /// a normal distribution created with numpy, with mu =
    /// 42 and
    /// sigma = 3.14
    ///
    fn numpy_normal_distribution() -> Vec<f64> {
        vec![
            43.67221552, 46.40865622, 43.44603147,
            43.16162571,
            40.94815816, 44.585914 , 45.84833022,
            37.77765835,
            40.23715928, 48.08791899, 44.80964938,
            42.13753315,
            38.80713956, 39.16183586, 42.61511209,
            42.25099062,
            41.2240736 , 44.59644304, 41.27516889,
            36.21238554
        ]
    }

    #[test]
    fn mean_tests() {
        // testing some aspects of the mean function
        assert_eq!(mean(&vec![1.0, 2.0, 3.0]), Some(2.0));
        assert_eq!(mean(&vec![]), None);
        assert_eq!(mean(&vec![0.0, 0.0, 0.0, 0.0, 0.0, 0.0,
        0.0]),
        Some(0.0));
    }
```

Then, we perform some testing on the new function:

```
    #[test]
    fn statisticstoolkit_new() {
        // require >= 3 elements in an array for a
```

```
        // plausible normal distribution
        assert!(StatisticsToolkit::new(&vec![]).is_none());
        assert!(StatisticsToolkit::new(&vec![2.0,
         2.0]).is_none());

        // a working example
        assert!(StatisticsToolkit::new(&vec![1.0, 2.0,
         1.0]).is_some());

        // not a normal distribution, but we don't mind
        assert!(StatisticsToolkit::new(&vec![2.0, 1.0,
         2.0]).is_some());
}
```

Next, let's test the actual statistics. In a single function, we are starting with some special input data:

```
#[test]
fn statisticstoolkit_statistics() {
    // simple best case test
    let a_sample = vec![1.0, 2.0, 1.0];
    let nd = StatisticsToolkit::
     new(&a_sample).unwrap();
    assert_eq!(nd.var(), 0.2222222222222222);
    assert_eq!(nd.std(), 0.4714045207910317);
    assert_eq!(nd.mean(), 1.3333333333333333);
    assert_eq!(nd.median(), 1.0);

    // no variance
    let a_sample = vec![1.0, 1.0, 1.0];
    let nd = StatisticsToolkit::
     new(&a_sample).unwrap();
    assert_eq!(nd.var(), 0.0);
    assert_eq!(nd.std(), 0.0);
    assert_eq!(nd.mean(), 1.0);
    assert_eq!(nd.median(), 1.0);
```

In order to check more sophisticated input data (for example, skewed distributions or edge cases), let's expand the test further:

```
    // double check with a real library
    let a_sample = numpy_normal_distribution();
    let nd =
     StatisticsToolkit::new(&a_sample).unwrap();
    assert_eq!(nd.var(), 8.580276516670548);
    assert_eq!(nd.std(), 2.9292109034124785);
    assert_eq!(nd.mean(), 42.36319998250001);
    assert_eq!(nd.median(), 42.61511209);
```

```
                    // skewed distribution
                    let a_sample = vec![1.0, 1.0, 5.0];
                    let nd =
                     StatisticsToolkit::new(&a_sample).unwrap();
                    assert_eq!(nd.var(), 3.555555555555556);
                    assert_eq!(nd.std(), 1.8856180831641267);
                    assert_eq!(nd.mean(), 2.3333333333333335);
                    assert_eq!(nd.median(), 1.0);

                    // median with even collection length
                    let a_sample = vec![1.0, 2.0, 3.0, 4.0] ;
                    let nd =
                     StatisticsToolkit::new(&a_sample).unwrap();
                    assert_eq!(nd.var(), 1.25);
                    assert_eq!(nd.std(), 1.118033988749895);
                    assert_eq!(nd.mean(), 2.5);
                    assert_eq!(nd.median(), 3.0);
                }
            }
```

6. Use `cargo test` to run the tests and verify that they are successful:

```
$ cargo test
   Compiling lifetimes v0.1.0 (Rust-Cookbook/Chapter02/lifetimes)
    Finished dev [unoptimized + debuginfo] target(s) in 1.16s
     Running target/debug/deps/lifetimes-69291f4a8f0af715

running 3 tests
test tests::mean_tests ... ok
test tests::statisticstoolkit_new ... ok
test tests::statisticstoolkit_statistics ... ok

test result: ok. 3 passed; 0 failed; 0 ignored; 0 measured; 0
filtered out

   Doc-tests lifetimes

running 0 tests

test result: ok. 0 passed; 0 failed; 0 ignored; 0 measured; 0
filtered out
```

Working with lifetimes is complex, so let's go behind the scenes to understand the code better.

How it works...

In this recipe, we created a simple statistics toolbox that allows normal distribution samples to be analyzed quickly and accurately. However, this example was only chosen to illustrate the ways of how lifetimes are useful and comparatively simple. In *Step 2*, we are creating a function to calculate the mean of a given collection. Since lifetimes can be inferred from using the functions/variables, explicit specification of the lifetime is optional. Nevertheless, the function explicitly ties the input parameter's lifetime to the function's lifetime, requiring any reference that is passed in to outlive `mean()`.

Steps 3 and *4* show how to deal with lifetimes in structs and their implementations. Since type instances can easily outlive the references they store (and each could even require a different lifetime), the explicit specification of the lifetimes becomes necessary. The lifetimes have to be stated every step of the way; in the struct declaration, in the `impl` block, and in the functions they are used with. The lifetime's name binds them together. In a way, it creates a virtual scope bound to the type instance's life.

Lifetime annotations are useful but verbose, which makes working with references sometimes cumbersome. However, once the annotations are in place, the program can be much more efficient and the interfaces can be a lot more convenient, removing `clone()` method and other things.

The choice for the lifetime name (`'a`) is common, but arbitrary. Other than the predefined `'static`, every word works just as fine and a readable choice is definitely better.

Working with explicit lifetimes was not too hard, right? We recommend that you keep on experimenting until you are ready to move on to the next recipe.

Enforcing behavior with trait bounds

When building a complex architecture, prerequisite behavior is very common. In Rust, this means that we cannot build either generic or other types without requiring them to conform to some prior behavior, or, in other words, we need to be able to specify which traits are required. Trait bounds are one way of doing that – and you have seen multiple instances of this already, even if you have skipped many recipes so far.

How to do it...

Follow these steps to learn more about traits:

1. Create a new project using `cargo new trait-bounds` and open it in your favorite editor.

2. Edit `src/main.rs` to add the following code, where we can easily print a variable's debug format since an implementation of that format is required on compilation:

```
///
/// A simple print function for printing debug formatted variables
///
fn log_debug<T: Debug>(t: T) {
    println!("{:?}", t);
}
```

3. If we were to call this using a custom type such as `struct AnotherType(usize)`, the compiler would quickly complain:

```
$ cargo run
   Compiling trait-bounds v0.1.0 (Rust-Cookbook/Chapter02/trait-
bounds)
error[E0277]: `AnotherType` doesn't implement `std::fmt::Debug`
  --> src/main.rs:35:5
   |
35 |     log_debug(b);
   |     ^^^^^^^^^ `AnotherType` cannot be formatted using `{:?}`
   |
   = help: the trait `std::fmt::Debug` is not implemented for
`AnotherType`
   = note: add `#[derive(Debug)]` or manually implement
`std::fmt::Debug`
note: required by `log_debug`
  --> src/main.rs:11:1
   |
11 | fn log_debug<T: Debug>(t: T) {
   | ^^^^^^^^^^^^^^^^^^^^^^^^^^^^^

error: aborting due to previous error

For more information about this error, try `rustc --explain E0277`.
error: Could not compile `trait-bounds`.

To learn more, run the command again with --verbose.
```

4. In order to fix this, we can either implement or derive the `Debug` trait, as it says in the error message. Deriving the implementation is very common for compositions of standard types. In traits, the trait bounds get a bit more interesting:

```
///
/// An interface that can be used for quick and easy logging
///
pub trait Loggable: Debug + Sized {
    fn log(self) {
        println!("{:?}", &self)
    }
}
```

5. We can then create and implement a suitable type:

```
#[derive(Debug)]
struct ArbitraryType {
    v: Vec<i32>
}

impl ArbitraryType {
    pub fn new() -> ArbitraryType {
        ArbitraryType {
            v: vec![1,2,3,4]
        }
    }
}
impl Loggable for ArbitraryType {}
```

6. Next, let's tie the code together in the `main` function:

```
fn main() {
    let a = ArbitraryType::new();
    a.log();
    let b = AnotherType(2);
    log_debug(b);
}
```

7. Execute `cargo run` and establish whether the output matches your expectations:

```
$ cargo run
   Compiling trait-bounds v0.1.0 (Rust-Cookbook/Chapter02/trait-
   bounds)
    Finished dev [unoptimized + debuginfo] target(s) in 0.38s
     Running `target/debug/trait-bounds`
    ArbitraryType { v: [1, 2, 3, 4] }
    AnotherType(2)
```

After creating an example program, let's explore the background for trait bounds.

How it works...

Trait bounds specify the requirements of the implementation to implementers. In this way, we can call functions on generic types without having a more in-depth knowledge of their structures.

In *Step 2*, we require any parameter type to implement the `std::fmt::Debug` trait in order to be able to use the debug formatter for printing. However, that does not generalize well, and we have to require that implementation for any *other* function as well. That's why, in *Step 4*, we require that any type that implements the `Loggable` trait also implements `Debug`.

As a result, we can expect to use all the required traits in the trait's functions, which makes expansion easier and provides the ability for all types to implement the trait to be compatible. In *Step 5* , we are implementing the `Loggable` trait for the type we created and using it in the remainder of the steps.

Decisions regarding the required traits are important for public APIs as well as for writing well-designed and maintainable code. Being mindful of what types are really required and how to provide them will lead to better interfaces and types. Notice also the + between two type bounds; it requires both (and more if more + symbols are added) traits to be present when implementing `Loggable`.

We've successfully learned how to enforce behavior with trait bounds. Now, let's move on to the next recipe.

Working with generic data types

Rust's function overloading is a bit more exotic than in other languages. Instead of redefining the same function with a different type signature, you can achieve the same result by specifying the actual types for a generic implementation. Generics are a great way to provide more general interfaces and are not too complex to implement thanks to helpful compiler messages.

In this recipe, we are going to implement a dynamic array (such as `Vec<T>`) in a generic way.

How to do it...

Learn how to use generics in just a few steps:

1. Start off by creating a new library project with `cargo new generics --lib` and open the project folder in Visual Studio Code.

2. A dynamic array is a data structure many of you will use every day. In Rust, the implementation is called `Vec<T>`, while other languages know it as `ArrayList` or `List`. First, let's establish the basic structure:

```
use std::boxed::Box;
use std::cmp;
use std::ops::Index;

const MIN_SIZE: usize = 10;

type Node<T> = Option<T>;

pub struct DynamicArray<T>
where
    T: Sized + Clone,
{
    buf: Box<[Node<T>]>,
    cap: usize,
    pub length: usize,
}
```

3. As the `struct` definition shows, the main element is a box of type `T`, a generic type. Let's see what the implementation looks like:

```
impl<T> DynamicArray<T>
where
    T: Sized + Clone,
{
    pub fn new_empty() -> DynamicArray<T> {
        DynamicArray {
            buf: vec![None; MIN_SIZE].into_boxed_slice(),
            length: 0,
            cap: MIN_SIZE,
        }
    }

    fn grow(&mut self, min_cap: usize) {
        let old_cap = self.buf.len();
        let mut new_cap = old_cap + (old_cap >> 1);
```

```
            new_cap = cmp::max(new_cap, min_cap);
            new_cap = cmp::min(new_cap, usize::max_value());
            let current = self.buf.clone();
            self.cap = new_cap;

            self.buf = vec![None; new_cap].into_boxed_slice();
            self.buf[..current.len()].clone_from_slice(&current);
        }

    pub fn append(&mut self, value: T) {
        if self.length == self.cap {
            self.grow(self.length + 1);
        }
        self.buf[self.length] = Some(value);
        self.length += 1;
    }

    pub fn at(&mut self, index: usize) -> Node<T> {
        if self.length > index {
            self.buf[index].clone()
        } else {
            None
        }
    }
}
```

4. So far, very straightforward. Instead of a type name, we'll simply use `T`. What happens if we wanted to implement a specific type for a generic definition? Let's implement the `Index` operation (a trait in Rust) for the `usize` type. Additionally, a `clone` operation will become very helpful in the future, so let's add that too:

```
impl<T> Index<usize> for DynamicArray<T>
where
    T: Sized + Clone,
{
    type Output = Node<T>;

    fn index(&self, index: usize) -> &Self::Output {
        if self.length > index {
            &self.buf[index]
        } else {
            &None
        }
    }
}

impl<T> Clone for DynamicArray<T>
```

```
where
    T: Sized + Clone,
{
    fn clone(&self) -> Self {
        DynamicArray {
            buf: self.buf.clone(),
            cap: self.cap,
            length: self.length,
        }
    }
}
```

5. In order to be certain that all of this works and we did not make any mistakes, let's start with a few tests for each implemented function:

```
#[cfg(test)]
mod tests {
    use super::*;

    #[test]
    fn dynamic_array_clone() {
        let mut list = DynamicArray::new_empty();
        list.append(3.14);
        let mut list2 = list.clone();
        list2.append(42.0);
        assert_eq!(list[0], Some(3.14));
        assert_eq!(list[1], None);
        assert_eq!(list2[0], Some(3.14));
        assert_eq!(list2[1], Some(42.0));
    }

    #[test]
    fn dynamic_array_index() {
        let mut list = DynamicArray::new_empty();
        list.append(3.14);

        assert_eq!(list[0], Some(3.14));
        let mut list = DynamicArray::new_empty();
        list.append("Hello");
        assert_eq!(list[0], Some("Hello"));
        assert_eq!(list[1], None);
    }
```

Now, let's add some more tests:

```
    #[test]
    fn dynamic_array_2d_array() {
        let mut list = DynamicArray::new_empty();
```

```
        let mut sublist = DynamicArray::new_empty();
        sublist.append(3.14);
        list.append(sublist);

        assert_eq!(list.at(0).unwrap().at(0), Some(3.14));
        assert_eq!(list[0].as_ref().unwrap()[0], Some(3.14));

    }

    #[test]
    fn dynamic_array_append() {
        let mut list = DynamicArray::new_empty();
        let max: usize = 1_000;
        for i in 0..max {
            list.append(i as u64);
        }
        assert_eq!(list.length, max);
    }

    #[test]
    fn dynamic_array_at() {
        let mut list = DynamicArray::new_empty();
        let max: usize = 1_000;
        for i in 0..max {
            list.append(i as u64);
        }
        assert_eq!(list.length, max);
        for i in 0..max {
            assert_eq!(list.at(i), Some(i as u64));
        }
        assert_eq!(list.at(max + 1), None);
    }
}
```

6. Once the tests are implemented, we can run the tests successfully with `cargo test`:

```
$ cargo test
    Compiling generics v0.1.0 (Rust-Cookbook/Chapter02/generics)
    Finished dev [unoptimized + debuginfo] target(s) in 0.82s
     Running target/debug/deps/generics-0c9bbd42843c67d5

running 5 tests
test tests::dynamic_array_2d_array ... ok
test tests::dynamic_array_index ... ok
test tests::dynamic_array_append ... ok
test tests::dynamic_array_clone ... ok
test tests::dynamic_array_at ... ok
```

```
test result: ok. 5 passed; 0 failed; 0 ignored; 0 measured; 0
filtered out

    Doc-tests generics

running 0 tests

test result: ok. 0 passed; 0 failed; 0 ignored; 0 measured; 0
filtered out
```

Now, let's look at using generics from behind the scenes.

How it works...

Generics work very well in Rust and, other than the verbose notation, they are very handy. In fact, you will find them all over the place and, as you progress in Rust, the need for better, more generic interfaces will increase.

In *Step 2*, we are creating a modified dynamic array (taken from the book *Hands-On Data Structures and Algorithms with Rust*: https://www.packtpub.com/application-development/hands-data-structures-and-algorithms-*rust*) that uses a generic type. Using a generic type in code works like any other type, writing T instead of i32. However, as discussed in a previous recipe, the compiler expects certain behaviors from the T type, such as implementing Clone, which is specified in the where clause of the struct and implementation. In more complex use cases, there could be multiple blocks for when T implements Clone and when it doesn't, but that would go beyond the scope of the recipe. *Step 3* shows the generic implementation of the dynamic array type and how the Clone and Sized traits come into play.

When implementing the Index trait in *Step 4*, something becomes more obvious. First, we specify the usize type for the trait implementation header. Therefore, this trait is only implemented if someone uses a usize variable (or constant/literal) for indexing, thereby ruling out any negative values. The second aspect is the associated type, which, in itself, has a generic type.

Another important aspect of generics is the term `Sized`. Variables in Rust are `Sized` when the size is known at compile time, so the compiler knows how much memory to allocate. Unsized types have an unknown size at compile time; that is, they are dynamically allocated and may grow at runtime. Examples include `str`, or slices of type `[T]`. Their actual size can change, which is why they are always behind a fixed-size reference, a pointer. If `Sized` is required, only the reference to an unsized type can be used (`&str`, `&[T]`), but there is also `?Sized` to make this behavior optional.

Steps 5 and *6* then create some tests and run them. The tests demonstrate that the main functions of the dynamic array continue to work, and we encourage you to try out any questions you have about the code in there as well.

If you want more details on the dynamic array and why/how it grows (it doubles in size, like Java's `ArrayList`), check out *Hands-On Data Structures and Algorithms with Rust*, where this dynamic array and other data structures are explained in more detail.

Managing Projects with Cargo

`cargo` is one of the unique selling points of Rust. It makes a developer's life easy by making the creating, developing, packaging, maintaining, testing, and deploying of application code or tools to production considerably more enjoyable. `cargo` is designed to be the single go-to tool for working on any type of Rust project across multiple stages such as the following:

- Project creation and management
- Configuring and executing builds
- Dependency installation and maintenance
- Testing
- Benchmarking
- Interfacing with other tools
- Packaging and publishing

Especially in the domain of systems programming, tools such as `cargo` are still rare—which is why many large-scale users developed their own versions. As a young language, Rust draws from the aspects that other tools got right: the versatility and central repository of `npm` (for Node.js), the ease of use of `pip` (for Python), and many more. In the end, `cargo` provides many great ways to enhance the Rust experience and has been cited as a major influence for developers who want to adopt the language.

In this chapter, we cover recipes that enable developers to utilize all of the features of `cargo` to create production-grade Rust projects. These fundamental recipes serve as building blocks for referencing dependencies, adjusting compiler behavior, customizing tools, and many more things that are common in everyday Rust development.

In this chapter, we will cover the following recipes:

- Organizing large projects with workspaces
- Uploading to `crates.io` (`https://crates.io`)
- Using dependencies and external crates
- Extending `cargo` with sub-commands
- Testing your project with `cargo`
- Continuous integration with `cargo`
- Customizing the build

Organizing large projects with workspaces

Creating a single project is easy: run `cargo new my-crate` and it's done. `cargo` creates everything from folder structure to a small source file (or unit test) in a breeze. However, what about larger projects consisting of multiple smaller crates and an executable? Or just a collection of related libraries? The `cargo` tool's answer to this is called **workspaces**.

How to do it...

Follow these steps to create your own workspace to manage multiple projects:

1. In a Terminal window (Windows PowerShell or a Terminal on macOS/Linux), change to a directory that will hold the workspace by running these commands:

```
$ mkdir -p my-workspace
$ cd my-workspace
```

2. Use the `cargo new` command followed by its name to create a project:

```
$ cargo new a-project
      Created binary (application) `a-project` package
```

3. Since we are talking about multiple projects, let's add another library project that we can use:

```
$ cargo new a-lib --lib
      Created library `a-lib` package
```

4. Edit `a-project/src/main.rs` to contain the following code:

```
use a_lib::stringify;
use rand::prelude::*;

fn main() {
    println!("{{ \"values\": {}, \"sensor\": {} }}",
stringify(&vec![random::<f64>(); 6]), stringify(&"temperature"));
}
```

5. Then, add some code to `a-lib/src/lib.rs` that will `stringify` (using the `Debug` trait) an incoming variable. Obviously, that also needs some tests to show that the function works. Let's add some tests to compare the outputs of number formatting and sequence formatting with `stringify`:

```
use std::fmt::Debug;

pub fn stringify<T: Debug>(v: &T) -> String {
    format!("{:#?}", v)
}

#[cfg(test)]
mod tests {
    use rand::prelude::*;
    use super::stringify;
    #[test]
    fn test_numbers() {
        let a_nr: f64 = random();
        assert_eq!(stringify(&a_nr), format!("{:#?}", a_nr));
        assert_eq!(stringify(&1i32), "1");
        assert_eq!(stringify(&1usize), "1");
        assert_eq!(stringify(&1u32), "1");
        assert_eq!(stringify(&1i64), "1");
    }

    #[test]
    fn test_sequences() {
        assert_eq!(stringify(&vec![0, 1, 2]), "[\n 0,\n 1,\n
2,\n]");
        assert_eq!(
            stringify(&(1, 2, 3, 4)),
            "(\n 1,\n 2,\n 3,\n 4,\n)"
        );
    }
}
```

6. Let's add some configuration to the `Cargo.toml` files of each project to reference dependencies:

```
$ cat a-project/Cargo.toml
[package]
name = "a-project"
version = "0.1.0"
authors = ["<git user email address>"]
edition = "2018"

[dependencies]
a-lib = { path = "../a-lib" }
rand = "0.5"

$ cat a-lib/Cargo.toml
[package]
name = "a-lib"
version = "0.1.0"
authors = ["<git user email address>"]
edition = "2018"

[dev-dependencies]
rand = "*"
```

a-project now makes use of the a-lib library, but if we are developing these at the same time, the switching back and forth (for example, for testing a-lib after changes) will soon become cumbersome. This is where workspaces come in.

7. To use cargo on both projects at the same time, we have to create Cargo.toml in my-workspace, the parent directory of a-lib and a-project. It only contains two lines:

```
[workspace]

members = [ "a-lib", "a-project" ]
```

8. With this file in place, cargo can execute commands on both projects simultaneously and thereby make handling them easier. Let's compile cargo test and see which tests are run, along with their (test) results:

```
$ cargo test
   Compiling a-project v0.1.0 (my-workspace/a-project)
    Finished dev [unoptimized + debuginfo] target(s) in 0.30s
     Running target/debug/deps/a_lib-bfd9c3226a734f51

running 2 tests
test tests::test_sequences ... ok
```

```
test tests::test_numbers ... ok

test result: ok. 2 passed; 0 failed; 0 ignored; 0 measured; 0
filtered out

     Running target/debug/deps/a_project-914dbee1e8606741

running 0 tests

test result: ok. 0 passed; 0 failed; 0 ignored; 0 measured; 0
filtered out

   Doc-tests a-lib

running 0 tests

test result: ok. 0 passed; 0 failed; 0 ignored; 0 measured; 0
filtered out
```

9. As there is only one project that has tests (a-lib), it runs those. Let's compile cargo run to see the output of running the binary executable project:

```
$  cargo run
   Compiling a-project v0.1.0 (my-workspace/a-project)
    Finished dev [unoptimized + debuginfo] target(s) in 0.41s
     Running `target/debug/a-project`
{ "values": [
    0.6798204591148014,
    0.6798204591148014,
    0.6798204591148014,
    0.6798204591148014,
    0.6798204591148014,
    0.6798204591148014,
], "sensor": "temperature" }
```

Now, let's go behind the scenes to understand the code better.

How it works...

In this recipe, we created a simple binary project (*step 2* and *step 4*) together with a library project (*step 3* and *step 5*) that depend on each other. We simply specify these dependencies in their Cargo.toml files in *step 6* and the workspace we created in *step 7* helps us to join the projects together. Now, any commands are run on the projects that support them.

By building this project (with `cargo run`, `cargo test`, or `cargo build`), the tool creates a file containing the current dependency tree (called `Cargo.lock`). As a workspace, the output directory for the binaries (`target/`) is also located in the workspace directory instead of the individual projects' directories. Let's check the contents of the directories to see what that looks like and where the compiled output can be found (emphasis has been added to the code):

```
$ ls -alh
total 28K
drwxr-xr-x. 5 cm cm 4.0K Apr 11 17:29 ./
drwx------. 63 cm cm 4.0K Apr 10 12:06 ../
drwxr-xr-x. 4 cm cm 4.0K Apr 10 00:42 a-lib/
drwxr-xr-x. 4 cm cm 4.0K Apr 11 17:28 a-project/
-rw-r--r--. 1 cm cm 187 Apr 11 00:05 Cargo.lock
-rw-r--r--. 1 cm cm 48 Apr 11 00:05 Cargo.toml
drwxr-xr-x. 3 cm cm 4.0K Apr 11 17:29 target/

$ ls -alh target/debug/
total 1.7M
drwxr-xr-x. 8 cm cm 4.0K Apr 11 17:31 ./
drwxr-xr-x. 3 cm cm 4.0K Apr 11 17:31 ../
-rwxr-xr-x. 2 cm cm 1.7M Apr 11 17:31 a-project*
-rw-r--r--. 1 cm cm 90 Apr 11 17:31 a-project.d
drwxr-xr-x. 2 cm cm 4.0K Apr 11 17:31 build/
-rw-r--r--. 1 cm cm 0 Apr 11 17:31 .cargo-lock
drwxr-xr-x. 2 cm cm 4.0K Apr 11 17:31 deps/
drwxr-xr-x. 2 cm cm 4.0K Apr 11 17:31 examples/
drwxr-xr-x. 4 cm cm 4.0K Apr 11 17:31 .fingerprint/
drwxr-xr-x. 4 cm cm 4.0K Apr 11 17:31 incremental/
-rw-r--r--. 1 cm cm 89 Apr 11 17:31 liba_lib.d
-rw-r--r--. 2 cm cm 3.9K Apr 11 17:31 liba_lib.rlib
drwxr-xr-x. 2 cm cm 4.0K Apr 11 17:31 native/
```

Another aspect of workspaces is its dependency management. `cargo` synchronizes the external project dependencies inside the `Cargo.lock` file for every project contained within that workspace. As a result, any external crate will have the same version across every project whenever possible. When we added the `rand` crate as a dependency, it picked the same version for both projects (because of the * version in `a-lib`). Here's part of the resulting `Cargo.lock` file:

```
# This file is automatically @generated by Cargo.
# It is not intended for manual editing.
[[package]]
name = "a-lib"
version = "0.1.0"
dependencies = [
```

```
  "rand 0.5.6 (registry+https://github.com/rust-lang/crates.io-index)",
]

[[package]]
name = "a-project"
version = "0.1.0"
dependencies = [
 "a-lib 0.1.0",
 "rand 0.5.6 (registry+https://github.com/rust-lang/crates.io-index)",
]
[...]
```

`cargo` workspaces are a way to handle larger projects by bundling some operations at a higher level while leaving most configurations to the individual crates and applications. The configuration is simple and results in predictable behavior that lets the user build processes around it (for example, collecting all binaries from the workspace's `target/` directory).

Another interesting aspect is that `cargo` travels upward to find the most parental `Cargo.toml` file before executing a command. Therefore, what seems like the running of the tests of a specific project from within its directory results in the running of *all* tests of that workspace. Consequently, the commands have to be more specific now, for example, by using `cargo test -p a-lib`.

We've successfully learned how to organize large projects with workspaces. Now, let's move on to the next recipe!

Uploading to crates.io

`crates.io` (`https://crates.io`) is Rust's public repository for community crates. This links dependencies together, enables discovery, and lets users search for packages. For crate maintainers, it offers usage statistics and a place to host a `readme` file. `cargo` makes it possible to publish crates quickly and easily, as well as to handle updates. Let's see how.

Getting ready

For this recipe, we are going to publish a crate with minimal functionality. If you already have source code to work on (that is, your own project), feel free to use it. If not, create a new library project using `cargo new public-crate --lib` and open it in VS Code:

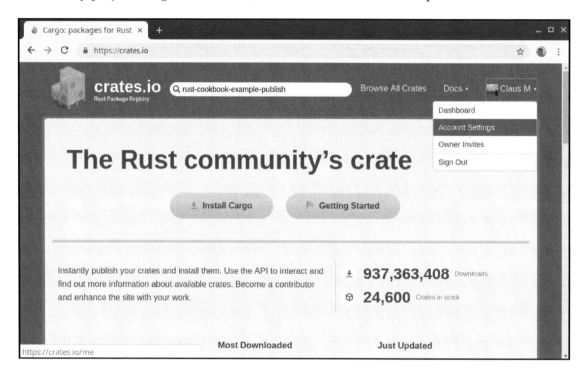

Go to `https://crates.io` and log in to your account (using `https://github.com`). Then, go to the **Account Settings** page to create a new token (follow the instructions on the page). Log in on the command line using your own token:

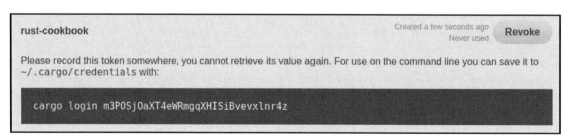

Let's take a look at the steps we need to perform to upload to `crates.io` (`https://crates.io`).

How to do it...

With `cargo` logged in and ready to go, follow these steps to publish the library to the repository:

1. Open `src/lib.rs` and add some code. The crate in our recipe is only going to publish the infamous bubble sort algorithm!

 At the moment, `crates.io` only uses names as identifiers, which means that you can't use the name `bubble-sort` any longer. However, instead of choosing a new name, we ask you not to publish a copy of this crate under a different name but focus your efforts on crates that are useful to the community.

Here is an implementation from the book *Hands-On Data Structures and Algorithms with Rust* (`https://www.packtpub.com/application-development/hands-data-structures-and-algorithms-rust`):

```
//! This is a non-optimized implementation of the [bubble sort]
algorithm for the book Rust Cookbook by Packt. This implementation
also clones the input vector.
//!
//! # Examples
//!```
//!# use bubble_sort::bubble_sort;
//! let v = vec![2, 2, 10, 1, 5, 4, 3];
//! assert_eq!(bubble_sort(&v), vec![1, 2, 2, 3, 4, 5, 10]);
//!```

///
/// See module level documentation.
///
pub fn bubble_sort<T: PartialOrd + Clone>(collection: &[T]) ->
Vec<T> {
    let mut result: Vec<T> = collection.into();
    for _ in 0..result.len() {
        let mut swaps = 0;
        for i in 1..result.len() {
            if result[i - 1] > result[i] {
                result.swap(i - 1, i);
                swaps += 1;
```

```
                }
            }
            if swaps == 0 {
                break;
            }
        }
        result
    }
```

This implementation also comes with tests:

```
#[cfg(test)]
mod tests {
    use super::bubble_sort;
    #[test]
    fn test_bubble_sort() {
        assert_eq!(bubble_sort(&vec![9, 8, 7, 6]), vec![6, 7, 8,
            9]);
        assert_eq!(bubble_sort(&vec![9_f32, 8_f32, 7_f32, 6_f32]),
            vec!
        [6_f32, 7_f32, 8_f32, 9_f32]);

        assert_eq!(bubble_sort(&vec!['c','f','a','x']), vec!['a',
            'c', 'f', 'x']);

        assert_eq!(bubble_sort(&vec![6, 8, 7, 9]), vec![6, 7, 8,
            9]);
        assert_eq!(bubble_sort(&vec![2, 1, 1, 1, 1]), vec![1, 1, 1,
            1, 2]);
    }
}
```

2. Additionally, `cargo` makes it possible to customize the landing page on `crates.io` using various fields in `Cargo.toml`. The landing page should inform the crate's users about the license (no license means everybody has to get your permission to use the code), where to find more information, and maybe even an example. On top of that, (quite fancy) badges provide information about the crate's build status, test coverage, and so on. Replace the content of `Cargo.toml` with the following snippet (and customize it if you want):

```
[package]
name = "bubble-sort"
description = "A quick and non-optimized, cloning version of the
bubble sort algorithm. Created as a showcase for publishing crates
in the Rust Cookbook 2018"
version = "0.1.0"
authors = ["Claus Matzinger <claus.matzinger+kb@gmail.com>"]
```

```
edition = "2018"
homepage = "https://blog.x5ff.xyz"
repository = "https://github.com/PacktPublishing/Rust-
             Programming-Cookbook"
license = "MIT"
categories = [
    "Algorithms",
    "Support"
]
keywords = [
    "cookbook",
    "packt",
    "x5ff",
    "bubble",
    "sort",
]
readme = "README.md"
maintenance = { status = "experimental" }
```

3. Now that all of the metadata is sorted out, let's run `cargo package` to see
   whether the package fulfills the formal criteria:

```
$ cargo package
error: 2 files in the working directory contain changes that were
not yet committed into git:

Cargo.toml
README.md

to proceed despite this, pass the `--allow-dirty` flag
```

4. As a friendly reminder, `cargo` makes sure that only committed changes are
   packaged, so the repository and `crates.io` are in sync. Commit the changes
   (read up on Git if you don't know how: `https://git-scm.com`) and re-run `cargo`
   `package`:

```
$ cargo package
   Packaging bubble-sort v0.1.0 (publish-crate)
   Verifying bubble-sort v0.1.0 (publish-crate)
   Compiling bubble-sort v0.1.0 (publish-
crate/target/package/bubble-sort-0.1.0)
    Finished dev [unoptimized + debuginfo] target(s) in 0.68s
```

5. Now, with an authorized `cargo`, let's make our crate public and run `cargo publish`:

```
$ cargo publish
    Updating crates.io index
    Packaging bubble-sort v0.2.0 (Rust-Cookbook/Chapter03/publish-
    crate)
    Verifying bubble-sort v0.2.0 (Rust-Cookbook/Chapter03/publish-
    crate)
    Compiling bubble-sort v0.2.0 (Rust-Cookbook/Chapter03/publish-
    crate/target/package/bubble-sort-0.2.0)
    Finished dev [unoptimized + debuginfo] target(s) in 6.09s
    Uploading bubble-sort v0.2.0 (Rust-Cookbook/Chapter03/publish-
    crate)
```

6. Once successful, check out your page at `https://crates.io/crates/bubble-sort`:

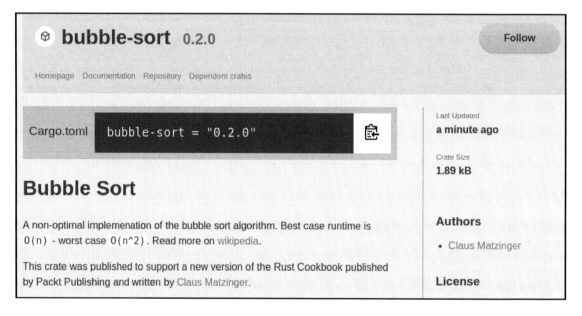

Now, let's go behind the scenes to understand the code better.

How it works...

Publishing crates is a great way to get recognized by the Rust community and make whatever you are creating available to a wider audience. For the community to be able to quickly adapt your crate, be sure to use appropriate keywords and categories, as well as examples and tests to make it clear and easy to use, something that we did in *step 1* and *step 2*. `Cargo.toml` provides many more options than specified previously, so check out the documentation, `https://doc.rust-lang.org/cargo/reference/manifest.html#package-metadata`, to find out more.

The most important property in that file is the package name, which uniquely identifies the crate. While there have been incidents on name squatting and selling names, this is generally frowned upon and the community strives to find a solution to that.

Once packaged (*step 3* and *step 4*), `cargo` creates a `target/package` directory, which contains everything that will be uploaded to `crates.io`. Inside, there is not only the source code but also an additional binary file named `project_name-version.crate`. If you don't want to upload everything—for example, leaving out videos or large example data—`Cargo.toml` allows for exclusion filters as well. By default, everything in the directory is included, but it is good practice to keep the size to a minimum!

Keep your API tokens secret and out of source control. If you are not sure whether a token has been compromised, revoke it!

In *step 5*, we are uploading the new crate. However, `crates.io` does not accept just any upload; here are some examples of the errors you might encounter (observe the error messages to fix them):

```
error: api errors (status 200 OK): crate version `0.1.0` is already
uploaded
error: api errors (status 200 OK): invalid upload request: invalid length
6, expected at most 5 keywords per crate at line 1 column 667
error: 1 files in the working directory contain changes that were not yet
committed into git:
error: api errors (status 200 OK): A verified email address is required to
publish crates to crates.io. Visit https://crates.io/me to set and verify
your email address.
```

These are actually great notifications since these barriers help programmers to avoid simple mistakes, reduce spam, and thereby raise quality. If you follow those terms, you'll easily see a version of the step 6 page for your own project.

We've successfully learned how to upload to `https://crates.io`. Now, let's move on to the next recipe!

Using dependencies and external crates

Reusing other libraries is a common task in software engineering, which is why easy dependency management was built into `cargo` from the start. Third-party dependencies (called **crates**) are stored in a registry called `crates.io` (`https://crates.io`), a public platform for users to find and discover crates. Private registries are also available, starting with Rust 1.34. With `Cargo.toml` as a central point in this process, let's dive into specifying those dependencies well.

How to do it...

Let's see how dependency management works in these steps:

1. As we are going to print on the command line, let's create a new binary application using `cargo new external-deps` and open it in VS Code.

2. Open the `Cargo.toml` file to add some dependencies:

```
[package]
name = "external-deps"
version = "0.1.0"
authors = ["Claus Matzinger <claus.matzinger+kb@gmail.com>"]
edition = "2018"

[dependencies]
regex = { git = "https://github.com/rust-lang/regex" } # bleeding
edge libraries

# specifying crate features
serde = { version = "1", features = ["derive"] }
serde_json = "*" # pick whatever version


[dev-dependencies]
criterion = "0.2.11"


[[bench]]
name = "cooking_with_rust"
harness = false
```

3. With these added, we need to add some code to the `src/main.rs` file as well:

```rust
use regex::Regex;
use serde::Serialize;

#[derive(Serialize)]
struct Person {
    pub full_name: String,
    pub call_me: String,
    pub age: usize,
}

fn main() {
    let a_person = Person {
        full_name: "John Smith".to_owned(),
        call_me: "Smithy".to_owned(),
        age: 42,
    };
    let serialized = serde_json::to_string(&a_person).unwrap();
    println!("A serialized Person instance: {}", serialized);

    let re = Regex::new(r"(?x)(?P<year>\d{4})-(?P<month>\d{2})-(?P<day>\d{2})").unwrap();
    println!("Some regex parsing:");
    let d = "2019-01-31";
    println!(" Is {} valid? {}", d, re.captures(d).is_some());
    let d = "9999-99-00";
    println!(" Is {} valid? {}", d, re.captures(d).is_some());
    let d = "2019-1-10";
    println!(" Is {} valid? {}", d, re.captures(d).is_some());
}
```

4. Then, there is `dev-dependency`, which we can use to create benchmarks with the stable Rust compiler. For that, create a new folder on the same level as `src/` and add a file, `cooking_with_rust.rs`, there. Open it in VS Code and add the following code to run a benchmark:

```rust
#[macro_use]
extern crate criterion;

use criterion::black_box;
use criterion::Criterion;

pub fn bubble_sort<T: PartialOrd + Clone>(collection: &[T]) ->
Vec<T> {
    let mut result: Vec<T> = collection.into();
    for _ in 0..result.len() {
```

```
                    let mut swaps = 0;
                    for i in 1..result.len() {
                        if result[i - 1] > result[i] {
                            result.swap(i - 1, i);
                            swaps += 1;
                        }
                    }
                    if swaps == 0 {
                        break;
                    }
                }
                result
            }

            fn bench_bubble_sort_1k_asc(c: &mut Criterion) {
                c.bench_function("Bubble sort 1k descending numbers", |b| {
                    let items: Vec<i32> = (0..1_000).rev().collect();
                    b.iter(|| black_box(bubble_sort(&items)))
                });
            }

            criterion_group!(benches, bench_bubble_sort_1k_asc);
            criterion_main!(benches);
```

5. Now, let's use these dependencies and see how `cargo` integrates them. Let's
    execute `cargo run` first:

```
$ cargo run
    Compiling proc-macro2 v0.4.27
    Compiling unicode-xid v0.1.0
    Compiling syn v0.15.30
    Compiling libc v0.2.51
    Compiling memchr v2.2.0
    Compiling ryu v0.2.7
    Compiling serde v1.0.90
    Compiling ucd-util v0.1.3
    Compiling lazy_static v1.3.0
    Compiling regex v1.1.5 (https://github.com/rust-
      lang/regex#9687986d)
    Compiling utf8-ranges v1.0.2
    Compiling itoa v0.4.3
    Compiling regex-syntax v0.6.6 (https://github.com/rust-
      lang/regex#9687986d)
    Compiling thread_local v0.3.6
    Compiling quote v0.6.12
    Compiling aho-corasick v0.7.3
    Compiling serde_derive v1.0.90
    Compiling serde_json v1.0.39
```

```
    Compiling external-deps v0.1.0 (Rust-Cookbook
     /Chapter03/external-deps)
      Finished dev [unoptimized + debuginfo] target(s) in 24.56s
       Running `target/debug/external-deps`
 A serialized Person instance: {"full_name":"John
 Smith","call_me":"Smithy","age":42}
 Some regex parsing:
   Is 2019-01-31 valid? true
   Is 9999-99-00 valid? true
   Is 2019-1-10 valid? false
```

6. It downloaded and compiled various crates (the download part was omitted as it is only done once)—but can you spot what's missing? It's the `criterion` crate that was specified as `dev-dependency`, and it's only required for development (`test/bench/..`) operations. Let's run `cargo bench` to see benchmark results of the crate, including some basic trends provided by `criterion` (output redacted):

```
$ cargo bench
    Compiling proc-macro2 v0.4.27
    Compiling unicode-xid v0.1.0
    Compiling arrayvec v0.4.10
    [...]
    Compiling tinytemplate v1.0.1
    Compiling external-deps v0.1.0 (Rust-Cookbook
     /Chapter03/external-deps)
    Compiling criterion v0.2.11
      Finished release [optimized] target(s) in 1m 32s
       Running target/release/deps/external_deps-09d742c8de9a2cc7

running 0 tests

test result: ok. 0 passed; 0 failed; 0 ignored; 0 measured; 0
filtered out

     Running target/release/deps/cooking_with_rust-b879dc4675a42592
Gnuplot not found, disabling plotting
Bubble sort 1k descending numbers
                        time: [921.90 us 924.39 us 927.17 us]
Found 12 outliers among 100 measurements (12.00%)
   6 (6.00%) high mild
   6 (6.00%) high severe

Gnuplot not found, disabling plotting
```

Now, let's go behind the scenes to understand the code better.

How it works...

By specifying the version and name in `Cargo.toml`, `cargo` can download and compile the required crates and link them into the project as needed. In fact, `cargo` maintains a cache for both crates on `crates.io` and raw `git` dependencies (check the `~/.cargo` directory), where it puts recently used crates. This is exactly what we did in the first steps by adding dependencies of mixed origin to the crate.

One of these origins is a `git` repository, but can alternatively take the shape of local paths to directories. Additionally, by passing an object (as seen in the `regex` crate in *step 1*), we can specify features for a crate (as shown in the `serde` dependency in *step 1*) or use an entire section called `dev-dependencies` for dependencies that are not shipped in the target output. The result is a dependency tree that is serialized in `Cargo.lock`. The use of the `dev-dependency` criterion is shown in *step 6*. The remaining steps show how to use external dependencies and the various versions downloaded and compiled by `cargo`.

The version specification in `Cargo.toml` is its own mini-language, and it will only upgrade with certain restrictions:

- A single number specifies the major version (a pattern of `<major>.<minor>.<patch>` is mandatory in Rust) but leaves the others open for `cargo` to decide (usually the latest version)
- More accurate versions leave less room for interpretation
- `*` means any available version, with the latest preferred

There are more characters and symbols to put into the version string, yet these will typically suffice. Check out `https://doc.rust-lang.org/cargo/reference/specifying-dependencies.html` for more examples. The `cargo upgrade` command will also check for the latest versions the specification allows and update them accordingly. If you plan to build a crate that is used by others, it's recommended to run `cargo upgrade` every once in a while to see it didn't miss any security/patch updates. The Rust project even recommends putting the `Cargo.lock` file in source control to avoid unintentionally breaking the crate.

It is good practice to minimize the number of required crates and to keep them as up to date as possible. Your users will want to do the same.

See also...

With 1.34, Rust also allows private repositories. Read more about this on the following blog post: `https://blog.rust-lang.org/2019/04/11/Rust-1.34.0.html#alternative-cargo-registries`. We've now successfully learned how to use dependencies and external crates. Now, let's move on to the next recipe!

Extending cargo with sub-commands

These days, everything is extensible. Whether they are called plugins, extensions, add-ons, or sub-commands—everything is about customizing the (developer) experience. `cargo` provides a very easy path to achieve this: by using a binary's name. This allows for quickly extending the `cargo` base to include functions that are specific to your own use case or way of working. In this recipe, we are going to build our own extension.

Getting ready

For this recipe, we will stay on the command line and we will use a sample code for a simple binary, so open a Terminal/PowerShell (we are using PowerShell features on Windows) to run the commands in this recipe.

How to do it...

Extending `cargo` is surprisingly easy. To do this, perform the following steps:

1. Create a new Rust binary application project with the following command: `cargo new cargo-hello`.
2. Change into the directory with `cd cargo-hello` and build it using `cargo build`.
3. Add the `target/debug` folder of the current project that is located at your PATH variable. On Linux and Mac (using bash), it's simply as follows:

   `export PATH=$PATH:/path/to/cargo-hello/target/debug`

   On Windows, you can use PowerShell to achieve the same goal with this code script:

   `$env:Path += ";C:/path/to/cargo-hello/target/debug"`

4. Within the same window, you should now be able to run `cargo-hello` (`cargo-hello.exe` on Windows) from any directory on the computer.

5. Additionally, `cargo` can now run `hello` as a sub-command. Try running `cargo hello` in any directory on the computer. From here, you will see the following output:

```
$ cargo hello
Hello, world!
```

Now let's go behind the scenes to understand the code better.

How it works...

`cargo` picks up any executable starting with `cargo-` that's available in the `PATH` environment variable. Directories listed in there are used to discover command-line executables in *nix systems.

For `cargo` to integrate these extensions seamlessly, their names have to meet a few conditions:

- These binaries have to be executable on the current platform
- The name starts with `cargo-`
- The containing folder is listed in the `PATH` variable

On Linux/macOS, these executables can also be shell scripts—something that's very useful for improving the developer workflow. However, these scripts have to look just like a binary and therefore have no file ending. Then, instead of running several commands, such as `cargo publish`, `git tag`, and `git push`, `cargo shipit` can significantly improve speed and consistency.

Additionally, any `cargo` sub-command can take command-line arguments that are passed after the command, and the working directory is the directory the command is run from by default. With that knowledge, we hope that you can now add to `cargo` features!

We've successfully learned how to extend cargo with sub-commands. Now, let's move on to the next recipe!

Testing your project with cargo

While in a previous recipe we focused on writing tests, this recipe is about *running* them. Tests are an important part of software engineering since it ensures that we put ourselves in the user's shoes and double-checked to see whether what we created is working. While many other languages require a separate test-runner, `cargo` comes with this functionality included!

Let's explore how `cargo` helps with this process in this recipe.

How to do it...

To explore `cargo` testing capabilities, follow these steps:

1. Create a new project on the command line with `cargo new test-commands -- lib` and open the resulting folder in VS Code.

2. Next, replace the content in `src/lib.rs` with the following:

```rust
#[cfg(test)]
mod tests {

    use std::thread::sleep;
    use std::time::Duration;

    #[test]
    fn it_works() {
        assert_eq!(2 + 2, 4);
    }

    #[test]
    fn wait_10secs() {
        sleep(Duration::from_secs(10));
        println!("Waited for 10 seconds");
        assert_eq!(2 + 2, 4);
    }

    #[test]
    fn wait_5secs() {
        sleep(Duration::from_secs(5));
        println!("Waited for 5 seconds");
        assert_eq!(2 + 2, 4);
    }

        #[test]
```

```
        #[ignore]
        fn ignored() {
            assert_eq!(2 + 2, 4);
        }
    }
```

3. As we did in other recipes, we can execute all tests with the `cargo test` command:

```
$ cargo test
    Compiling test-commands v0.1.0 (Rust-Cookbook/Chapter03/test-
    commands)
    Finished dev [unoptimized + debuginfo] target(s) in 0.37s
     Running target/debug/deps/test_commands-06e02dadda81dfcd

running 4 tests
test tests::ignored ... ignored
test tests::it_works ... ok
test tests::wait_5secs ... ok
test tests::wait_10secs ... ok

test result: ok. 3 passed; 0 failed; 1 ignored; 0 measured; 0
filtered out

    Doc-tests test-commands

running 0 tests

test result: ok. 0 passed; 0 failed; 0 ignored; 0 measured; 0
filtered out
```

4. To iterate quickly, `cargo` allows us to carry out a specific test as well by using `cargo test <test-name>`:

```
$ cargo test tests::it_works
    Finished dev [unoptimized + debuginfo] target(s) in 0.05s
     Running target/debug/deps/test_commands-06e02dadda81dfcd

running 1 test
test tests::it_works ... ok

test result: ok. 1 passed; 0 failed; 0 ignored; 0 measured; 3
filtered out
```

5. Another useful way to run tests is without capturing their output. By default, the testing harness won't print anything from inside the tests. Sometimes, it's useful to have some testing output, so let's use `cargo test -- --nocapture` to see the output:

```
$ cargo test -- --nocapture
    Finished dev [unoptimized + debuginfo] target(s) in 0.01s
     Running target/debug/deps/test_commands-06e02dadda81dfcd

running 4 tests
test tests::ignored ... ignored
test tests::it_works ... ok
Waited for 5 seconds
test tests::wait_5secs ... ok
Waited for 10 seconds
test tests::wait_10secs ... ok

test result: ok. 3 passed; 0 failed; 1 ignored; 0 measured; 0
filtered out

    Doc-tests test-commands

running 0 tests

test result: ok. 0 passed; 0 failed; 0 ignored; 0 measured; 0
filtered out
```

6. All tests are run in parallel, which sometimes leads to unexpected results. To adjust this behavior, we can use `cargo test -- --test-threads <no-of-threads>` to control the number of threads. Let's compare using four threads and one thread to see the difference. We will use the `time` program to show the runtime in seconds (this is optional if you don't have `time`). Let's start with four:

```
$ time -f "%e" cargo test -- --test-threads 4
   Compiling test-commands v0.1.0 (/home/cm/workspace/Mine/Rust-
   Cookbook/Chapter03/test-commands)
    Finished dev [unoptimized + debuginfo] target(s) in 0.35s
     Running target/debug/deps/test_commands-06e02dadda81dfcd

running 4 tests
test tests::ignored ... ignored
test tests::it_works ... ok
test tests::wait_5secs ... ok
test tests::wait_10secs ... ok

test result: ok. 3 passed; 0 failed; 1 ignored; 0 measured; 0
filtered out
```

```
        Doc-tests test-commands

running 0 tests

test result: ok. 0 passed; 0 failed; 0 ignored; 0 measured; 0
filtered out

10.53
```

This is fast, compared to a single thread:

```
$ time -f "%e" cargo test -- --test-threads 1
    Finished dev [unoptimized + debuginfo] target(s) in 0.03s
     Running target/debug/deps/test_commands-06e02dadda81dfcd

running 4 tests
test tests::ignored ... ignored
test tests::it_works ... ok
test tests::wait_10secs ... ok
test tests::wait_5secs ... ok

test result: ok. 3 passed; 0 failed; 1 ignored; 0 measured; 0
filtered out

    Doc-tests test-commands

running 0 tests

test result: ok. 0 passed; 0 failed; 0 ignored; 0 measured; 0
filtered out

15.17
```

7. Lastly, we can also filter multiple tests as well, such as all tests starting with
   `wait`:

```
$ cargo test wait
    Finished dev [unoptimized + debuginfo] target(s) in 0.03s
     Running target/debug/deps/test_commands-06e02dadda81dfcd

running 2 tests
test tests::wait_5secs ... ok
test tests::wait_10secs ... ok
```

Now, let's go behind the scenes to understand the code better.

How it works...

Rust's built-in testing library is called `libtest` and it is what's invoked by `cargo`. Regardless of the type of project created (binary application or library), `libtest` runs the associated test and outputs the result. In this recipe, we are examining running the tests of a previously created project—however, these steps obviously work for any project with tests.

In *step 2*, we created a small library that features four tests, two of which print things to the command line just after waiting for a few seconds (five and ten seconds). This allows us to show threaded test running and that the test harness captures the output by default.

Other than filtering the list of available tests (we do that in *step 4* and *step 7*) in the project, `libtest` takes command-line arguments to customize the output, logging, threads, and many more things. Find out more by invoking `cargo test -- --help`. Note the double dashes (`--`), which tell `cargo` to pass any following arguments into `libtest`.

As the options already indicate: all tests are run in parallel unless stated otherwise, an option that we change in *step 6* with noticeable results (15 seconds with a single thread versus 10 seconds multi-threaded—just like the longest sleep time). Use this option to debug race conditions or other runtime behavior.

Step 5 uses an option to show the standard output, which appears in a different order than how we wrote the test functions. This is the result of concurrent execution, so combining the options to limit the number of threads with the output capture will linearly execute the tests. We conclude the steps by filtering for multiple tests in *step 7*.

We've successfully learned how to test our project with `cargo`. Now, let's move on to the next recipe!

Continuous integration with cargo

Automation is an important aspect of today's software engineering. Whether it is infrastructure as code or functions as a service, many things are expected to automatically work as expected. However, the notion of a central testing and deployment infrastructure based on certain rules is much older (called **ALM—Application Lifecycle Management**) and with modern tools, it is incredibly easy. `cargo` was built to support this stateless infrastructure with reasonable defaults and an easy interface to customize them.

In this recipe, we will take a look at how to build Rust applications using Microsoft's Azure DevOps platform as an example.

Getting ready

While the Azure DevOps repository (`https://azure.microsoft.com/en-us/services/devops/?nav=min`) is accessible for anyone, it is highly recommended to create a Microsoft account and make use of the free tier to reproduce the example. Go to `https://azure.microsoft.com/en-us/services/devops/` and follow the instructions to get started.

To have a ready-made project to work on, we are re-using the `bubble-sort` crate from the *Uploading to crates.io* recipe earlier in this chapter and uploading it to a source code hosting service such as Azure DevOps or GitHub.

How to do it...

Open a browser window and navigate to `https://dev.azure.com`, sign in, and find the project you created. Then, follow these steps:

1. Azure DevOps is an all-in-one solution for project management, so we are pushing our source code to the available repository. Follow the repository setup guide to do that.
2. Pipelines are the continuous integration part of Azure DevOps. They orchestrate build agents (machines to run the build on) and provide a visual interface to put together a step-by-step build process. Create a new pipeline from an empty job template:

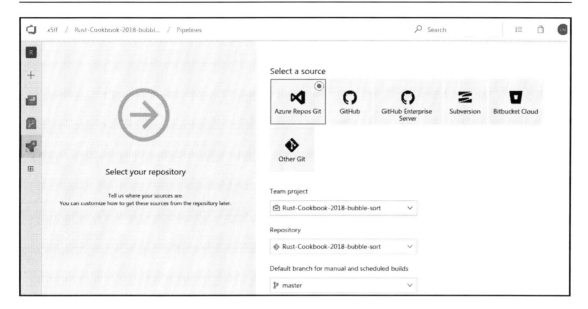

3. Inside each pipeline, there are several jobs—several steps that run on the same agent, but we only need one. Click on the + symbol on the right of the predefined **Agent job 1** and search for a build task named `rust`:

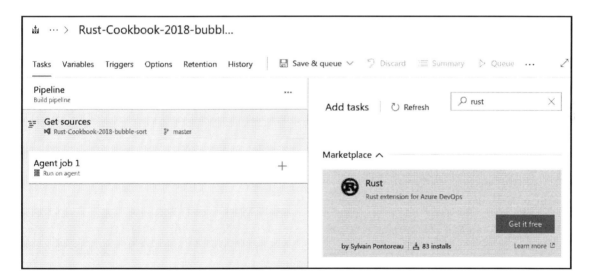

4. Since that particular build task is available on the Marketplace (thanks to Sylvain Pontoreau: `https://github.com/spontoreau/rust-azure-devops`), we have to add it to our project.

5. After *purchasing* (it's free) the task blueprint, we can add and configure it in our pipeline. It's useful to have a build that runs tests, but CI systems are very flexible and you can get very creative. Your screen should now look like this:

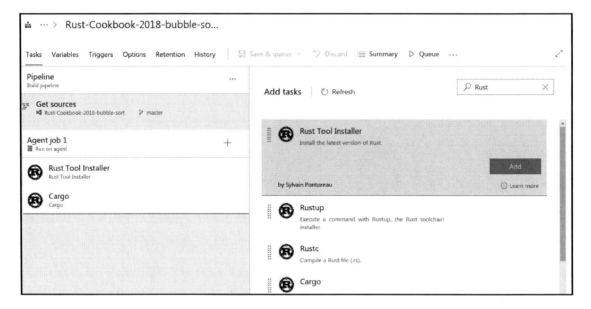

6. Use the first task as it is (no configuration needed) since it is only installing the tools using `rustup`. The second task simply runs `cargo test`:

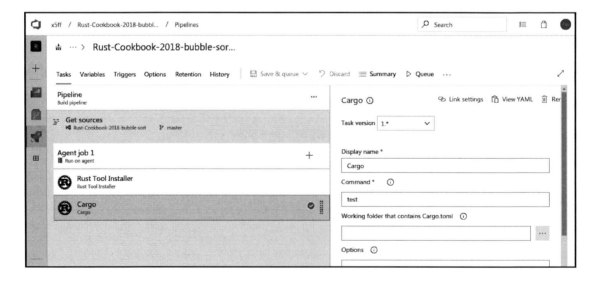

7. As the last step, queue the build and check its progress. If you followed the recipe, it will result in a successful build and you can start using it to check pull requests, add badges on `crates.io`, and much more:

Now, let's go behind the scenes to understand the code better.

How it works...

Azure DevOps is a fully integrated solution for project management, issue tracking, source code hosting, and building and deploying solutions. Similar offerings are GitHub (also owned by Microsoft), GitLab (`https://about.gitlab.com`), or Atlassian's Bitbucket (`https://bitbucket.org`). Together with CircleCI (`https://circleci.com`) or Travis CI (`https://travis-ci.org/`), these platforms offer powerful tools for teams to make sure that every new deployment reliably meets their goals without large management overhead.

The basic idea is simple: by making the build work on a neutral platform, most of the obvious mistakes (missing dependencies or relying on environment specifics) can easily be avoided while running the same tests that have to run locally. On top of that, running every test might be demanding on large projects, and dedicated infrastructure takes care of that.

Since computers are notoriously picky, the results of running tests are also visible and can be used to prohibit certain actions, such as deploying to production with failing tests. In a way, a continuous integration system holds the developer accountable to their own rules (tests).

`cargo` support is implicit by being a good citizen in stateless systems. Instead of failing if certain conditions are not met, it tries to mitigate late terminations and requires little configuration to begin with. Its ability to handle dependencies easily and well adds to that and the support for sub-commands makes it a great way to build across platforms.

Here are some ideas of what you can do besides running `cargo test`:

- Run benchmarks
- Run integration tests
- Format code
- Accept PRs only on successful tests
- Generate documentation
- Do static code analysis

Azure DevOps also supports release pipelines, which should be used for tasks such as publishing to `crates.io` (or other package repositories), updating the hosted documentation, and more. Read the Azure DevOps documentation (`https://docs.microsoft.com/en-us/azure/devops/?view=azure-devops`) on how to do that. For anyone who prefers YAML (`https://yaml.org/`) files to configure CI pipelines, Azure DevOps supports these as well.

Thanks to Sylvain Pontoreau's work (`https://twitter.com/bla`) on creating easy-to-use task templates, we can quickly set build, test, or other pipelines. Doing it manually can be tricky to get right for every platform and maintaining downloads and shell scripts is a hassle for most developers. If you are using his work, he is happy to hear about it as well—for example, on Twitter (`https://twitter.com/spontoreau`).

We've successfully learned how to continuously integrate with `cargo`. Now, let's move on to the next recipe!

Customizing the build

`cargo` is versatile—something that we have already established in the previous recipes in this chapter. However, we did not touch configuring the tools `cargo` uses to compile and run Rust projects. For this, there are multiple ways, as they apply to different domains.

In this recipe, we are going to explore two ways by customizing the build of a new project.

How to do it...

Here's how to customize a build:

1. Create a new binary project using `cargo new custom-build` and open the project folder using VS Code.

2. Open `src/main.rs` and replace the hello world code with the following:

```
fn main() {
    println!("Overflow! {}", 128u8 + 129u8);
}
```

3. The code in our binary is now creating an overflow situation that a compiler can easily catch. However, the default release build has that feature turned off. Run `cargo run --release` to see it in action:

```
$ cargo run --release
 Finished release [optimized] target(s) in 0.02s
 Running `target/release/custom-build`
Overflow! 1
```

4. If we wanted to change the fact that the compiler verifies overflow errors at compile time in release mode (even though overflows can be *useful*, for example, in hardware drivers), we have to edit `Cargo.toml` and customize the profile for `release` (there are others as well, for example, `dev` and `test`). While we are there we can change a few other options for faster builds (important for larger projects):

```
# Let's modify the release build
[profile.release]
opt-level = 2
incremental = true # default is false
overflow-checks = true
```

5. When we run `cargo run --release` now, the output has changed:

```
$ cargo run --release
    Compiling custom-build v0.1.0 (Rust-Cookbook/Chapter03/custom-
build)
error: attempt to add with overflow
 --> src/main.rs:2:30
  |
2 |     println!("Overflow! {}", 128u8 + 129u8);
  |                              ^^^^^^^^^^^^^
  |
  = note: #[deny(const_err)] on by default

error: aborting due to previous error

error: Could not compile `custom-build`.

To learn more, run the command again with --verbose.
```

6. That was easy—but there is more! Create a `.cargo` directory at the root of the project and add a `config` file inside. Since the file (and directory) is inside the project, that's its scope. However, it's possible to make it valid for a larger number of projects by moving the `.cargo` directories up several levels. Be aware that the user's home directory represents *global scope*, which means the `cargo` configuration applies to all of the user's projects. The following settings switch the default build target to WASM output (https://webassembly.org/) and rename the build artifact directory `out` (the default is `target`):

```
[build]
target = "wasm32-unknown-unknown" # the new default target
target-dir = "out"                # custom build output directory
```

7. Now, let's remove the overflow from `src/main.rs`:

```
fn main() {
    println!("Overflow! {}", 128 + 129);
}
```

8. Compile with `cargo build` and `cargo run` to see what's happening:

```
$ cargo build
    Compiling custom-build v0.1.0 (Rust-Cookbook/Chapter03/custom-
    build)
    Finished dev [unoptimized + debuginfo] target(s) in 0.37s
$ cargo run
    Compiling custom-build v0.1.0 (Rust-Cookbook/Chapter03/custom-
    build)
```

```
Finished dev [unoptimized + debuginfo] target(s) in 0.15s
 Running `out/wasm32-unknown-unknown/debug/custom-build.wasm`
out/wasm32-unknown-unknown/debug/custom-build.wasm:
 out/wasm32-unknown-unknown/debug/custom-build.wasm: cannot
  execute binary file
```

Now, let's go behind the scenes to understand the code better.

How it works...

There are many aspects of a project that can be configured, most of which are not needed for smaller programs and libraries (unless it's for special architectures). This recipe can only show a few—easy—examples of what's possible, but there is more in the `cargo` book about configuration (`https://doc.rust-lang.org/cargo/reference/config.html`) and the manifest (`https://doc.rust-lang.org/cargo/reference/manifest.html#the-profile-sections`).

In the first steps, `cargo` is configured to overlook overflow errors by changing a flag in the `cargo` configuration. While it might seem a foolish step at first, it is sometimes necessary to allow overflows for drivers or other low-level electronics to operate.

Many other options customize the developer experience (for example, setting the name and email address for new projects, aliases, and many more) or prove useful in non-standard settings, for example, when creating device drivers, operating systems, or real-time software for specialized hardware. We might use some of these later on in `Chapter 9`, *Systems Programming Made Easy*.

However, changing the `build` section (as in `cargo build`) has grave consequences as it represents the standard output format for the project. It might seem arbitrary to change it to something like WASM, but as a default, it can save many steps for the developer to set up the development environment—or to simply make CI build scripts less verbose.

In any case, `cargo` is very flexible and easy to configure, but it's tailored to each project individually. Check out the manifest and documentation to find out how it can make your project (and your life) easier.

4
Fearless Concurrency

Concurrency and parallelism are important parts of modern-day programming and Rust is perfectly equipped to deal with these challenges. The borrowing and ownership model is great for preventing data races (**anomalies**, as they are called in the database world) since variables are immutable by default and if mutability is required, there cannot be any other reference to the data. This makes any type of concurrency safe and less complex in Rust (compared to many other languages).

In this chapter, we will cover several ways of employing concurrency to solve problems and will even look at futures, which are—at the time of writing—not part of the language yet. If you are reading this in the future (no pun intended), this may be part of the core language already and you can check out the *Asynchronous programming with futures* recipe for historical reference.

In this chapter, we will cover the following recipes:

- Moving data into new threads
- Managing multiple threads
- Message passing between threads
- Shared mutable states
- Multiprocessing
- Making sequential code parallel
- Concurrent data processing in vectors
- Shared immutable states
- Actors and asynchronous messages
- Async programming with futures

Moving data into new threads

Rust threads operate just like in any other language—in scopes. Any other scope (such as closures) can easily borrow the variables from the parent scope since it's easy to determine if and when variables are dropped. However, when spawning a thread, its lifetime, compared to its parent's lifetime, is impossible to know and therefore the reference can become invalid at any time.

To tackle this problem, the threaded scope can take ownership of its variables—the memory is **moved** into the thread's scope. Let's see how this is done!

How to do it...

Follow these steps to see how to move memory between threads:

1. Use `cargo new simple-threads` to create a new application project and open the directory in Visual Studio Code.
2. Edit `src/main.rs` and spawn a simple thread that does not move data into its scope. Since it's the simplest form of a thread, let's print something to the command line and wait:

```
use std::thread;
use std::time::Duration;

fn start_no_shared_data_thread() -> thread::JoinHandle<()> {
    thread::spawn(|| {
        // since we are not using a parent scope variable in here
        // no move is required
        println!("Waiting for three seconds.");
        thread::sleep(Duration::from_secs(3));
        println!("Done")
    })
}
```

3. Now, let's call the new function from within `fn main()`. Replace the `hello world` snippet with the following:

```
let no_move_thread = start_no_shared_data_thread();
for _ in 0..10 {
    print!(":");
}

println!("Waiting for the thread to finish ... {:?}",
    no_move_thread.join());
```

4. Let's run the code to see if it works:

```
$ cargo run
 Compiling simple-threads v0.1.0 (Rust-Cookbook/Chapter05/simple-
 threads)
    Finished dev [unoptimized + debuginfo] target(s) in 0.35s
     Running `target/debug/simple-threads`
:::::::::::Waiting for three seconds.
Done
Waiting for the thread to finish ... Ok(())
```

5. Now, let's get some outside data into a thread. Add another function to
   src/main.rs:

```
fn start_shared_data_thread(a_number: i32, a_vec: Vec<i32>) ->
thread::JoinHandle<Vec<i32>> {
    // thread::spawn(move || {
    thread::spawn(|| {
        print!(" a_vec ---> [");
        for i in a_vec.iter() {
            print!(" {} ", i);
        }
        println!("]");
        println!(" A number from inside the thread: {}", a_number);
        a_vec // let's return ownership
    })
}
```

6. To demonstrate what's happening under the hood, we have left out the move
   keyword for now. Expand the main function with the following code:

```
let a_number = 42;
let a_vec = vec![1,2,3,4,5];

let move_thread = start_shared_data_thread(a_number, a_vec);

println!("We can still use a Copy-enabled type: {}", a_number);
println!("Waiting for the thread to finish ... {:?}",
move_thread.join());
```

7. Does it work? Let's try cargo run:

```
$ cargo run
Compiling simple-threads v0.1.0 (Rust-Cookbook/Chapter04/simple-
threads)
error[E0373]: closure may outlive the current function, but it
borrows `a_number`, which is owned by the current function
  --> src/main.rs:22:20
```

```
     |
22  |  thread::spawn(|| {
     |                  ^^ may outlive borrowed value `a_number`
...
29  |     println!(" A number from inside the thread: {}", a_number);
     |                                                       --------
`a_number` is borrowed here
     |
note: function requires argument type to outlive `'static`
  --> src/main.rs:22:6
     |
23  | /     thread::spawn(|| {
24  | |         print!(" a_vec ---> [");
25  | |         for i in a_vec.iter() {
... | |
30  | |         a_vec // let's return ownership
31  | |     })
     | |_____^
help: to force the closure to take ownership of `a_number` (and any
other referenced variables), use the `move` keyword
     |
23  | thread::spawn(move || {
     |               ^^^^^^^

error: aborting due to previous error

For more information about this error, try `rustc --explain E0373`.
error: Could not compile `simple-threads`.

To learn more, run the command again with --verbose.
```

8. There we have it: to get any kind of data into a threaded scope, we need to transfer ownership by moving the value into the scope using the move keyword. Let's follow the compiler's instructions:

```
///
/// Starts a thread moving the function's input parameters
///
fn start_shared_data_thread(a_number: i32, a_vec: Vec<i32>) ->
thread::JoinHandle<Vec<i32>> {
    thread::spawn(move || {
    // thread::spawn(|| {
        print!(" a_vec ---> [");
        for i in a_vec.iter() {
            print!(" {} ", i);
        }
        println!("]");
        println!(" A number from inside the thread: {}", a_number);
```

```
        a_vec // let's return ownership
    })
}
```

9. Let's try again with `cargo run`:

```
$ cargo run
    Compiling simple-threads v0.1.0 (Rust-Cookbook/Chapter04/simple-
    threads)
     Finished dev [unoptimized + debuginfo] target(s) in 0.38s
      Running `target/debug/simple-threads`
:::::::::::Waiting for three seconds.
Done
Waiting for the thread to finish ... Ok(())
We can still use a Copy-enabled type: 42
    a_vec ---> [ 1 2 3 4 5 ]
    A number from inside the thread: 42
Waiting for the thread to finish ... Ok([1, 2, 3, 4, 5])
```

Now, let's go behind the scenes to understand the code better.

How it works...

Threads in Rust behave a lot like regular functions: they can take ownership and operate on the same syntax as closures (|| {} is an empty/noop function without parameters). Therefore, we have to treat them like we treat functions and think of them in terms of ownership and borrowing, or more specifically: lifetimes. Passing a reference (the default behavior) into this thread function makes it impossible for the compiler to keep track of the validity of the reference, which is a problem for code safety. Rust solves this by introducing the move keyword.

Using the move keyword changes the default behavior of borrowing to moving the ownership of every variable into the scope. Hence, unless these values implement the Copy trait (like i32), or have a longer lifetime than the thread when borrowing (like the 'static lifetime for str literals), they become unavailable to the thread's parent scope.

Giving back ownership also works just like in a function—via the return statement. The thread that waits for the other (using join()) can then retrieve the return value by unwrapping the join() result.

Threads in Rust are native threads for each operating system and have their own local state and execution stack. When they panic, only the thread stops, not the entire program.

We've successfully gone through moving data into new threads. Now let's move on to the next recipe.

Managing multiple threads

Single threads are great, but in reality, many use cases demand a wealth of threads to execute on a large-scale data set in parallel. This has been popularized by the map/reduce pattern, published several years ago, and is still a great way to process something distinct such as multiple files, rows in a database result, and many more in parallel. Whatever the source, as long as the processing is not inter-dependent, it can be chunked and **mapped**—both of which Rust can make easy and free of data-race conditions.

How to do it...

In this recipe, we'll add some more threads to do map-style data processing. Follow these steps:

1. Run `cargo new multiple-threads` to create a new application project and open the directory in Visual Studio Code.
2. In `src/main.rs`, add the following function on top of `main()`:

```
use std::thread;


///
/// Doubles each element in the provided chunks in parallel and
returns the results.
///
fn parallel_map(data: Vec<Vec<i32>>) ->
Vec<thread::JoinHandle<Vec<i32>>> {
    data.into_iter()
        .map(|chunk| thread::spawn(move ||
        chunk.into_iter().map(|c|
        c * 2).collect())))
        .collect()
}
```

3. In this function, we spawn a thread for each chunk that has been passed in. This thread only doubles the number and therefore the function returns Vec<i32> for each chunk containing the results of this transformation. Now we need to create input data and call the function. Let's extend main to do that:

```
fn main() {

    // Prepare chunked data
    let data = vec![vec![1, 2, 3], vec![4, 4, 5], vec![6, 7, 7]];

    // work on the data in parallel
    let results: Vec<i32> = parallel_map(data.clone())
        .into_iter() // an owned iterator over the results
        .flat_map(|thread| thread.join().unwrap()) // join each
        thread
        .collect(); // collect the results into a Vec

    // flatten the original data structure
    let data: Vec<i32> = data.into_iter().flat_map(|e| e)
        .collect();

    // print the results
    println!("{:?} -> {:?}", data, results);
}
```

4. With cargo run we can now see the results:

```
$ cargo run
    Compiling multiple-threads v0.1.0 (Rust-
    Cookbook/Chapter04/multiple-threads)
    Finished dev [unoptimized + debuginfo] target(s) in 0.45s
    Running `target/debug/multiple-threads`
    [1, 2, 3, 4, 4, 5, 6, 7, 7] -> [2, 4, 6, 8, 8, 10, 12, 14, 14]
```

Now, let's go behind the scenes to understand the code better.

How it works...

Admittedly, working with multiple threads in Rust is just the same as if we were working on single threads since there are no convenient methods for joining a list of threads or similar. Instead, we can use the power of Rust's iterators to do that in an expressive way. With these functional constructs, the need for for loops can be replaced by a chain of functions that lazily process collections, which makes the code easier to handle and more efficient.

After setting up the project in *step 1*, we implement a multithreaded function to apply an operation to every chunk. These chunks are simply parts of a vector, and an operation—a simple function that doubles the input variable in this example—can be done with any type of task. *Step 3* shows how to call the multithreaded `mapping` function and how to get results by using the `JoinHandle` in a future/promise (`http://dist-prog-book.com/chapter/2/futures.html`) way. *Step 4* then simply shows that it works as intended by outputting the doubled chunks as a flat list.

What is also interesting is the number of times we have had to clone data. Since passing data into the threads is only possible by moving the values into each thread's memory space, cloning is often the only way to work around these sharing issues. However, we'll cover a method similar to multiple `Rc` in a later recipe (*Shared immutable states*) in this chapter, so let's move on to the next recipe.

Using channels to communicate between threads

Message passing between threads has been an issue in many standard libraries and programming languages since many rely on the user to apply locking. This leads to deadlocks and is somewhat intimidating for newcomers, which is why many developers were excited when Go popularized the concept of channels, something that we can also find in Rust. Rust's channels are great for designing a safe, event-driven application in just a few lines of code without any explicit locking.

How to do it...

Let's create a simple application that visualizes incoming values on the command line:

1. Run `cargo new channels` to create a new application project and open the directory in Visual Studio Code.
2. First, let's get the basics out of the way. Open `src/main.rs` and add the imports and an `enum` structure to the file:

```
use std::sync::mpsc::{Sender, Receiver};
use std::sync::mpsc;
use std::thread;

use rand::prelude::*;
use std::time::Duration;
```

```
enum ChartValue {
    Star(usize),
    Pipe(usize)
}
```

3. Then, inside the `main` function, we create a channel with the `mpsc::channel()` function along with two threads that take care of the sending. Afterward, we are going to use two threads to send messages to the main thread with a variable delay. Here's the code:

```
fn main() {
    let (tx, rx): (Sender<ChartValue>, Receiver<ChartValue>) =
    mpsc::channel();

    let pipe_sender = tx.clone();

    thread::spawn(move || {
        loop {
            pipe_sender.send(ChartValue::Pipe(random::<usize>() %
            80)).unwrap();
            thread::sleep(Duration::from_millis(random::<u64>() %
            800));
        }
    });

    let star_sender = tx.clone();
    thread::spawn(move || {
        loop {
            star_sender.send(ChartValue::Star(random::<usize>() %
            80)).unwrap();
            thread::sleep(Duration::from_millis(random::<u64>() %
            800));
        }
    });
```

4. Both of the threads are sending data to the channel, so what's missing is the channel's receiving end to take care of the input data. The receiver offers two functions, `recv()` and `recv_timeout()`, both of which block the calling thread until an item is received (or the timeout is reached). We are just going to print the character multiplied by the passed-in value:

```
    while let Ok(val) = rx.recv_timeout(Duration::from_secs(3)) {

        println!("{}", match val {
            ChartValue::Pipe(v) => "|".repeat(v + 1),
            ChartValue::Star(v) => "*".repeat(v + 1)
        });
```

```
        }
    }
```

5. In order to use `rand` when we finally run the program, we still need to add it to `Cargo.toml` with the following:

```
[dependencies]
rand = "^0.5"
```

6. Lastly, let's see how the program runs—it's going to run infinitely. To stop it, press *Ctrl* + *C*. Run it with `cargo run`:

```
$ cargo run
   Compiling channels v0.1.0 (Rust-Cookbook/Chapter04/channels)
    Finished dev [unoptimized + debuginfo] target(s) in 1.38s
     Running `target/debug/channels`
| | | | | | | | | | | | | | | | | | | | | | | | | | | | | | | | | | | | | | | | | | | | | | | | | | | | | | | | | | | | | | | | | |
|
* * * * * * * * * * * * * * * * * * * * * * * * * *
| | | | | | | | | | | | | | | | | | | | | | | | | | | | | | | | | | | | | | | | | | | | | | | | | | | | | | | | | | | | | | | | | | | |
| | | | | | | | | | |
| | | | | | | | | | | | | | | | | | | | | | | | | | | | | | | | | |
* * * * * * * * * * * * * * * * * * * * * * * * * * * * * * * * * * * * * * * * * * * * * * * * * * * *
| | | | | | | | | | | | | | | | | | | | | | | | | | | |
* * * * * * * * * * * * * * * * * * * * * * * * * * * * * * * * * * * * * * * * * * * * * * * * * * * * *
* * * * * * * * * * * * * * * * * * * * * * * * * * *
| | | | | | | | | | | | | | | | | |
* * * * * * * * * * *
| | | | | | | | | | | | | | | | | | | | | | | | | | | | | | | | | | | | | | | | | | | | | | | | | | | | | | | | | | | | | | | | |
* * * * * * * * * * * * * * * * * * * * * * * * * * * *
| | | | | | | | | | | | | | | | | | | | | | | | | | | | | | | | | | | | | | | | | | | |
* * * * * * * * * * * * * * * * * * * * * * * * * * * * * * * * * * * * * * * * * * * * * * * * * * * * *
| | | | | | | | | | | | | | | | | | | | | | | | | | | | | | | | | | | | | | | | | | | | | | |
* * * * * * * * * * * * * * * * * * * * * * * * * * * * *
* * * * * * * * * * * * * * * * * * * * * * * * * * * * * * * * * * * * * * * * * * * * * * * * * * * * * * * * * * * * * * * *
* * * * *
* * * * * * * * * * * * * * * * * * *
* * * * * * * * * * * * * * * * * * * * * * * * * * * * * * * * * * * * * * * * * * * * * *
| | | | | | | | | | | | | | | | | | | | | | | | | | | | | | | | | | | | | | | | | | | | | | | | | | | | | | | | | | | | | | | |
| | | | | | | | | | |
| | | | | | | | | | | | | | | | | | | | | | | | | | | | | | | | | | | | |
* * * * * * * * * * * * * * * * * * * * * * * * * * * * * * * * * * * * * * * * * * * * * *
*
| | | | | | | | | | | | | | | | | | | | | | | | | | | | | | | | | | | | | | | | |
* * * * * * * * * * * * * * * * * * * * * * * * * * * * * * * * * * * * * * * * *
| | | | | |
* * * * * * * * * * * * * * * * * * * * * * * *
| | | | | | | | | | | | | | | | | | | | | |
```

^C⏎

How does this work? Let's go behind the scenes to understand the code better.

How it works...

Channels are **multi-producer-single-consumer** data structures, consisting of many senders (with a lightweight clone) but only a single receiver. Under the hood, the channel does not lock but relies on an `unsafe` data structure that allows the detection and management of the state of the stream. The channel handles simply sending data across threads well and can be used to create an actor-style framework or a reactive map-reduce style data-processing engine.

This is one example of how Rust does **fearless concurrency**: the data going in is owned by the channel until the receiver retrieves it, which is when a new owner takes over. The channel also acts as a queue and holds elements until they are retrieved. This not only frees the developer from implementing the exchange but also adds concurrency for regular queues for free as well.

We create the channel in *step 3* of this recipe and pass the senders into different threads, which start sending the previously defined (in *step 2*) `enum` types for the receiver to print. This printing is done in *step 4* by looping over the blocking iterator with a three-second timeout. *Step 5* then shows how to add the dependency to `Cargo.toml`, and in *step 6* we see the output: multiple full lines with a random number of elements that are either asterisks (*) or pipes (|).

We've successfully covered how to use channels to communicate between threads effortlessly. Now let's move on to the next recipe.

Sharing mutable states

Rust's ownership and borrowing model simplifies immutable data access and transfer considerably—but what about shared states? There are many applications that require mutable access to a shared resource from multiple threads. Let's see how this is done!

How to do it...

In this recipe, we will create a very simple simulation:

1. Run `cargo new black-white` to create a new application project and open the directory in Visual Studio Code.

2. Open `src/main.rs` to add some code. First, we are going to need some imports and an `enum` to make our simulation interesting:

```
use std::sync::{Arc, Mutex};
use std::thread;
use std::time::Duration;

///
/// A simple enum with only two variations: black and white
///
#[derive(Debug)]
enum Shade {
    Black,
    White,
}
```

3. In order to show a shared state between two threads, we obviously need a thread that works on something. This will be a coloring task, where each thread is only adding white to a vector if black was the previous element and vice versa. Thus, each thread is required to read and—depending on the output—write into a shared vector. Let's look at the code that does this:

```
fn new_painter_thread(data: Arc<Mutex<Vec<Shade>>>) ->
thread::JoinHandle<()> {
    thread::spawn(move || loop {
        {
            // create a scope to release the mutex as quickly as
            // possible
            let mut d = data.lock().unwrap();
            if d.len() > 0 {
                match d[d.len() - 1] {
                    Shade::Black => d.push(Shade::White),
                    Shade::White => d.push(Shade::Black),
                }
            } else {
                d.push(Shade::Black)
            }
            if d.len() > 5 {
                break;
            }
```

```
        }
        // slow things down a little
        thread::sleep(Duration::from_secs(1));
    })
}
```

4. All that remains at this stage is to create multiple threads and hand them an `Arc` instance of the data to work on:

```
fn main() {
    let data = Arc::new(Mutex::new(vec![]));
    let threads: Vec<thread::JoinHandle<()>> =
        (0..2)
        .map(|_| new_painter_thread(data.clone()))
        .collect();

    let _: Vec<()> = threads
        .into_iter()
        .map(|t| t.join().unwrap())
        .collect();

    println!("Result: {:?}", data);
}
```

5. Let's run the code with `cargo run`:

```
$ cargo run
   Compiling black-white v0.1.0 (Rust-Cookbook/Chapter04/black-
white)
    Finished dev [unoptimized + debuginfo] target(s) in 0.35s
     Running `target/debug/black-white`
     Result: Mutex { data: [Black, White, Black, White, Black,
White, Black] }
```

Now, let's go behind the scenes to understand the code better.

How it works...

Rust's ownership principle is a double-edged sword: on the one hand, it protects from unintended consequences and enables compile-time memory management; on the other hand, mutable access is significantly more difficult to obtain. While it is more complex to manage, shared mutable access can be great for performance.

Arc stands for **Atomic Reference Counter**. This makes them very similar to regular reference counters (Rc), with the exception that an Arc does its job with an *atomic increment*, which is thread-safe. Therefore, they're the only choice for cross-threaded reference counting.

In Rust, this is done in a way similar to interior mutability (https://doc.rust-lang.org/book/ch15-05-interior-mutability.html), but using Arc and Mutex types (instead of Rc and RefCell), where Mutex owns the actual part of the memory it restricts access to (in step 3's snippet, we create the Vec just like that). As shown in *step 2*, to obtain a mutable reference to the value, locking the Mutex instance is strictly required and it will only be returned after the returned data instance is dropped (for example, when the scope ends). Hence, it is important to keep the scope of the Mutex as small as possible (note the additional { ... } in *step 2*)!

In many use cases, a channel-based approach can achieve the same goal without having to deal with Mutex and the fear of a deadlock occurring (when several Mutex locks wait for each other to unlock).

We've successfully learned how to use channels to share mutable states. Now let's move on to the next recipe.

Multiprocessing in Rust

Threading is great for in-process concurrency and certainly the preferred method of spreading workloads over multiple cores. Whenever other programs need to be called, or an independent, heavyweight task is required, sub-processes are the way to go. With the recent rise of orchestrator-type applications (Kubernetes, Docker Swarm, Mesos, and many others), managing child processes has become a more important topic as well. In this recipe, we will communicate with and manage child processes.

How to do it...

Follow these steps to create a simple application that searches the filesystem:

1. Create a new project using `cargo new child-processes` and open it in Visual Studio Code.
2. On Windows, execute `cargo run` (the last step) from a PowerShell window, since it contains all the required binaries.

3. After importing a few (standard library) dependencies, let's write the basic
`struct` to hold the result data. Add this on top of the `main` function:

```
use std::io::Write;
use std::process::{Command, Stdio};

#[derive(Debug)]
struct SearchResult {
    query: String,
    results: Vec<String>,
}
```

4. The function calling the `find` binary (which does the actual searching) translates
the results into the `struct` from *step 1*. This is what the function looks like:

```
fn search_file(name: String) -> SearchResult {
    let ps_child = Command::new("find")
        .args(&[".", "-iname", &format!("{}", name)])
        .stdout(Stdio::piped())
        .output()
        .expect("Could not spawn process");

    let results = String::from_utf8_lossy(&ps_child.stdout);
    let result_rows: Vec<String> = results
        .split("\n")
        .map(|e| e.to_string())
        .filter(|s| s.len() > 1)
        .collect();

    SearchResult {
        query: name,
        results: result_rows,
    }
}
```

5. Great! Now we know how to call an external binary, pass arguments in, and
forward any `stdout` output to the Rust program. How about writing into the
external program's `stdin`? We'll add the following function to do that:

```
fn process_roundtrip() -> String {
    let mut cat_child = Command::new("cat")
        .stdin(Stdio::piped())
        .stdout(Stdio::piped())
        .spawn()
        .expect("Could not spawn process");

    let stdin = cat_child.stdin.as_mut().expect("Could
```

```
        not attach to stdin");

    stdin
        .write_all(b"datadatadata")
        .expect("Could not write to child process");
    String::from_utf8(
        cat_child
            .wait_with_output()
            .expect("Something went wrong")
            .stdout
            .as_slice()
            .iter()
            .cloned()
            .collect(),
    )
    .unwrap()
}
```

6. To see it in action, we also need to call the functions in the `main()` part of the program. Replace the contents of the default `main()` function with the following:

```
fn main() {
    println!("Reading from /bin/cat > {:?}", process_roundtrip());
    println!(
        "Using 'find' to search for '*.rs': {:?}",
        search_file("*.rs".to_owned())
    )
}
```

7. Now we should see if it works by issuing `cargo run`:

```
$ cargo run
    Compiling child-processes v0.1.0 (Rust-Cookbook/Chapter04/child-
    processes)
    Finished dev [unoptimized + debuginfo] target(s) in 0.59s
    Running `target/debug/child-processes`
    Reading from /bin/cat > "datadatadata"
    Using 'find' to search for '*.rs': SearchResult { query: "
    *.rs", results: ["./src/main.rs"] }
```

Now, let's go behind the scenes to understand the code better.

How it works...

By using Rust's ability to run sub-processes and manipulate their inputs and outputs, it's easy to integrate existing applications into the new program's workflow. In *step 1*, we do exactly that by using the `find` program with parameters and parse the output into our own data structure.

In *step 3*, we go further and send data into a sub-process and recover the same text (using `cat` in an echo-like fashion). You'll notice the parsing of a string in each function, which is required as Windows and Linux/macOS use different byte sizes to encode their characters (**UTF-16** and **UTF-8** respectively). Similarly, the b`"string"` transforms the literal into a byte-literal appropriate for the current platform.

The key ingredient for these operations is **piping**, an operation that is available on the command line using a | (**pipe**) symbol. We encourage you to try out other variants of the `Stdio` struct as well and see where they lead!

We've successfully learned about multiprocessing in Rust. Now let's move on to the next recipe.

Making sequential code parallel

Creating highly concurrent applications from scratch is relatively simple in many technologies and languages. However, when multiple developers have to build on pre-existing work of some kind (legacy or not), creating these highly concurrent applications gets complicated. Thanks to API differences across languages, best practices, or technical limitations, existing operations on sequences cannot be run in parallel without in-depth analysis. Who would do that if the potential benefit is not significant? With Rust's powerful iterators, can we run operations in parallel without major code changes? Our answer is yes!

How to do it...

This recipe shows you how to simply make an application run in parallel without massive effort using `rayon-rs` in just a few steps:

1. Create a new project using `cargo new use-rayon --lib` and open it in Visual Studio Code.

2. Open `Cargo.toml` to add the required dependencies to the project. We are going to build on `rayon` and use the benchmarking abilities of `criterion`:

```
# replace the default [dependencies] section...
[dependencies]
rayon = "1.0.3"


[dev-dependencies]
criterion = "0.2.11"
rand = "^0.5"


[[bench]]
name = "seq_vs_par"
harness = false
```

3. As an example algorithm, we are going to use merge sort, a sophisticated, divide-and-conquer algorithm similar to quicksort (`https://www.geeksforgeeks.org/quick-sort-vs-merge-sort/`). Let's start off with the sequential version by adding the `merge_sort_seq()` function to `src/lib.rs`:

```
///
/// Regular, sequential merge sort implementation
///
pub fn merge_sort_seq<T: PartialOrd + Clone + Default>(collection:
&[T]) -> Vec<T> {
    if collection.len() > 1 {
        let (l, r) = collection.split_at(collection.len() / 2);
        let (sorted_l, sorted_r) = (merge_sort_seq(l),
         merge_sort_seq(r));
        sorted_merge(sorted_l, sorted_r)
    } else {
        collection.to_vec()
    }
}
```

4. The high-level view of merge sort is simple: split the collection in half until it's impossible to do it again, then merge the halves back *in order*. The splitting part is done; what's missing is the merging part. Insert this snippet into `lib.rs`:

```
///
/// Merges two collections into one.
///
fn sorted_merge<T: Default + Clone + PartialOrd>(sorted_l: Vec<T>,
sorted_r: Vec<T>) -> Vec<T> {
    let mut result: Vec<T> = vec![Default::default();
sorted_l.len()
        + sorted_r.len()];

    let (mut i, mut j) = (0, 0);
    let mut k = 0;
    while i < sorted_l.len() && j < sorted_r.len() {
        if sorted_l[i] <= sorted_r[j] {
            result[k] = sorted_l[i].clone();
            i += 1;
        } else {
            result[k] = sorted_r[j].clone();
            j += 1;
        }
        k += 1;
    }
    while i < sorted_l.len() {
        result[k] = sorted_l[i].clone();
        k += 1;
        i += 1;
    }

    while j < sorted_r.len() {
        result[k] = sorted_r[j].clone();
        k += 1;
        j += 1;
    }
    result
}
```

5. Lastly, we will have to import `rayon`, a crate for creating parallel applications with ease, and then add a changed, parallelized version of merge sort:

```
use rayon;
```

6. Next, we add a modified version of merge sort:

```
///
/// Merge sort implementation using parallelism.
///
pub fn merge_sort_par<T>(collection: &[T]) -> Vec<T>
where
    T: PartialOrd + Clone + Default + Send + Sync,
{
    if collection.len() > 1 {
        let (l, r) = collection.split_at(collection.len() / 2);
        let (sorted_l, sorted_r) = rayon::join(||
merge_sort_par(l),
            || merge_sort_par(r));
        sorted_merge(sorted_l, sorted_r)
    } else {
        collection.to_vec()
    }
}
```

7. Great—but can you spot the change? To make sure both variants deliver the same results, let's add a few tests:

```
#[cfg(test)]
mod tests {
    use super::*;

    #[test]
    fn test_merge_sort_seq() {
        assert_eq!(merge_sort_seq(&vec![9, 8, 7, 6]), vec![6, 7, 8,
            9]);
        assert_eq!(merge_sort_seq(&vec![6, 8, 7, 9]), vec![6, 7, 8,
            9]);
        assert_eq!(merge_sort_seq(&vec![2, 1, 1, 1, 1]), vec![1, 1,
            1, 1, 2]);
    }

    #[test]
    fn test_merge_sort_par() {
        assert_eq!(merge_sort_par(&vec![9, 8, 7, 6]), vec![6, 7, 8,
            9]);
        assert_eq!(merge_sort_par(&vec![6, 8, 7, 9]), vec![6, 7, 8,
            9]);
```

```
        assert_eq!(merge_sort_par(&vec![2, 1, 1, 1, 1]), vec![1, 1,
            1, 1, 2]);
    }
}
```

8. Run `cargo test` and you should see successful tests:

```
$ cargo test
    Compiling use-rayon v0.1.0 (Rust-Cookbook/Chapter04/use-rayon)
     Finished dev [unoptimized + debuginfo] target(s) in 0.67s
      Running target/debug/deps/use_rayon-1fb58536866a2b92

running 2 tests
test tests::test_merge_sort_seq ... ok
test tests::test_merge_sort_par ... ok

test result: ok. 2 passed; 0 failed; 0 ignored; 0 measured; 0
filtered out

    Doc-tests use-rayon

running 0 tests

test result: ok. 0 passed; 0 failed; 0 ignored; 0 measured; 0
filtered out
```

9. However, we are really interested in the benchmarks—will it be faster? For that, create a `benches` folder containing a `seq_vs_par.rs` file. Open the file and add the following code:

```
#[macro_use]
extern crate criterion;
use criterion::black_box;
use criterion::Criterion;
use rand::prelude::*;
use std::cell::RefCell;
use use_rayon::{merge_sort_par, merge_sort_seq};

fn random_number_vec(size: usize) -> Vec<i64> {
    let mut v: Vec<i64> = (0..size as i64).collect();
    let mut rng = thread_rng();
    rng.shuffle(&mut v);
    v
}

thread_local!(static ITEMS: RefCell<Vec<i64>> =
RefCell::new(random_number_vec(100_000)));
```

```
fn bench_seq(c: &mut Criterion) {
    c.bench_function("10k merge sort (sequential)", |b| {
        ITEMS.with(|item| b.iter(||
        black_box(merge_sort_seq(&item.borrow())))));
    });
}

fn bench_par(c: &mut Criterion) {
    c.bench_function("10k merge sort (parallel)", |b| {
        ITEMS.with(|item| b.iter(||
        black_box(merge_sort_par(&item.borrow())))));
    });
}
criterion_group!(benches, bench_seq, bench_par);

criterion_main!(benches);
```

10. When we run `cargo bench`, we are getting actual numbers to compare parallel versus sequential implementations (the change refers to previous runs of the same benchmark):

```
$ cargo bench
    Compiling use-rayon v0.1.0 (Rust-Cookbook/Chapter04/use-rayon)
     Finished release [optimized] target(s) in 1.84s
      Running target/release/deps/use_rayon-eb085695289744ef

running 2 tests
test tests::test_merge_sort_par ... ignored
test tests::test_merge_sort_seq ... ignored

test result: ok. 0 passed; 0 failed; 2 ignored; 0 measured; 0
filtered out

Running target/release/deps/seq_vs_par-6383ba0d412acb2b
Gnuplot not found, disabling plotting
10k merge sort (sequential)
                        time:   [13.815 ms 13.860 ms 13.906 ms]
                        change: [-6.7401% -5.1611% -3.6593%] (p =
                        0.00 < 0.05)
                        Performance has improved.
Found 5 outliers among 100 measurements (5.00%)
  3 (3.00%) high mild
  2 (2.00%) high severe

10k merge sort (parallel)
                        time:   [10.037 ms 10.067 ms 10.096 ms]
                        change: [-15.322% -13.276% -11.510%] (p =
                        0.00 < 0.05)
```

```
                    Performance has improved.
    Found 6 outliers among 100 measurements (6.00%)
       1 (1.00%) low severe
       1 (1.00%) high mild
       4 (4.00%) high severe

    Gnuplot not found, disabling plotting
```

Now, let's check what all of this means and pull back the curtains on the code.

How it works...

rayon-rs (https://github.com/rayon-rs/rayon) is a popular data-parallelism crate that only requires a few modifications to introduce automatic concurrency into the code. In our example, we are using the rayon::join operation to create a parallel version of the popular merge sort algorithm.

In *step 1*, we are adding dependencies for benchmarks ([dev-dependencies]) and to actually build the library ([dependencies]). But in *step 2* and *step 3*, we are implementing a regular merge sort variation. Once we add the rayon dependency in *step 4*, we can add rayon::join in *step 5* to run each branch (to sorting of the left and right parts) in its own closure (|/*no params*/| {/* do work */}, or |/*no params*/| /*do work*/ for short) in parallel *if possible*. The docs on join can be found at https://docs.rs/rayon/1.2. 0/rayon/fn.join.html, go into the details about when it speeds things up.

In *step 8*, we are creating a benchmark test as required by the criterion. The library compiles a file outside the src/ directory to run within the benchmark harness and output numbers (as shown in *step 9*)—and in these numbers, we can see a slight but consistent improvement in performance just by adding one line of code. Within the benchmark file, we are sorting a copy of the same random vector (thread_local!() is somewhat akin to static) of 100,000 random numbers.

We've successfully learned how to make sequential code parallel. Now let's move on to the next recipe.

Concurrent data processing in vectors

Rust's `Vec` is a great data structure that is used not only for holding data but also as a management tool of sorts. In an earlier recipe (*Managing multiple threads*) in this chapter, we saw that when we captured the handles of multiple threads in `Vec` and then used the `map()` function to join them. This time, we are going to focus on concurrently processing regular `Vec` instances without additional overhead. In the previous recipe, we saw the power of `rayon-rs` and now we are going to use it to parallelize data processing.

How to do it...

Let's use `rayon-rs` some more in the following steps:

1. Create a new project using `cargo new concurrent-processing --lib` and open it in Visual Studio Code.
2. 2 First, we have to add `rayon` as a dependency by adding a few lines to `Cargo.toml`. Additionally, the `rand` crate and criterion for benchmarking will be useful later on, so let's add those as well and configure them appropriately:

```
[dependencies]
rayon = "1.0.3"

[dev-dependencies]
criterion = "0.2.11"
rand = "^0.5"

[[bench]]
name = "seq_vs_par"
harness = false
```

3. Since we are going to add a significant statistical error measure, that is, the sum of squared errors, open `src/lib.rs`. In its sequential incarnation, we simply iterate over the predictions and their original value to find out the difference, then square it, and sum up the results. Let's add that to the file:

```
pub fn ssqe_sequential(y: &[f32], y_predicted: &[f32]) ->
Option<f32> {
    if y.len() == y_predicted.len() {
```

```
            let y_iter = y.iter();
            let y_pred_iter = y_predicted.iter();

            Some(
                y_iter
                    .zip(y_pred_iter)
                    .map(|(y, y_pred)| (y - y_pred).powi(2))
                    .sum()
            )
        } else {
            None
        }
    }
```

4. That seems easily parallelizable, and `rayon` offers us just the tools for it. Let's create almost the same code using concurrency:

```
use rayon::prelude::*;

pub fn ssqe(y: &[f32], y_predicted: &[f32]) -> Option<f32> {
    if y.len() == y_predicted.len() {
        let y_iter = y.par_iter();
        let y_pred_iter = y_predicted.par_iter();

        Some(
            y_iter
                .zip(y_pred_iter)
                .map(|(y, y_pred)| (y - y_pred).powi(2))
                .reduce(|| 0.0, |a, b| a + b),
        ) // or sum()
    } else {
        None
    }
}
```

5. While the differences to the sequential code are very subtle, the changes have a substantial impact on execution speed! Before we proceed, we should add some tests to see the results of actually calling the functions. Let's start with the parallel version first:

```
#[cfg(test)]
mod tests {
    use super::*;

    #[test]
    fn test_sum_of_sq_errors() {
        assert_eq!(
            ssqe(&[1.0, 1.0, 1.0, 1.0], &[2.0, 2.0, 2.0, 2.0]),
```

```
                    Some(4.0)
            );
            assert_eq!(
                ssqe(&[-1.0, -1.0, -1.0, -1.0], &[-2.0, -2.0, -2.0,
                    -2.0]),
                Some(4.0)
            );
            assert_eq!(
                ssqe(&[-1.0, -1.0, -1.0, -1.0], &[2.0, 2.0, 2.0, 2.0]),
                Some(36.0)
            );
            assert_eq!(
                ssqe(&[1.0, 1.0, 1.0, 1.0], &[2.0, 2.0, 2.0, 2.0]),
                Some(4.0)
            );
            assert_eq!(
                ssqe(&[1.0, 1.0, 1.0, 1.0], &[2.0, 2.0, 2.0, 2.0]),
                Some(4.0)
            );
        }
```

6. The sequential code should have the same results, so let's duplicate the test for the sequential version of the code:

```
#[test]
fn test_sum_of_sq_errors_seq() {
    assert_eq!(
        ssqe_sequential(&[1.0, 1.0, 1.0, 1.0], &[2.0, 2.0, 2.0,
            2.0]),
        Some(4.0)
    );
    assert_eq!(
        ssqe_sequential(&[-1.0, -1.0, -1.0, -1.0], &[-2.0,
            -2.0, -2.0, -2.0]),
        Some(4.0)
    );
    assert_eq!(
        ssqe_sequential(&[-1.0, -1.0, -1.0, -1.0], &[2.0, 2.0,
            2.0, 2.0]),
        Some(36.0)
    );
    assert_eq!(
        ssqe_sequential(&[1.0, 1.0, 1.0, 1.0], &[2.0, 2.0, 2.0,
            2.0]),
        Some(4.0)
    );
    assert_eq!(
        ssqe_sequential(&[1.0, 1.0, 1.0, 1.0], &[2.0, 2.0, 2.0,
```

```
                    2.0]),
                Some(4.0)
            );
        }
    }
```

7. In order to check that everything works as expected, run `cargo test` in between:

```
$ cargo test
    Compiling concurrent-processing v0.1.0 (Rust-
    Cookbook/Chapter04/concurrent-processing)
    Finished dev [unoptimized + debuginfo] target(s) in 0.84s
     Running target/debug/deps/concurrent_processing-
     250eef41459fd2af

running 2 tests
test tests::test_sum_of_sq_errors_seq ... ok
test tests::test_sum_of_sq_errors ... ok

test result: ok. 2 passed; 0 failed; 0 ignored; 0 measured; 0
filtered out

    Doc-tests concurrent-processing

running 0 tests

test result: ok. 0 passed; 0 failed; 0 ignored; 0 measured; 0
filtered out
```

8. As an additional feat of `rayon`, let's also add some more functions to `src/lib.rs`. This time, they are related to counting alphanumeric characters in `str`:

```
pub fn seq_count_alpha_nums(corpus: &str) -> usize {
    corpus.chars().filter(|c| c.is_alphanumeric()).count()
}


pub fn par_count_alpha_nums(corpus: &str) -> usize {
    corpus.par_chars().filter(|c| c.is_alphanumeric()).count()
}
```

9. Now let's see which performs better and let's add a benchmark. To do that, create a `benches/` directory next to `src/` with a `seq_vs_par.rs` file. Add the following benchmark and helper functions to see what the speedups are. Let's start with a few helpers that define the basic data the benchmark is processing:

```
#[macro_use]
extern crate criterion;
use concurrent_processing::{ssqe, ssqe_sequential,
seq_count_alpha_nums, par_count_alpha_nums};
use criterion::{black_box, Criterion};
use std::cell::RefCell;
use rand::prelude::*;

const SEQ_LEN: usize = 1_000_000;
thread_local!(static ITEMS: RefCell<(Vec<f32>, Vec<f32>)> = {
    let y_values: (Vec<f32>, Vec<f32>) = (0..SEQ_LEN).map(|_|
      (random::<f32>(), random::<f32>()) )
    .unzip();
    RefCell::new(y_values)
});


const MAX_CHARS: usize = 100_000;
thread_local!(static CHARS: RefCell<String> = {
    let items: String = (0..MAX_CHARS).map(|_| random::<char>
      ()).collect();
    RefCell::new(items)
});
```

10. Next, we are going to create the benchmarks themselves:

```
fn bench_count_seq(c: &mut Criterion) {
    c.bench_function("Counting in sequence", |b| {
        CHARS.with(|item| b.iter(||
          black_box(seq_count_alpha_nums(&item.borrow())))))
    });
}

fn bench_count_par(c: &mut Criterion) {
    c.bench_function("Counting in parallel", |b| {
        CHARS.with(|item| b.iter(||
          black_box(par_count_alpha_nums(&item.borrow())))))
    });
}
```

11. Let's create another benchmark:

```
fn bench_seq(c: &mut Criterion) {
    c.bench_function("Sequential vector operation", |b| {
        ITEMS.with(|y_values| {
            let y_borrowed = y_values.borrow();
            b.iter(|| black_box(ssqe_sequential(&y_borrowed.0,
            &y_borrowed.1)))
        })
    });
}

fn bench_par(c: &mut Criterion) {
    c.bench_function("Parallel vector operation", |b| {
        ITEMS.with(|y_values| {
            let y_borrowed = y_values.borrow();
            b.iter(|| black_box(ssqe(&y_borrowed.0,
            &y_borrowed.1)))
        })
    });
}

criterion_group!(benches, bench_seq, bench_par,bench_count_par,
bench_count_seq);

criterion_main!(benches);
```

12. With that available, run `cargo bench` and (after a while) check the outputs to
    see the improvements and timings (the changed part refers to the changes from
    the previous run of the same benchmark):

```
$ cargo bench
    Compiling concurrent-processing v0.1.0 (Rust-
    Cookbook/Chapter04/concurrent-processing)
    Finished release [optimized] target(s) in 2.37s
     Running target/release/deps/concurrent_processing-
     eedf0fd3b1e51fe0

running 2 tests
test tests::test_sum_of_sq_errors ... ignored
test tests::test_sum_of_sq_errors_seq ... ignored

test result: ok. 0 passed; 0 failed; 2 ignored; 0 measured; 0
filtered out

Running target/release/deps/seq_vs_par-ddd71082d4bd9dd6
Gnuplot not found, disabling plotting
Sequential vector operation
```

```
                              time: [1.0631 ms 1.0681 ms 1.0756 ms]
                              change: [-4.8191% -3.4333% -2.3243%] (p =
                              0.00 < 0.05)
                              Performance has improved.
Found 4 outliers among 100 measurements (4.00%)
  2 (2.00%) high mild
  2 (2.00%) high severe

Parallel vector operation
                              time: [408.93 us 417.14 us 425.82 us]
                              change: [-9.5623% -6.0044% -2.2126%] (p =
                              0.00 < 0.05)
                              Performance has improved.
Found 15 outliers among 100 measurements (15.00%)
  2 (2.00%) low mild
  7 (7.00%) high mild
  6 (6.00%) high severe

Counting in parallel time: [552.01 us 564.97 us 580.51 us]
                              change: [+2.3072% +6.9101% +11.580%] (p =
                              0.00 < 0.05)
                              Performance has regressed.
Found 4 outliers among 100 measurements (4.00%)
  3 (3.00%) high mild
  1 (1.00%) high severe

Counting in sequence time: [992.84 us 1.0137 ms 1.0396 ms]
                              change: [+9.3014% +12.494% +15.338%] (p =
                              0.00 < 0.05)
                              Performance has regressed.
Found 4 outliers among 100 measurements (4.00%)
  4 (4.00%) high mild

Gnuplot not found, disabling plotting
```

Now, let's go behind the scenes to understand the code better.

How it works...

Again, `rayon-rs`—a fantastic library—has made roughly a 50% improvement in the benchmark performance (parallel versus sequential) by changing **a single line of code**. This is significant for many applications but in particular for machine learning, where the loss function of an algorithm is required to run hundreds or thousands of times during a training cycle. Cutting this time in half would immediately have a large impact on productivity.

In the first steps after setting everything up (*step 3*, *step 4*, and *step 5*), we are creating a sequential and parallel implementation of the sum of squared errors (`https://hlab.stanford.edu/brian/error_sum_of_squares.html`) with the only difference being `par_iter()` versus the `iter()` call including some tests. Then we add some—more common—counting functions to our benchmark suite, which we'll create and call in *step 7* and *step 8*. Again, the sequential and parallel algorithms work on exactly the same dataset every time to avoid any unfortunate incidents.

We've successfully learned how to process data concurrently in vectors. Now let's move on to the next recipe.

Shared immutable states

Sometimes, when a program operates on multiple threads, the current version of settings and many more are available to the threads as a single point of truth. Sharing a state between threads is straightforward in Rust—as long as the variable is immutable and the types are marked as safe to share. In order to mark types as thread-safe, it's important that the implementation makes sure that accessing the information can be done without any kind of inconsistency occurring.

Rust uses two marker traits—`Send` and `Sync`—to manage these options. Let's see how.

How to do it...

In just a few steps, we'll explore immutable states:

1. Run `cargo new immutable-states` to create a new application project and open the directory in Visual Studio Code.
2. First, we'll add the imports and a `noop` function to call to our `src/main.rs` file:

```
use std::thread;
use std::rc::Rc;
use std::sync::Arc;
use std::sync::mpsc::channel;


fn noop<T>(_: T) {}
```

3. Let's explore how different types can be shared across threads.
   The `mpsc::channel` type provides a great out-of-the-box example of a shared state. Let's start off with a baseline that works as expected:

```
fn main() {
    let (sender, receiver) = channel::<usize>();

    thread::spawn(move || {
        let thread_local_read_only_clone = sender.clone();
        noop(thread_local_read_only_clone);
    });
}
```

4. To see it working, execute `cargo build`. Any errors with respect to illegal state sharing will be found by the compiler:

```
$ cargo build
    Compiling immutable-states v0.1.0 (Rust-Cookbook/Chapter04
    /immutable-states)
warning: unused import: `std::rc::Rc`
 --> src/main.rs:2:5
  |
2 | use std::rc::Rc;
  | ^^^^^^^^^^^
  |
  = note: #[warn(unused_imports)] on by default

warning: unused import: `std::sync::Arc`
 --> src/main.rs:3:5
  |
3 | use std::sync::Arc;
  | ^^^^^^^^^^^^^^
  |

warning: unused variable: `receiver`
  --> src/main.rs:10:18
   |
10 | let (sender, receiver) = channel::<usize>();
   | ^^^^^^^^ help: consider prefixing with an underscore:
`_receiver`
   |
   = note: #[warn(unused_variables)] on by default

    Finished dev [unoptimized + debuginfo] target(s) in 0.58s
```

5. Now we'll try the same thing with the receiver. Will it work? Add this to the `main` function:

```
let c = Arc::new(receiver);
thread::spawn(move || {
    noop(c.clone());
});
```

6. Run `cargo build` to get a more extensive message:

```
$ cargo build
   Compiling immutable-states v0.1.0 (Rust-Cookbook/Chapter04
     /immutable-states)
warning: unused import: `std::rc::Rc`
 --> src/main.rs:2:5
  |
2 | use std::rc::Rc;
  |     ^^^^^^^^^^^
  |
  = note: #[warn(unused_imports)] on by default

error[E0277]: `std::sync::mpsc::Receiver<usize>` cannot be shared
between threads safely
   --> src/main.rs:26:5
   |
26 | thread::spawn(move || {
   | ^^^^^^^^^^^^^ `std::sync::mpsc::Receiver<usize>` cannot be
shared between threads safely
   |
   = help: the trait `std::marker::Sync` is not implemented for
`std::sync::mpsc::Receiver<usize>`
   = note: required because of the requirements on the impl of
`std::marker::Send` for
`std::sync::Arc<std::sync::mpsc::Receiver<usize>>`
   = note: required because it appears within the type
`[closure@src/main.rs:26:19: 28:6
c:std::sync::Arc<std::sync::mpsc::Receiver<usize>>]`
   = note: required by `std::thread::spawn`

error: aborting due to previous error

For more information about this error, try `rustc --explain E0277`.
error: Could not compile `immutable-states`.

To learn more, run the command again with --verbose.
```

7. Since the receiver is only made for a single thread to fetch data out of the channel, it's to be expected that this cannot be avoided using `Arc`. Similarly, it's impossible to simply wrap `Rc` into `Arc` to make it available across threads. Add the following to see the error:

```
let b = Arc::new(Rc::new(vec![]));
 thread::spawn(move || {
     let thread_local_read_only_clone = b.clone();
     noop(thread_local_read_only_clone);
 });
```

8. `cargo build` reveals the consequences again—an error about how the type is unable to be sent across threads:

```
$ cargo build
    Compiling immutable-states v0.1.0 (Rust-Cookbook/Chapter04
    /immutable-states)
error[E0277]: `std::rc::Rc<std::vec::Vec<_>>` cannot be sent
between threads safely
   --> src/main.rs:19:5
    |
19 | thread::spawn(move || {
    | ^^^^^^^^^^^^^ `std::rc::Rc<std::vec::Vec<_>>` cannot be sent
between threads safely
    |
    = help: the trait `std::marker::Send` is not implemented for
`std::rc::Rc<std::vec::Vec<_>>`
    = note: required because of the requirements on the impl of
`std::marker::Send` for
`std::sync::Arc<std::rc::Rc<std::vec::Vec<_>>>`
    = note: required because it appears within the type
`[closure@src/main.rs:19:19: 22:6
b:std::sync::Arc<std::rc::Rc<std::vec::Vec<_>>>]`
    = note: required by `std::thread::spawn`

error[E0277]: `std::rc::Rc<std::vec::Vec<_>>` cannot be shared
between threads safely
   --> src/main.rs:19:5
    |
19 | thread::spawn(move || {
    | ^^^^^^^^^^^^^ `std::rc::Rc<std::vec::Vec<_>>` cannot be shared
between threads safely
    |
    = help: the trait `std::marker::Sync` is not implemented for
`std::rc::Rc<std::vec::Vec<_>>`
    = note: required because of the requirements on the impl of
`std::marker::Send` for
```

```
`std::sync::Arc<std::rc::Rc<std::vec::Vec<_>>>`
   = note: required because it appears within the type
`[closure@src/main.rs:19:19: 22:6
b:std::sync::Arc<std::rc::Rc<std::vec::Vec<_>>>]`
   = note: required by `std::thread::spawn`

error: aborting due to 2 previous errors

For more information about this error, try `rustc --explain E0277`.
error: Could not compile `immutable-states`.

To learn more, run the command again with --verbose.
```

Now, let's go behind the scenes to understand the code better.

How it works...

Since this recipe actually failed to build and pointed to an error message in the last step, what happened? We learned about Send and Sync. These marker traits and the types of errors will cross your path in the most surprising and critical situations. Since they work seamlessly when they are present, we had to create a failing example to show you what magic they do and how.

In Rust, marker traits (https://doc.rust-lang.org/std/marker/index.html) signal something to the compiler. In the case of concurrency, it's the ability to be shared across threads. The Sync (shared access from multiple threads) and Send (ownership can transfer safely from one thread to another) traits are implemented for almost all default data structures, but if unsafe code is required, then the marker traits have to be added manually—which is also unsafe.

Hence, most of the data structures will be able to inherit Send and Sync from their properties, which is what happens in *step 2* and *step 3*. Mostly, you'll wrap your instance in Arc as well for easier handling. However, multiple instances of Arc require their contained types to implement Send and Sync. In *step 4* and *step 6*, we try to get the available types into Arc—without implementing either Sync or Send. *Step 5* and *step 7* show the compiler's error messages for either try. If you want to know more and see how to add the marker trait (https://doc.rust-lang.org/std/marker/index.html) to custom types, check out the documentation at https://doc.rust-lang.org/nomicon/send-and-sync.html.

Now that we know more about `Send` and `Sync`, sharing states in concurrent programs is less of a mystery. Let's move on to the next recipe.

Handling asynchronous messages with actors

Scalable architectures and asynchronous programming have led to a rise of actors and actor-based designs (`https://mattferderer.com/what-is-the-actor-model-and-when-should-you-use-it`), facilitated by frameworks such as Akka (`https://akka.io/`). Regardless of Rust's powerful concurrency features, actors in Rust are still tricky to get right and they lack the documentation that many other libraries have. In this recipe, we are going to explore the basics of `actix`, Rust's actor framework, which was created after the popular Akka.

How to do it...

Implement an actor-based sensor data reader in just a few steps:

1. Create a new binary application using `cargo new actors` and open the directory in Visual Studio Code.
2. Include the required dependencies in the `Cargo.toml` configuration file:

```
[package]
name = "actors"
version = "0.1.0"
authors = ["Claus Matzinger <claus.matzinger+kb@gmail.com>"]
edition = "2018"

[dependencies]
actix = "^0.8"
rand = "0.5"
```

3. Open `src/main.rs` to add the code before the `main` function. Let's start with the imports:

```
use actix::prelude::*;
use std::thread;
use std::time::Duration;
use rand::prelude::*;
```

4. In order to create an actor system, we'll have to think about the application's structure. An actor can be thought of as a message receiver with a postbox where messages are piled up until they are processed. For simplicity, let's mock up some sensor data mock as messages, each consisting of a `u64` timestamp and a `f32` value:

```
///
/// A mock sensor function
///
fn read_sensordata() -> f32 {
    random::<f32>() * 10.0
}

#[derive(Debug, Message)]
struct Sensordata(pub u64, pub f32);
```

5. In a typical system, we would use an I/O loop to read from the sensor(s) in scheduled intervals. Since `actix` (https://github.com/actix/actix/) builds on Tokio (https://tokio.rs/), that can be explored outside this recipe. To simulate the fast reading and slow processing steps, we'll implement it as a `for` loop:

```
fn main() -> std::io::Result<()> {
    System::run(|| {
        println!(">> Press Ctrl-C to stop the program");
        // start multi threaded actor host (arbiter) with 2 threads
        let sender = SyncArbiter::start(N_THREADS, ||
        DBWriter);
        // send messages to the actor
        for n in 0..10_000 {
            let my_timestamp = n as u64;
            let data = read_sensordata();
            sender.do_send(Sensordata(my_timestamp, data));
        }
    })
}
```

6. Let's take care of implementing the most important part: the actor's message handling. `actix` requires you to implement the `Handler<T>` trait. Add the following implementation just before the `main` function:

```
struct DBWriter;

impl Actor for DBWriter {
    type Context = SyncContext<Self>;
}
```

```
impl Handler<Sensordata> for DBWriter {
    type Result = ();

    fn handle(&mut self, msg: Sensordata, _: &mut Self::Context) ->
    Self::Result {

        // send stuff somewhere and handle the results
        println!(" {:?}", msg);
        thread::sleep(Duration::from_millis(300));
    }
}
```

7. Use `cargo run` to run the program and see how it generates artificial sensor data (press *Ctrl* + *C* if you don't want to wait for it to finish):

```
$ cargo run
   Compiling actors v0.1.0 (Rust-Cookbook/Chapter04/actors)
    Finished dev [unoptimized + debuginfo] target(s) in 2.05s
     Running `target/debug/actors`
>> Press Ctrl-C to stop the program
 Sensordata(0, 2.2577233)
 Sensordata(1, 4.039347)
 Sensordata(2, 8.981095)
 Sensordata(3, 1.1506838)
 Sensordata(4, 7.5091066)
 Sensordata(5, 2.5614727)
 Sensordata(6, 3.6907816)
 Sensordata(7, 7.907603)
^C⏎
```

Now, let's go behind the scenes to understand the code better.

How it works...

The actor model solves the shortcomings of passing data around threads using an object-oriented approach. By utilizing an implicit queue for messages to and from actors, it can prevent expensive locking and corrupt states. There is extensive content on the topic, for example, in Akka's documentation at `https://doc.akka.io/docs/akka/current/guide/actors-intro.html`.

After preparing the project in the first two steps, *step 3* shows the implementation of the `Message` trait using a macro (`[#derive()]`). With that available, we proceed to set up the main *system*—the main loop that runs the actor scheduling and message passing behind the scenes.

`actix` uses `Arbiters` to run different actors and tasks. A regular Arbiter is basically a single-threaded event loop, helpful for working in a non-concurrent setting. `SyncArbiter`, on the other hand, is a multithreaded version that allows the use of actors across threads. In our case, we used three threads.

In *step 5*, we see the required minimum implementation of a handler. Using `SyncArbiter` does not allow sending messages back via the return value, which is why the result is an empty tuple for now. The handler is also specific to the message type and the handle function simulates a long-running action by issuing `thread::sleep`—this only works because it's the only actor running in that particular thread.

We have only scraped the surface of what `actix` can do (leaving out the all-powerful Tokio tasks and streams). Check out their book (`https://actix.rs/book/actix/`) on the topic and the examples in their GitHub repositories.

We've successfully learned how to handle asynchronous messages with actors. Now let's move on to the next recipe.

Asynchronous programming with futures

Using futures is a common technique in JavaScript, TypeScript, C#, and similar technologies—made popular by the addition of the `async`/`await` keywords in their syntax. In a nutshell, futures (or promises) is a function's guarantee that, at some point, the handle will be resolved and the actual value will be returned. However, there is no explicit time when this is going to happen—but you can schedule entire chains of promises that are resolved after each other. How does this work in Rust? Let's find out in this recipe.

 At the time of writing, `async`/`await` were under heavy development. Depending on when you are reading this book, the examples may have stopped working. In this case, we ask you to open an issue in the accompanying repository so we can fix the issues. For updates, check the Rust `async` working group's repository at `https://github.com/rustasync/team`.

How to do it...

In a few steps, we'll be able to use `async` and `await` in Rust for seamless concurrency:

1. Create a new binary application using `cargo new async-await` and open the directory in Visual Studio Code.

2. As usual, when we are integrating a library, we'll have to add the dependencies to `Cargo.toml`:

```
[package]
name = "async-await"
version = "0.1.0"
authors = ["Claus Matzinger <claus.matzinger+kb@gmail.com>"]
edition = "2018"

[dependencies]
runtime = "0.3.0-alpha.6"
surf = "1.0"
```

3. In `src/main.rs`, we have to import the dependencies. Add the following lines at the top of the file:

```
use surf::Exception;
use surf::http::StatusCode;
```

4. The classic example is waiting for a web request to finish. This is notoriously difficult to judge since the web resources and/or the network in between is owned by someone else and might be down. `surf` (https://github.com/rustasync/surf) is `async` by default and therefore requires using the `.await` syntax heavily. Let's declare an `async` function to do the fetching:

```
async fn response_code(url: &str) -> Result<StatusCode, Exception>
{
    let res = surf::get(url).await?;
    Ok(res.status())
}
```

5. Now we need an `async main` function in order to call the `response_code()` `async` function:

```
#[runtime::main]
async fn main() -> Result<(), Exception> {
    let url = "https://www.rust-lang.org";
    let status = response_code(url).await?;
    println!("{} responded with HTTP {}", url, status);
    Ok(())
}
```

6. Let's see if the code works by running `cargo run` (a `200 OK` is expected):

```
$ cargo +nightly run
   Compiling async-await v0.1.0 (Rust-Cookbook/Chapter04/async-await)
    Finished dev [unoptimized + debuginfo] target(s) in 1.81s
     Running `target/debug/async-await`
   https://www.rust-lang.org responded with HTTP 200 OK
```

`async` and `await` have been worked on for a long time in the Rust community. Let's see how this recipe works.

How it works...

Futures (often called promises) are typically fully integrated into the language and come with a built-in runtime. In Rust, the team chose a more ambitious approach and left the runtime open for the community to implement (for now). Right now the two projects Tokio and Romio (`https://github.com/withoutboats/romio`) and `juliex` (`https://github.com/withoutboats/juliex`) have the most sophisticated support for these futures. With the recent addition of `async/await` in the Rust syntax in the 2018 edition, it's only a matter of time until the various implementations mature.

After setting up the dependencies in *step 1*, *step 2* shows that we don't have to enable the `async` and `await` macros/syntax to use them in the code—this was a requirement for a long time. Then, we import the required crates. Coincidentally, a new async web library—called `surf`—was built by the Rust async working group while we were busy with this book. Since this crate was built fully asynchronous, we preferred it over more established crates such as `hyper` (`https://hyper.rs`).

In *step 3*, we declare an `async` function, which automatically returns a `Future` (https://doc.rust-lang.org/std/future/trait.Future.html) type and can only be called from within another `async` scope. *Step 4* shows the creation of such a scope with the `async` main function. Does it end there? No—the `#[runtime::main]` attribute gives it away: a runtime is seamlessly started and assigned to execute anything async.

While the `runtime` crate (https://docs.rs/runtime/0.3.0-alpha.7/runtime/) is agnostic of the actual implementation, the default is a native runtime based on `romio` and `juliex` (check your `Cargo.lock` file), but you can also enable the much more feature-laden `tokio` runtime to enable streams, timers, and so on to use on top of async.

Inside the `async` functions, we can make use of the `await` keyword attached to a `Future` implementor (https://doc.rust-lang.org/std/future/trait.Future.html), such as the `surf` request (https://github.com/rustasync/surf/blob/master/src/request.rs#L563), where the runtime calls `poll()` until a result is available. This can also result in an error, which means that we have to handle errors as well, which is generally done with the `?` operator. `surf` also provides a generic `Exception` type (https://docs.rs/surf/1.0.2/surf/type.Exception.html) alias to handle anything that might happen.

While there are some things that could still change in Rust's fast-moving ecosystem, using `async`/`await` is finally coming together without requiring highly unstable crates. Having that available is a significant boost to Rust's usefulness. Now, let's move on to another chapter.

Handling Errors and Other Results

5

Handling errors is always an interesting challenge in every programming language. There are many styles available: returning numeric values, exceptions (software interrupts), result and option types, and so on. Each way requires different architectures and has implications for performance, readability, and maintainability. Rust's approach is—just like many functional programming languages—based on integrating failure as part of the regular workflow. This means that whatever the return value, an error is not a special case but integrated into the handling. `Option` and `Result` are the central types that allow for returning results as well as errors. `panic!` is an additional macro to halt the thread immediately in case it cannot/should not continue.

In this chapter, we'll cover some basic recipes and architectures to use Rust's error handling effectively so that your code is easy to read, understand, and maintain. For this reason, in this chapter, you can look forward to learning about the following recipes:

- Panicking responsibly
- Handling multiple errors
- Working with exceptional results
- Seamless error handling
- Customizing errors
- Resilient programming
- Working with external crates for error handling
- Moving between Option and Result

Panicking responsibly

Sometimes, there is no way for an execution thread to continue. This may be due to things such as invalid configuration files, unresponsive peers or servers, or OS-related errors. Rust has many ways to panic, explicitly or implicitly. The most ubiquitous one is probably `unwrap()` for multiple `Option` types and related types, which panic on error or `None`. Yet, for more complex programs, it is essential to take control of the panicking (for example, by avoiding multiple `unwrap()` calls and libraries that use it) and the `panic!` macro supports that.

How to do it...

Let's examine how we can take control of multiple `panic!` instances:

1. Create a new project with `cargo new panicking-responsibly --lib` and open it with VS Code.

2. Open `src/lib.rs` and replace the default tests with a regular, straightforward panic instances:

```
#[cfg(test)]
mod tests {

    #[test]
    #[should_panic]
    fn test_regular_panic() {
        panic!();
    }
}
```

3. There are many other ways to halt the program too. Let's add another `test` instance:

```
#[test]
#[should_panic]
fn test_unwrap() {
    // panics if "None"
    None::<i32>.unwrap();
}
```

4. However, these panics all have a generic error message, which is not very informative with regard to what the application was doing. Using `expect()` lets you provide an error message to explain the causes of the error:

```
#[test]
#[should_panic(expected = "Unwrap with a message")]
fn test_expect() {
    None::<i32>.expect("Unwrap with a message");
}
```

5. The `panic!` macro provides a similar way of explaining the sudden halt:

```
#[test]
#[should_panic(expected = "Everything is lost!")]
fn test_panic_message() {
    panic!("Everything is lost!");
}

#[test]
#[should_panic(expected = "String formatting also works")]
fn test_panic_format() {
    panic!("{} formatting also works.", "String");
}
```

6. The macro can also return numerical values, something that is very important for Unix-type OSes that can check for those values. Add another test to return an integer code to indicate a specific failure:

```
#[test]
#[should_panic]
fn test_panic_return_value() {
    panic!(42);
}
```

7. Another great way of halting the program based on invalid values is by using the `assert!` macro. It should be well-known from writing tests, so let's add a few to see Rust's variants:

```
#[test]
#[should_panic]
fn test_assert() {
    assert!(1 == 2);
}

#[test]
#[should_panic]
fn test_assert_eq() {
```

```
        assert_eq!(1, 2);
    }

    #[test]
    #[should_panic]
    fn test_assert_neq() {
        assert_ne!(1, 1);
    }
```

8. The last step is, as usual, to compile and run the code we have just written using `cargo test`. The output shows whether the tests have passed (which they should):

```
$ cargo test
 Compiling panicking-responsibly v0.1.0 (Rust- Cookbook/Chapter05
 /panicking-responsibly)
Finished dev [unoptimized + debuginfo] target(s) in 0.29s
Running target/debug/deps/panicking_responsibly-6ec385e96e6ee9cd

running 9 tests
test tests::test_assert ... ok
test tests::test_assert_eq ... ok
test tests::test_assert_neq ... ok
test tests::test_panic_format ... ok
test tests::test_expect ... ok
test tests::test_panic_message ... ok
test tests::test_panic_return_value ... ok
test tests::test_regular_panic ... ok
test tests::test_unwrap ... ok

test result: ok. 9 passed; 0 failed; 0 ignored; 0 measured; 0
filtered out

    Doc-tests panicking-responsibly

running 0 tests

test result: ok. 0 passed; 0 failed; 0 ignored; 0 measured; 0
filtered out
```

But how does this allow us to panic responsibly? Let's see how it works.

How it works...

Thanks to Rust's ability to check panic results, we can verify the messages and the fact that the panic occurred. From *step 2* to *step 4*, we are simply panicking using various (common) methods, such as `unwrap()` (`https://doc.rust-lang.org/std/option/enum.Option.html#method.unwrap`) or `panic!()` (`https://doc.rust-lang.org/std/macro.panic.html`). These methods return messages such as `'called `Option::unwrap()` on a `None` value', src/libcore/option.rs:347:21`, or `panicked at 'explicit panic', src/lib.rs:64:9`, which are not easy to debug.

However, there is a variation of `unwrap()` called `expect()`, which takes a `&str` parameter as a simple message for users to debug the issue further. *Steps 4* to *6* show how messages and return values are incorporated. In *step 7*, we cover the additional `assert!` macro that is typically seen in tests but finds its way into productive systems as well to guard against rare and irrecoverable values.

Halting the execution of a thread or program should always be the last resort, especially when you are creating a library for others to use. Think about it—some bug leads to an unexpected value in a third-party library, which then panics and brings the service to an immediate unexpected halt. Imagine if that happened thanks to a call to `unwrap()` instead of using more robust methods.

We've successfully learned how to panic responsibly. Now, let's move on to the next recipe.

Handling multiple errors

Whenever an application becomes more complex and includes third-party frameworks, all kinds of error types need to be taken care of *consistently* without having a condition for each one. For example, a web service's large range of possible errors can bubble up to the handler where they need to be translated into HTTP codes with informative messages. These expected errors can range from parser errors to invalid authentication details, failed database connections, or an application-specific error with an error code. In this recipe, we'll cover how to deal with this variety of errors using wrappers.

How to do it...

Let's create an error wrapper in a few steps:

1. Open the project you created with `cargo new multiple-errors` with VS Code.

2. Open `src/main.rs` to and add some imports at the top:

```
use std::fmt;
use std::io;
use std::error::Error;
```

3. In our application, we will deal with three user-defined errors. Let's declare them right after the imports:

```
#[derive(Debug)]
pub struct InvalidDeviceIdError(usize);
#[derive(Debug)]
pub struct DeviceNotPresentError(usize);
#[derive(Debug)]
pub struct UnexpectedDeviceStateError {}
```

4. Now for the wrapper: since we are dealing with multiple variations of something, `enum` will fit the purpose perfectly:

```
#[derive(Debug)]
pub enum ErrorWrapper {
    Io(io::Error),
    Db(InvalidDeviceIdError),
    Device(DeviceNotPresentError),
    Agent(UnexpectedDeviceStateError)
}
```

5. However, it would be nice to have the same interface as other errors, so let's implement the `std::error::Error` trait:

```
impl Error for ErrorWrapper {
    fn description(&self) -> &str {
        match *self {
            ErrorWrapper::Io(ref e) => e.description(),
            ErrorWrapper::Db(_) | ErrorWrapper::Device(_) => "No
            device present with this id, check formatting.",
            _ => "Unexpected error. Sorry for the inconvenience."
        }
    }
}
```

6. The trait makes it necessary to implement `std::fmt::Display` as well, so this will be the next `impl` block:

```
impl fmt::Display for ErrorWrapper {
    fn fmt(&self, f: &mut fmt::Formatter<'_>) -> fmt::Result {
        match *self {
            ErrorWrapper::Io(ref e) => write!(f, "{} [{}]", e,
                self.description()),
            ErrorWrapper::Db(ref e) => write!(f, "Device with id \"
                {}\" not found [{}]", e.0, self.description()),
            ErrorWrapper::Device(ref e) => write!(f, "Device with
                id\"{}\" is currently unavailable [{}]", e.0,
                self.description()),
            ErrorWrapper::Agent(_) => write!(f, "Unexpected device
                state [{}]", self.description())
        }
    }
}
```

7. Now, we want to see the results of our labor. Replace the existing `main` function as follows:

```
fn main() {
    println!("{}",
    ErrorWrapper::Io(io::Error::from(io::ErrorKind::InvalidData)));
    println!("{}", ErrorWrapper::Db(InvalidDeviceIdError(42)));
    println!("{}", ErrorWrapper::Device
      (DeviceNotPresentError(42)));
    println!("{}", ErrorWrapper::Agent(UnexpectedDeviceStateError
{}));
}
```

8. Finally, we execute `cargo run` to see that the output matches what we expected before:

```
$ cargo run
 Compiling multiple-errors v0.1.0 (Rust-Cookbook/Chapter05
 /multiple-errors)
 Finished dev [unoptimized + debuginfo] target(s) in 0.34s
 Running `target/debug/multiple-errors`
invalid data [invalid data]
Device with id "42" not found [No device present with this id,
check formatting.]
Device with id "42" is currently unavailable [No device present
with this id, check formatting.]
Unexpected device state [Unexpected error. Sorry for the
inconvenience.]
```

Now, let's go behind the scenes to understand the code better.

How it works...

Multiple errors may not seem much of an issue at first, but for a clean, readable architecture, it is necessary to address them somehow. An enum that wraps possible variants has been shown to be the most practical solution, and, by implementing `std::error::Error` (and the `std::fmt::Display` requirement), the handling of the new error type should be seamless. In *steps 3* to *6*, we show an example implementation of the required traits in a reductionist fashion. *Step 7* shows how to use the wrapping enum and how to use the `Display` and `Error` implementations to help match the variants.

Implementing the `Error` trait will allow interesting aspects in the future, including recursive nesting. Check the documentation at `https://doc.rust-lang.org/std/error/trait.Error.html#method.source` to find out more. Typically, we would not create these error variants themselves if we can avoid it, which is why there are supportive crates taking care of all of the boilerplate code—we'll cover that in a different recipe in this chapter.

Let's move on to the next recipe to complement our newfound skills in handling multiple errors!

Working with exceptional results

Other than the `Option` type, a `Result` type can have two custom types, which means that `Result` provides additional information about the cause of the error. This is more expressive than returning `Option`, which returns a single type instance or `None`. However, this `None` instance can mean anything from *failure to process* to *wrong input*. This way, the `Result` type can be seen as a similar system as exceptions in other languages, but they are part of the regular workflow of a program. One example is a search, where a multitude of scenarios can happen:

- The desired value is found.
- The desired value is not found.
- The collection was invalid.
- The value was invalid.

How can you use the `Result` type effectively? Let's find out in this recipe!

How to do it...

Here are some steps for working with `Result` and `Option`:

1. Create a new project with `cargo new exceptional-results --lib` and open it with VS Code.

2. Open `src/lib.rs` and add a function before the `test` module:

```
///
/// Finds a needle in a haystack, returns -1 on error
///
pub fn bad_practice_find(needle: &str, haystack: &str) -> i32 {
    haystack.find(needle).map(|p| p as i32).unwrap_or(-1)
}
```

3. As the name suggests, this is not the best way to communicate failure in Rust. What is a better way, though? One answer is to utilize the `Option` enum. Add another function underneath the first one:

```
///
/// Finds a needle in a haystack, returns None on error
///
pub fn better_find(needle: &str, haystack: &str) -> Option<usize> {
    haystack.find(needle)
}
```

4. This makes it possible to reason about the expected return values, but Rust allows a more expressive variation—such as the `Result` type. Add the following to the current collection of functions:

```
#[derive(Debug, PartialEq)]
pub enum FindError {
    EmptyNeedle,
    EmptyHaystack,
    NotFound,
}

///
/// Finds a needle in a haystack, returns a proper Result
///
pub fn best_find(needle: &str, haystack: &str) -> Result<usize,
FindError> {
    if needle.len() <= 0 {
```

```
        Err(FindError::EmptyNeedle)
    } else if haystack.len() <= 0 {
        Err(FindError::EmptyHaystack)
    } else {
        haystack.find(needle).map_or(Err(FindError::NotFound), |n|
Ok(n))
    }
}
```

5. Now that we implemented a few variations of the same function, let's test them. For the first function, add the following to the test module and replace the existing (default) test:

```
use super::*;

#[test]
fn test_bad_practice() {
    assert_eq!(bad_practice_find("a", "hello world"), -1);
    assert_eq!(bad_practice_find("e", "hello world"), 1);
    assert_eq!(bad_practice_find("", "hello world"), 0);
    assert_eq!(bad_practice_find("a", ""), -1);
}
```

6. The other test functions look very similar. To have consistent outcomes and show the differences between the return types, add these to the test module:

```
#[test]
fn test_better_practice() {
    assert_eq!(better_find("a", "hello world"), None);
    assert_eq!(better_find("e", "hello world"), Some(1));
    assert_eq!(better_find("", "hello world"), Some(0));
    assert_eq!(better_find("a", ""), None);
}

#[test]
fn test_best_practice() {
    assert_eq!(best_find("a", "hello world"),
    Err(FindError::NotFound));
    assert_eq!(best_find("e", "hello world"), Ok(1));
    assert_eq!(best_find("", "hello world"),
    Err(FindError::EmptyNeedle));
    assert_eq!(best_find("e", ""),
    Err(FindError::EmptyHaystack));
}
```

7. Let's run `cargo test` to see the test results:

```
$ cargo test
Compiling exceptional-results v0.1.0 (Rust-Cookbook/Chapter05
 /exceptional-results)
Finished dev [unoptimized + debuginfo] target(s) in 0.53s
Running target/debug/deps/exceptional_results-97ca0d7b67ae4b8b

running 3 tests
test tests::test_best_practice ... ok
test tests::test_bad_practice ... ok
test tests::test_better_practice ... ok

test result: ok. 3 passed; 0 failed; 0 ignored; 0 measured; 0
filtered out

    Doc-tests exceptional-results

running 0 tests

test result: ok. 0 passed; 0 failed; 0 ignored; 0 measured; 0
filtered out
```

Now, let's see what's behind the scenes to understand the code better.

How it works...

Rust and many other programming languages use the `Result` type to communicate multiple function outcomes at once. This way, the function can return just as it was designed without (unexpected) jumps such as the exception mechanism.

In *step 3* of this recipe, we show one way of communicating errors that is common in other languages (for example, Java)—however, as we can see in the test (*step 6*), the outcome for an empty string is unexpected (0 instead of –1). In *step 3*, we define a better return type, but is it enough? No, it isn't. In *step 4*, we implement the best version of the function where each `Result` type is easy to interpret and clearly defined.

One even greater example of how to use `Result` can be found in the standard library. It's the `quick_search` function on the `slice` trait, which returns `Ok()` with the position that it found the item in and `Err()` with the position that the item should have been found at. Check out the documentation at `https://doc.rust-lang.org/std/primitive.slice.html#method.binary_search` for more details.

Others will love your expressive APIs once you master using multiple `Result` and `Option` types to communicate beyond success and failure. Keep learning by moving on to the next recipe.

Seamless error handling

Exceptions represent a special case in many programs: they have their own execution path and the program can jump into this path any time. Is this ideal, though? This depends on the size of the `try` block (or whatever the name); this might cover several statements and debugging a runtime exception stops being fun quickly. A better way to achieve safe error handling could be to integrate errors in the results of a function call—a practice that can already be seen in C functions where the parameters do the data transfer and the return code indicates success/failure. Newer, more functional paradigms suggest something akin to the `Result` type in Rust—which comes with functions to elegantly deal with the various outcomes. This makes the errors an expected outcome of a function and enables smooth error handling without additional `if` conditions for every call.

In this recipe, we'll go over several methods to work with errors seamlessly.

How to do it...

Let's go through some steps to handle errors seamlessly:

1. Create a new project with `cargo new exceptional-results --lib` and open it with VS Code.

2. Open `src/lib.rs` and replace the existing test with a new test:

   ```
   #[test]
   fn positive_results() {
       // code goes here
   }
   ```

3. As the name suggests, we'll add some positive result tests in the function's body. Let's start with a declaration and something simple. Replace the preceding `// code goes here` section with the following:

   ```
   let ok: Result<i32, f32> = Ok(42);

   assert_eq!(ok.and_then(|r| Ok(r + 1)), Ok(43));
   assert_eq!(ok.map(|r| r + 1), Ok(43));
   ```

4. Let's add some more variation since multiple `Result` types can behave just like Booleans. Add some more code into the `good_results` test:

```
// Boolean operations with Results. Take a close look at
// what's returned
assert_eq!(ok.and(Ok(43)), Ok(43));
let err: Result<i32, f32> = Err(-42.0);
assert_eq!(ok.and(err), err);
assert_eq!(ok.or(err), ok);
```

5. However, where there are good results, bad results may happen too! In the case of the `Result` type, it is about the `Err` variant. Add another empty test called `negative_results`:

```
#[test]
fn negative_results() {
    // code goes here
}
```

6. Just like before, we are replacing the `//code goes here` comment with some actual tests:

```
let err: Result<i32, f32> = Err(-42.0);
let ok: Result<i32, f32> = Ok(-41);

assert_eq!(err.or_else(|r| Ok(r as i32 + 1)), ok);
assert_eq!(err.map(|r| r + 1), Err(-42.0));
assert_eq!(err.map_err(|r| r + 1.0), Err(-41.0));
```

7. Other than the positive results, the negative results often have their own functions such as `map_err`. Contrary to that, the Boolean functions behave consistently and treat the `Err` result as false. Add the following to the `negative_results` test:

```
let err2: Result<i32, f32> = Err(43.0);
let ok: Result<i32, f32> = Ok(42);
assert_eq!(err.and(err2), err);
assert_eq!(err.and(ok), err);
assert_eq!(err.or(ok), ok);
```

8. As the last step, we run `cargo test` to see the test results:

```
$ cargo test
  Compiling seamless-errors v0.1.0 (Rust-Cookbook/Chapter05
  /seamless-errors)
  Finished dev [unoptimized + debuginfo] target(s) in 0.37s
  Running target/debug/deps/seamless_errors-7a2931598a808519
```

```
running 2 tests
test tests::positive_results ... ok
test tests::negative_results ... ok

test result: ok. 2 passed; 0 failed; 0 ignored; 0 measured; 0
filtered out

    Doc-tests seamless-errors

running 0 tests

test result: ok. 0 passed; 0 failed; 0 ignored; 0 measured; 0
filtered out
```

Do you want to know more? Keep reading to find out how it works.

How it works...

The `Result` type is important for creating code that integrates all of the possible function outcomes into the regular workflow. This eliminates the need for special handling of exceptions, making the code less verbose and easier to reason about. Since these types are known beforehand, the library can offer specialized functions as well, which is what we are looking at in this recipe.

In the first few steps (*step 2* to *step 4*), we are working with positive results, which means values that are wrapped in the `Ok` enum variant. First, we covered the `and_then` function, which provides chaining of various functions that should only be executed when the initial `Result` is `Ok`. In the case of an `Err` return value of one of the functions in the chain, the `Err` result is passed through, skipping the positive handlers (such as `and_then` and `map`). Similarly, `map()` allows transformation within the `Result` type. Both `map` and `and_then` only make it possible to transform `Result<i32, i32>` into `Result<MyOwnType, i32>` but not `MyOwnType` alone. Lastly, the test covers Boolean operations with the multiple `Result` types summarized in this table:

A	B	A and B
Ok	Ok	Ok (B)
Ok	Err	Err
Err	Ok	Err
Err	Err	Err (A)
Ok	Ok	Ok (A)

The remaining steps (*step 5* to *step 7*) show the same process with a negative result type: Err. In the same manner that map() handles only Ok results, map_err() transforms Err. A special case of that is the or_else() function, which executes the provided closure whenever Err was returned. The last parts of the test cover the Boolean functions of multiple Result types and show how they work with various Err parameters.

Now that we have seen many different variations of working with Ok and Err, let's move on to the next recipe.

Customizing errors

While the Result type doesn't care about the type it returns in the Err branch, returning String instances for error messages is not ideal either. Typical errors have several things to consider:

- Is there a root cause or error?
- What is the error message?
- Is there a more in-depth message to output?

The standard library's errors all follow a common trait from std::error::Error—let's see how they are implemented.

How to do it...

Defining error types is not hard—just follow these steps:

1. Create a new project with cargo new custom-errors and open it with VS Code.
2. Using VS Code, open src/main.rs and create a basic struct called MyError:

```
use std::fmt;
use std::error::Error;

#[derive(Debug)]
pub struct MyError {
    code: usize,
}
```

3. There is an `Error` trait that we can implement, as follows:

```
impl Error for MyError {
    fn description(&self) -> &str {
        "Occurs when someone makes a mistake"
    }
}
```

4. However, the trait also requires us (next to `Debug`—which we derived) to implement `std::fmt::Display`:

```
impl fmt::Display for MyError {
    fn fmt(&self, f: &mut fmt::Formatter<'_>) -> fmt::Result {
        write!(f, "Error code {:#X}", self.code)
    }
}
```

5. Lastly, let's see these traits in action and replace the `main` function:

```
fn main() {
    println!("Display: {}", MyError{ code: 1535 });
    println!("Debug: {:?}", MyError{ code: 42 });
    println!("Description: {:?}", (MyError{ code: 42
    }).description());
}
```

6. Then, we can see everything work together using `cargo run`:

```
$ cargo run
Compiling custom-errors v0.1.0 (Rust-Cookbook/Chapter05/custom-
errors)
 Finished dev [unoptimized + debuginfo] target(s) in 0.23s
 Running `target/debug/custom-errors`
Display: Error code 0x5FF
Debug: MyError { code: 42 }
Description: "Occurs when someone makes a mistake"
```

Let's see whether we can get behind the scenes of this short recipe.

How it works...

Although any type will work just fine in a `Result` arm, Rust offers an error trait that can be implemented for better integration into other crates. An example of that is the `actix_web` framework's error handling (`https://actix.rs/docs/errors/`) that works with `std::error::Error` as well as with its own types (we will look at that in more depth in `Chapter 8`, *Safe Programming for the Web*).

In addition to that, the `Error` trait also offers nesting, and, using dynamic dispatch, all `Errors` can follow a common API. In *step 2*, we declare the type and derive the (mandatory) `Debug` trait. In *step 3* and *step 4*, the remaining implementations follow. The rest of the recipe executes the code.

In this short and sweet recipe, we can create custom error types. Now, let's move on to the next recipe.

Resilient programming

Returning `Result` or `Option` will always follow a certain pattern that generates a lot of boilerplate code—especially for uncertain operations such as reading or creating files and searching for values. In particular, the pattern produces either code that uses early returns a lot (remember `goto`?) or nested statements, both of which produce code that is hard to reason about. Therefore, early versions of the Rust library implemented a `try!` macro, which has been replaced with the `?` operator as a quick early return option. Let's see how that influences the code.

How to do it...

Follow these steps to write more resilient programs:

1. Create a new project with `cargo new resilient-programming` and open it with VS Code.
2. Open `src/main.rs` to add a function:

```
use std::fs;
use std::io;

fn print_file_contents_qm(filename: &str) -> Result<(), io::Error>
{
    let contents = fs::read_to_string(filename)?;
```

```
println!("File contents, external fn: {:?}", contents);
Ok(())
}
```

3. The preceding function prints the file contents if it finds the file; in addition to that, we have to call this function. For that, replace the existing `main` function with this:

```
fn main() -> Result<(), std::io::Error> {
    println!("Ok: {:?}", print_file_contents_qm("testfile.txt"));
    println!("Err: {:?}", print_file_contents_qm("not-a-file"));
    let contents = fs::read_to_string("testfile.txt")?;
    println!("File contents, main fn: {:?}", contents);
    Ok(())
}
```

4. That's it—run `cargo run` to find out what the results are:

```
$ cargo run
 Compiling resilient-programming v0.1.0 (Rust-Cookbook/Chapter05
 /resilient-programming)
 Finished dev [unoptimized + debuginfo] target(s) in 0.21s
 Running `target/debug/resilient-programming`
File contents, external fn: "Hello World!"
Ok: Ok(())
Err: Err(Os { code: 2, kind: NotFound, message: "No such file or
directory" })
File contents, main fn: "Hello World!"
```

Now, let's go behind the scenes to understand the code better.

How it works...

In these four steps, we saw the use of the question mark operator and how it can avoid the boilerplate typically associated with guards. In *step 3*, we create a function that prints the file contents if the file has been found (and was readable), and, by using the `?` operator, we can skip checking the return value and exiting the function if necessary—it's all done with a simple `?` operator.

In *step 4*, we not only call the previously created function, but we are also printing the result to show how it works. On top of that, the same pattern is applied to the (special) `main` function, which now has a return value. Therefore, `?` is not limited to sub-functions but can be applied throughout the application.

In just a few simple steps, we have seen how to use the `?` operator to unwrap
`Result` safely. Now, let's move on to the next recipe.

Working with external crates for error handling

Creating and wrapping errors is a common task in modern programs. However, as we have
seen in various recipes in this chapter, it can be quite tedious to handle every possible case
and, on top of that, care about each possible variation that might be returned. This problem
is well known and the Rust community has come up with ways to make that a lot easier.
We'll touch on macros in the next chapter (Chapter 6, *Expressing Yourself with Macros*), but
creating error types leans a lot on using macros. Additionally, this recipe mirrors a previous
recipe (*Handling multiple errors*) to show the differences in code.

How to do it...

Let's pull in some external crates to handle errors better in just a few steps:

1. Create a new project with `cargo new external-crates` and open it with VS
   Code.
2. Edit `Cargo.toml` to add the `quick-error` dependency:

   ```
   [dependencies]
   quick-error = "1.2"
   ```

3. To use the provided macros in `quick-error`, we need to import them explicitly.
   Add the following `use` statements to `src/main.rs`:

   ```
   #[macro_use] extern crate quick_error;

   use std::convert::From;
   use std::io;
   ```

4. In one step, we are then going to add all of the errors we want to declare inside
   the `quick_error!` macro:

   ```
   quick_error! {
       #[derive(Debug)]
       pub enum ErrorWrapper {
           InvalidDeviceIdError(device_id: usize) {
               from(device_id: usize) -> (device_id)
   ```

```
                    description("No device present with this id, check
                    formatting.")
            }

            DeviceNotPresentError(device_id: usize) {
                display("Device with id \"{}\" not found", device_id)
            }

            UnexpectedDeviceStateError {}

            Io(err: io::Error) {
                from(kind: io::ErrorKind) -> (io::Error::from(kind))
                description(err.description())
                display("I/O Error: {}", err)
            }
        }
    }
```

5. The code is only complete when the `main` function is added as well:

```
fn main() {
    println!("(IOError) {}",
    ErrorWrapper::from(io::ErrorKind::InvalidData));
    println!("(InvalidDeviceIdError) {}",
    ErrorWrapper::InvalidDeviceIdError(42));
    println!("(DeviceNotPresentError) {}",
    ErrorWrapper::DeviceNotPresentError(42));
    println!("(UnexpectedDeviceStateError) {}",
    ErrorWrapper::UnexpectedDeviceStateError {});
}
```

6. Use `cargo run` to find the output of the program:

```
$ cargo run
 Compiling external-crates v0.1.0 (Rust-Cookbook/Chapter05
  /external-crates)
 Finished dev [unoptimized + debuginfo] target(s) in 0.27s
   Running `target/debug/external-crates`
(IOError) I/O Error: invalid data
(InvalidDeviceIdError) No device present with this id, check
formatting.
(DeviceNotPresentError) Device with id "42" not found
(UnexpectedDeviceStateError) UnexpectedDeviceStateError
```

Did you understand the code? Let's find out how it works.

How it works...

Compared to the previous recipe where we declared multiple errors, this declaration is much shorter and has several added benefits. The first benefit is that each error type can be created using the `From` trait (first `IOError` in *step 4*). Secondly, each type generates an automated description and `Display` implementation (see *step 3*, `UnexpectedDeviceStateError`, and then *step 5*) with the error's name. This is not perfect, but OK as a first step.

Under the hood, `quick-error` generates one enum that handles all possible cases and generates the implementations if necessary. Check out the `main` macro—quite impressive (`http://tailhook.github.io/quick-error/quick_error/macro.quick_error.html`)! To tailor the use of `quick-error` to your needs, check out the rest of their documentation at `http://tailhook.github.io/quick-error/quick_error/index.html`. Alternatively, there is the `error-chain` crate (`https://github.com/rust-lang-nursery/error-chain`), which takes a different approach to create those error types. Either of these options lets you vastly improve the readability and implementation speed of your errors while removing all of the boilerplate code.

We've successfully learned how to improve our error handling by using external crates. Now, let's move on to the next recipe.

Moving between Option and Result

Whenever a binary result is to be returned from a function, the choice is between using `Result` or `Option`. Both can communicate a failed function call—but the former provides too much specificity, while the latter may give too little. While this is a decision to make for the specific situation, Rust's types provide the tools to move between them with ease. Let's go over them in this recipe.

How to do it...

In a few quick steps, you'll know how to move between `Option` and `Result`:

1. Create a new project with `cargo new options-results --lib` and open it with VS Code.

2. Let's edit `src/lib.rs` and replace the existing test (inside `mod tests`) with the following:

```
#[derive(Debug, Eq, PartialEq, Copy, Clone)]
struct MyError;

#[test]
fn transposing() {
    // code will follow
}
```

3. We have to replace `// code will follow` with an example of how to use the `transpose()` function:

```
let this: Result<Option<i32>, MyError> = Ok(Some(42));
let other: Option<Result<i32, MyError>> = Some(Ok(42));
assert_eq!(this, other.transpose());
```

4. This works with `Err` as well and, for proof, add this to the `transpose()` test:

```
let this: Result<Option<i32>, MyError> = Err(MyError);
let other: Option<Result<i32, MyError>> = Some(Err(MyError));
assert_eq!(this, other.transpose());
```

5. What's left is the special case of `None`. Complete the `transpose()` test with this:

```
assert_eq!(None::<Result<i32, MyError>>.transpose(), Ok(None::
<i32>));
```

6. Moving between the two types is not only about transposing—there are more complex ways to do that too. Create another `test`:

```
#[test]
fn conversion() {
    // more to follow
}
```

7. As a first test, let's replace `// more to follow` with something that can be used instead of `unwrap()`:

```
let opt = Some(42);
assert_eq!(opt.ok_or(MyError), Ok(42));

let res: Result<i32, MyError> = Ok(42);
assert_eq!(res.ok(), opt);
assert_eq!(res.err(), None);
```

8. To complete the conversion test, also add the following to `test`. These are conversions but from the `Err` side:

```
let opt: Option<i32> = None;
assert_eq!(opt.ok_or(MyError), Err(MyError));

let res: Result<i32, MyError> = Err(MyError);
assert_eq!(res.ok(), None);
assert_eq!(res.err(), Some(MyError));
```

9. Lastly, we should run the code using `cargo test` and see successful test results:

```
$ cargo test
Compiling options-results v0.1.0 (Rust-Cookbook/Chapter05/options-
results)
 Finished dev [unoptimized + debuginfo] target(s) in 0.44s
 Running target/debug/deps/options_results-111cad5a9a9f6792

running 2 tests
test tests::conversion ... ok
test tests::transposing ... ok

test result: ok. 2 passed; 0 failed; 0 ignored; 0 measured; 0
filtered out

   Doc-tests options-results

running 0 tests

test result: ok. 0 passed; 0 failed; 0 ignored; 0 measured; 0
filtered out
```

Now, let's go behind the scenes to understand the code better.

How it works...

While the discussion of when to use `Option` and when to use `Result` takes place on a high level, Rust supports the transition between the two types with several functions. In addition to `map()`, `and_then()`, and so on (discussed in the *Seamless error handling* section in this chapter), these functions provide powerful and elegant ways to work with a variety of errors. In *step 1* to *step 4*, we are slowly building a simple test that shows the applicability of the transpose function. It makes it possible to switch from `Ok(Some(42))` to `Some(Ok(42))` (notice the subtle difference) with a single call to a function. Similarly, the `Err` variation of the call goes from a regular `Err(MyError)` function to `Some(Err(MyError))`.

The remaining steps (*step 6* to *step 8*) show more traditional ways to convert between the two types. These include fetching the values of `Ok` and `Err`, as well as providing an error instance for positive results. In general, these functions should be enough to replace most `unwrap()` or `expect()` calls and have a single execution path through the program without having to resort to `if` and `match` conditionals. This adds the bonus of robustness and readability, and your future colleagues and users will thank you!

6
Expressing Yourself with Macros

In the previous century, many languages featured a preprocessor (most prominently, C/C++) that often did unassuming text replacement. While this is handy for expressing constants (`#define MYCONST 1`), it also leads to potentially unexpected outcomes once the replacement gets more complex (for example, `#define MYCONST 1 + 1` and when applied as `5 * MYCONST` yields *5 * 1 + 1 = 6* instead of the expected 10 (from *5 * (1 + 1))*) .

However, a preprocessor allows program programming (metaprogramming) and therefore makes things easier for the developer. Instead of copying and pasting expressions and excessive boilerplate code, a quick macro definition leads to a smaller code base and reusable calls and—as a consequence—fewer errors. In order to make the best use of Rust's type system, macros cannot simply search and replace text; they have to work on a higher level: the abstract syntax tree. Not only does this require a different calling syntax (such as an exclamation mark at the end of a call; for example, `println!`) for the compiler to know what to do, the parameter *types* are different as well.

At this level, we are talking about expressions, statements, identifiers, types, and many more that can be passed into a macro. Ultimately, however, the macro preprocessor still inserts the macro's body into the calling scope before compilation, so the compiler catches type mismatches or borrowing violations. If you want to read more on macros, check out the blog post at `https://blog.x5ff.xyz/blog/easy-programming-with-rust-macros/`, *The Little Book of Rust Macros* (`https://danielkeep.github.io/tlborm/book/index.html`), and the Rust book (`https://doc.rust-lang.org/book/ch19-06-macros.html`). Macros are best tried out to get a feel for them—we'll cover the following in this chapter:

- Building custom macros in Rust
- Implementing matching with macros
- Using predefined Rust macros
- Code generation using macros

- Macro overloading
- Using `repeat` for parameter ranges
- Don't Repeat Yourself (DRY)

Building custom macros in Rust

Previously, we have mostly used predefined macros—it's now time to look at creating custom macros. There are several types of macros in Rust—derive-based, function-like, and attributes, all of which have their own respective use cases. In this recipe, we'll experiment with the function-like variety to get started.

How to do it...

You are only a few steps from creating macros:

1. Run `cargo new custom-macros` in Terminal (or PowerShell on Windows) and open the directory with Visual Studio Code.
2. Open `src/main.rs` in the editor. Let's create a new macro called `one_plus_one` at the top of the file:

```
// A simple macro without arguments
macro_rules! one_plus_one {
    () => { 1 + 1 };
}
```

3. Let's call this simple macro inside the `main` function:

```
fn main() {
    println!("1 + 1 = {}", one_plus_one!());
}
```

4. This was a very simple macro, but macros can do so much more! How about one that lets us decide on the operation. Add a very simple macro to the top of the file:

```
// A simple pattern matching argument
macro_rules! one_and_one {
  (plus) => { 1 + 1 };
  (minus) => { 1 - 1 };
  (mult) => { 1 * 1 };
}
```

5. Since the words in the **matcher** part of the macro are required, we have to call the macro exactly like that. Add the following inside the `main` function:

```
println!("1 + 1 = {}", one_and_one!(plus));
println!("1 - 1 = {}", one_and_one!(minus));
println!("1 * 1 = {}", one_and_one!(mult));
```

6. As the last part, we should think of keeping things in order; creating modules, structs, files, and so on. To group similar behavior is a common way to organize stuff, and if we want to use it outside of our module we need to make it publicly available. Just like the `pub` keyword, macros have to be exported explicitly—but with an attribute. Add this module to `src/main.rs` as follows:

```
mod macros {
    #[macro_export]
    macro_rules! two_plus_two {
        () => { 2 + 2 };
    }
}
```

7. Thanks to the export, we can now also call this function in `main()`:

```
fn main() {
    println!("1 + 1 = {}", one_plus_one!());
    println!("1 + 1 = {}", one_and_one!(plus));
    println!("1 - 1 = {}", one_and_one!(minus));
    println!("1 * 1 = {}", one_and_one!(mult));
    println!("2 + 2 = {}", two_plus_two!());
}
```

8. By issuing `cargo run` from Terminal inside the project's directory, we will then find out whether it worked:

```
$ cargo run
  Compiling custom-macros v0.1.0 (Rust-Cookbook/Chapter06/custom-
  macros)
   Finished dev [unoptimized + debuginfo] target(s) in 0.66s
    Running `target/debug/custom-macros`
1 + 1 = 2
1 + 1 = 2
1 - 1 = 0
1 * 1 = 1
2 + 2 = 4
```

In order to understand the code better, let's decipher these steps.

How it works...

As appropriate, we use a macro—`macro_rules!`—to create a custom macro as we did in *step 3*. A single macro matches a pattern and consists of three parts:

- A name (for example, `one_plus_one`)
- A matcher (for example, `(plus) => ...`)
- A transcriber (for example, `... => { 1 + 1 }`)

Calling a macro is always done using its name followed by an exclamation mark (*step 4*), and for specific patterns, with the required characters/words (*step 6*). Note that `plus` and others are not variables, types, or otherwise defined—which gives you the power to create your own **domain-specific language** (DSL)! More on that in other recipes in this chapter.

By calling a macro, the compiler takes note of the position in the **abstract syntax tree** (AST) and, instead of pure text replacement, inserts the macro's transcriber sub-tree right there. Afterward, the compiler tries to finish the compilation, leading to regular type-safety checks, borrowing rules enforcement, and so on, but with awareness for macros. This makes it easier for you, as the developer, to find errors and trace them back into the macros they originate from.

In *step 6*, we create a module to export a macro from—something that will improve the code structure and maintainability, especially in larger code bases. However, the export step is required since macros are private by default. Try removing the `#[macro_export]` attribute to see what happens.

Step 8 shows how to call every macro variation in the project as a comparison. For more information, you can also check out the blog post at `https://blog.rust-lang.org/2018/12/21/Procedural-Macros-in-Rust-2018.html`, which goes into more detail about providing macro crates on `crates.io` (`https://crates.io`).

Now that we know how to build custom macros in Rust, we can move on to the next recipe.

Implementing matching with macros

When we created custom macros, we had already seen pattern matching at play: a command was only executed if particular words were present *before compilation*. In other words, the macro system compares raw text as patterns before they become expressions or types. Consequently, creating a DSL is really easy. Defining a web request handler? Use method names in the pattern: `GET`, `POST`, `HEAD`. There is an endless variety, however, so let's see how we can define some patterns in this recipe!

How to do it...

By following these next few steps, you will be able to use macros:

1. Run `cargo new matching --lib` in Terminal (or PowerShell on Windows) and open the directory with Visual Studio Code.

2. In `src/lib.rs`, we add a macro to work with specific types as inputs. Insert the following at the top of the file:

```
macro_rules! strange_patterns {
    (The pattern must match precisely) => { "Text" };
    (42) => { "Numeric" };
    (;<=,<=;) => { "Alpha" };
}
```

3. Clearly, this should be tested to see whether it works. Replace the `it_works()` test with a different test function:

```
#[test]
fn test_strange_patterns() {
    assert_eq!(strange_patterns!(The pattern must match
    precisely), "Text");
    assert_eq!(strange_patterns!(42), "Numeric");
    assert_eq!(strange_patterns!(;<=,<=;), "Alpha");
}
```

4. The patterns can also contain actual input parameters:

```
macro_rules! compare {
    ($x:literal => $y:block) => { $x == $y };
}
```

5. A simple test to round it off is as follows:

```
#[test]
fn test_compare() {
    assert!(compare!(1 => { 1 }));
}
```

6. Handling HTTP requests has always been an architectural challenge, with added layers and special routes for every business case. As some web frameworks (https://github.com/seanmonstar/warp) show, macros can provide useful support to enable composing handlers together. Add another macro and support functions to the file—the register_handler() function, which mocks registering a handler function for our hypothetical web framework:

```
#[derive(Debug)]
pub struct Response(usize);
pub fn register_handler(method: &str, path: &str, handler:
&Fn() -> Response ) {}

macro_rules! web {
    (GET $path:literal => $b:block) => {
        register_handler("GET", $path, &|| $b) };
    (POST $path:literal => $b:block) => {
        register_handler("POST", $path, &|| $b) };
}
```

7. In order to make sure everything works, we should also add a test for the web! macro. When the function is empty, a macro that doesn't match the pattern it holds leads to a compile-time error:

```
use super::*;

#[test]
fn test_web() {
    web!(GET "/" => { Response(200) });
    web!(POST "/" => { Response(403) });
}
```

8. As the final step, let's run cargo test (note: add #![allow(unused_variables, unused_macros)] at the top of the file to remove warnings):

```
$ cargo test
   Compiling matching v0.1.0 (Rust-Cookbook/Chapter06/matching)
    Finished dev [unoptimized + debuginfo] target(s) in 0.31s
     Running target/debug/deps/matching-124bc24094676408

running 3 tests
test tests::test_compare ... ok
test tests::test_strange_patterns ... ok
test tests::test_web ... ok

test result: ok. 3 passed; 0 failed; 0 ignored; 0 measured; 0
```

```
filtered out

    Doc-tests matching

running 0 tests

test result: ok. 0 passed; 0 failed; 0 ignored; 0 measured; 0
filtered out
```

Now let's look at what the code does.

How it works...

In *step 2* of this recipe, we define a macro that explicitly provides the different patterns that the engine can match to. Specifically, the alphanumeric characters are limited to , , ; , and => . While this allows Ruby-style map initialization, it also limits the elements that a DSL can have. However, macros are still great for creating a more expressive way to deal with situations. In *step 6* and *step 7*, we show a way to create a web request handler using a more expressive way than the usual chained function calls. *Step 4* and *step 5* show the usage of the arrow (=>) inside macros and *step 8* ties it all together by running the tests.

In this recipe, we created matching arms for the macro invocation to use, where the arms use a literal matching (instead of matching on the types, which will come later in this chapter) to decide on a replacement. This shows that not only can we use parameters and literals in one arm but we can also automate tasks without the constraints of regularly allowed names.

We've successfully learned how to implement matching in macros. Now let's move on to the next recipe.

Using predefined macros

As we saw in the previous recipes in this chapter, macros can save a lot of writing and provide convenience functions without having to rethink the entire application architecture. Consequently, the Rust standard library provides several macros for a range of features that might otherwise be surprisingly complex to implement. One example is cross-platform prints—how would that work? Is there an equivalent way to output console text for every platform? What about color support? What is the default encoding? There are a lot of questions, which is an indicator of how many things need to be configurable—yet in a typical program, we only call print!("hello") and it works. Let's see what else there is.

How to do it...

Follow these few steps to implement this recipe:

1. Run `cargo new std-macros` in Terminal (or PowerShell on Windows) and open the directory with Visual Studio Code. Then, create a a.txt file inside the project's `src` directory with the following content:

    ```
    Hello World!
    ```

2. First, the default implementation of `main()` (in `src/main.rs`) already provides us with a macro call to `println!`:

    ```
    fn main() {
        println!("Hello, world!");
    }
    ```

3. We can extend the function by printing more. Insert the following after the `println!` macro call in the `main()` function:

    ```
    println!("a vec: {:?}", vec![1, 2, 3]);
    println!("concat: {}", concat!(0, 'x', "5ff"));
    println!("MyStruct stringified: {}", stringify!(MyStruct(10)));
    println!("some random word stringified: {}", stringify!
      (helloworld));
    ```

4. The definition for `MyStruct` is also simple and involves a procedural macro that comes with the standard library. Insert this before the `main()` function:

    ```
    #[derive(Debug)]
    struct MyStruct(usize);
    ```

5. The Rust standard library also includes macros to interact with the outside world. Let's add a few more calls to the `main` function:

    ```
    println!("Running on Windows? {}", cfg!(windows));
    println!("From a file: {}", include_str!("a.txt"));
    println!("$PATH: {:?}", option_env!("PATH"));
    ```

6. As a final step, let's add two alternatives to the well-known `println!` and `assert!` macros to `main()`:

    ```
    eprintln!("Oh no!");
    debug_assert!(true);
    ```

7. If you haven't already, we have to run the entire project using `cargo run` to see some output:

```
$ cargo run
    Compiling std-macros v0.1.0 (Rust-Cookbook/Chapter06/std-macros)
     Finished dev [unoptimized + debuginfo] target(s) in 0.25s
      Running `target/debug/std-macros`
Hello, world!
a vec: [1, 2, 3]
concat: 0x5ff
MyStruct stringified: MyStruct ( 10 )
some random word stringified: helloworld
Running on Windows? false
From a file: Hello World!
$PATH:
Some("/home/cm/.cargo/bin:/home/cm/.cargo/bin:/home/cm/.cargo/bin:/
usr/local/bin:/usr/bin:/bin:/home/cm/.cargo/bin:/home/cm/Apps:/home
/cm/.local/bin:/home/cm/.cargo/bin:/home/cm/Apps:/home/cm/.local/bi
n")
Oh no!
```

We should now pull back the curtain to understand the code a bit better.

How it works...

Inside the `main` function, we now have a few macros that are more or less well known. Each of them is doing something we thought was useful. We'll skip *step 2* since it only shows the `println!` macro—something that we are using constantly. In *step 3*, however, some more exotic macros turn up:

- `vec!` creates and initializes a vector and famously uses `[]` to do so. However, while this makes visual sense, the compiler will accept `vec!()` just as well as `vec!{}`.
- `concat!` joins literals from left to right like a static string.
- `stringify!` creates a string literal from the input tokens, regardless of whether they exist or not (see the word `helloworld`, which got translated to a string).

Step 4 includes working with a procedural macro in Rust. While the word *derive* and the syntax bring to mind inheritance in classic OOP fashion, they are not actually deriving anything but are providing an actual implementation. For us, `#[derive(Debug)]` has certainly been the most useful, but there is also `PartialEq`, `Eq`, and `Clone`, which are closely behind.

Step 5 of the recipe returns to function-like macros:

- `cfg!` is similar to the `#[cfg]` attribute, which makes it possible to determine conditions at compile time, which allows you—for example—to include platform-specific code.
- `include_str!` is a very interesting one. There are other includes, but this is very useful to provide translation to your applications since it reads the provided file's contents as a `'static str` (just like a literal).
- `option_env!` reads environment variables at **compile time** to provide an `Option` result of their values. Be aware that, in order to reflect the changes to the variable, the program has to be re-compiled!

Step 6's macros are alternatives to other popular macros that we know:

- `debug_assert!` is a variation of `assert!`, which is not included in `--release` builds.
- `eprintln!` outputs stuff on standard error instead of standard out.

While this is a pretty stable selection, future releases of the Rust Standard Library will include more macros to make working with Rust more convenient. The most popular example—at the time of writing—for unfinished macros is `await!`, which might never be stabilized due to a different approach to `async`/`await`. Check out the full list in the document at `https://doc.rust-lang.org/std/#macros`.

Now we've learned more about using predefined macros, we can move on to the next recipe.

Code generation using macros

Something derive-type macros already show us is that we can generate entire trait implementations using macros. Similarly, we can generate entire structs and functions using macros and avoid copy-and-paste programming, as well as tedious boilerplate code. Since macros are executed right before compilation, the generated code will be checked accordingly while avoiding the details of strictly typed languages. Let's see how!

How to do it...

Code generation can be as easy as these few steps:

1. Run `cargo new code-generation --lib` in Terminal (or PowerShell on Windows) and open the directory with Visual Studio Code.

2. Open `src/lib.rs` and add the first simple macro:

```
// Repeat the statement that was passed in n times
macro_rules! n_times {
    // `()` indicates that the macro takes no argument.
    ($n: expr, $f: block) => {
        for _ in 0..$n {
            $f()
        }
    }
}
```

3. Let's do another one, this time a bit more generative. Add this outside of the testing module (for example, underneath the previous macro):

```
// Declare a function in a macro!
macro_rules! make_fn {
    ($i: ident, $body: block) => {
        fn $i () $body
    }
}
```

4. Both of those macros are also very straightforward to use. Let's replace the `tests` module with relevant tests:

```
#[cfg(test)]
mod tests {
    #[test]
    fn test_n_times() {
        let mut i = 0;
        n_times!(5, {
            i += 1;
        });
        assert_eq!(i, 5);
    }

    #[test]
    #[should_panic]
    fn test_failing_make_fn() {
        make_fn!(fail, {assert!(false)});
        fail();
```

```
    }

    #[test]
    fn test_make_fn() {
        make_fn!(fail, {assert!(false)});
        // nothing happens if we don't call the function
    }
}
```

5. So far, the macros have not done a sophisticated code generation, however. In fact, the first one simply repeats a block several times—something that is already available through iterators (https://doc.rust-lang.org/std/iter/fn.repeat_ with.html). The second macro creates a function, but that's available, too, via the closure syntax (https://doc.rust-lang.org/stable/rust-by-example/fn/ closures.html). Let's add something more interesting then, such as enum with a Default implementation:

```
macro_rules! default_enum {
    ($name: ident, $($variant: ident => $val:expr),+) => {
        #[derive(Eq, PartialEq, Clone, Debug)]
        pub enum $name {
            Invalid,
            $($variant = $val),+
        }

        impl Default for $name {
            fn default() -> Self { $name::Invalid }
        }
    };
}
```

6. Nothing can go untested, so here is a test to see whether it works as expected. Add this to the preceding tests:

```
    #[test]
    fn test_default_enum() {
        default_enum!(Colors, Red => 0xFF0000, Blue => 0x0000FF);
        let color: Colors = Default::default();
        assert_eq!(color, Colors::Invalid);
        assert_eq!(Colors::Red as i32, 0xFF0000);
        assert_eq!(Colors::Blue as i32, 0x0000FF);
    }
```

7. If we are writing tests, we also want to see them running:

```
$ cargo test
Compiling custom-designators v0.1.0 (Rust-Cookbook/Chapter06/code-
generation)
warning: function is never used: `fail`
  --> src/lib.rs:20:9
   |
20 | fn $i () $body
   | ^^^^^^^^^^^^^^
...
56 | make_fn!(fail, {assert!(false)});
   | ------------------------------- in this macro invocation
   |
   = note: #[warn(dead_code)] on by default

    Finished dev [unoptimized + debuginfo] target(s) in 0.30s
      Running target/debug/deps/custom_designators-ebc95554afc8c09a

running 4 tests
test tests::test_default_enum ... ok
test tests::test_make_fn ... ok
test tests::test_failing_make_fn ... ok
test tests::test_n_times ... ok

test result: ok. 4 passed; 0 failed; 0 ignored; 0 measured; 0
filtered out

    Doc-tests custom-designators

running 0 tests

test result: ok. 0 passed; 0 failed; 0 ignored; 0 measured; 0
filtered out
```

In order to understand the code, let's talk about what's going on behind the scenes.

How it works...

Thanks to the compiler executing macros before the actual compilation, we can generate code that will show up in the final program but that was actually created via a macro invocation. This lets us reduce boilerplate code, enforce defaults (such as implementing certain traits, adding metadata, and many others), or simply provide a nicer interface for users of our crate.

In *step 2*, we are creating a simple macro to repeat a block (these curly braces—{ }—and their content are called a **block**) several times—using a `for` loop. The tests created in *step 4* show how this operates and what it can do—it executes as if we were to write a `for` loop right in the test.

Step 3 creates a more interesting thing: a function. Together with the tests in *step 4*, we can see how the macro operates and note the following:

- The provided block is evaluated lazily (the test only fails when the function is called).
- The compiler complains about an unused function if it is not called.
- Creating a parameterized function in this way leads to a compiler error (it can't find the value).

Step 5 creates a more complex macro that is able to create an entire `enum`. It lets the user define the variants (even using an arrow—=>—notation), and adds a default value. Let's look at the pattern the macro expects: (`$name: ident, $($variant: ident =>` `$val:expr),+`). The first parameter (`$name`) is an identifier, something that names something (that is, the rules of identifiers are enforced). The second parameter is a repeated parameter and it is required to be present at least once (indicated by +), but if you provide more instances, they have to be separated by , . The expected pattern for those repetitions is as follows: identifier, =>, and expression (for example, `bla => 1 + 1`, `Five => 5`, or `blog => 0x5ff`, and many others).

What follows inside the macro is a classic definition of `enum` with the repeated parameter inserted just as often as it occurs in the input. Then, we can add derive attributes on top of `enum` and implement the `std::default::Default` trait (`https://doc.rust-lang.org/` `std/default/trait.Default.html`) to provide something sensible for when a default value is required.

Let's learn some more about macros and parameters and move on to the next recipe.

Macro overloading

Method/function overloading is a technique to have duplicate method/function names but different parameters for each. Many statically typed languages, such as C# and Java, support this in order to provide many ways to call a method without having to come up with a new name each time (or use generics). Rust, however, does not support that for functions—with good reason (https://blog.rust-lang.org/2015/05/11/traits.html). Where Rust does support overloading is with macro patterns: you can create a macro and have multiple arms that only differ in their input parameters.

How to do it...

Let's implement some overloaded macros in a few simple steps:

1. Run `cargo new macro-overloading --lib` in Terminal (or PowerShell on Windows) and open the directory with Visual Studio Code.
2. In `src/lib.rs`, we add the following before the `mod tests` module declaration:

```
#![allow(unused_macros)]

macro_rules! print_debug {
    (stdout, $($o:expr),*) => {
        $(print!("{:?}", $o));*;
        println!();
    };
    (error, $($o:expr),*) => {
        $(eprint!("{:?}", $o));*;
        eprintln!();
    };
    ($stream:expr, $($o:expr),*) => {
        $(let _ = write!($stream, "{:?}", $o));*;
        let _ = writeln!($stream);
    }
}
```

3. Let's see how we apply this macro. Inside the `tests` module, let's see if the printer macro serializes strings to a stream by adding the following unit test (replace the existing `it_works` test):

```
use std::io::Write;

#[test]
fn test_printer() {
    print_debug!(error, "hello std err");
    print_debug!(stdout, "hello std out");
    let mut v = vec![];
    print_debug!(&mut v, "a");
    assert_eq!(v, vec![34, 97, 34, 10]);

}
```

4. In order to facilitate testing in the future, we should add another macro inside the `tests` module. This time, the macro is mocking (`https://martinfowler.com/articles/mocksArentStubs.html`) a function with a static return value. Write this after the previous test:

```
macro_rules! mock {
    ($type: ty, $name: ident, $ret_val: ty, $val: block) => {
        pub trait $name {
            fn $name(&self) -> $ret_val;
        }

        impl $name for $type {
            fn $name(&self) -> $ret_val $val
        }
    };
    ($name: ident, $($variant: ident => $type:ty),+) => {
        #[derive(PartialEq, Clone, Debug)]
        struct $name {
            $(pub $variant: $type),+
        }
    };
}
```

5. Then, we should test the `mock!` macro as well. Add another test underneath:

```
mock!(String, hello, &'static str, { "Hi!" });
mock!(HelloWorld, greeting => String, when => u64);

#[test]
fn test_mock() {
    let mystr = "Hello".to_owned();
```

```
        assert_eq!(mystr.hello(), "Hi!");

        let g = HelloWorld { greeting: "Hello World".to_owned(),
        when: 1560887098 };

        assert_eq!(g.greeting, "Hello World");
        assert_eq!(g.when, 1560887098);
    }
```

6. As a final step, we run `cargo test` to see if it works. However, this time, we pass `--nocapture` into the test harness to see what's been printed (for *step 3*):

```
$ cargo test -- --nocapture
Compiling macro-overloading v0.1.0 (Rust-Cookbook/Chapter06
/macro-overloading)
warning: trait `hello` should have an upper camel case name
  --> src/lib.rs:53:19
   |
53 | mock!(String, hello, &'static str, { "Hi!" });
   | ^^^^^ help: convert the identifier to upper camel case:
`Hello`
   |
   = note: #[warn(non_camel_case_types)] on by default

    Finished dev [unoptimized + debuginfo] target(s) in 0.56s
     Running target/debug/deps/macro_overloading-bd8b38e609ddd77c

running 2 tests
"hello std err"
"hello std out"
test tests::test_mock ... ok
test tests::test_printer ... ok

test result: ok. 2 passed; 0 failed; 0 ignored; 0 measured; 0
filtered out

   Doc-tests macro-overloading

running 0 tests

test result: ok. 0 passed; 0 failed; 0 ignored; 0 measured; 0
filtered out
```

Now, let's go behind the scenes to understand the code better.

How it works...

Overloading is a very simple concept—so simple, in fact, that it's hard to find usable examples that can't be done using a sufficiently complex function. However, in this recipe, we think that we have come up with something useful.

In *step 2*, we created a wrapper around `println!` and similar functions that allow writing to standard streams such as standard output and standard error, or any other arbitrary stream type, with only a token to make the difference. There are a few interesting details to this implementation outside of this as well:

- Each call to `print!` is followed by `;`—except for the last one, which is why there is an extra `;` after the `*`.
- The pattern allows for an arbitrary number of expressions to be passed in.

This macro can be useful to avoid repeating `println!("{:?}", "hello")` just to quickly see the current value of a variable. Additionally, it facilitates output redirection to standard error.

In *step 3*, we create a test for this macro invocation. In a quick check, we print to `error`, `stdout`, and `vec!` (which is why we import `std::io::Write`). There, we can see the new line at the end and that it's written as a string (the numbers are bytes). In either call, it finds the required macro pattern and inserts its contents.

Step 4 creates a macro for mocking functions on structs or entire structs. This is very useful for isolating the tests to really only test the target implementation without running the risk of adding more errors by trying to implement a supporting function. In this case, the macro's arms are easy to distinguish. The first one creates a mock implementation of a function and matches the parameters it requires: the type it attaches to, the function's identifier, which return type, and a block that returns that type. The second arm creates a struct and therefore only requires an identifier to name the struct and properties together with their data types.

 Mocking—or creating a mock object—is a testing technique that allows the creation of shallow constructs to simulate the desired behavior. This is very useful for things that cannot be implemented otherwise (external hardware, third-party web services, and many more) or complex internal systems (database connection and logic).

Next, we have to test these outcomes, which is done in *step 5*. There, we call the `mock!` macro and define its behavior along with a test to prove it works. We run the tests in *step 6* without the harness capturing the console outputs: it works!

We are certain that overloading macros were a breeze to learn. Now let's move on to the next recipe.

Using repeat for parameter ranges

Rust's `println!` macro has a curious characteristic: there is no upper limit on the number of parameters that you can pass into it. Since regular Rust does not support arbitrary parameter ranges, it has to be a macro feature—but which? In this recipe, find out how to handle and implement parameter ranges for macros.

How to do it...

You'll know how to use parameter ranges after these few steps:

1. Run `cargo new parameter-ranges --lib` in Terminal (or PowerShell on Windows) and open the directory with Visual Studio Code.
2. In `src/lib.rs`, add the following code to initialize a set in `vec!` style:

```
#![allow(unused_macros)]

macro_rules! set {
  ( $( $item:expr ),* ) => {
      {
          let mut s = HashSet::new();
          $(
              s.insert($item);
          )*
          s
      }
  };
}
```

3. Next, we'll add a simple macro to create a DTO—a data transmission object:

```
macro_rules! dto {
    ($name: ident, $($variant: ident => $type:ty),+) => {
        #[derive(PartialEq, Clone, Debug)]
        pub struct $name {
            $(pub $variant: $type),+
        }

        impl $name {
            pub fn new($($variant:$type),+) -> Self {
                $name {
                    $($variant: $variant),+
                }
            }
        }
    };
}
```

4. This needs to be tested as well, so let's add a test to use the new macro to create a set:

```
#[cfg(test)]
mod tests {
    use std::collections::HashSet;

    #[test]
    fn test_set() {
        let actual = set!("a", "b", "c", "a");
        let mut desired = HashSet::new();
        desired.insert("a");
        desired.insert("b");
        desired.insert("c");
        assert_eq!(actual, desired);
    }
}
```

5. With the set initializer tested, let's also test creating a DTO. Add the following under the previous test:

```
#[test]
fn test_dto() {
    dto!(Sensordata, value => f32, timestamp => u64);
    let s = Sensordata::new(1.23f32, 123456);
    assert_eq!(s.value, 1.23f32);
    assert_eq!(s.timestamp, 123456);
}
```

6. As a final step, we also run `cargo test` to show that it works:

```
$ cargo test
 Compiling parameter-ranges v0.1.0 (Rust-Cookbook/Chapter06
  /parameter-ranges)
  Finished dev [unoptimized + debuginfo] target(s) in 1.30s
  Running target/debug/deps/parameter_ranges-7dfb9718c7ca3bc4

running 2 tests
test tests::test_dto ... ok
test tests::test_set ... ok

test result: ok. 2 passed; 0 failed; 0 ignored; 0 measured; 0
filtered out

    Doc-tests parameter-ranges

running 0 tests

test result: ok. 0 passed; 0 failed; 0 ignored; 0 measured; 0
filtered out
```

Now, let's go behind the scenes to understand the code better.

How it works...

Parameter ranges in Rust's macro system work a little bit like regular expressions. There are several parts to the syntax: `$()` indicates repetition, the character that follows its separator (`,`, `;`, and `=>` are allowed), and lastly, the qualifier for how often the repetition is expected (+ or *—just like regular expressions, one or more and zero or more respectively).

Step 2 shows the implementation of a set initializer macro akin to `vec!`. There, we expect a single expression to populate `std::collections::HashSet` and return the result in a sub-block from the transcriber. This is necessary to allow things such as variable assignments (which are not allowed directly within the transcriber block), but don't hinder the expansion of the parameters that were passed into the macro. In a similar fashion to the declaration, the expansion is done using a `$()` area, but instead of a separator, the repetition qualifier follows directly. Whatever is contained in there will be run as many times as there are parameters.

The second macro is defined in *step 3* and is much more complex. The name `dto!` (data transmission object) indicates a business object such as a data container that is only used to pass data around the program without being sent outside the program. Since these DTOs contain a significant amount of boilerplate code, they can be initialized similarly to a key-value store. By using the => sign in the parameter range specification, we can create identifier/type pairs that are used to create properties in `struct` and its constructor function. Note that the comma that separates the properties is located right before the + sign so it gets repeated as well.

Step 4 shows an invocation of the macro designed in *step 2* to populate a set and test to confirm it was populated properly. Similarly, *step 5* shows the creation and instantiation of a DTO instance (`struct` called `Sensordata`) along with a test to confirm that the properties were created as expected. The last step confirms this by running the tests.

We've successfully learned how to use repeat for parameter ranges. Now let's move on to the next recipe.

Don't Repeat Yourself

In a previous recipe, we were using macros to generate almost arbitrary code, thereby reducing the amount of code to write. Let's dive deeper into this topic since this is a great way not only to reduce bugs but also to achieve consistent quality in code. One repetitive task that everyone should do is testing (especially if it's a public-facing API), and if we copy and paste those tests we expose ourselves to errors. Instead, let's see how we can generate boilerplate code with macros to stop repeating ourselves.

How to do it...

Automated testing with macros is only a few steps away:

1. Run `cargo new dry-macros --lib` in Terminal (or PowerShell on Windows) and open the directory with Visual Studio Code.
2. In `src/lib.rs`, we want to create a helper macro and import the stuff we need:

```
use std::ops::{Add, Mul, Sub};

macro_rules! assert_equal_len {
    // The `tt` (token tree) designator is used for
    // operators and tokens.
    ($a:ident, $b: ident, $func:ident) => (
```

```
                assert_eq!($a.len(), $b.len(),
                        "{:?}: dimension mismatch: {:?} {:?}",
                        stringify!($func),
                        ($a.len(),),
                        ($b.len(),));
        )
    }
```

3. Next, we define a macro to auto-implement an operator. Let's add this underneath the `assert_equal_len` macro:

```
macro_rules! op {
    ($func:ident, $bound:ident, $method:ident) => (
        pub fn $func<T: $bound<T, Output=T> + Copy>(xs: &mut
        Vec<T>, ys: &Vec<T>) {
            assert_equal_len!(xs, ys, $func);

            for (x, y) in xs.iter_mut().zip(ys.iter()) {
                *x = $bound::$method(*x, *y);
            }
        }
    )
}
```

4. Now, let's call the macro and actually generate the implementation:

```
op!(add_assign, Add, add);
op!(mul_assign, Mul, mul);
op!(sub_assign, Sub, sub);
```

5. With these functions in place, we can now generate the test cases as well! Add the following instead of the `test` module:

```
#[cfg(test)]
mod test {

    use std::iter;
    macro_rules! test {
        ($func: ident, $x:expr, $y:expr, $z:expr) => {
            #[test]
            fn $func() {
                for size in 0usize..10 {
                    let mut x: Vec<_> =
                    iter::repeat($x).take(size).collect();
                    let y: Vec<_> =
                    iter::repeat($y).take(size).collect();
                    let z: Vec<_> =
                    iter::repeat($z).take(size).collect();
```

```
                            super::$func(&mut x, &y);

                            assert_eq!(x, z);
                    }
                }
            }
        }

        // Test `add_assign`, `mul_assign` and `sub_assign`
        test!(add_assign, 1u32, 2u32, 3u32);
        test!(mul_assign, 2u32, 3u32, 6u32);
        test!(sub_assign, 3u32, 2u32, 1u32);
    }
```

6. As a final step, let's see the generated code in action by running `cargo test` to see the (positive) test results:

```
$ cargo test
  Compiling dry-macros v0.1.0 (Rust-Cookbook/Chapter06/dry-macros)
   Finished dev [unoptimized + debuginfo] target(s) in 0.64s
    Running target/debug/deps/dry_macros-bed1682b386b41c3

running 3 tests
test test::add_assign ... ok
test test::mul_assign ... ok
test test::sub_assign ... ok

test result: ok. 3 passed; 0 failed; 0 ignored; 0 measured; 0
filtered out

    Doc-tests dry-macros

running 0 tests

test result: ok. 0 passed; 0 failed; 0 ignored; 0 measured; 0
filtered out
```

In order to understand the code better, let's decipher the steps.

How it works...

While design patterns, `if-else` constructs, and API design, in general, facilitate reusing code, it becomes tricky when it's time to hardcode tokens (for example, certain names) to remain loosely coupled. Rust's macros can help with that. As an example, we generate functions and tests for those functions in an effort to avoid copying and pasting test code around files.

In *step 3*, we declare a macro that wraps around comparing the lengths of two sequences and provides a better error message. *Step 4* uses this macro right away and creates a function with the name provided, but only if the lengths of the multiple input `Vec` instances match.

In *step 5*, we call the macros and provide them with the required input: a name (for the function) and types for the generic binding. This creates the functions using a provided interface without the need to copy and paste code.

Step 6 creates the associated tests by declaring the `test` module, a macro to generate the tests, and the call to finally create the test code as well. This allows you to generate the tests on the fly, right before compiling them, which significantly reduces the amount of static, repeated code—which has always been an issue in testing. The last step shows that these tests are actually created and executed when running `cargo test`.

Integrating Rust with Other Languages

7

In today's application landscape, integration is key. Whether you are slowly modernizing a legacy service or starting from scratch with using a new language, programs rarely run in isolation nowadays. Rust is still an exotic technology for many companies and—unfortunately—is usually not considered in the typical SDK. This is why Rust made a point of *playing nicely with others*, which is why the community can (and will) supply a large number of drivers, service integrations, and so on, by wrapping other (native) libraries.

As developers, we rarely have the luxury of starting completely from scratch (greenfield projects), so in this chapter, we will cover the various ways the Rust language integrates with other languages and technologies. We'll focus on the most popular and useful integrations at the time of writing, but these fundamentals should provide a basis for greater interoperability as well since many languages provide an interface for native binaries (such as .NET (`https://docs.microsoft.com/en-us/cpp/dotnet/calling-native-functions-from-managed-code?view=vs-2019`) or Java's JNI (`https://docs.oracle.com/javase/7/docs/technotes/guides/jni/spec/intro.html#wp9502`)). With that knowledge, adding Rust to enhance your web application should be just as easy as creating a sensor driver wrapper for the manufacturer's code.

We believe that good integration is important for the success of a language. In this chapter, we will cover the following recipes:

- Including legacy C code
- Calling into Rust from Node.js using FFI
- Running Rust in the browser
- Using Rust and Python
- Generating bindings for legacy applications

Including legacy C code

C is still among the most popular programming languages (https://www.tiobe.com/tiobe-index/) thanks to its versatility, speed, and simplicity. Due to this, many applications—legacy or not—are developed using C, with all of its upsides and downsides. Rust shares a domain with C—systems programming, which is why more and more companies replace their C code with Rust thanks to its safety and appeal as a modern programming language. However, changes are not always made in one big bang (https://www.linkedin.com/pulse/big-bang-vs-iterative-dilemma-martijn-endenburg/); it's usually a much more gradual (iterative) approach that includes swapping out components and replacing parts of an application.

Here, we use the C code as an analogy because it's popular and well known. However, these techniques apply to any (natively) compiled technology, such as Go, C++, or even Fortran. So let's get to it!

Getting ready

In this recipe, we are not only building Rust but also C. For this, we need a C compiler toolchain—gcc (https://gcc.gnu.org/) and make: https://www.gnu.org/software/make/manual/make.html, which is a rule-based scripting engine for executing the build.

Check whether the tools are installed by opening a Terminal window (note that the versions should be similar—at least the major release—to avoid any unexpected differences):

```
$ cc --version
cc (GCC) 9.1.1 20190503 (Red Hat 9.1.1-1)
Copyright (C) 2019 Free Software Foundation, Inc.
This is free software; see the source for copying conditions. There is NO
warranty; not even for MERCHANTABILITY or FITNESS FOR A PARTICULAR PURPOSE.
$ make --version
GNU Make 4.2.1
Built for x86_64-redhat-linux-gnu
Copyright (C) 1988-2016 Free Software Foundation, Inc.
License GPLv3+: GNU GPL version 3 or later
<http://gnu.org/licenses/gpl.html>
This is free software: you are free to change and redistribute it.
There is NO WARRANTY, to the extent permitted by law.
```

If these commands are not available on your machine, check how to install them on your operating system. In any **Linux/Unix** environment (including the WSL—the **Windows Subsystem for Linux**: `https://docs.microsoft.com/en-us/windows/wsl/install-win10`), they can require the installation of `gcc` and `make` via the default package repositories. On some distributions (for example, Ubuntu), bundles such as `build_essentials` (`https://packages.ubuntu.com/xenial/build-essential`) provide these tools as well.

On macOS, check out Homebrew, which provides a similar experience and provides `gcc` as well as `make`: `https://brew.sh/`.

Windows users have a choice between the WSL (and then following the Linux instructions) or using Cygwin (`https://www.cygwin.com`) to find `gcc-core` and `make` there. We recommended adding these tools (by default, `C:\cygwin64\bin`) to the `PATH` variable on Windows (`https://www.java.com/en/download/help/path.xml`), so a regular (PowerShell) Terminal can access Cygwin's executables.

Once ready, use the same shell to create a `legacy-c-code` directory and, inside, run `cargo new rust-digest --lib` and create a directory named `C` alongside it:

```
$ ls legacy-c-code
C/  rust-digest/
```

Inside the `C` directory, create an `src` folder to mirror the Rust project. Open the entire `legacy-c-code` in Visual Studio Code or your Rust development environment.

How to do it...

Follow these steps to be able to include legacy code in your project:

1. Let's implement the Rust library first. Open `rust-digest/Cargo.toml` to adjust the configuration to output a dynamic library (`*.so` or `*.dll`):

```
[lib]
name = "digest"
crate-type = ["cdylib"]
```

2. Another thing to add is the dependencies. Here, we are using types from `libc` and a cryptography library called `ring`, so let's add those dependencies:

```
[dependencies]
libc = "0.2"
ring = "0.14"
```

3. Next, we can take care of the code itself. Let's open `rust-digest/src/lib.rs` and replace the default code with the following snippet. This snippet creates an interface from the outside world that accepts a string (a mutable character pointer) and returns a string digest of the input:

```
use std::ffi::{CStr, CString};
use std::os::raw::{c_char, c_void};

use ring::digest;

extern "C" {
    fn pre_digest() -> c_void;
}

#[no_mangle]
pub extern "C" fn digest(data: *mut c_char) -> *mut c_char {
    unsafe {
        pre_digest();

        let data = CStr::from_ptr(data);
        let signature = digest::digest(&digest::SHA256,
        data.to_bytes());

        let hex_digest = signature
            .as_ref()
            .iter()
            .map(|b| format!("{:X}", b))
            .collect::<String>();

        CString::new(hex_digest).unwrap().into_raw()
    }
}
```

4. This should be a full Rust library now. Let's run `cargo build` inside `rust-digest` to check the output:

```
$ cd rust-digest; cargo build
   Compiling libc v0.2.58
   Compiling cc v1.0.37
   Compiling lazy_static v1.3.0
   Compiling untrusted v0.6.2
   Compiling spin v0.5.0
   Compiling ring v0.14.6
   Compiling rust-digest v0.1.0 (Rust-Cookbook/Chapter07/legacy-c-
   code/rust-digest)
    Finished dev [unoptimized + debuginfo] target(s) in 7.53s
```

5. There should be a `libdigest.so` library (or `digest.dll` on Windows):

```
$  ls -al rust-digest/target/debug/
total 3756
drwxr-xr-x. 8 cm cm 4096 Jun 23 20:17 ./
drwxr-xr-x. 4 cm cm 4096 Jun 23 20:17 ../
drwxr-xr-x. 6 cm cm 4096 Jun 23 20:17 build/
-rw-r--r--. 1 cm cm 0 Jun 23 20:17 .cargo-lock
drwxr-xr-x. 2 cm cm 4096 Jun 23 20:17 deps/
drwxr-xr-x. 2 cm cm 4096 Jun 23 20:17 examples/
drwxr-xr-x. 13 cm cm 4096 Jun 23 20:17 .fingerprint/
drwxr-xr-x. 3 cm cm 4096 Jun 23 20:17 incremental/
-rw-r--r--. 1 cm cm 186 Jun 23 20:17 libdigest.d
-rwxr-xr-x. 2 cm cm 3807256 Jun 23 20:17 libdigest.so*
drwxr-xr-x. 2 cm cm 4096 Jun 23 20:17 native/
```

6. However, let's do a release build as well. Run `cargo build --release` in `rust-digest`:

```
$ cargo build --release
    Compiling rust-digest v0.1.0 (Rust-Cookbook/Chapter07/legacy-c-
    code/rust-digest)
    Finished release [optimized] target(s) in 0.42s
```

7. To implement the C part of the project, create and open `C/src/main.c` to add the following code:

```c
#include <stdio.h>

// A function with that name is expected to be linked to the
project
extern char* digest(char *str);

// This function is exported under the name pre_digest
extern void pre_digest() {
    printf("pre_digest called\n");
}

int main() {
    char *result = digest("Hello World");
    printf("SHA digest of \"Hello World\": %s", result);
    return 0;
}
```

8. `make` is the traditional (and simplest) tool to build C code. `make` runs a file called `Makefile` to adhere to the rules that it defines. Create and open `C/Makefile` and add the following:

```
# Include the Rust library
LIBS := -ldigest -L../rust-digest/target/release

ifeq ($(shell uname),Darwin)
    LDFLAGS := -Wl,-dead_strip $(LIBS)
else
    LDFLAGS := -Wl,--gc-sections $(LIBS)
endif

all: target/main

target:
  @mkdir -p $@

target/main: target/main.o
  @echo "Linking ... "
  $(CC) -o $@ $^ $(LDFLAGS)

target/main.o: src/main.c | target
  @echo "Compiling ..."
  $(CC) -o $@ -c $<

clean:
  @echo "Removing target/"
  @rm -rf target
```

9. If everything is in place, we should be able to switch to the C directory and run `make all` there:

```
$ make all
Compiling ...
cc -o target/main.o -c src/main.c
Linking ...
cc -o target/main target/main.o -Wl,--gc-sections -ldigest -
L../rust-digest/target/release
```

Afterward, there is a `C/target` directory, which contains two files: `main.o` and `main` (`main.exe` on Windows).

10. To be able to run the executable (the `.o` file is just the object file; not for running), we also need to tell it where our dynamic library is located. For that, the `LD_LIBRARY_PATH` environment variable is typically used. Open `bash` and run the following command inside the `legacy-c-code` directory to—temporarily—overwrite the variable with the appropriate path:

```
$ cd rust-digest/target/release
$ LD_LIBRARY_PATH=$(pwd)
$ echo $LD_LIBRARY_PATH
/tmp/Rust-Cookbook/Chapter07/legacy-c-code/rust-
digest/target/release
```

11. Now it's time to finally run the C program and check whether everything worked out. Switch to the `C/target` directory and run the following command:

```
$ ./main
pre_digest called
SHA digest of "Hello World":
A591A6D4BF420404A11733CFB7B190D62C65BFBCDA32B57B277D9AD9F146E
```

With that done, let's take a look behind the scenes to understand how it was done.

How it works...

Replacing legacy C code with Rust is a step-by-step process that is often done in order to improve developer productivity, safety, and potential innovation. This has been done in countless applications (for example, in Microsoft's public cloud offering, Azure: `https://azure.microsoft.com/en-gb/`) and requires two technologies to work together flawlessly.

Thanks to Rust's LLVM-based compiler, the compilation outputs native code (for example, ELF on Linux: `https://en.wikipedia.org/wiki/Executable_and_Linkable_Format`), which makes it accessible—in particular—for C/C++. In this recipe, we are taking a look at how to link those two outputs together into a single program using a dynamic library built in Rust.

The prerequisites for creating a dynamic library (`*.so/*.dll`) in Rust are surprisingly simple: *step 1* shows the required changes to `Cargo.toml` for `rustc` to output the required format. There are other formats, so if you are looking for something specific, check out the nomicon (`https://doc.rust-lang.org/cargo/reference/manifest.html#building-dynamic-or-static-libraries`) and docs at `https://doc.rust-lang.org/cargo/reference/manifest.html#building-dynamic-or-static-libraries`.

Step 3 shows the code to create an SHA256 (`https://www.thesslstore.com/blog/difference-sha-1-sha-2-sha-256-hash-algorithms/`) digest of an incoming string, but only after it calls a simple callback function, `pre_digest()`, to showcase the bi-directional bindings. There are a few things of note here:

- Importing a function from a linked library is done using an `extern "C" {}` declaration (the `"C"` isn't actually necessary). After declaring a construct like that, it can be used just like any other function.
- In order to export a function compatible with the ELF format, the `#[no_mangle]` attribute is required since the compiler runs a name-mangling scheme that changes the function name. Since compilers don't have a common scheme, `no_mangle` makes sure it stays just as it is. To learn more about name mangling, check out this link: `https://doc.rust-lang.org/book/ch19-01-unsafe-rust.html#using-extern-functions-to-call-external-code`.
- The use of `unsafe` inside the `digest` function is required for a few reasons. First, calling an external function is always unsafe (`pre_digest()`). Second, the conversion from a `char` pointer to `CStr` is unsafe, requiring the scope as well.

> **Note:** `ring` (`https://github.com/briansmith/ring`) is a pure Rust implementation of several cryptography algorithms, so there are no OpenSSL (`https://www.openssl.org/`) or LibreSSL (`https://www.libressl.org`) requirements. Since both of those libraries are built on the respective native libraries, they always present a headache to even experienced Rust developers. Being pure Rust, `ring` avoids any of their linking/compilation issues, however.

From *steps 4* to *6*, we are building the Rust library just as we used to, but instead of a `.rlib` file, a `.so` or `.dll` file is the result of this process.

Step 7 shows the C code required to import and call a dynamically linked function. C keeps this admirably simple with an `extern` declaration for the interface, which enables you to call the function just like that. The callback is also implemented and exported using the `extern` declaration and it simply prints out that it was called.

Rust's build system really shines when we get to *step 8*, where the rules for `Makefile` are created. Making rules is simple, but it leaves a lot of room for complexity, as many C developers know. In our recipe, however, we want to keep it easy to understand. Each rule consists of a target (for example, `all`) and its dependencies (for example, `target/main`), as well as a body of bash commands to run (for example, `@mkdir -p $@`).

These dependencies can be files (such as `target/main.o` or `target/main`) or other rules. If they are files, check when they were modified last and, if there was a change, that they run the rule and its dependencies. The resulting dependency tree gets resolved automatically. As fascinating as this highly useful, 30-year-old tool may be, there are books written that are devoted to how it works. It is certainly a deep dive into history, and Linux conventions. Check out a short tutorial here: `http://www.cs.colby.edu/maxwell/courses/ tutorials/maketutor/` or go straight to the make manual (`https://www.gnu.org/ software/make/manual/make.html`).

Step 9 compiles the C code into an executable and links it to `libdigest.so`, which `rustc` created. We are also pointing the linker to the right path in the `LDFLAGS` variable in `Makefile`.

Only in *step 10* will it become apparent how a static library is different from a dynamic library. The latter has to be available at runtime because it isn't baked into the executable and relies on other mechanisms to be found. One such mechanism is the `LD_LIBRARY_PATH` environment variable, which points to directories with `libXXXX.so` files for the program to find its dependencies (by name). For this recipe, we are **replacing** the original value with wherever your `rust- digest/target/release` directory is located (`$(pwd)` outputs the current directory); however, this is only for the current Terminal session, so whenever you close and reopen the window, the setting will be gone. If the path is improperly set or the directory/file is missing, executing `main` will give you something along the lines of the following:

```
$ ./main
./main: error while loading shared libraries: libdigest.so: cannot open
shared object file: No such file or directory
```

Step 11 shows the correct output since the `pre_digest` function was called and we were able to create the correct SHA256 digest for "`Hello World`" (without the ").

Now that we know a little more about integrating Rust into a C-type application, we can move on to the next recipe.

Calling into Rust from Node.js using FFI

JavaScript is a language that excels in its flat learning curve and flexibility, which leads to impressive adoption rates in various areas outside of the original browser animation. Node.js (`https://nodejs.org/en/`) is a runtime based on Google's V8 JavaScript engine, which allows JavaScript code to run directly on the operating system (without the browser), including access to various low-level APIs in order to enable IoT-type applications and web services, or even to create and display virtual/augmented reality environments (`https://github.com/microsoft/HoloJS`). All of this is possible because the Node runtime provides access to native libraries on the host operating system. Let's see how we create a Rust library to call from JavaScript into this.

Getting ready

Since we are working with Node.js, please install `npm` and the Node.js runtime, as explained on their official website: `https://nodejs.org/en/download/`. Once ready, you should be able to run these commands from a Terminal (PowerShell or bash):

```
$ node --version
v11.15.0
$ npm --version
6.7.0
```

The actual versions may be higher at the time of reading. The node dependency we are using also requires C/C++ tools, as well as having Python 2 installed. Follow the instructions for your OS on GitHub: `https://github.com/nodejs/node-gyp#installation`. Then, let's set up a folder structure similar to the previous recipe:

1. Create a `node-js-rust` folder.
2. Create a sub-folder called `node`, change into it, and run `npm init` to generate `package.json`—basically, Node's `Cargo.toml`.
3. Inside the `node` folder, add a directory called `src`.
4. At the same level as the `node` folder, create a new Rust project called `cargo new rust-digest --lib` (or reuse the one from the previous recipe).

At the end, you should have a directory setup like this:

```
$ tree node-js-rust/
node-js-rust/
├── node
│   ├── package.json
│   └── src
```

```
|           └── index.js
└── rust-digest
        ├── Cargo.toml
        └── src
              └── lib.rs
4 directories, 4 files
```

Open the entire directory in Visual Studio Code to work on the code.

How to do it ...

Let's repeat a few steps from the SHA256 library from the previous recipe:

1. First, let's take care of the Rust part. Open `rust-digest/Cargo.toml` to add `ring`, a dependency for the hashing part, as well as the `crate-type` configuration for cross-compilation:

```
[lib]
name = "digest"
crate-type = ["cdylib"]

[dependencies]
libc = "0.2"
ring = "0.14"
```

2. Next, let's look at the Rust code. Just as in other recipes in this chapter, we are creating a fast way to generate an SHA digest via Rust to be used from Node.js:

```
use std::ffi::{CStr, CString};
use std::os::raw::c_char;

use ring::digest;

#[no_mangle]
pub extern "C" fn digest(data: *mut c_char) -> *mut c_char {
    unsafe {

        let data = CStr::from_ptr(data);
        let signature = digest::digest(&digest::SHA256,
        data.to_bytes());

        let hex_digest = signature
            .as_ref()
            .iter()
            .map(|b| format!("{:X}", b))
            .collect::<String>();
```

```
            CString::new(hex_digest).unwrap().into_raw()
        }
    }

    // No tests :(
```

3. `cargo build` now creates a native library. You can find the library in `target/debug` inside the Rust project directory:

```
$ cargo build
    Compiling libc v0.2.58
    Compiling cc v1.0.37
    Compiling untrusted v0.6.2
    Compiling spin v0.5.0
    Compiling lazy_static v1.3.0
    Compiling ring v0.14.6
    Compiling rust-digest v0.1.0 (Rust-Cookbook/Chapter07/node-js-
    rust/rust-digest)
    Finished dev [unoptimized + debuginfo] target(s) in 5.88s
$ ls rust-digest/target/debug/
build/ deps/ examples/ incremental/ libdigest.d libdigest.so*
native/
```

4. If the JavaScript part calls into the Rust binary, there are a few declarations to be made in order to make the function known. We finish off the code by printing out the result of a call to the Rust library. Add this to `node/src/index.js`:

```javascript
const ffi = require('ffi');
const ref = require('ref');

const libPath = '../rust-digest/target/debug/libdigest';


const libDigest = ffi.Library(libPath, {
  'digest': [ "string", ["string"]],
});

const { digest } = libDigest;
console.log('Hello World SHA256', digest("Hello World"));
```

5. The `require` statement already hints toward a dependency, so let's integrate this as well. Open `node/package.json` to add the following:

```json
{
  [...]
  "dependencies": {
    "ffi": "^2.3.0"
```

```
        }
    }
```

6. With everything in place, we can now issue an `npm install` command from
   within the `node` directory:

   $ npm install

   ```
   > ref@1.3.5 install Rust-Cookbook/Chapter07/node-js-
   rust/node/node_modules/ref
   > node-gyp rebuild

   make: Entering directory 'Rust-Cookbook/Chapter07/node-js-
   rust/node/node_modules/ref/build'
     CXX(target) Release/obj.target/binding/src/binding.o
   In file included from ../src/binding.cc:7:
   ../../nan/nan.h: In function 'void
   Nan::AsyncQueueWorker(Nan::AsyncWorker*)':
   ../../nan/nan.h:2298:62: warning: cast between incompatible
   function types from 'void (*)(uv_work_t*)' {aka 'void
   (*)(uv_work_s*)'} to 'uv_after_work_cb' {aka 'void (*)(uv_work_s*,
   int)'} [-Wcast-function-type]
    2298 | , reinterpret_cast<uv_after_work_cb>(AsyncExecuteComplete)
   [...]
     COPY Release/ffi_bindings.node
   make: Leaving directory 'Rust-Cookbook/Chapter07/node-js-
   rust/node/node_modules/ffi/build'
   npm WARN node@1.0.0 No description
   npm WARN node@1.0.0 No repository field.

   added 7 packages from 12 contributors and audited 18 packages in
   4.596s
   found 0 vulnerabilities
   ```

7. After the dependencies have been installed, the `node` application is ready to run.
   Issue `node src/index.js` to execute the JavaScript file:

   $ node src/index.js
   ```
   Hello World SHA256
   A591A6D4BF420404A11733CFB7B190D62C65BFBCDA32B57B277D9AD9F146E
   ```

Having done the work, let's take a look at why and how it all comes together.

How it works...

Node.js, as a native runtime environment for JavaScript, provides easy-to-access native libraries that can be built with Rust. In order to do that, the `node-ffi` (`https://github.com/node-ffi/node-ffi`) package is required to dynamically find and load the desired libraries. First, however, we start with the Rust code and project: *steps 1 to 3* show how to build a native dynamic library, which we discussed earlier in this chapter, in the *Including legacy C code* recipe, in the *How it works...* section.

In *step 4*, we create the JavaScript code. Thanks to the dynamic nature of JavaScript, defining the function signature can be done using strings and objects and the actual invocation looks just like a regular function that can be imported from a module. The FFI library also takes away the data type conversion, and the call across technology boundaries is seamless. Another important note is that, with `node-ffi` (`https://github.com/node-ffi/node-ffi`), the actual module path is required, which makes handling the different artifacts a lot easier (compared to using environment variables in C/C++ interop).

In *step 5* and *step 6*, we take care of adding and installing the required dependencies for Node.js using the famous `npm` package manager (`https://www.npmjs.com/`), with `node-ffi` (`https://github.com/node-ffi/node-ffi`) requiring some compiler tools to work properly.

The last step shows how the program executes and creates the same hash as other recipes in this chapter.

We've learned how to call into Rust from Node.js using FFI, so now let's move on to the next recipe.

Running Rust in the browser

Running Rust in the browser may seem like a similar task to using Rust binaries with Node.js. However, the modern browser environment is exceedingly more difficult. Sandboxing limits access to local resources (which is a good thing!) and browsers provide a small number of scripting languages to run within the website. While the most successful language is JavaScript, it comes with many drawbacks in the area of animation, caused by the scripting nature of the technology. On top of that, there is garbage collection, a type system with many flaws, and the lack of a coherent programming paradigm—all of which manifests itself in unpredictable and poor performance for real-time applications such as games.

However, these issues are being resolved. A technology called WebAssembly has been introduced to be able to distribute binaries (as an assembler language for the web) that can be run in a specialized execution environment—just like JavaScript. In fact, JavaScript is able to seamlessly interact with these binaries, akin to native libraries in a Node.js application, which speeds things up considerably. Thanks to Rust's LLVM base, it can compile to WebAssembly, and, with its memory management, it's a great choice for running these real-time applications. While this technology is still in its infancy, let's see how this works!

Getting ready

For this project, we are setting up a directory called `browser-rust`, containing a `web` directory and a `cargo` library project called `rust-digest` (`cargo new rust-digest --lib`). For the compilation, we need an additional compilation target, `wasm23-unknown-unknown`, which can be installed via `rustup`. Issue the following command in a Terminal to install the target:

```
$ rustup target add wasm32-unknown-unknown
info: downloading component 'rust-std' for 'wasm32-unknown-unknown'
 10.9 MiB / 10.9 MiB (100 %) 5.3 MiB/s in 2s ETA: 0s
info: installing component 'rust-std' for 'wasm32-unknown-unknown'
```

Use `cargo` to install a tool called `wasm-bindgen-cli` (`cargo install wasm-bindgen-cli`), and check whether it works by invoking `wasm-bindgen` in your current console window.

Inside the `web` directory, we create a file named `index.html`, which will host and show our Rust output. In order to be able to render the index file, a web server is also required. Here are a few options:

- Python (3.x)'s standard library comes with an `http.server` module, which can be called like this: `python3 -m http.server 8080`.
- Fans of JavaScript and Node.js can use `http-server` (https://www.npmjs.com/package/http-server), installable via `npm` (https://www.npmjs.com/package/http-server).
- Recent versions of Ruby come with a web server as well: `ruby -run -ehttpd . -p8080`.

- On Windows, you can use IIS Express (`https://www.npmjs.com/package/http-server`), also via the command line: `C:\> "C:\Program Files (x86)\IIS Express\iisexpress.exe" /path:C:\Rust-Cookbook\Chapter07\browser-rust\web /port:8080`.

Any web server that serves static files will do, and it should be able to provide the files appropriately. You should end up with a directory structure like this:

```
$ tree browser-rust/
browser-rust/
├── rust-digest
│   ├── Cargo.lock
│   ├── Cargo.toml
│   ├── src
│   └── └── lib.rs
└── web
    └── index.html

3 directories, 4 files
```

Your project should now be set up and ready to go. Let's see how we can get Rust to run in the browser.

How to do it...

Here's how to write low-latency web applications in just a few steps:

1. Let's start by implementing the Rust part. We'll again create a hashing library, so we start by creating the API basics. Open `rust-digest/src/lib.rs` and insert the following above the tests:

```rust
use sha2::{Sha256, Digest};
use wasm_bindgen::prelude::*;

fn hex_digest(data: &str) -> String {
    let mut hasher = Sha256::new();
    hasher.input(data.as_bytes());
    let signature = hasher.result();
    signature
        .as_ref()
        .iter()
        .map(|b| format!("{:X}", b))
        .collect::<String>()
}
```

2. Let's bind the `hex_digest()` function to a public API that we can call from outside the module. This enables us to invoke the code using WASM types and even autogenerate most of these bindings. Add some of those just below the preceding code:

```
#[wasm_bindgen]
pub extern "C" fn digest(data: String) -> String {
    hex_digest(&data)
}

#[wasm_bindgen]
pub extern "C" fn digest_attach(data: String, elem_id: String) ->
Result<(), JsValue> {
    web_sys::window().map_or(Err("No window found".into()), |win| {
        if let Some(doc) = win.document() {
            doc.get_element_by_id(&elem_id).map_or(Err(format!("No
            element with id {} found", elem_id).into()), |val|{
                let signature = hex_digest(&data);
                val.set_inner_html(&signature);
                Ok(())
            })
        }
        else {
            Err("No document found".into())
        }
    })
}
// No tests :(
```

3. It's sometimes handy to have a callback once the module is instantiated, so let's add one of those as well:

```
#[wasm_bindgen(start)]
pub fn start() -> Result<(), JsValue> {
    // This function is getting called when initializing the WASM
    // module
    Ok(())
}
```

4. We have used two imports that require additional dependencies: `wasm-bindgen` and `sha2` (as a web-compatible version of `ring::digest`). Additionally, we are pretending to be a native library for external linking, so the library type and name should be adjusted. Modify `rust-digest/Cargo.toml` to include these changes:

```
[lib]
name = "digest"
crate-type = ["cdylib"]

[dependencies]
sha2 = "0.8"
wasm-bindgen = "0.2.48"

[dependencies.web-sys]
version = "0.3.25"
features = [
  'Document',
  'Element',
  'HtmlElement',
  'Node',
  'Window',
]
```

5. Now, let's compile the library and check the output. Run `cargo build --target wasm32-unknown-unknown`:

```
$ cargo build --target wasm32-unknown-unknown
   Compiling proc-macro2 v0.4.30
   [...]
   Compiling js-sys v0.3.24
   Compiling rust-digest v0.1.0 (Rust-Cookbook/Chapter07/browser-
   rust/rust-digest)
    Finished dev [unoptimized + debuginfo] target(s) in 54.49s
$ ls target/wasm32-unknown-unknown/debug/
build/ deps/ digest.d digest.wasm* examples/ incremental/ native/
```

6. The resulting `digest.wasm` file is what we want to include in our web application using JavaScript. While this can be done directly (`https://developer.mozilla.org/en-US/docs/WebAssembly/Using_the_JavaScript_API`), the data type conversion can be quite cumbersome. This is why there is a CLI tool to help out. Run `wasm-bindgen target/wasm32-unknown-unknown/debug/digest.wasm --out-dir ../web/ --web` from within `browser-rust/rust-digest` to generate the necessary JavaScript bindings for web browsers:

```
$ wasm-bindgen target/wasm32-unknown-unknown/debug/digest.wasm --out-dir ../web/ --web
$ ls ../web/
digest_bg.d.ts digest_bg.wasm digest.d.ts digest.js index.html
```

7. These bindings need to be included in our `web/index.html` file (which is empty at the moment):

```html
<!DOCTYPE html>
<html>
    <head>
        <meta content="text/html;charset=utf-8" http-equiv="Content-
            Type"/>
        <script type="module">
            import init, { digest, digest_attach } from
             './digest.js';
            async function run() {
                await init();
                const result = digest("Hello World");
                console.log(`Hello World SHA256 = ${result}`);
                digest_attach("Hello World", "sha_out")
            }
            run();
        </script>
    </head>
    <body>
        <h1>Hello World in SHA256 <span id="sha_out"></span></h1>
    </body>
</html>
```

8. Save and exit the `index.html` file and start the web server you prepared earlier inside the web directory:

```
py -m http.server 8080
Serving HTTP on 0.0.0.0 port 8080 (http://0.0.0.0:8080/) ...
```

9. Access `http://localhost:8080` in your browser (be sure to allow the server through the firewall) and check whether your output matches the following:

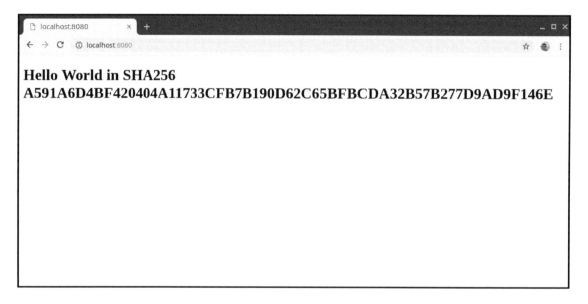

Having done the work, let's take a look at why and how it all comes together.

How it works...

Modern browsers provide a JavaScript engine alongside a web assembly virtual machine (`https://webassembly.org/`). With this capability, web applications can run binary code that is safely executed inside its own runtime environment with easy access from the outside. The main benefits include the following:

- A smaller-sized application, thanks to binary compilation
- Faster end-to-end execution times (no compilation step)
- No garbage collection—the WASM virtual machine is a stack machine

On top of that, WASM can be converted into a text-based format for visual inspection and manual optimization. Rust is one of the few languages to even compile to these formats (text and binary), and it's largely thanks to LLVM and Rust's approach to memory management.

In *steps 1, 2,* and *3,* we create the Rust module to do the work. Notice the `#[wasm_bindgen]` attributes over the `extern` functions, which allow the macro preprocessor to fetch the input and output types of the function and generate bindings from this interface definition. There is also a special (`https://rustwasm.github.io/wasm-bindgen/reference/attributes/on-rust-exports/start.html`) `#[wasm_bindgen(start)]` macro on top of one of the functions, which designates the initializer function to run whenever the module is instantiated. Both this function and `digest_attach()` feature a `Result` return type, which allows the `?` operator and rusty error handling in general.

`digest_attach()` is special (compared to `digest()`) since it directly accesses the DOM (`https://www.w3.org/TR/WD-DOM/introduction.html`) from the WASM module, which is provided by the `web_sys` crate. All of these macros and functions are imported in the `wasm_bindgen::prelude::*` statement.

Step 4 adjusts `Cargo.toml` accordingly to provide everything in order for the compilation to work. Note that any errors here that work on a different target (for example, the default target) hint toward an incompatible crate for WASM. Only in *step 5* do we execute the compilation for the wasm32 target, which produces a WASM binary file. *Step 6* runs the binding generator using the `wasm-bindgen` CLI, which produces a few files for easier integration. In this case, they are the following:

- `digest_bg.d.ts`: TypeScript (`https://www.typescriptlang.org/`) definitions for the exported WASM functions
- `digest_bg.wasm`: The WASM file itself
- `digest.d.ts`: TypeScript definitions for the integration file
- `digest.js`: The JavaScript implementation for loading and converting the exported WASM functions into regular JavaScript calls

The tool includes more options and examples (`https://rustwasm.github.io/docs/wasm-bindgen/examples/without-a-bundler.html`) for other integrations so, check out the documentation for specifics (`https://rustwasm.github.io/docs/wasm-bindgen/`).

 Not every crate can be compiled to `wasm32-unknown-unknown`, especially if they are using hardware access or operating system features. Some crates implement compatibility layers that are often specified as `cargo` features.

Step 7 shows how to include the generated WASM bindings into a regular HTML page. Outside of the ES6 syntax (`http://es6-features.org/#Constants`) (which may be unfamiliar to some), the Rust code is neatly wrapped in JavaScript functions, so no additional conversion is needed. For those interested in how this works, check out the `digest.js` file, which is quite readable but shows the complexity involved in transforming the data. That's it—the last step only shows how to serve the files and that the hosting actually works.

Now that we have learned how to run Rust in the browser, let's move on to the next recipe!

Using Rust and Python

Python has become a staple language for many applications, from the web to data science. However, Python itself is an interpreted language and is famously quite slow—which is why it integrates well with much faster C code. Many well-liked libraries are implemented in C/C++ and Cython (`https://cython.org/`) in order to achieve the required performance (for example, `numpy`, `pandas`, `keras`, and PyTorch are largely native code). Since Rust produces native binaries as well, let's look at how we can write Rust modules for Python.

Getting ready

We will work on creating an SHA256 digest again and will use the same folder structure as we have in every recipe in this chapter. Create a `python-rust` directory and initialize a new Rust project there using `cargo new rust-digest --lib`.

For the Python part of the project, install Python (3.6/3.7) by following the instructions on the website. Then, create the following folder structure and files (empty is OK for now) inside `python-rust/python`:

```
$ tree python
python
├── setup.py
└── src
    └── digest.py

1 directory, 2 files
```

Open the entire `python-rust` folder in VS Code and you are ready to go.

How to do it...

Python is a great language to integrate with—find out why in just a few steps:

1. Open `rust-digest/src/lib.rs` to start off with the Rust code. Let's add the required `use` statements for FFI and `ring` and declare a `digest()` function to be exported. Note that this function is the same as in most other recipes in this chapter:

```rust
use std::ffi::{CStr, CString};
use std::os::raw::c_char;

use ring::digest;

#[no_mangle]
pub extern "C" fn digest(data: *mut c_char) -> *mut c_char {
    unsafe {

        let data = CStr::from_ptr(data);
        let signature = digest::digest(&digest::SHA256,
         data.to_bytes());

        let hex_digest = signature
            .as_ref()
            .iter()
            .map(|b| format!("{:X}", b))
            .collect::<String>();

        CString::new(hex_digest).unwrap().into_raw()

    }
}

// No tests :(
```

2. Since we are using `ring` and a third-party dependency to create the hash, let's declare them (and the library type) in `rust-digest/Cargo.toml`:

```toml
[lib]
name = "digest"
crate-type = ["cdylib"]

[dependencies]
libc = "0.2"
ring = "0.14"
```

3. Now, let's build the library to obtain `libdigest.so` (or `digest.dll` or `libdigest.dylib`). Run `cargo build` inside `rust-digest`:

```
$ cargo build
    Updating crates.io index
  Compiling cc v1.0.37
  Compiling libc v0.2.58
  Compiling untrusted v0.6.2
  Compiling spin v0.5.0
  Compiling lazy_static v1.3.0
  Compiling ring v0.14.6
  Compiling rust-digest v0.1.0 (Rust-Cookbook/Chapter07/python-
  rust/rust-digest)
    Finished dev [unoptimized + debuginfo] target(s) in 8.29s
$ ls target/debug/
build/ deps/ examples/ incremental/ libdigest.d libdigest.so*
native/
```

4. In order to load this library in Python, we need to write some code as well. Open `python/src/digest.py` and add the following content:

```python
from ctypes import cdll, c_char_p
from sys import platform

def build_lib_name(name):
    prefix = "lib"
    ext = "so"

    if platform == 'darwin':
        ext = 'dylib'
    elif platform == 'win32':
        prefix = ""
        ext = 'dll'

    return "{prefix}{name}.{ext}".format(prefix=prefix, name=name,
ext=ext)

def main():
    lib = cdll.LoadLibrary(build_lib_name("digest"))
    lib.digest.restype = c_char_p
    print("SHA256 of Hello World =", lib.digest(b"Hello World"))

if __name__ == "__main__":
    main()
```

5. While this file can be run by invoking `python3 digest.py`, it's not what a larger project will look like. Python's setuptools (`https://setuptools.readthedocs.io/en/latest/`) provide a better-structured approach to create and even install runnable scripts for the current OS. The common point of entry is the `setup.py` script, which declares metadata along with dependencies and entry points. Create `python/setup.py` with the following content:

```python
#!/usr/bin/env python
# -*- coding: utf-8 -*-

# Courtesy of https://github.com/kennethreitz/setup.py

from setuptools import find_packages, setup, Command

# Package meta-data.
NAME = 'digest'
DESCRIPTION = 'A simple Python package that loads and executes a
Rust function.'
URL = 'https://blog.x5ff.xyz'
AUTHOR = 'Claus Matzinger'
REQUIRES_PYTHON = '>=3.7.0'
VERSION = '0.1.0'
LICENSE = 'MIT'
```

The file continues to input the declared variables into the `setup()` method, which generates the required metadata:

```python
setup(
    # Meta stuff
    name=NAME,
    version=VERSION,
    description=DESCRIPTION,
    long_description=DESCRIPTION,
    long_description_content_type='text/markdown',
    # ---
    package_dir={'':'src'}, # Declare src as root folder
    packages=find_packages(exclude=["tests", "*.tests",
"*.tests.*",
        "tests.*"]), # Auto discover any Python packages
    python_requires=REQUIRES_PYTHON,
    # Scripts that will be generated invoke this method
    entry_points={
        'setuptools.installation': ['eggsecutable=digest:main'],
    },
    include_package_data=True,
    license=LICENSE,
    classifiers=[
```

```
                  # Trove classifiers
                  # Full list: https://pypi.python.org/pypi?
                   %3Aaction=list_classifiers
                  'License :: OSI Approved :: MIT License',
                  'Programming Language :: Python',
                  'Programming Language :: Python :: 3',
                  'Programming Language :: Python :: 3.7',
                  'Programming Language :: Python :: Implementation ::
                   CPython',
                  'Programming Language :: Python :: Implementation :: PyPy'
          ],
      )
```

6. *Steps 6, 7,* and *8* are for Linux/macOS only (or WSL). Windows users, please continue with *step 9*. Python's standalone modules are called eggs, so let's make one and run python3 setup.py bdist_egg:

```
$ python3 setup.py bdist_egg
running bdist_egg
running egg_info
writing src/digest.egg-info/PKG-INFO
writing dependency_links to src/digest.egg-
info/dependency_links.txt
writing entry points to src/digest.egg-info/entry_points.txt
writing top-level names to src/digest.egg-info/top_level.txt
reading manifest file 'src/digest.egg-info/SOURCES.txt'
writing manifest file 'src/digest.egg-info/SOURCES.txt'
installing library code to build/bdist.linux-x86_64/egg
running install_lib
warning: install_lib: 'build/lib' does not exist -- no Python
modules to install

creating build/bdist.linux-x86_64/egg
creating build/bdist.linux-x86_64/egg/EGG-INFO
copying src/digest.egg-info/PKG-INFO -> build/bdist.linux-
x86_64/egg/EGG-INFO
copying src/digest.egg-info/SOURCES.txt -> build/bdist.linux-
x86_64/egg/EGG-INFO
copying src/digest.egg-info/dependency_links.txt ->
build/bdist.linux-x86_64/egg/EGG-INFO
copying src/digest.egg-info/entry_points.txt -> build/bdist.linux-
x86_64/egg/EGG-INFO
copying src/digest.egg-info/top_level.txt -> build/bdist.linux-
x86_64/egg/EGG-INFO
zip_safe flag not set; analyzing archive contents...
creating 'dist/digest-0.1.0-py3.7.egg' and adding
'build/bdist.linux-x86_64/egg' to it
removing 'build/bdist.linux-x86_64/egg' (and everything under it)
```

7. This creates a `.egg` file in `python/dist`, which is built to run the `main()` function from the preceding script when invoked. On Mac/Linux, you have to run `chmod +x python/dist/digest-0.1.0-py3.7.egg` to be able to run it. Let's see what happens when we run it right away:

```
$ cd python/dist
$  ./digest-0.1.0-py3.7.egg
Traceback (most recent call last):
  File "<string>", line 1, in <module>
  File "Rust-Cookbook/Chapter07/python-rust/python/src/digest.py",
line 17, in main
    lib = cdll.LoadLibrary(build_lib_name("digest"))
  File "/usr/lib64/python3.7/ctypes/__init__.py", line 429, in
LoadLibrary
    return self._dlltype(name)
  File "/usr/lib64/python3.7/ctypes/__init__.py", line 351, in
__init__
    self._handle = _dlopen(self._name, mode)
OSError: libdigest.so: cannot open shared object file: No such file
or directory
```

8. Right, the library is only dynamically linked! We have to point our binary to the library or move the library where it can find it. On Mac/Linux, this can be accomplished by setting the `LD_LIBRARY_PATH` environment variable to wherever the Rust build output is located. The result is a Python program that calls into the compiled Rust code for an SHA256 digest of a string:

```
$ LD_LIBRARY_PATH=$(pwd)/../../rust-digest/target/debug/
./digest-0.1.0-py3.7.egg
SHA256 of Hello World =
b'A591A6D4BF420404A11733CFB7B190D62C65BFBCDA32B57B277D9AD9F146E'
```

9. For Windows users, the execution is a little bit simpler. First, make the library available to Python and then run the script directly. Run the following from within the `python` directory to use Rust from within Python to generate the SHA256 digest:

```
$ cp ../rust-digest/target/debug/digest.dll .
$ python.exe src/digest.py
SHA256 of Hello World =
b'A591A6D4BF420404A11733CFB7B190D62C65BFBCDA32B57B277D9AD9F146E'
```

Let's look at how and why this works.

How it works...

Enhancing Python's capabilities with Rust is a great way to get the best of both worlds: Python is famously easy to learn and use; Rust is fast and safe (and does not fail at runtime as easily).

In *steps 1 to 3*, we again create a dynamic native library that creates an SHA256 hash out of a provided string argument. The required changes in `Cargo.toml` and `lib.rs` are the same as if we were to create a library for C/C++ inter-op: `#[no_mangle]`. The *Including legacy C code* recipe earlier in this chapter describes the inner workings in more detail, so be sure to read the *How it works...* section there as well.

The `cdylib` library type describes a dynamic library for C, and other types are available for different purposes. Check out the nomicon (`https://doc.rust-lang.org/nomicon/ffi.html`) and docs (`https://doc.rust-lang.org/cargo/reference/manifest.html#building-dynamic-or-static-libraries`) for more details.

Our Python code uses the `ctypes` (`https://docs.python.org/3/library/ctypes.html`) part of the standard library to load the Rust module. In *step 4*, we show that Python's dynamic invocation capabilities seamlessly instantiate and integrate the type. However, the data types need to be interpreted accordingly, which is why the return type is set as a character pointer and the input is of the bytes type to achieve the same result as the other recipes in this chapter. Since platforms and programming languages use their own ways of encoding bytes to strings (UTF-8, UTF-16, ...), we have to pass a bytes literal (which translates to a `char*` in C) into the function.

In *steps 5 and 6*, we use Python's setuptools to create a `.egg` file, which is a distribution format for Python modules. In this particular case, we even create an eggsecutable (`https://setuptools.readthedocs.io/en/latest/setuptools.html#eggsecutable-scripts`), which makes it possible to run the function by executing the `.egg` file. As shown in *step 7*, simply running it is not enough, since we also need to make the library known to the execution environment. In *step 8*, we are doing that and checking the result (more on `LD_LIBRARY_PATH` in the *How to do it...* section of the *Including legacy C code* recipe earlier in this chapter).

In *step 9*, we run the script on Windows. Windows uses a different mechanism to load dynamic libraries, so the `LD_LIBRARY_PATH` method does not work. On top of that, Python eggsecutables are only available on Linux/macOS, and setuptools provides great mechanisms for deployment right away, but not for local development (without further installations/complexities). This is why, on Windows, we are executing the script directly—which is the reason for `if __name__ == "__main__"`.

Now that we have learned how to successfully run Rust from within Python, let's move on to the next recipe.

Generating bindings for legacy applications

As we saw in the first recipe, Rust's interop capabilities with other native languages require specific structures to be present on either side to declare the memory layout properly. This task is easy to automate using `rust-bindgen`. Let's see how this makes integrating with native code easier.

Getting ready

Just like the first recipe in this chapter, *Including legacy C code*, this recipe has the following prerequisites:

- `gcc` (`https://gcc.gnu.org/`) (includes `ar` and `cc`)
- `git` (`https://git-scm.com/`) (command-line or UI tools are fine)
- `llvm` (`https://releases.llvm.org/2.7/docs/UsingLibraries.html`) (library and header files for the LLVM compiler project)
- `libclang` (`https://clang.llvm.org/doxygen/group__CINDEX.html`) (library and header files for the CLang compiler)

The tools are available in any Linux/Unix environment (on Windows, you can use the WSL (`https://docs.microsoft.com/en-us/windows/wsl/install-win10`)) and might require additional installs. Check your distribution's package repositories for the packages in the list.

On macOS, check out Homebrew, which is a package manager for Mac: `https://brew.sh/`.

Windows users best use the WSL and follow the Linux instructions, or install MinGW (`http://www.mingw.org/`), in an effort to provide GNU Linux tools for Windows.

Check whether the tools are properly installed by opening a Terminal window and issuing the following command:

```
$ cc --version
cc (GCC) 9.1.1 20190503 (Red Hat 9.1.1-1)
Copyright (C) 2019 Free Software Foundation, Inc.
This is free software; see the source for copying conditions. There is NO
warranty; not even for MERCHANTABILITY or FITNESS FOR A PARTICULAR PURPOSE.
$  ar --version
```

```
GNU ar version 2.31.1-29.fc30
Copyright (C) 2018 Free Software Foundation, Inc.
This program is free software; you may redistribute it under the terms of
the GNU General Public License version 3 or (at your option) any later
version.
This program has absolutely no warranty.
$ git --version
git version 2.21.0
```

The versions should be similar (at least the major release) to avoid any unexpected differences.

Once ready, use the same shell to create a `bindgen` directory, and inside it run `cargo new rust-tinyexpr` and clone the TinyExpr GitHub repository (`https://github.com/codeplea/tinyexpr`) using `git clone https://github.com/codeplea/tinyexpr`.

How to do it...

Let's create some bindings in just a few steps:

1. Open `rust-tinyexpr/Cargo.toml` and add the appropriate build dependencies:

   ```
   [build-dependencies]
   bindgen = "0.49"
   ```

2. Create a new `rust-tinyexpr/build.rs` file and add the following content to create a custom build of the C library:

   ```
   use std::env;
   use std::env::var;
   use std::path::PathBuf;
   const HEADER_FILE_NAME: &'static str = "../tinyexpr/tinyexpr.h";

   fn main() {
       let project_dir = var("CARGO_MANIFEST_DIR").unwrap();
       println!("cargo:rustc-link-search={}/../tinyexpr/",
        project_dir);
       println!("cargo:rustc-link-lib=static=tinyexpr");

       if cfg!(target_env = "msvc") {
           println!("cargo:rustc-link-
             lib=static=legacy_stdio_definitions");
       }
       let bindings = bindgen::Builder::default()
   ```

```
        .header(HEADER_FILE_NAME)
        .generate()
        .expect("Error generating bindings");

    let out_path = PathBuf::from(env::var("OUT_DIR").unwrap());
    bindings
        .write_to_file(out_path.join("bindings.rs"))
        .expect("Error writing bindings");
}
```

3. Now for the actual Rust code. Open rust-tinyexpr/src/main.rs and add some code to include the file generated by rust-bindgen (which is called from build.rs):

```
#![allow(non_upper_case_globals)]
#![allow(non_camel_case_types)]
#![allow(non_snake_case)]
use std::ffi::CString;

include!(concat!(env!("OUT_DIR"), "/bindings.rs"));

fn main() {
    let expr = "sqrt(5^2+7^2+11^2+(8-2)^2)".to_owned();
    let result = unsafe {
        te_interp(CString::new(expr.clone()).unwrap().into_raw(), 0
as *mut i32)
    };
    println!("{} = {}", expr, result);
}
```

4. If we run cargo build now (inside rust-tinyexpr), we will see the following result:

```
$   cargo build
    Compiling libc v0.2.58
    Compiling cc v1.0.37
    Compiling autocfg v0.1.4
    Compiling memchr v2.2.0
    Compiling version_check v0.1.5
    Compiling rustc-demangle v0.1.15
    Compiling proc-macro2 v0.4.30
    Compiling bitflags v1.1.0
    Compiling ucd-util v0.1.3
    Compiling byteorder v1.3.2
    Compiling lazy_static v1.3.0
    Compiling regex v1.1.7
    Compiling glob v0.2.11
    Compiling cfg-if v0.1.9
```

```
    Compiling quick-error v1.2.2
    Compiling utf8-ranges v1.0.3
    Compiling unicode-xid v0.1.0
    Compiling unicode-width v0.1.5
    Compiling vec_map v0.8.1
    Compiling ansi_term v0.11.0
    Compiling termcolor v1.0.5
    Compiling strsim v0.8.0
    Compiling bindgen v0.49.3
    Compiling peeking_take_while v0.1.2
    Compiling shlex v0.1.1
    Compiling backtrace v0.3.31
    Compiling nom v4.2.3
    Compiling regex-syntax v0.6.7
    Compiling thread_local v0.3.6
    Compiling log v0.4.6
    Compiling humantime v1.2.0
    Compiling textwrap v0.11.0
    Compiling backtrace-sys v0.1.28
    Compiling libloading v0.5.1
    Compiling clang-sys v0.28.0
    Compiling atty v0.2.11
    Compiling aho-corasick v0.7.3
    Compiling fxhash v0.2.1
    Compiling clap v2.33.0
    Compiling quote v0.6.12
    Compiling cexpr v0.3.5
    Compiling failure v0.1.5
    Compiling which v2.0.1
    Compiling env_logger v0.6.1
    Compiling rust-tinyexpr v0.1.0 (Rust-
Cookbook/Chapter07/bindgen/rust-tinyexpr)
error: linking with `cc` failed: exit code: 1
[...]
"-Wl,-Bdynamic" "-ldl" "-lrt" "-lpthread" "-lgcc_s" "-lc" "-lm" "-
lrt" "-lpthread" "-lutil" "-lutil"
  = note: /usr/bin/ld: cannot find -ltinyexpr
          collect2: error: ld returned 1 exit status

error: aborting due to previous error

error: Could not compile `rust-tinyexpr`.

To learn more, run the command again with --verbose.
```

5. This is a linker error—the linker could not find the library! This is because we never actually created it. Change into the `tinyexpr` directory and run these commands to create a static library from the source code on Linux/macOS:

```
$ cc -c -ansi -Wall -Wshadow -O2 tinyexpr.c -o tinyexpr.o -fPIC
$ ar rcs libtinyexpr.a tinyexpr.o
```

With Windows, the process is a little bit different:

```
$ gcc -c -ansi -Wall -Wshadow -O2 tinyexpr.c -o tinyexpr.lib -fPIC
```

6. Going back into the `rust-tinyexpr` directory, we can run `cargo build` again:

```
$ cargo build
    Compiling rust-tinyexpr v0.1.0 (Rust-
Cookbook/Chapter07/bindgen/rust-tinyexpr)
    Finished dev [unoptimized + debuginfo] target(s) in 0.31s
```

7. As a bonus, `bindgen` also generates tests, so we can run `cargo test` to make sure the binary layout is validated. Then, let's parse an expression using the TinyExpr C library from Rust:

```
$ cargo test
    Compiling rust-tinyexpr v0.1.0 (Rust-
    Cookbook/Chapter07/bindgen/rust-tinyexpr)
    Finished dev [unoptimized + debuginfo] target(s) in 0.36s
    Running target/debug/deps/rust_tinyexpr-fbf606d893dc44c6

running 3 tests
test bindgen_test_layout_te_expr ... ok
test bindgen_test_layout_te_expr__bindgen_ty_1 ... ok
test bindgen_test_layout_te_variable ... ok

test result: ok. 3 passed; 0 failed; 0 ignored; 0 measured; 0
filtered out
$ cargo run
    Finished dev [unoptimized + debuginfo] target(s) in 0.04s
    Running `target/debug/rust-tinyexpr`
    sqrt(5^2+7^2+11^2+(8-2)^2) = 15.198684153570664
```

Let's see how we achieved this result.

How it works...

`bindgen` is an amazing tool that generates Rust code from C/C++ headers *on the fly*. In *step 1* and 2, we added the dependency and used the `bindgen` API to load the header and generate and output a file called `bindings.rs` in the temporary `build` directory. The `OUT_DIR` variable is only available from within `cargo`'s build environment and leads to a directory containing several build artifacts.

Additionally, the linker needs to know about the library that has been created so it can link to it. This is done by printing out the required parameters to standard with a special syntax. In this case, we pass the library's name (`link-lib`) and the directory it should check (`link-search`) to the `rustc` linker. `cargo` can do much more with these outputs. Check the docs (`https://doc.rust-lang.org/cargo/reference/build-scripts.html`) for more information.

 Microsoft's `msvc` compiler introduced a breaking change by removing the standard `printf` functions in favor of more secure variations. In order to minimize the complexity of cross-platform compilation, a simple compiler switch was introduced in *step 4* to bring back the `printf` legacy.

Step 3 creates the Rust code to call the linked functions (while discarding several warnings about naming) by including the file. While `bindgen` takes away the generation of the interface, it's still necessary to use C-compatible types for passing parameters. This is why we have to create the pointer when we call the function.

If we compiled the Rust code right after this step, we would end up with a huge error message, as shown in *step 4*. To remedy this, we create the static library from the C code in *step 5*, using a few compiler flags for `cc` (the `gcc` C compiler), such as `-fPIC` (which stands for *position independent code*), which creates consistent positions within the file, so it's usable as a library. The output of the `cc` call is an object file, which is then *archived* in a static library using the `ar` tool.

If the library is properly available, we can use `cargo build` and `cargo run`—as shown in the last two steps—to execute the code.

Now that we know how to integrate Rust with other languages, let's move on to another chapter to deep dive into a different topic.

Safe Programming for the Web

8

Ever since the popular Rails framework for the Ruby programming language, creating backend web services seemed like a domain for dynamically typed languages. This trend was only reinforced by the rise of Python and JavaScript as primary languages for these tasks. After all, the nature of these technologies made creating these services especially fast and changes to services (for example, a new field in the JSON response) are simple to do. Returning to static types for web services feels strange for many of us; after all, it takes a lot longer to get *something* going.

However, there is a cost to these: many services are deployed in the cloud nowadays, which means that a pay-as-you-go model is employed together with (practically) infinite scalability. Since—most notably—Python is not known for its execution speed, we can now see the cost of this overhead on the bill from the cloud provider. A 10% faster execution time can mean serving 10% more customers on the same hardware at the same level of quality (for example, response time). Similarly, smaller devices benefit from lower resource usage, which translates into faster software and therefore less energy consumed. Rust, as a systems programming language, was built with zero overhead in mind and is a close rival to C in many aspects such as speed or efficiency. It is therefore not unreasonable for heavily used web services to write critical parts in Rust, a move that has famously been made by Dropbox to improve its service quality and save costs.

Rust is a great language for the web and, in this chapter, we are looking at creating a regular RESTful API using a framework that is in use at many different applications and developed at Microsoft. You can look forward to learning about the following:

- Setting up a web server
- Designing a RESTful API
- Handling JSON payloads
- Web error handling
- Rendering HTML templates

- Using an ORM to save data to a database
- Running advanced queries using an ORM
- Authentication on the web

Setting up a web server

Over the last few years, web servers have changed. Where early web applications have been deployed behind some sort of web server application such as Apache Tomcat (`http://tomcat.apache.org/`), IIS (`https://www.iis.net/`), and nginx (`https://www.nginx.com/`), it is now more common to embed the serving part into the application as well. Not only is this easier on the Ops people, it also allows developers to have tight control over the entire application. Let's see how we can get started and set up a basic static web server.

Getting ready

Let's set up a Rust binary project using `cargo new static-web`. Since we are going to serve stuff on local port `8081`, make sure that the port is accessible as well. Inside the newly created project folder, we need an additional folder, `static/`, where you can put an interesting `.jpg` image and serve it. We are going to assume that this image is called `foxes.jpg`.

Finally, open the entire directory with VS Code.

How to do it...

We are going to set up and run our own web server in just a few steps:

1. Open `src/main.rs` first, and let's add some code. We will work our way down to the `main` function, starting with imports and a simple index handler:

```
#[macro_use]
extern crate actix_web;

use actix_web::{web, App, middleware, HttpServer, Responder, Result};
use std::{env};
use actix_files as fs;
```

```
fn index() -> Result<fs::NamedFile> {
    Ok(fs::NamedFile::open("static/index.html")?)
}
```

2. This is not going to be the only request handler, however, so let's add a few more to see how request-handling works:

```
fn path_parser(info: web::Path<(String, i32)>) -> impl Responder {
    format!("You tried to reach '{}/{}'", info.0, info.1)
}

fn rust_cookbook() -> impl Responder {
    format!("Welcome to the Rust Cookbook")
}

#[get("/foxes")]
fn foxes() -> Result<fs::NamedFile> {
    Ok(fs::NamedFile::open("static/foxes.jpg")?)
}
```

3. What's missing is the `main` function. This `main` function starts the server and attaches the services we created in the previous step:

```
fn main() -> std::io::Result<()> {
    env::set_var("RUST_LOG", "actix_web=debug");
    env_logger::init();
    HttpServer::new(
        || App::new()
            .wrap(middleware::Logger::default())
            .service(foxes)
            .service(web::resource("/").to(index))
            .service(web::resource("/welcome").to(rust_cookbook))
    .service(web::resource("/{path}/{id}").to(path_parser)))
        .bind("127.0.0.1:8081")?
        .run()
}
```

4. In the first handler, we mention a static `index.html` handle, which we haven't yet created. Add a simple `marquee` output to a new file and save it as `static/index.html`:

```
<html>
    <body>
        <marquee><h1>Hello World</h1></marquee>
    </body>
</html>
```

5. One important thing that we are still need to do is adjust `Cargo.toml`. Declare the dependencies in `Cargo.toml` as follows:

```
[dependencies]
actix-web = "1"
env_logger = "0.6"
actix-files = "0"
```

6. Use a Terminal to execute `cargo run` and run the code, then open a browser window at `http://localhost:8081/`, `http://localhost:8081/welcome`, `http://localhost:8081/foxes`, and `http://localhost:8081/somethingarbitrary/10`:

```
$ cargo run
    Compiling autocfg v0.1.4
    Compiling semver-parser v0.7.0
    Compiling libc v0.2.59
[...]
    Compiling static-web v0.1.0 (Rust-Cookbook/Chapter08/static-web)
     Finished dev [unoptimized + debuginfo] target(s) in 1m 51s
      Running `target/debug/static-web`
```

Here is the output for `http://localhost:8081`, handled by the `index` function:

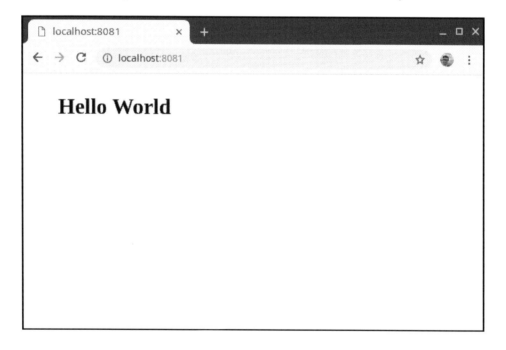

You can also call the welcome handler at `http://localhost:8081/welcome`:

Our static handler returns a photo of the Mozilla office in Berlin at `http://localhost:8081/foxes`:

Lastly, we added a path handler that parses a string and an integer from the path, only to return the values:

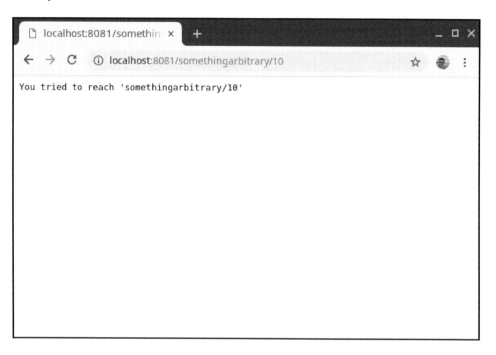

To verify the requests were actually handled by our web server, you should view the individual requests in the log output of the Terminal running `cargo run`:

```
[...]
    Finished dev [unoptimized + debuginfo] target(s) in 1m 51s
     Running `target/debug/static-web`
[2019-07-17T06:20:27Z INFO actix_web::middleware::logger]
127.0.0.1:35358 "GET / HTTP/1.1" 200 89 "-" "Mozilla/5.0 (X11;
Fedora; Linux x86_64) AppleWebKit/537.36 (KHTML, like Gecko)
Chrome/73.0.3683.86 Safari/537.36" 0.004907
[2019-07-17T06:21:58Z INFO actix_web::middleware::logger]
127.0.0.1:36154 "GET /welcome HTTP/1.1" 200 28 "-" "Mozilla/5.0
(X11; Fedora; Linux x86_64) AppleWebKit/537.36 (KHTML, like Gecko)
Chrome/73.0.3683.86 Safari/537.36" 0.000844
^[[B[2019-07-17T06:22:34Z INFO actix_web::middleware::logger]
127.0.0.1:36476 "GET /somethingarbitrary/10 HTTP/1.1" 200 42 "-"
"Mozilla/5.0 (X11; Fedora; Linux x86_64) AppleWebKit/537.36 (KHTML,
like Gecko) Chrome/73.0.3683.86 Safari/537.36" 0.000804
[2019-07-17T06:24:22Z INFO actix_web::middleware::logger]
127.0.0.1:37424 "GET /foxes HTTP/1.1" 200 1416043 "-" "Mozilla/5.0
```

```
(X11; Fedora; Linux x86_64) AppleWebKit/537.36 (KHTML, like Gecko)
Chrome/73.0.3683.86 Safari/537.36" 0.010263
```

Now, let's go behind the scenes to understand the code better.

How it works...

`actix-web` (`https://actix.rs`) is a versatile web framework and it—among other things—efficiently serves static files as well. In this recipe, we covered how to declare and register request handlers, as well as some ways to provide responses. In a typical web framework, there are several ways to achieve these tasks (declaring handlers, creating responses) and *steps 1* to *3* show two ways to do this with `actix-web`:

- Using an attribute (`#[get("/foxes")]`)
- Via the service registration call
  (`.service(web::resource("/welcome").to(rust_cookbook))`)

Regardless of the way we associate a handler with a route, each of them is wrapped into a factory that creates new handler instances on demand, which is very visible when a compiler error points to the `#[get(...)]` attribute instead of the actual function. The paths include typed placeholders for passing data from the path into the handler function—but more on that in the next recipe (*Designing a RESTful API*).

In *step 3*, we also add logging middleware that logs the user agent, time, and IP address so we can see requests also on the server side. All of this is done using `actix-web` method chaining, which structures the calls nicely. The call to `run()` blocks the application and starts the actix main loop.

 The photo in *step 6* was taken in Mozilla's Berlin office during Rust All Hands 2019. Yes, those are Firefox pillows.

Step 4 adds a very basic `index.html` file to be served, while *step 5* declares the dependencies in `Cargo.toml` as we have done before.

In the last step, we are running the code and showing the output—both in the browser and the logging.

We've successfully learned the basics of setting up a web server. Equipped with this knowledge of serving static files and images, as well as parsed path parameters, we can move on to the next recipe.

Designing a RESTful API

Almost everything relies on web resources—from a single page application that
dynamically fetches data via JavaScript and displays it in HTML to the app integration for a
particular service. A resource on a web service can be anything but it's typically expressed
using readable URIs so information is already transferred by using a specific path, which
then only accepts the required information it needs to process. This allows structuring code
internally and globally utilizes all HTTP methods to create an expressive interface that
developers can use. RESTful APIs (https://www.codecademy.com/articles/what-is-rest)
ideally capture all of these benefits.

Getting ready

Let's set up a Rust binary project using `cargo new api`. Since we are going to serve stuff
on local port 8081, make sure that the port is accessible as well. Inside the newly created
project folder, we need an additional `static/` folder, where you can put an
interesting `.jpg` image to serve. Additionally, make sure that there is a program such
as curl (https://curl.haxx.se/) available on your command line. Alternatively, Postman
(https://www.getpostman.com/) is a tool that does the same thing with a graphical
interface.

Finally, open the entire directory with VS Code.

How to do it...

Let's build an API with a few steps:

1. Open `src/main.rs` to add the primary code for the server and handling
   requests. Let's go step by step and start with the imports:

```
#[macro_use]
extern crate actix_web;

use actix_files as fs;
use actix_web::{ guard,
    http::header, http::Method, middleware, web, App, HttpRequest,
HttpResponse, HttpServer,
    Responder, Result,
};
use std::env;
use std::path::PathBuf;
```

2. Next, we are defining a few handlers that take requests and use that data somehow. Add these lines to `main.rs`:

```
#[get("by-id/{id}")]
fn bookmark_by_id(id: web::Path<(i32)>) -> impl Responder {
    format!("{{ \"id\": {}, \"url\": \"https://blog.x5ff.xyz\" }}",
id)
}


fn echo_bookmark(req: HttpRequest) -> impl Responder {
    let id: i32 = req.match_info().query("id").parse().unwrap();
    format!("{:?}", id)
}


#[get("/captures/{tail:.*}")]
fn captures(req: HttpRequest) -> Result<fs::NamedFile> {
    let mut root = PathBuf::from("static/");
    let tail: PathBuf =
req.match_info().query("tail").parse().unwrap();
    root.push(tail);

    Ok(fs::NamedFile::open(root)?)
}


#[get("from-bitly/{bitlyid}")]
fn bit_ly(req: HttpRequest) -> HttpResponse {
    let bitly_id = req.match_info().get("bitlyid").unwrap();
    let url = req.url_for("bitly", &[bitly_id]).unwrap();
    HttpResponse::Found()
        .header(header::LOCATION, url.into_string())
        .finish()
        .into_body()
}


#[get("/")]
fn bookmarks_index() -> impl Responder {
    format!("Welcome to your quick and easy bookmarking service!")
}
```

3. Next, we should also register the handlers with the web server. The following is the `main` function for `main.rs`:

```
fn main() -> std::io::Result<()> {
    env::set_var("RUST_LOG", "actix_web=debug");
    env_logger::init();
    HttpServer::new(|| {
        App::new()
            .wrap(middleware::Logger::default())
```

```
                        .service(
                            web::scope("/api")
                            .service(
                                web::scope("/bookmarks")
                                .service(captures)
                                .service(bookmark_by_id)
                                .service(bit_ly)
                                .service(web::resource("add/{id}")
                                    .name("add")
                                    .guard(guard::Any(guard::Put())
                                    .or(guard::Post()))
                                    .to(echo_bookmark))
                        ))
                        .service(
                            web::scope("/bookmarks")
                                .service(bookmarks_index)
                        )
                        .external_resource("bitly", "https://bit.ly/{bitly}")
            })
            .bind("127.0.0.1:8081")?
            .run()
    }
```

4. Lastly, we should adapt `Cargo.toml` to include these new dependencies as well:

```
[dependencies]
actix-web = "1"
env_logger = "0.6"
actix-files = "0"
```

5. Now we can build and run the app using `cargo run`. Then, let's see whether we can reach the APIs using `curl` or Postman, which should result in a similar logging output to the following:

```
$ cargo run
 Finished dev [unoptimized + debuginfo] target(s) in 0.09s
 Running `target/debug/api`
[2019-07-17T15:38:14Z INFO actix_web::middleware::logger]
127.0.0.1:50426 "GET /bookmarks/ HTTP/1.1" 200 51 "-" "curl/7.64.0"
0.000655
[2019-07-17T15:40:07Z INFO actix_web::middleware::logger]
127.0.0.1:51386 "GET /api/bookmarks/by-id/10 HTTP/1.1" 200 44 "-"
"curl/7.64.0" 0.001103
[2019-07-17T15:40:41Z INFO actix_web::middleware::logger]
127.0.0.1:51676 "GET /api/bookmarks/from-bitly/2NOMT6Q HTTP/1.1"
302 0 "-" "curl/7.64.0" 0.007269
[2019-07-17T15:42:26Z INFO actix_web::middleware::logger]
127.0.0.1:52566 "PUT /api/bookmarks/add/10 HTTP/1.1" 200 2 "-"
```

```
"curl/7.64.0" 0.000704
[2019-07-17T15:42:33Z INFO actix_web::middleware::logger]
127.0.0.1:52626 "POST /api/bookmarks/add/10 HTTP/1.1" 200 2 "-"
"curl/7.64.0" 0.001098
[2019-07-17T15:42:39Z INFO actix_web::middleware::logger]
127.0.0.1:52678 "DELETE /api/bookmarks/add/10 HTTP/1.1" 404 0 "-"
"curl/7.64.0" 0.000630
[2019-07-17T15:43:30Z INFO actix_web::middleware::logger]
127.0.0.1:53094 "GET /api/bookmarks/captures/does-not/exist
HTTP/1.1" 404 38 "-" "curl/7.64.0" 0.003554
[2019-07-17T15:43:39Z INFO actix_web::middleware::logger]
127.0.0.1:53170 "GET /api/bookmarks/captures/foxes.jpg HTTP/1.1"
200 59072 "-" "curl/7.64.0" 0.013600
```

The following are the `curl` requests—they should be easy to replicate with Postman:

```
$ curl localhost:8081/bookmarks/
Welcome to your quick and easy bookmarking service!↵
$ curl localhost:8081/api/bookmarks/by-id/10
{ "id": 10, "url": "https://blog.x5ff.xyz" }↵
$ curl -v localhost:8081/api/bookmarks/from-bitly/2NOMT6Q
*   Trying ::1...
* TCP_NODELAY set
* connect to ::1 port 8081 failed: Connection refused
*   Trying 127.0.0.1...
* TCP_NODELAY set
* Connected to localhost (127.0.0.1) port 8081 (#0)
> GET /api/bookmarks/from-bitly/2NOMT6Q HTTP/1.1
> Host: localhost:8081
> User-Agent: curl/7.64.0
> Accept: */*
>
< HTTP/1.1 302 Found
< content-length: 0
< location: https://bit.ly/2NOMT6Q
< date: Wed, 17 Jul 2019 15:40:45 GMT
<
$ curl -X PUT localhost:8081/api/bookmarks/add/10
10↵
$ curl -X POST localhost:8081/api/bookmarks/add/10
10↵
$ curl -v -X DELETE localhost:8081/api/bookmarks/add/10
*   Trying ::1...
* TCP_NODELAY set
* connect to ::1 port 8081 failed: Connection refused
*   Trying 127.0.0.1...
* TCP_NODELAY set
```

```
* Connected to localhost (127.0.0.1) port 8081 (#0)
> DELETE /api/bookmarks/add/10 HTTP/1.1
> Host: localhost:8081
> User-Agent: curl/7.64.0
> Accept: */*
>
< HTTP/1.1 404 Not Found
< content-length: 0
< date: Wed, 17 Jul 2019 15:42:51 GMT
<
* Connection #0 to host localhost left intact
$ curl localhost:8081/api/bookmarks/captures/does-not/exist
No such file or directory (os error 2)⏎ 17:43:31
$ curl localhost:8081/api/bookmarks/captures/foxes.jpg
Warning: Binary output can mess up your terminal. Use "--output -"
to tell
Warning: curl to output it to your terminal anyway, or consider "--
output
Warning: <FILE>" to save to a file.
```

That's it, but there is a lot to unpack so let's see why this works the way it does.

How it works...

Designing *good* APIs is hard and requires a good grasp of what's possible—especially with new frameworks and languages. `actix-web` has proven itself to be a versatile tool that proficiently uses types to achieve great results. *Step 1* sets this up by importing a few types and traits.

Only in *step 2* and *step 3* does it get more interesting. Here, we define the various handlers in almost all of the ways `actix-web` allows us to, by either using the attribute that wraps a function into a factory (underneath it's all asynchronous actors; check out *Handle asynchronous messages with actors* in Chapter 4, *Fearless Concurrency*) or letting the `web::resource()` type do that. Either way, every handler function has a route associated with it and will be called in parallel. The routes also contain parameters that can be specified using a {} syntax that also allows regular expression (see the route containing `"{tail:.*}"` – a shorthand that receives the path's remainder under the `tail` key.

Don't let users directly access files on your filesystem as we did here. This is a bad idea in many ways, but most importantly offers a way to execute potentially any file in the filesystem. A better way is to provide a white list of abstracted files—for example, Base64 (`https://developer.mozilla.org/en-US/docs/Web/API/WindowBase64/Base64_encoding_and_decoding`)-encoded—using an independent key: for example, a UUID (`https://tools.ietf.org/html/rfc4122`).

If a function provides an input parameter of the `Path<T>` type, then `T` is what's checked for in the corresponding path variable. Therefore, if a function header expects `i32`, the request will fail for anyone trying to pass a string. You can verify that yourself with the `bookmarks/by-id/{id}` path. As an alternative to `Path<T>`, you can also receive the entire `HttpRequest` (`https://docs.rs/actix-web/1.0.3/actix_web/struct.HttpRequest.html`) as a parameter and extract the required information with the `.query()` function. Both the `echo_bookmark` and `bit_ly` functions demonstrate how to use these.

The responses behave similarly. `actix-web` provides a `Responder` trait that is implemented for standard types such as `String` (along with the correct response content type as far as we saw), which makes the handler more readable. Again, returning an `HttpResponse` type provides more finely controllable returns. Additionally, there are results and similar types that are automatically converted into appropriate responses, but showing all of these would go beyond the scope of this book. Check out the `actix-web` documentation to find out more.

One downside to the attributes is the fact that only one of them can go on top of a function—so how can we reuse a function for two different `HTTP` methods? `echo_bookmark` is registered to respond to the input ID only on `PUT` and `POST`, not on `DELETE`, `HEAD`, `GET`, and more. This is done by guards that forward a request only if a condition is met. Check out the docs (`https://docs.rs/actix-web/1.0.3/actix_web/guard/index.html`) for more.

Step 4 shows adaptations to `Cargo.toml` to make it all work and, in *step 5,* we get to try out the web service. If you take some time to observe the `curl` responses, we receive the expected results. `curl` also does not follow redirects by default, hence the `HTTP` response code, `302`, with the location header set pointing to where I would go. This redirect is provided by an external resource that `actix-web` provides, which is useful for these situations.

Now that we have learned more about designing APIs in `actix-web`, let's move on to the next recipe.

Handling JSON payloads

After learning how to create APIs, we need to pass data back and forth. While the path provides one method to do that, anything a little more sophisticated (for example, a long list of things) will quickly show the limitations of these methods. This is why other formats are typically used to structure the data—JSON (http://json.org/) is the most popular for web services. In this chapter, we are going to use the previous API and enhance it by handling and returning JSON.

Getting ready

Let's set up a Rust binary project using `cargo new json-handling`. Since we are going to serve stuff on the local port 8081, make sure that the port is accessible as well. Additionally, a program such as `curl` or Postman is required to test the web service.

Finally, open the entire directory with VS Code.

How to do it...

Perform the following steps to implement this recipe:

1. In `src/main.rs`, we are going to add the imports first:

```
#[macro_use]
extern crate actix_web;

use actix_web::{
    guard, http::Method, middleware, web, App, HttpResponse,
HttpServer,
};
use serde_derive::{Deserialize, Serialize};
use std::env;
```

2. Next, let's create some handler functions along with a serializable JSON type. Add the following code to `src/main.rs`:

```
#[derive(Debug, Clone, Serialize, Deserialize)]
struct Bookmark {
    id: i32,
    url: String,
}
```

```
#[get("by-id/{id}")]
fn bookmarks_by_id(id: web::Path<(i32)>) -> HttpResponse {
    let bookmark = Bookmark {
        id: *id,
        url: "https://blog.x5ff.xyz".into(),
    };
    HttpResponse::Ok().json(bookmark)
}


fn echo_bookmark(bookmark: web::Json<Bookmark>) -> HttpResponse {
    HttpResponse::Ok().json(bookmark.clone())
}
```

3. Lastly, we are registering the handlers with the web server in the `main` function:

```
fn main() -> std::io::Result<()> {
    env::set_var("RUST_LOG", "actix_web=debug");
    env_logger::init();
    HttpServer::new(|| {
        App::new().wrap(middleware::Logger::default()).service(
            web::scope("/api").service(
                web::scope("/bookmarks")
                    .service(bookmarks_by_id)
                    .service(
                        web::resource("add/{id}")
                            .name("add")
                            .guard(guard::Any(guard::Put()).
                             or(guard::Post()))
                            .to(echo_bookmark),
                    )
                    .default_service(web::route().method
                     (Method::GET)),
            ),
        )
    })
    .bind("127.0.0.1:8081")?
    .run()
}
```

4. We also need to specify the dependencies in `Cargo.toml`. Replace the existing dependencies with the following:

```
[dependencies]
actix-web = "1"
serde = "1"
serde_derive = "1"
env_logger = "0.6"
```

5. Then, we can see whether it works by running `cargo run` and issuing requests with `curl` from a different Terminal. The commands and their responses should look as follows:

```
$ curl -d "{\"id\":10,\"url\":\"https://blog.x5ff.xyz\"}"
localhost:8081/api/bookmarks/add/10
Content type error⏎
$ curl -d "{\"id\":10,\"url\":\"https://blog.x5ff.xyz\"}" -H
"Content-Type: application/json"
localhost:8081/api/bookmarks/add/10
{"id":10,"url":"https://blog.x5ff.xyz"}⏎
$ curl localhost:8081/api/bookmarks/by-id/1
{"id":1,"url":"https://blog.x5ff.xyz"}⏎
```

Meanwhile, the logging output of `cargo run` shows the requests from the server side:

```
$ cargo run
    Finished dev [unoptimized + debuginfo] target(s) in 0.08s
     Running `target/debug/json-handling`
[2019-07-13T17:06:22Z INFO actix_web::middleware::logger]
127.0.0.1:48880 "POST /api/bookmarks/add/10 HTTP/1.1" 400 63 "-"
"curl/7.64.0" 0.001955
[2019-07-13T17:06:51Z INFO actix_web::middleware::logger]
127.0.0.1:49124 "POST /api/bookmarks/add/10 HTTP/1.1" 200 39 "-"
"curl/7.64.0" 0.001290
[2019-07-18T06:34:18Z INFO actix_web::middleware::logger]
127.0.0.1:54900 "GET /api/bookmarks/by-id/1 HTTP/1.1" 200 39 "-"
"curl/7.64.0" 0.001636
```

This was quick and easy, right? Let's see how it works.

How it works...

Adding JSON handling to an `actix-web` web service is easy—thanks to the deep integration of the popular `serde` crate (`https://crates.io/crates/serde`). After some imports in *step 1*, we declare a `Bookmark` struct as `Serialize` and `Deserialize` in *step 2*, which enables `serde` to generate and parse JSON for this data type.

The change in the handler functions is also minimal since returning and ingesting JSON is a very common task. The required function to return a JSON payload with the response is attached to the `HttpResponse` factory method that does everything, including setting the appropriate content type. On the ingest part, there is a `web::Json<T>` type to take care of deserializing and checking whatever is forwarded into the request handler. We can rely on the framework to do most of the heavy lifting here as well.

The registering of the handlers in *step 3* is no different from previous recipes; the JSON input is only declared in the handler function. There are more variations in the `actix-web` docs (`https://actix.rs/docs/request/#json-request`) and their examples (`https://github.com/actix/examples/tree/master/json`). Similarly, *step 4* contains the required dependencies we have also used in other recipes.

In *step 5*, we run the whole project and see how it works: if we pass JSON, the input `content-type` header has to be set to the appropriate mime type (`application/json`); the return values have this header set as well (and the `content-length` header) so browsers or other programs can easily work with the results.

Let's move on and look at another recipe.

Web error handling

The various layers of web services make error handling tricky, even without security requirements: what to communicate and when? Should an error bubble up only to be handled at the last minute or earlier? What about cascades? In this recipe, we will uncover some options to do that elegantly in `actix-web`.

Getting ready

Let's set up a Rust binary project using `cargo new web-errors`. Since we are going to serve stuff on the local port `8081`, make sure that the port is accessible as well. Additionally, a program such as `curl` or Postman is required to test the web service.

Finally, open the entire directory with VS Code.

How to do it...

You are just a few steps away from understanding error handling with `actix-web`:

1. In `src/main.rs`, we are going to add the basic imports:

```
#[macro_use]
extern crate actix_web;
use failure::Fail;

use actix_web::{ http, middleware, web, App, HttpResponse,
HttpServer, error
};
use serde_derive::{Deserialize, Serialize};
use std::env;
```

2. As a next step, we are going to define our error types and augment them with attributes to make the types known to the framework:

```
#[derive(Fail, Debug)]
enum WebError {
    #[fail(display = "Invalid id '{}'", id)]
    InvalidIdError { id: i32 },
    #[fail(display = "Invalid request, please try again later")]
    RandomInternalError,
}

impl error::ResponseError for WebError {
    fn error_response(&self) -> HttpResponse {
        match *self {
            WebError::InvalidIdError { .. } =>
HttpResponse::new(http::StatusCode::BAD_REQUEST),
            WebError::RandomInternalError =>
HttpResponse::new(http::StatusCode::INTERNAL_SERVER_ERROR)
        }
    }
}
```

3. Then, we add the handler function to `src/main.rs` and register it in `main()`:

```
#[derive(Debug, Clone, Serialize, Deserialize)]
struct Bookmark {
    id: i32,
    url: String,
}

#[get("by-id/{id}")]
fn bookmarks_by_id(id: web::Path<(i32)>) -> Result<HttpResponse,
```

```
WebError> {
    if *id < 10 {
        Ok(HttpResponse::Ok().json(Bookmark {
            id: *id,
            url: "https://blog.x5ff.xyz".into(),
        }))
    }
    else {
        Err(WebError::InvalidIdError { id: *id })
    }
}

fn main() -> std::io::Result<()> {
    env::set_var("RUST_LOG", "actix_web=debug");
    env_logger::init();
    HttpServer::new(|| {
        App::new()
            .wrap(middleware::Logger::default())
            .service(
                web::scope("/bookmarks")
                    .service(bookmarks_by_id)
            )
            .route(
                "/underconstruction",
                web::get().to(|| Result::<HttpResponse,
                WebError>::Err(WebError::RandomInternalError)),
            )
    })
    .bind("127.0.0.1:8081")?
    .run()
}
```

4. To import the dependencies, we also have to adapt `Cargo.toml`:

```
[dependencies]
actix-web = "1"
serde = "1"
serde_derive = "1"
env_logger = "0.6"
failure = "0"
```

5. To finish this recipe, let's see how everything works together with `cargo run` and `curl`. Here is the server output after the requests have been handled:

```
$ cargo run
  Compiling web-errors v0.1.0 (Rust-Cookbook/Chapter08/web-errors)
    Finished dev [unoptimized + debuginfo] target(s) in 7.74s
      Running `target/debug/web-errors`
[2019-07-19T17:33:43Z INFO actix_web::middleware::logger]
127.0.0.1:46316 "GET /bookmarks/by-id/1 HTTP/1.1" 200 38 "-"
"curl/7.64.0" 0.001529
[2019-07-19T17:33:47Z INFO actix_web::middleware::logger]
127.0.0.1:46352 "GET /bookmarks/by-id/100 HTTP/1.1" 400 16 "-"
"curl/7.64.0" 0.000952
[2019-07-19T17:33:54Z INFO actix_web::middleware::logger]
127.0.0.1:46412 "GET /underconstruction HTTP/1.1" 500 39 "-"
"curl/7.64.0" 0.000275
```

The following is what the requests look like with `curl`'s verbose mode:

```
$ curl -v localhost:8081/bookmarks/by-id/1
* Trying ::1...
* TCP_NODELAY set
* connect to ::1 port 8081 failed: Connection refused
* Trying 127.0.0.1...
* TCP_NODELAY set
* Connected to localhost (127.0.0.1) port 8081 (#0)
> GET /bookmarks/by-id/1 HTTP/1.1
> Host: localhost:8081
> User-Agent: curl/7.64.0
> Accept: */*
>
< HTTP/1.1 200 OK
< content-length: 38
< content-type: application/json
< date: Fri, 19 Jul 2019 17:33:43 GMT
<
* Connection #0 to host localhost left intact
{"id":1,"url":"https://blog.x5ff.xyz"}
```

Requesting the wrong ID returns an appropriate HTTP status code as well:

```
$ curl -v localhost:8081/bookmarks/by-id/100
* Trying ::1...
* TCP_NODELAY set
* connect to ::1 port 8081 failed: Connection refused
* Trying 127.0.0.1...
* TCP_NODELAY set
* Connected to localhost (127.0.0.1) port 8081 (#0)
```

```
> GET /bookmarks/by-id/100 HTTP/1.1
> Host: localhost:8081
> User-Agent: curl/7.64.0
> Accept: */*
>
< HTTP/1.1 400 Bad Request
< content-length: 16
< content-type: text/plain
< date: Fri, 19 Jul 2019 17:33:47 GMT
<
* Connection #0 to host localhost left intact
Invalid id '100'⏎
```

Just as expected, a request to /underconstruction yields an HTTP 500 error (internal server error):

```
$ curl -v localhost:8081/underconstruction
* Trying ::1...
* TCP_NODELAY set
* connect to ::1 port 8081 failed: Connection refused
* Trying 127.0.0.1...
* TCP_NODELAY set
* Connected to localhost (127.0.0.1) port 8081 (#0)
> GET /underconstruction HTTP/1.1
> Host: localhost:8081
> User-Agent: curl/7.64.0
> Accept: */*
>
< HTTP/1.1 500 Internal Server Error
< content-length: 39
< content-type: text/plain
< date: Fri, 19 Jul 2019 17:33:54 GMT
<
* Connection #0 to host localhost left intact
Invalid request, please try again later⏎
```

Since that worked well, let's see how it works.

How it works...

`actix-web` uses an error trait to convert Rust errors into `HttpResponses`. This trait is automatically implemented for a range of default errors but only by responding with the default *Internal Server Error* message.

In *step 1* and *step 2*, we are setting up custom errors so that we can return messages that are relevant to what the user is currently doing (or trying to do). As with other errors (see `Chapter 5`, *Handling Errors and Other Results*), we are using enums to provide an umbrella to match error variations to. Each of the variants is augmented with an attribute that provides a corresponding error message with a format string—an ability provided by the `failure` crate (`https://crates.io/crates/failure`). The message here is a last-resort type message for a response code 500 (the default). This HTTP response code, along with the body of the error—such as an HTML page—can be customized by implementing the `actix_web::error::ResponseError` trait. Whichever `HttpResponse` is supplied using the `error_response()` function will be returned to the client.

> If you call the function yourself, then the `#[fail(display="...")]` message won't be attached. Always use Rust's `Result` enum to communicate errors to `actix_web`.

Step 3 defines the handler functions of the web service and, since it uses a JSON response, a struct for serializing the information. In this example, we are also using the arbitrary number 10 as a cutoff point for returning an error—using a Rust `Result` enum. This provides a framework-agnostic way to handle bad outcomes just as if we were working with plain Rust. The second route, `/underconstruction`, provides an insight into how `actix-web` routes can be implemented: as a closure. Since this immediately returns an error, we have to explicitly tell the compiler about the return types and that it's a `Result` enum that could either be `HttpResponse` or `WebError`. We then directly return the latter. *Step 4* shows the required dependencies and tells us we have to include the failure crate. In the last step, we are running the code and testing it by issuing `curl` requests and checking the logs on the server side. That's nothing too complex, right? If you want to go deeper, also check out the `actix-web` docs (`https://actix.rs/docs/errors/`).

Let's move on to the next recipe.

Rendering HTML templates

While JSON is a very human-readable format and easy to work with, many people still prefer a more interactive experience—such as websites. While this is not native to `actix-web`, some template engines provide seamless integration to minimize the calls required to assemble and output HTML. The major difference compared to simply delivering a static site is that template engines render variable output and Rust code into an augmented HTML page to produce content adapted to whatever the application's state is. In this recipe, we are taking a look at **Yet Another Rust Template Engine (Yarte)** (`https://crates.io/crates/yarte`) and its integration with `actix-web`.

Getting ready

Create a Rust binary project using `cargo new html-templates` and make sure that port `8081` is accessible from the localhost. After creating the project directory, you'll have to create some additional folders and files. The image files inside the static directory can be any image, as long as there is a Base64-encoded version of it available as a text file. Use an online service or the Base64 binary (`https://linux.die.net/man/1/base64` on Linux) to create your own (you'll have to change the names in the code accordingly) or use ours from the repository. The `.hbs` files will be filled (created) in this recipe:

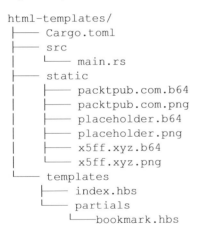

```
html-templates/
├──── Cargo.toml
├──── src
│      └──── main.rs
├──── static
│      ├──── packtpub.com.b64
│      ├──── packtpub.com.png
│      ├──── placeholder.b64
│      ├──── placeholder.png
│      ├──── x5ff.xyz.b64
│      └──── x5ff.xyz.png
└──── templates
       ├──── index.hbs
       └──── partials
              └──bookmark.hbs
```

Finally, open the entire directory with VS Code.

How to do it...

Create templated web pages in just a few steps:

1. First, let's add some code to `src/main.rs`. Replace the default snippet with the following (note: the Base64-encoded string in `PLACEHOLDER_IMG` is abbreviated here. Get the full Base64-encoded image at `https://blog.x5ff.xyz/other/placeholder.b64`):

```
#[macro_use]
extern crate actix_web;

use actix_web::{middleware, web, App, HttpServer, Responder};
use chrono::prelude::*;
use std::env;
use yarte::Template;

const PLACEHOLDER_IMG: &str =
    "iVBORw0KGgoAAAANS[...]s1NR+4AAAAASUVORK5CYII=";

#[derive(Template)]
#[template(path = "index.hbs")]
struct IndexViewModel {
    user: String,
    bookmarks: Vec<BookmarkViewModel>,
}

#[derive(Debug, Clone)]
struct BookmarkViewModel {
    timestamp: Date<Utc>,
    url: String,
    mime: String,
    base64_image: String,
}
```

After adjusting `src/main.rs`, add the required dependencies to `Cargo.toml`:

```
[dependencies]
actix-web = "1"
serde = "1"
serde_derive = "1"
env_logger = "0.6"
base64 = "0.10.1"
yarte = {version = "0", features=["with-actix-web"]}
chrono = "0.4"
```

2. After declaring the templates, we need to register a handler to serve them as well:

```
#[get("/{name}")]
pub fn index(name: web::Path<(String)>) -> impl Responder {
    let user_name = name.as_str().into();
```

First, let's add the bookmark data for the recognized user:

```
if &user_name == "Claus" {
    IndexViewModel {
        user: user_name,
        bookmarks: vec![
            BookmarkViewModel {
                timestamp: Utc.ymd(2019, 7, 20),
                url: "https://blog.x5ff.xyz".into(),
                mime: "image/png".into(),
                base64_image: std::fs::read_to_string
                ("static/x5ff.xyz.b64")
                    .unwrap_or(PLACEHOLDER_IMG.into()),
            },
            BookmarkViewModel {
                timestamp: Utc.ymd(2017, 9, 1),
                url: "https://microsoft.com".into(),
                mime: "image/png".into(),
                base64_image: std::fs::read_to_string
                ("static/microsoft.com.b64")
                    .unwrap_or(PLACEHOLDER_IMG.into()),
            },
            BookmarkViewModel {
                timestamp: Utc.ymd(2019, 2, 2),
                url: "https://www.packtpub.com/".into(),
                mime: "image/png".into(),
                base64_image: std::fs::read_to_string
                ("static/packtpub.com.b64")
                    .unwrap_or(PLACEHOLDER_IMG.into()),
            },
        ],
    }
```

For everyone else (unrecognized users), we can simply return an empty vector:

```
    } else {
        IndexViewModel {
            user: user_name,
            bookmarks: vec![],
        }
    }
}
```

Finally, let's start the server in the `main` function:

```
fn main() -> std::io::Result<()> {
    env::set_var("RUST_LOG", "actix_web=debug");
    env_logger::init();
    HttpServer::new(|| {
        App::new()
            .wrap(middleware::Logger::default())
            .service(web::scope("/bookmarks").service(index))
    })
    .bind("127.0.0.1:8081")?
    .run()
}
```

3. The code is ready, but we still lack templates. This is where we add some content to the `.hbs` files. First, let's add code to `templates/index.hbs`:

```
<!DOCTYPE html>
<html>
<head>
    <meta charset="UTF-8">
    <link
href="https://stackpath.bootstrapcdn.com/bootstrap/4.3.1/css/bootst
rap.min.css" rel="stylesheet" integrity="sha384-
ggOyR0iXCbMQv3Xipma34MD+dH/1fQ784/j6cY/iJTQUOhcWr7x9JvoRxT2MZw1T"
crossorigin="anonymous">
    <meta name="viewport" content="width=device-width, initial-
scale=1, shrink-to-fit=no">
</head>
```

After the head, we need an HTML body that marks up the data:

```
<body>
    <div class="container">
        <div class="row">
            <div class="col-lg-12 pb-3">
                <h1>Welcome {{ user }}.</h1>
                <h2 class="text-muted">Your bookmarks:</h2>
            </div>
        </div>

        {{#if bookmarks.is_empty() }}
        <div class="row">
            <div class="col-lg-12">
            No bookmarks :(
            </div>
        </div>
        {{~/if}}
        {{#each bookmarks}}
            <div class="row {{# if index % 2 == 1 }} bg-light text-
            dark {{/if }} mt-2 mb-2">
            {{> partials/bookmark }}
            </div>
        {{~/each}}
    </div>
</body>
</html>
```

4. We are calling a partial inside this last template, so let's add some code to it as well. Open `templates/partials/bookmark.hbs` and insert the following:

```
<div class="col-lg-2">
    <img class="rounded img-fluid p-1" src="data:{{ mime }};base64,
    {{ base64_image }}"> </div>
<div class="col-lg-10">
    <a href="{{ url }}">
        <h3>{{ url.replace("https://", "") }}</h3>
    </a>
    <i class="text-muted">Added {{ timestamp.format("%Y-%m-
    %d").to_string() }}</i>
</div>
```

5. It's time to try this out! Use `cargo run` to start the server logging output and open a browser window at `localhost:8081/bookmarks/Hans` as well as `localhost:8081/bookmarks/Claus` to see whether it works. Here is what `cargo run` shows after the browser window has been opened at the URLs:

```
$ cargo run
    Compiling html-templates v0.1.0 (Rust-Cookbook/Chapter08/html-
templates)
 Finished dev [unoptimized + debuginfo] target(s) in 2m 38s
     Running `target/debug/html-templates`
[2019-07-20T16:36:06Z INFO actix_web::middleware::logger]
127.0.0.1:50060 "GET /bookmarks/Claus HTTP/1.1" 200 425706 "-"
"Mozilla/5.0 (X11; Fedora; Linux x86_64) AppleWebKit/537.36 (KHTML,
like Gecko) Chrome/73.0.3683.86 Safari/537.36" 0.013246
[2019-07-20T16:37:34Z INFO actix_web::middleware::logger]
127.0.0.1:50798 "GET /bookmarks/Hans HTTP/1.1" 200 821 "-"
"Mozilla/5.0 (X11; Fedora; Linux x86_64) AppleWebKit/537.36 (KHTML,
like Gecko) Chrome/73.0.3683.86 Safari/537.36" 0.000730
```

The following are the results for an unrecognized user:

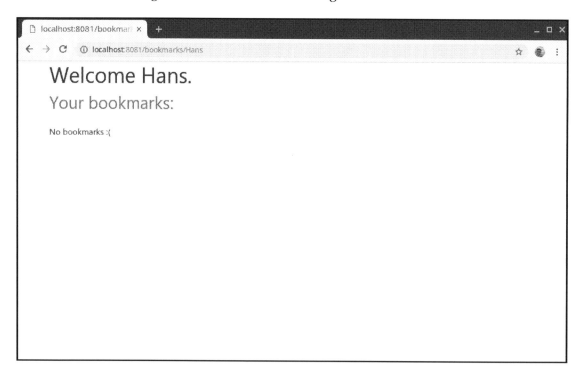

For a recognized user, the system returns the appropriate content:

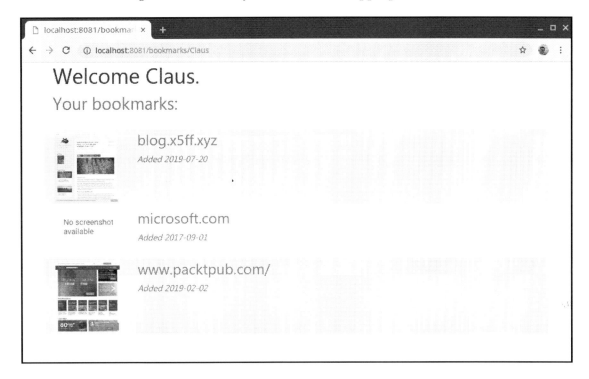

Let's find out why this works.

How it works...

In many languages, creating a template engine is somewhat like an introduction tutorial—which is probably where the name Yarte comes from. While the choices are many, `actix-web` provides examples with three other engines as well; we recommend checking them out in their GitHub repository (`https://github.com/actix/examples`). *Step 1* of this recipe already covers some of the important work: importing stuff and declaring the view models (as in the MVVM pattern: `https://blogs.msdn.microsoft.com/msgulfcommunity/2013/03/13/understanding-the-basics-of-mvvm-design-pattern/`). Yarte provides macro attributes that associate a particular model with a template file—and it automatically finds the `templates` folder. If that does not suit your project, they allow you to configure the framework accordingly. Find out more on their website (`https://yarte.netlify.com/`). We are using a nested model, where the inner struct does not need its own associated template.

In *step 2*, we are registering the handler function under the `/bookmarks` scope and the `/{name}` path, which leads to the URL: `/bookmarks/{name}`. `actix-web` is strict in checking the routes, so `/bookmarks/{name}/` is going to return an error (404). The handler function returns a small list of bookmarks for the name Claus but not for anyone else, which—in a more realistic scenario—would come out of a database. Regardless, we are using this hardcoded version, and we added the logger middleware so we can see what's going on. We are also using a constant for the placeholder image, which you can download at `https://blog.x5ff.xyz/other/placeholder.b64`.

The templates we are defining in *step 3* are the main difference between engines. Using the well-known `{{ rust-code }}` notation, we can augment regular HTML to generate more sophisticated output. There are loops of all kinds, conditionals, variables, and partials. Partials are important because they let you split the view parts into reusable components, which don't even have to be HTML/Yarte templates but can be any text.

The compilation process pulls in these templates, combining them with the types we declared earlier—with an important consequence. Currently, changing the template requires the `main.rs` file to be recompiled, reflect the changes, so using touch or similar to set the modified date of `src/main.rs` is recommended. After that, `cargo` behaves as if there was a change to `src/main.rs`.

Step 4 implements the partial that shows each bookmark, similarly to the index template in *step 3*. Only in *step 5* do we run and look at the results: a simple website showing the list of associated bookmarks for when a user is recognized (read: has data associated with the name) and when a user is not recognized. The minimal design is achieved by using the popular Bootstrap CSS framework (`https://getbootstrap.com`).

Now, let's move on to the next recipe.

Using an ORM to save data to a database

Opinions about object-relational mappers vary considerably: their use was strongly encouraged when SQL databases stored all of the World's data but they quickly fell out of favor when it was actually the whole World's data. Typically these frameworks provide a trade-off between ease of use, language integration, and scalability. While it's true that querying terabytes of data requires a fundamentally different approach, simple CRUD-type business applications work well with frameworks that do the heavy lifting for you and—most importantly—are somewhat independent of the actual database they connect to. Rust's macros come in very handy here—they allow the ORM framework to do these things largely at compile time, so it's memory-safe, type-safe, and fast. Let's see how it's done.

Getting ready

Create a Rust binary project using `cargo new orm` and make sure that port `8081` is accessible from the localhost. To access the services, get a program such as `curl` or Postman to execute `POST`, `GET`, and more type web requests, as well as a program to create and manage SQLite (`https://www.sqlite.org/index.html`) databases (for example, sqlitebrowser: `https://github.com/sqlitebrowser/sqlitebrowser`).

Using a SQLite database manager, create a new database, `bookmarks.sqlite`, in a folder, `db`. Then, add a table that follows this schema:

```
CREATE TABLE bookmarks(id TEXT PRIMARY KEY, url TEXT);
```

Next, we are going to use the `libsqlite3` library and headers in the project. On Linux, WSL, and macOS, install the appropriate packages from the package repository. On Ubuntu and the WSL, you can use something such as `apt-get install libsqlite3-dev`. For other distributions and macOS, please use your preferred package manager to install `libsqlite3` and its headers.

 Native Windows 10 users may have to download the `dll` binaries from `https://www.sqlite.org/download.html` and place them into the project directory. However, using Linux/macOS is highly recommended.

Finally, open the entire directory with VS Code.

How to do it...

Get your database queries running in just a few steps:

1. In `src/main.rs`, we are going to add the basic imports:

   ```
   #[macro_use]
   extern crate diesel;
   mod models;
   mod schema;

   use actix_web::{middleware, web, App, Error, HttpResponse,
   HttpServer};

   use std::env;

   use diesel::prelude::*;
   use diesel::sqlite::SqliteConnection;
   ```

```
use futures::Future;
use models::{Bookmark, NewBookmark};
use serde_derive::{Deserialize, Serialize};
```

2. Let's set up some more helper types and a constant for the connection string in `main.rs`:

```
// Helpers
const SQLITE_DB_URL: &str = "db/bookmarks.sqlite";

#[derive(Debug, Serialize, Deserialize)]
struct WebBookmark {
    url: String,
}

fn connect(db_url: &str) -> SqliteConnection {
    SqliteConnection::establish(&SQLITE_DB_URL)
      .expect(&format!("Error connecting to {}", db_url))
}
```

3. We are going to need some handlers as well, so let's add them to the file, starting with retrieving bookmarks by their IDs:

```
// Handlers
fn bookmarks_by_id(req_id: web::Path<(String)>) -> impl
 Future<Item = HttpResponse, Error = Error> {
    web::block(move || {
        use self::schema::bookmarks::dsl::*;

        let conn = connect(&SQLITE_DB_URL);
        bookmarks
            .filter(id.eq(req_id.as_str()))
            .limit(1)
            .load::<Bookmark>(&conn)
    })
    .then(|res| match res {
        Ok(obj) => Ok(HttpResponse::Ok().json(obj)),
        Err(_) => Ok(HttpResponse::InternalServerError().into()),
    })
}
```

To find out all IDs, we also want to have a handler that returns all bookmarks:

```
fn all_bookmarks() -> impl Future<Item = HttpResponse, Error =
Error> {
    web::block(move || {
        use self::schema::bookmarks::dsl::*;
```

```
        let conn = connect(&SQLITE_DB_URL);
        bookmarks.load::<Bookmark>(&conn)
    })
    .then(|res| match res {
        Ok(obj) => Ok(HttpResponse::Ok().json(obj)),
        Err(_) => Ok(HttpResponse::InternalServerError().into()),
    })
}
```

Next, let's see whether we can add some bookmarks:

```
fn bookmarks_add(
    bookmark: web::Json<WebBookmark>,
    ) -> impl Future<Item = HttpResponse, Error = Error> {
    web::block(move || {
        use self::schema::bookmarks::dsl::*;

        let conn = connect(&SQLITE_DB_URL);
        let new_id = format!("{}", uuid::Uuid::new_v4());
        let new_bookmark = NewBookmark {
            id: &new_id,
            url: &bookmark.url,
        };
        diesel::insert_into(bookmarks)
            .values(&new_bookmark)
            .execute(&conn)
            .map(|_| new_id)
    })
    .then(|res| match res {
        Ok(obj) => Ok(HttpResponse::Ok().json(obj)),
        Err(_) => Ok(HttpResponse::InternalServerError().into()),
    })
}
```

What's missing for almost full CRUD is the `delete` function:

```
fn bookmarks_delete(
    req_id: web::Path<(String)>,
    ) -> impl Future<Item = HttpResponse, Error = Error> {
    web::block(move || {
        use self::schema::bookmarks::dsl::*;

        let conn = connect(&SQLITE_DB_URL);
        diesel::delete(bookmarks.filter(id.eq(req_id.as_str())))
          .execute(&conn)
    })
    .then(|res| match res {
        Ok(obj) => Ok(HttpResponse::Ok().json(obj)),
```

```
            Err(_) => Ok(HttpResponse::InternalServerError().into()),
    })
}
```

Lastly, we tie them all together in the `main` function that starts the server and attaches these handlers:

```
fn main() -> std::io::Result<()> {
    env::set_var("RUST_LOG", "actix_web=debug");
    env_logger::init();
    HttpServer::new(move || {
        App::new().wrap(middleware::Logger::default()).service(
            web::scope("/api").service(
                web::scope("/bookmarks")
                    .service(web::resource("/all").route(web::get()
                    .to_async(all_bookmarks)))
                    .service(
                        web::resource("by-id/{id}").route(web
                        ::get().to_async(bookmarks_by_id)),
                    )
                    .service(
                        web::resource("/")
                            .data(web::JsonConfig::default())
                            .route(web::post().to_async
                            (bookmarks_add)),
                    )
                    .service(
                        web::resource("by-
                        id/{id}").route(web::delete()
                        .to_async(bookmarks_delete)),
                    ),
            ),
        )
    })
    .bind("127.0.0.1:8081")?
    .run()
}
```

4. So, where are the models? They are in their own file, `src/models.rs`. Create it and add the following content:

```
use crate::schema::bookmarks;
use serde_derive::Serialize;

#[derive(Debug, Clone, Insertable)]
#[table_name = "bookmarks"]
pub struct NewBookmark<'a> {
    pub id: &'a str,
```

```
        pub url: &'a str,
    }

    #[derive(Serialize, Queryable)]
    pub struct Bookmark {
        pub id: String,
        pub url: String,
    }
```

5. There is still another import that we have not yet created: `src/schema.rs`. Create that file as well with the following code:

```
    table! {
        bookmarks (id) {
            id -> Text,
            url -> Text,
        }
    }
```

6. As usual, we need to adapt `Cargo.toml` to download the dependencies:

```
[dependencies]
actix-web = "1"
serde = "1"
serde_derive = "1"
env_logger = "0.6"
diesel = {version = "1.4", features = ["sqlite"] }
uuid = { version = "0.7", features = ["serde", "v4"] }
futures = "0.1"
```

7. This should set everything up to run the web service with `cargo run` and observe the logging output (after the requests):

```
$ cargo run
    Finished dev [unoptimized + debuginfo] target(s) in 0.16s
     Running `target/debug/orm`
[2019-07-20T19:33:33Z INFO actix_web::middleware::logger]
127.0.0.1:54560 "GET /api/bookmarks/all HTTP/1.1" 200 2 "-"
"curl/7.64.0" 0.004737
[2019-07-20T19:33:52Z INFO actix_web::middleware::logger]
127.0.0.1:54722 "POST /api/bookmarks/ HTTP/1.1" 200 1 "-"
"curl/7.64.0" 0.017087
[2019-07-20T19:33:55Z INFO actix_web::middleware::logger]
127.0.0.1:54750 "GET /api/bookmarks/all HTTP/1.1" 200 77 "-"
"curl/7.64.0" 0.002248
[2019-07-20T19:34:11Z INFO actix_web::middleware::logger]
127.0.0.1:54890 "GET /api/bookmarks/by-
id/9b2a4264-3db6-4c50-88f1-807b20b5841e HTTP/1.1" 200 77 "-"
```

```
"curl/7.64.0" 0.003298
[2019-07-20T19:34:23Z INFO actix_web::middleware::logger]
127.0.0.1:54992 "DELETE /api/bookmarks/by-
id/9b2a4264-3db6-4c50-88f1-807b20b5841e HTTP/1.1" 200 1 "-"
"curl/7.64.0" 0.017980
[2019-07-20T19:34:27Z INFO actix_web::middleware::logger]
127.0.0.1:55030 "GET /api/bookmarks/all HTTP/1.1" 200 2 "-"
"curl/7.64.0" 0.000972
```

We can interact with the web service with `curl`, and here are the expected calls and output:

```
$ curl localhost:8081/api/bookmarks/all
[]⏎
$ curl -d "{\"url\":\"https://blog.x5ff.xyz\"}" -H "Content-Type:
application/json" localhost:8081/api/bookmarks/
"9b2a4264-3db6-4c50-88f1-807b20b5841e"⏎
$ curl localhost:8081/api/bookmarks/all
[{"id":"9b2a4264-3db6-4c50-88f1-807b20b5841e","url":"https://blog.x
5ff.xyz"}]⏎
$ curl localhost:8081/api/bookmarks/by-
id/9b2a4264-3db6-4c50-88f1-807b20b5841e
[{"id":"9b2a4264-3db6-4c50-88f1-807b20b5841e","url":"https://blog.x
5ff.xyz"}]⏎
$ curl -X "DELETE" localhost:8081/api/bookmarks/by-
id/9b2a4264-3db6-4c50-88f1-807b20b5841e
1⏎
$ curl localhost:8081/api/bookmarks/all
[]⏎
```

Let's see how this works.

How it works...

`diesel-rs` is Rust's most well-known database connection framework and provides a fast, type-safe, and easy-to-use experience with mapping database tables. This is, again, possible thanks to the power of macros, which enable the creation of zero-cost abstractions at compile time. However, there is a trade-off for a few things and it's important to learn how to use the framework.

SQLite does not have a very rigid type system. This is why we get away with using a generic type for strings called text. Other databases may have more nuanced types. Check out SQLite3 types (`https://www.sqlite.org/datatype3.html`) for more information.

In *step 1*, we are preparing the imports—nothing too interesting but you'll notice the declaration of `models.rs` and `schema.rs`. One step further, in *step 2* we see a connection string (actually just a file path) constant that we'll use to connect to the database in the connect function. Additionally, we are making a JSON web service so we create the transfer object type, `WebBookmark`. We are creating these handlers in *step 3*, one for adding, retrieving (all and by ID), and deleting a bookmark entity.

All of these handlers return a `Future` object and run asynchronously. While handlers always run asynchronously (they are actors), these return the type explicitly since they use a synchronous section to connect to the database—`diesel-rs` is not thread-safe right now. This synchronous section is implemented using a `web::block` statement that returns a result that is mapped onto `Future` and an appropriate `HttpResponse` type. In the case of the `bookmarks_add` handler, it returns the newly created ID as a JSON string, while `bookmarks_delete` returns the number of rows affected by the delete. All of the handlers return a 500 in the case of an error.

> If you want to know how to use connection pooling and properly manage those, check out the `actix-web` example for diesel (https://github.com/ actix/examples/tree/master/diesel). It uses Rust's r2d2 crate (https:/ /github.com/sfackler/r2d2).

Step 3 also registers these functions with their respective routes. The `by-id` route accepts two different methods (`GET` and `DELETE`) and, thanks to the asynchronous nature of the `bookmarks_add` function, the data has to be declared to explicitly declare `JsonConfig` to automatically parse JSON input. All of the registrations are done using the `to_async` method as well, which makes the attribute method impossible to use.

Only in *step 4* and *step 5* are we creating `diesel-rs`-specific code. `models.rs` is a file that contains all of our models, and both of them are abstractions for a row in the table, but the `NewBookmark` type takes care of inserting new objects (the `table_name` and `Insertable` attributes attach it to the DSL), while `Bookmark` is returned to the user (diesel's `Queryable` and Serde's `Serialize` enable that). `schema.rs` contains a macro call declaring the table name (`bookmarks`), its primary key (`id`), and its columns (`id` and `url`) along with their datatypes as understood by diesel. There are many more types; check out diesel's in-depth explanation of `table!` (https://diesel.rs/guides/schema-in-depth/).

Step 6 shows how `diesel-rs` works with different databases; all of them are features that have to be declared. Additionally, diesel has a CLI for database migrations and other fun stuff, so check out its getting started guide (https://diesel.rs/guides/getting-started/) for more information. In *step 7*, we finally get to run the web service and insert/query some of the data.

However, let's move on to do more advanced stuff with the ORM framework.

Running advanced queries using an ORM

One major downside of ORMs is typically the complexity of doing things that are outside the happy path. SQL—the language relational databases use—is standardized but its types are not always compatible with what the application is doing. In this recipe, we'll explore a few ways to run more advanced queries in Rust's `diesel-rs`.

Getting ready

Create a Rust binary project using `cargo new advanced-orm` and make sure that port `8081` is accessible from the localhost. To access the services, get a program such as `curl` or Postman to execute `POST`, `GET`, and more type web requests, as well as a program to create and manage SQLite (`https://www.sqlite.org/index.html`) databases (for example, sqlitebrowser: `https://github.com/sqlitebrowser/sqlitebrowser`).

You can reuse and expand the code from the previous recipe (*Using an ORM to save data to a database*) if you ensure you update the database tables.

Using a SQLite database manager, create a new database, `bookmarks.sqlite`, in a folder, `db`. Then, add tables that follow these schemas:

```
CREATE TABLE bookmarks(id TEXT PRIMARY KEY, url TEXT, added TEXT);
CREATE TABLE comments(id TEXT PRIMARY KEY, bookmark_id TEXT, comment TEXT);
```

Next, we are going to use the `libsqlite3` library and headers in the project. On Linux, WSL, and macOS, install the appropriate packages from the package repository. On Ubuntu and the WSL, you can use something like `apt-get install libsqlite3-dev`.

Native Windows 10 users may have to download the `dll` binaries from `https://www.sqlite.org/download.html` and place them into the project directory. However, using Linux/macOS is highly recommended.

Finally, open the entire directory with VS Code.

How to do it...

Use templates in just a few steps:

1. `src/main.rs` is going to contain the handlers and main function. Let's start by adding some helper types and functions:

```
#[macro_use]
extern crate diesel;
mod models;
mod schema;

use actix_web::{middleware, web, App, Error, HttpResponse,
HttpServer};

use std::env;

use crate::schema::{date, julianday};
use chrono::prelude::*;
use diesel::prelude::*;
use diesel::sqlite::SqliteConnection;
use futures::Future;
use serde_derive::{Deserialize, Serialize};
```

After some imports, let's set up the helpers:

```
// Helpers
const SQLITE_DB_URL: &str = "db/bookmarks.sqlite";

#[derive(Debug, Serialize, Deserialize)]
struct WebBookmark {
    url: String,
    comment: Option<String>,
}

#[derive(Debug, Serialize, Deserialize)]
struct WebBookmarkResponse {
    id: String,
    added: String,
    url: String,
    comment: Option<String>,
}

fn connect(db_url: &str) -> SqliteConnection {
SqliteConnection::establish(&SQLITE_DB_URL).expect(&format!("Error
connecting to {}", db_url))
}
```

2. A new handler will fetch bookmarks with a Julian date. Let's add it along with some other, well-known handlers:

```
fn bookmarks_as_julian_by_date(
    at: web::Path<(String)>,
    ) -> impl Future<Item = HttpResponse, Error = Error> {
    web::block(move || {
        use self::schema::bookmarks::dsl::*;
        let conn = connect(&SQLITE_DB_URL);
        bookmarks
            .select((id, url, julianday(added)))
            .filter(date(added).eq(at.as_str()))
            .load::<models::JulianBookmark>(&conn)
    })
    .then(|res| match res {
        Ok(obj) => Ok(HttpResponse::Ok().json(obj)),
        Err(_) => Ok(HttpResponse::InternalServerError().into()),
    })
}
```

Adding bookmarks is one of these well-known handlers:

```
fn bookmarks_add(
    bookmark: web::Json<WebBookmark>,
    ) -> impl Future<Item = HttpResponse,
    Error = Error> {
    web::block(move || {
        use self::schema::bookmarks::dsl::*;
        use self::schema::comments::dsl::*;

        let conn = connect(&SQLITE_DB_URL);
        let new_id = format!("{}", uuid::Uuid::new_v4());
        let now = Utc::now().to_rfc3339();
        let new_bookmark = models::NewBookmark {
            id: &new_id,
            url: &bookmark.url,
            added: &now,
        };

        if let Some(comment_) = &bookmark.comment {
            let new_comment_id = format!("{}",
            uuid::Uuid::new_v4());
            let new_comment = models::NewComment {
                comment_id: &new_comment_id,
                bookmark_id: &new_id,
                comment: &comment_,
            };
            let _ = diesel::insert_into(comments)
```

```
                        .values(&new_comment)
                        .execute(&conn);
            }

        diesel::insert_into(bookmarks)
            .values(&new_bookmark)
            .execute(&conn)
            .map(|_| new_id)
    })
    .then(|res| match res {
        Ok(obj) => Ok(HttpResponse::Ok().json(obj)),
        Err(_) => Ok(HttpResponse::InternalServerError().into()),
    })
}
```

Next, deleting bookmarks is an important handler:

```
fn bookmarks_delete(
    req_id: web::Path<(String)>,
    ) -> impl Future<Item = HttpResponse, Error = Error> {
    web::block(move || {
        use self::schema::bookmarks::dsl::*;
        use self::schema::comments::dsl::*;

        let conn = connect(&SQLITE_DB_URL);
        diesel::delete(bookmarks.filter(id.eq(req_id.as_str())))
            .execute(&conn)
            .and_then(|_| {
                diesel::delete(comments.filter(bookmark_id.eq
                (req_id.as_str()))).execute(&conn)
            })
    })
    .then(|res| match res {
        Ok(obj) => Ok(HttpResponse::Ok().json(obj)),
        Err(_) => Ok(HttpResponse::InternalServerError().into()),
    })
}
```

3. Now that we can add and delete comments and bookmarks, all we have to do is
    fetch them all at once:

```
fn all_bookmarks() -> impl Future<Item = HttpResponse, Error =
Error> {
    web::block(move || {
        use self::schema::bookmarks::dsl::*;
        use self::schema::comments::dsl::*;

        let conn = connect(&SQLITE_DB_URL);
```

```
        bookmarks
            .left_outer_join(comments)
            .load::<(models::Bookmark, Option<models::Comment>)>
            (&conn)
            .map(
                |bookmarks_: Vec<(models::Bookmark,
                Option<models::Comment>)>| {
                    let responses: Vec<WebBookmarkResponse> =
                    bookmarks_
                        .into_iter()
                        .map(|(b, c)| WebBookmarkResponse {
                            id: b.id,
                            url: b.url,
                            added: b.added,
                            comment: c.map(|c| c.comment),
                        })
                        .collect();
                    responses
                },
            )
    })
    .then(|res| match res {
        Ok(obj) => Ok(HttpResponse::Ok().json(obj)),
        Err(_) => Ok(HttpResponse::InternalServerError().into()),
    })
}
```

Lastly, we wire everything up in `main()`:

```
fn main() -> std::io::Result<()> {
    env::set_var("RUST_LOG", "actix_web=debug");
    env_logger::init();
    HttpServer::new(move || {
        App::new().wrap(middleware::Logger::default()).service(
            web::scope("/api").service(
                web::scope("/bookmarks")
                    .service(web::resource("/all").route
                    (web::get().to_async(all_bookmarks)))
                    .service(
                        web::resource("added_on/{at}/julian")
                            .route(web::get().to_async
                            (bookmarks_as_julian_by_date)),
                    )
                    .service(
                        web::resource("/")
                            .data(web::JsonConfig::default())
                            .route(web::post().to_async
                            (bookmarks_add)),
```

```
                    )
                    .service(
                        web::resource("by-
                        id/{id}").route(web::delete().
                        to_async(bookmarks_delete)),
                    ),
                ),
            )
        })
        .bind("127.0.0.1:8081")?
        .run()
}
```

4. To save comments alongside bookmarks, we had to expand the schema and models as well. Create (or edit) `src/schema.rs` with the following content:

```
use diesel::sql_types::Text;
joinable!(comments -> bookmarks (bookmark_id));
allow_tables_to_appear_in_same_query!(comments, bookmarks);

sql_function! {
    fn julianday(t: Text) -> Float;
}
sql_function! {
    fn date(t: Text) -> Text;
}

table! {
    bookmarks (id) {
        id -> Text,
        url -> Text,
        added -> Text,
    }
}

table! {
    comments (comment_id) {
        comment_id -> Text,
        bookmark_id -> Text,
        comment -> Text,
    }
}
```

5. Next, create or update `src/models.rs` to create the Rust representation of these types:

```
use crate::schema::{bookmarks, comments};
use serde_derive::Serialize;
```

```
#[derive(Debug, Clone, Insertable)]
#[table_name = "bookmarks"]
pub struct NewBookmark<'a> {
    pub id: &'a str,
    pub url: &'a str,
    pub added: &'a str,
}


#[derive(Debug, Serialize, Queryable)]
pub struct Bookmark {
    pub id: String,
    pub url: String,
    pub added: String,
}


#[derive(Serialize, Queryable)]
pub struct JulianBookmark {
    pub id: String,
    pub url: String,
    pub julian: f32,
}


#[derive(Debug, Serialize, Queryable)]
pub struct Comment {
    pub bookmark_id: String,
    pub comment_id: String,
    pub comment: String,
}


#[derive(Debug, Clone, Insertable)]
#[table_name = "comments"]
pub struct NewComment<'a> {
    pub bookmark_id: &'a str,
    pub comment_id: &'a str,
    pub comment: &'a str,
}
```

6. To import the dependencies, we also have to adapt `Cargo.toml`:

```
[dependencies]
actix-web = "1"
serde = "1"
serde_derive = "1"
env_logger = "0.6"
diesel = {version = "1.4", features = ["sqlite"] }
uuid = { version = "0.7", features = ["serde", "v4"] }
futures = "0.1"
chrono = "0.4"
```

7. To finish this recipe, let's see how everything works together with `cargo run` and `curl`. The requests should respond in line with the following logging output:

```
$ curl http://localhost:8081/api/bookmarks/all
[]
$ curl -d "{\"url\":\"https://blog.x5ff.xyz\"}" -H "Content-Type:
application/json" localhost:8081/api/bookmarks/
"db5538f4-e2f9-4170-bc38-02af42e6ef59"
$ curl -d "{\"url\":\"https://www.packtpub.com\", \"comment\":
\"Great books\"}" -H "Content-Type:
  application/json" localhost:8081/api/bookmarks/
"5648b8c3-635e-4d55-9592-d6dfab59b32d"
$ curl http://localhost:8081/api/bookmarks/all
[{
    "id": "db5538f4-e2f9-4170-bc38-02af42e6ef59",
    "added": "2019-07-23T10:32:51.020749289+00:00",
    "url": "https://blog.x5ff.xyz",
    "comment": null
  },
  {
    "id": "5648b8c3-635e-4d55-9592-d6dfab59b32d",
    "added": "2019-07-23T10:32:59.899292263+00:00",
    "url": "https://www.packtpub.com",
    "comment": "Great books"
  }]
$ curl
http://localhost:8081/api/bookmarks/added_on/2019-07-23/julian
[{
    "id": "db5538f4-e2f9-4170-bc38-02af42e6ef59",
    "url": "https://blog.x5ff.xyz",
    "julian": 2458688.0
  },
  {
    "id": "5648b8c3-635e-4d55-9592-d6dfab59b32d",
    "url": "https://www.packtpub.com",
    "julian": 2458688.0
  }]
```

Here are the server logs generated by the requests, printed to the Terminal that `cargo run` runs in:

```
$ cargo run
   Compiling advanced-orm v0.1.0 (Rust-Cookbook/Chapter08/advanced-
orm)
 Finished dev [unoptimized + debuginfo] target(s) in 4.75s
 Running `target/debug/advanced-orm`
[2019-07-23T10:32:36Z INFO actix_web::middleware::logger]
127.0.0.1:39962 "GET /api/bookmarks/all HTTP/1.1" 200 2 "-"
"curl/7.64.0" 0.004323
[2019-07-23T10:32:51Z INFO actix_web::middleware::logger]
127.0.0.1:40094 "POST /api/bookmarks/ HTTP/1.1" 200 38 "-"
"curl/7.64.0" 0.018222
[2019-07-23T10:32:59Z INFO actix_web::middleware::logger]
127.0.0.1:40172 "POST /api/bookmarks/ HTTP/1.1" 200 38 "-"
"curl/7.64.0" 0.025890
[2019-07-23T10:33:06Z INFO actix_web::middleware::logger]
127.0.0.1:40226 "GET /api/bookmarks/all HTTP/1.1" 200 287 "-"
"curl/7.64.0" 0.001803
[2019-07-23T10:34:18Z INFO actix_web::middleware::logger]
127.0.0.1:40844 "GET /api/bookmarks/added_on/2019-07-23/julian
HTTP/1.1" 200 194 "-" "curl/7.64.0" 0.001653
```

Behind the scenes, a lot is going on. Let's find out what.

How it works...

Working with `diesel-rs` requires a good understanding of how it works internally to achieve the desired results. Check out the previous recipe (*Using an ORM to save data to a database*) for some details on the basics. In this recipe, we are diving straight into the more advanced stuff.

After some basic setup in *step 1*, *step 2* creates a new handler that fetches all bookmarks added on a particular day and returns the date as a Julian date (https://en.wikipedia.org/wiki/Julian_day). The calculation is done using one of SQLite's few scalar functions: `juliandate()` (https://www.sqlite.org/lang_datefunc.html). So, how did we get the function into Rust? *Step 4* shows the `diesel-rs` way: by using a `sql_function!` macro (https://docs.diesel.rs/diesel/macro.sql_function.html) that maps the data types and output appropriately. Since we are mapping a pre-existing function here, there are no further steps required (this should work the same for stored procedures).

Another aspect that *step 2* covers is inserting into and deleting from multiple tables, which is easy thanks to SQLite's disabled referential integrity constraint (`https://www.w3resource.com/sql/joins/joining-tables-through-referential-integrity.php`). If this constraint is enforced, take a look at the `diesel-rs` transactions (`https://docs.diesel.rs/diesel/connection/trait.Connection.html#method.transaction`). *Step 3* goes on to show how to retrieve this data—using a left outer join. Left joins take every row from the left side (`bookmarks` if the join looks as follows: `bookmarks LEFT JOIN comments`) and try to match it to rows in the table on the right, which means we get every bookmark regardless of whether they have comments or not. To map this result set, we have to provide a corresponding data type to parse to, which `diesel-rs` expects to be `(Bookmark, Option<Comment>)`. Since the `left_join()` call does not mention which columns to join on, how does the framework know? Again, in *step 4*, we declare the two tables as `joinable` via two macros: `joinable` (`https://docs.diesel.rs/diesel/macro.joinable.html`) and `allow_tables_to_appear_in_same_query` (`https://docs.diesel.rs/diesel/macro.allow_tables_to_appear_in_same_query.html`). After the results are fetched, we map them to a `Serializable` combined type to hide this implementation detail from the user.

Only in *step 4* and *step 5* do we take care of mapping out the database tables and rows for diesel—nothing too surprising here. The `Queryable` attribute is important for `diesel-rs` to map tuples to types—regardless of the actual table. For more ad hoc queries, we could work with tuples directly as well. *Step 6* takes care of the dependencies.

Step 7 runs the server and avid readers will have noticed one thing: compilation takes longer than usual. We suspect that `diesel-rs` is doing a lot of work behind the scenes, creating type-safe code to keep the dynamic runtime overhead low. However, this may significantly factor into bigger projects, but once compiled, the types help to avoid errors and make the service work smoothly.

We formatted the `curl` output to make it more readable and the output works just as expected. `serde` provides consistent serialization and deserialization of JSON objects; thus, the `comment` field is optional on input but is rendered as `null` on output.

 While `diesel-rs` tries to abstract many database operations, it uses a `sql_query` interface (`https://docs.diesel.rs/diesel/fn.sql_query.html`) to work with other SQL statements as well. However, more complex group by aggregations are not yet supported—even in the raw SQL interface—which is unfortunate. You can follow the progress on GitHub (`https://github.com/diesel-rs/diesel/issues/210`).

Now that we know more about running queries with `diesel-rs`, let's move on to the next recipe.

Authentication on the web

Running web services safely on public interfaces is itself challenge and a lot of things need to be taken care of. While many details fall within the job description of a security engineer, developers should adhere to at least a minimum set of best practices so they rightfully earn the trust of their users. At the start, there is transport encryption (TLS), which is something we did not include in any recipes in this chapter since reverse proxies and load balancers provide amazing and simple integration for this (and let's encrypt: `https://letsencrypt.org/` provides free certificates). This chapter focuses on using the `actix-web` middleware infrastructure to authenticate requests via JWT (`https://jwt.io/`) at the application layer.

Getting ready

Create a Rust binary project using `cargo new authentication` and make sure that port `8081` is accessible from the localhost. To access the services, get a program such as `curl` or Postman to execute `POST`, `GET`, and more type web requests.

Finally, open the entire directory with VS Code.

How to do it...

Authenticate your users in just a few steps:

1. In `src/main.rs`, we start by declaring the required imports:

```
#[macro_use]
extern crate actix_web;
mod middlewares;
use actix_web::{http, middleware, web, App, HttpResponse,
HttpServer, Responder};
use jsonwebtoken::{encode, Header};
use middlewares::Claims;
use serde_derive::{Deserialize, Serialize};
use std::env;
```

2. With that out of the way, we can take care of the more relevant bits. Let's declare a few basics for authentication and a handler that we want to access:

```
const PASSWORD: &str = "swordfish";
pub const TOKEN_SECRET: &str = "0fd2af6f";

#[derive(Debug, Serialize, Deserialize)]
struct Login {
    password: String,
}

#[get("/secret")]
fn authed() -> impl Responder {
    format!("Congrats, you are authenticated")
}
```

3. Next, we need a handler to log users in and create the token if they provide the expected password, as well as the `main()` function to set everything up:

```
fn login(login: web::Json<Login>) -> HttpResponse {
    // TODO: have a proper security concept
    if &login.password == PASSWORD {
        let claims = Claims {
            user_id: "1".into(),
        };
        encode(&Header::default(), &claims, TOKEN_SECRET.as_ref())
            .map(|token| {
                HttpResponse::Ok()
                    .header(http::header::AUTHORIZATION, format!
                    ("Bearer {}", token))
                    .finish()
            })
            .unwrap_or(HttpResponse::InternalServerError().into())
    } else {
        HttpResponse::Unauthorized().into()
    }
}

fn main() -> std::io::Result<()> {
    env::set_var("RUST_LOG", "actix_web=debug");
    env_logger::init();
    HttpServer::new(|| {
        App::new()
            .wrap(middleware::Logger::default())
            .wrap(middlewares::JwtLogin)
            .service(authed)
.service(web::resource("/login").route(web::post().to(login)))
    })
```

```
        .bind("127.0.0.1:8081")?
        .run()
}
```

4. The `wrap()` call in the `main()` function already gives away some details—we are
   going to need middleware to take care of authentication. Let's create a new
   file, `src/middlewares.rs`, with the following code:

```rust
use actix_service::{Service, Transform};
use actix_web::dev::{ServiceRequest, ServiceResponse};
use actix_web::{http, Error, HttpResponse};
use futures::future::{ok, Either, FutureResult};
use futures::Poll;
use jsonwebtoken::{decode, Validation};
use serde_derive::{Deserialize, Serialize};

#[derive(Debug, Serialize, Deserialize)]
pub struct Claims {
    pub user_id: String,
}

pub struct JwtLogin;

impl<S, B> Transform<S> for JwtLogin
where
    S: Service<Request = ServiceRequest, Response =
ServiceResponse<B>, Error = Error>,
    S::Future: 'static,
{
    type Request = ServiceRequest;
    type Response = ServiceResponse<B>;
    type Error = Error;
    type InitError = ();
    type Transform = JwtLoginMiddleware<S>;
    type Future = FutureResult<Self::Transform, Self::InitError>;

    fn new_transform(&self, service: S) -> Self::Future {
        ok(JwtLoginMiddleware { service })
    }
}
```

5. In the code in *step 4*, we see another struct that needs implementation:
   `JwtLoginMiddleware`. Let's add it to `src/middlewares.rs`:

```rust
pub struct JwtLoginMiddleware<S> {
    service: S,
}
```

```
impl<S, B> Service for JwtLoginMiddleware<S>
where
    S: Service<Request = ServiceRequest, Response =
    ServiceResponse<B>, Error = Error>,
    S::Future: 'static,
{
    type Request = ServiceRequest;
    type Response = ServiceResponse<B>;
    type Error = Error;
    type Future = Either<S::Future, FutureResult<Self::Response,
    Self::Error>>;

    fn poll_ready(&mut self) -> Poll<(), Self::Error> {
        self.service.poll_ready()
    }
```

The most important code can be found in the call function implementation where
the request is passed through to apply the middleware (and authenticate the
token):

```
fn call(&mut self, req: ServiceRequest) -> Self::Future {
    if req.path() == "/login" {
        Either::A(self.service.call(req))
    } else {
        if let Some(header_value) =
        req.headers().get(http::header::AUTHORIZATION) {
            let token = header_value.to_str().unwrap().
            replace("Bearer", "");
            let mut validation = Validation::default();
            validation.validate_exp = false; // our logins don't
            // expire
            if let Ok(_) =
                decode::<Claims>(&token.trim(),
                crate::TOKEN_SECRET.as_ref(), &validation)
            {
                Either::A(self.service.call(req))
            } else {
                Either::B(ok(
                    req.into_response(HttpResponse::Unauthorized()
                    .finish().into_body())
                ))
            }
        } else {
            Either::B(ok(
                req.into_response(HttpResponse::Unauthorized().
                finish().into_body())
            ))
        }
    }
```

```
        }
    }
}
```

6. Before we can run the server, we also have to update `Cargo.toml` with the current dependencies:

```
[dependencies]
actix-web = "1"
serde = "1"
serde_derive = "1"
env_logger = "0.6"
jsonwebtoken = "6"
futures = "0.1"
actix-service = "0.4"
```

7. Exciting—let's try it out! Start the server with `cargo run` and issue some `curl` requests:

```
$ cargo run
    Compiling authentication v0.1.0 (Rust-
Cookbook/Chapter08/authentication)
    Finished dev [unoptimized + debuginfo] target(s) in 6.07s
     Running `target/debug/authentication`
[2019-07-22T21:28:07Z INFO actix_web::middleware::logger]
127.0.0.1:33280 "POST /login HTTP/1.1" 401 0 "-" "curl/7.64.0"
0.009627
[2019-07-22T21:28:13Z INFO actix_web::middleware::logger]
127.0.0.1:33334 "POST /login HTTP/1.1" 200 0 "-" "curl/7.64.0"
0.009191
[2019-07-22T21:28:21Z INFO actix_web::middleware::logger]
127.0.0.1:33404 "GET /secret HTTP/1.1" 200 31 "-" "curl/7.64.0"
0.000784
```

The following is the `curl` output for each request. First, the unauthorized request:

```
$ curl -v localhost:8081/secret
* Trying ::1...
* TCP_NODELAY set
* connect to ::1 port 8081 failed: Connection refused
* Trying 127.0.0.1...
* TCP_NODELAY set
* Connected to localhost (127.0.0.1) port 8081 (#0)
> GET /secret HTTP/1.1
> Host: localhost:8081
> User-Agent: curl/7.64.0
> Accept: */*
>
```

```
< HTTP/1.1 401 Unauthorized
< content-length: 0
< date: Mon, 22 Jul 2019 21:27:48 GMT
<
* Connection #0 to host localhost left intact
```

Next, we try to log in using an invalid password:

```
$ curl -d "{\"password\":\"a-good-guess\"}" -H "Content-Type:
application/json"
  http://localhost:8081/login -v
* Trying ::1...
* TCP_NODELAY set
* connect to ::1 port 8081 failed: Connection refused
* Trying 127.0.0.1...
* TCP_NODELAY set
* Connected to localhost (127.0.0.1) port 8081 (#0)
> POST /login HTTP/1.1
> Host: localhost:8081
> User-Agent: curl/7.64.0
> Accept: */*
> Content-Type: application/json
> Content-Length: 27
>
* upload completely sent off: 27 out of 27 bytes
< HTTP/1.1 401 Unauthorized
< content-length: 0
< date: Mon, 22 Jul 2019 21:28:07 GMT
<
* Connection #0 to host localhost left intact
```

Then, we use the real password and receive a token back:

```
$ curl -d "{\"password\":\"swordfish\"}" -H "Content-Type:
application/json"
  http://localhost:8081/login -v
* Trying ::1...
* TCP_NODELAY set
* connect to ::1 port 8081 failed: Connection refused
* Trying 127.0.0.1...
* TCP_NODELAY set
* Connected to localhost (127.0.0.1) port 8081 (#0)
> POST /login HTTP/1.1
> Host: localhost:8081
> User-Agent: curl/7.64.0
> Accept: */*
> Content-Type: application/json
> Content-Length: 24
```

```
>
* upload completely sent off: 24 out of 24 bytes
< HTTP/1.1 200 OK
< content-length: 0
< authorization: Bearer
eyJ0eXAiOiJKV1QiLCJhbGciOiJIUzI1NiJ9.eyJ1c2VyX2lkIjoiMSJ9.V_Po0UCGZ
qNmbXw0hYozeFLsNpjTZeSh8wcyELavx-c
< date: Mon, 22 Jul 2019 21:28:13 GMT
<
* Connection #0 to host localhost left intact
```

With this token in the `authorization` **header** (`https://developer.mozilla.
org/en-US/docs/Web/HTTP/Headers/Authorization`)**, we can then access the
secret resource:**

```
$ curl -H "authorization: Bearer
eyJ0eXAiOiJKV1QiLCJhbGciOiJIUzI1NiJ9.eyJ1c2VyX2lkIjoiMSJ9.V_Po0UCGZ
qNmbXw0hYozeFLsNpjTZeSh8wcyELavx-
  c" http://localhost:8081/secret -v
* Trying ::1...
* TCP_NODELAY set
* connect to ::1 port 8081 failed: Connection refused
* Trying 127.0.0.1...
* TCP_NODELAY set
* Connected to localhost (127.0.0.1) port 8081 (#0)
> GET /secret HTTP/1.1
> Host: localhost:8081
> User-Agent: curl/7.64.0
> Accept: */*
> authorization: Bearer
eyJ0eXAiOiJKV1QiLCJhbGciOiJIUzI1NiJ9.eyJ1c2VyX2lkIjoiMSJ9.V_Po0UCGZ
qNmbXw0hYozeFLsNpjTZeSh8wcyELavx-c
>
< HTTP/1.1 200 OK
< content-length: 31
< content-type: text/plain; charset=utf-8
< date: Mon, 22 Jul 2019 21:28:21 GMT
<
* Connection #0 to host localhost left intact
Congrats, you are authenticated⏻
```

Let's pull back the curtain and see how it works.

How it works...

JWTs are a great way to provide authentication combined with authorization in a web application. As demonstrated on the official website, a JWT consists of three parts:

- The header, providing meta-information about the token
- Its payload, which is where the information is sent (JSON-serialized)
- A signature to guarantee that the token wasn't changed in transport

These parts are Base64-encoded and joined with . to form a single string. This string is put into the `authorization` header of an HTTP request (`https://developer.mozilla.org/en-US/docs/Web/HTTP/Headers/Authorization`). One important remark is that TLS is mandatory for this kind of authentication since the headers as well as everything else are sent in plaintext—everyone would be able to see the token.

The payload can contain anything you wish to carry back and forth as user information. However, there are special fields as well: `iss`, `sub`, and `exp`. `iss` provides the issuer's credentials (in whichever way), `sub` is the subject, and `exp` is the expiration timestamp. This is because JWTs can be used to authenticate via federation, that is, third-party services, as well. For this implementation, we are using a crate called `jsonwebtoken` (`https://github.com/Keats/jsonwebtoken`).

In *step 1*, we are simply setting up the imports—nothing special here. Only *step 2* provides something interesting: a hardcoded password (**BAD** security practice, but good enough for demonstration) as well as a hardcoded secret (also **BAD**). Real applications can use a secret store for the secret (for example, Azure Key Vault: `https://azure.microsoft.com/en-in/services/key-vault/`) and a hash stored in a database for the password. In the same step, we are also declaring the input data structure for logging in—we care only about the password—as well as the handler for the path/secret, which should only work once we are logged in.

The following step creates the handler for logging in: if the password matches, the handler creates a new token containing the payload data (a struct called `Claims`) and the HMAC (`https://searchsecurity.techtarget.com/definition/Hash-based-Message-Authentication-Code-HMAC`) algorithm (HS256 by default) used to sign the token, and returns it. The handlers are then registered with the `App` instance, together with the new JWT authentication middleware implemented in the following steps.

Step 4 and *step 5* take care of creating the middleware for validating JWT tokens. *Step 4* contains the Claims type mentioned previously; however, the rest of the code is a largely required boilerplate if the request and response types remains default. If we wanted to retrieve user information to pass to the handlers, we would look into defining custom requests. Only in *step 5* are we implementing the important part: the call() function. This function is called before every request is processed and decides whether to continue or stop propagating it. Obviously, the /login route is the exception and will always be passed on the handlers.

Every other route has to contain a header field called authorization and a type called Bearer, along with the token, for example, (truncated) authorization: Bearer eyJ0eXAiOiJKV1QiLCJhbGciOiJ[...]8wcyELavx-c. The call() function extracts the token and tries to decode it with its secret. If that works, the call is forwarded to the handler; if not, the user is clearly not authorized to access the resource—the same happens if there is no authorization header at all. jsonwebtoken validates the exp field by default as well (our Claims type does not have this), which is what we are turning off for this example. For brevity, we used unwrap() when parsing the header's bytes into a string. However, this can crash the thread if unknown bytes are encountered.

The return types here are imported from the futures library (https:// docs.rs/futures/) and provide the Either type (https://docs.rs/ futures/0.1.28/futures/future/enum.Either.html) as well as the ok() function (https://docs.rs/futures/0.1.28/futures/future/fn.ok. html). Check their documentation to learn more.

Step 6 simply declares the additional dependencies, and in *step 7*, we get to run the server! Check the curl requests first—can you see what's off? Requests without authorization are blocked *before* logging happens. Additionally, we have marked the important bits in bold.

This concludes this chapter. We hope you enjoyed the web programming recipes. The next chapter covers something a lot closer to the metal: systems programming.

Systems Programming Made Easy

9

Rust was originally envisioned as a systems programming language in the same way as C (and maybe C++). Although its appeal led to significant growth outside this field (somewhat like C/C++), there are still many features that significantly facilitate working on low-level projects. We suspect that the novelty aspect (as well as the powerful compiler, error messages, and community) led to very interesting projects in that space—such as operating systems. One of them is intermezzOS (`https://intermezzos.github.io/`), an operating system for learning programming (in Rust); another is Redox OS (`https://www.redox-os.org/`), a microkernel effort in pure Rust. However, it doesn't stop there—the Rust embedded working group has compiled a list of resources and highlight projects on their GitHub (`https://github.com/rust-embedded/awesome-embedded-rust`).

 Linux is the most widely adopted operating system for embedded devices, but we tried to show the principles without requiring you to run Linux. In order to fully implement, for example, an I2C device driver, macOS and Windows users can use virtual machines with Hyper-V (`https://docs.microsoft.com/en-us/virtualization/hyper-v-on-windows/`), VirtualBox (`https://www.virtualbox.org/`), or Parallels (`https://www.parallels.com/`), or rent a machine on the cloud (`https://azure.microsoft.com/en-us/`). With the exception of the first recipe, the recipes in this chapter work across OSes.

This list is truly awesome, and we are aiming to get you to a place where you can start building embedded drivers and cross-compile them to various CPU architectures. With that in mind, this chapter covers the following topics:

- Cross-compiling Rust
- Implementing device drivers
- Reading from these drivers

Cross-compiling Rust

Surprisingly, one of the more challenging aspects of implementing low-level projects is cross-compilation. Thanks to its LLVM underpinnings, `rustc` comes with a lot of toolchains for different CPU architectures. However, cross-compiling an application means that its (native) dependencies have to be available for this CPU architecture as well. This is challenging for small projects since it requires lots of management for versions across architectures and grows more and more complex with every added requirement. This is why there have been several tools that relate to this issue. In this recipe, we will explore at a few tools and learn how to use them.

Getting ready

This recipe is highly platform-specific; at the time of writing, cross-compiling Rust on platforms other than Linux is tricky. On macOS and Windows, you can use virtual machines with Hyper-V (`https://docs.microsoft.com/en-us/virtualization/hyper-v-on-windows/`), VirtualBox (`https://www.virtualbox.org/`), or Parallels (`https://www.parallels.com/`), or rent a machine from your favorite cloud provider (`https://azure.microsoft.com/en-us/`).

> The **Windows Subsystem for Linux (WSL)** on Windows 10 doesn't support Docker at the time of writing. There might be ways around this limitation, but we will leave the required tinkering to our readers. If you find a solution, be sure to share it on our GitHub repository (`https://github.com/PacktPublishing/Rust-Programming-Cookbook`).

Then, install Docker (`https://docs.docker.com/install/`) and make sure you can run Docker without `sudo` (`https://docs.docker.com/install/linux/linux-postinstall/`) to proceed.

How to do it...

With Docker available, take these steps to cross-compile to many targets:

1. Create a project using `cargo new cross-compile` for a binary executable and open the folder using VS Code.
2. Open `src/main.rs` and replace the default with the following:

```
#[cfg(target_arch = "x86")]
const ARCH: &str = "x86";
```

```
#[cfg(target_arch = "x86_64")]
const ARCH: &str = "x64";

#[cfg(target_arch = "mips")]
const ARCH: &str = "mips";

#[cfg(target_arch = "powerpc")]
const ARCH: &str = "powerpc";

#[cfg(target_arch = "powerpc64")]
const ARCH: &str = "powerpc64";

#[cfg(target_arch = "arm")]
const ARCH: &str = "ARM";

#[cfg(target_arch = "aarch64")]
const ARCH: &str = "ARM64";

fn main() {
    println!("Hello, world!");
    println!("Compiled for {}", ARCH);
}
```

3. Use `cargo run` to see if it works and what architecture you are on:

```
$ cargo run
   Compiling cross-compile v0.1.0 (Rust-Cookbook/Chapter09/cross-
   compile)
    Finished dev [unoptimized + debuginfo] target(s) in 0.25s
     Running `target/debug/cross-compile`
Hello, world!
Compiled for x64
```

4. Let's do some cross-compilation. First, install a tool called cross using `cargo install cross`:

```
$ cargo install cross
    Updating crates.io index
  Installing cross v0.1.14
   Compiling libc v0.2.60
   Compiling cc v1.0.38
   Compiling cfg-if v0.1.9
   Compiling rustc-demangle v0.1.15
   Compiling semver-parser v0.7.0
   Compiling rustc-serialize v0.3.24
   Compiling cross v0.1.14
   Compiling lazy_static v0.2.11
   Compiling semver v0.9.0
```

```
Compiling semver v0.6.0
Compiling rustc_version v0.2.3
Compiling backtrace-sys v0.1.31
Compiling toml v0.2.1
Compiling backtrace v0.3.33
Compiling error-chain v0.7.2
 Finished release [optimized] target(s) in 15.64s
Replacing ~/.cargo/bin/cross
 Replaced package `cross v0.1.14` with `cross v0.1.14`
 (executable `cross`)
$ cross --version
cross 0.1.14
cargo 1.36.0 (c4fcfb725 2019-05-15)
```

5. As mentioned in the rust-cross (https://github.com/rust-embedded/cross) repository, start the Docker daemon to run a cross-build for ARMv7:

```
$ sudo systemctl start docker
$ cross build --target armv7-unknown-linux-gnueabihf -v
+ "rustup" "target" "list"
+ "cargo" "fetch" "--manifest-path" "/home/cm/workspace/Mine/Rust-
Cookbook/Chapter09/cross-compile/Cargo.toml"
+ "rustc" "--print" "sysroot"
+ "docker" "run" "--userns" "host" "--rm" "--user" "1000:1000" "-e"
"CARGO_HOME=/cargo" "-e" "CARGO_TARGET_DIR=/target" "-e" "USER=cm"
"-e" "XARGO_HOME=/xargo" "-v" "/home/cm/.xargo:/xargo" "-v"
"/home/cm/.cargo:/cargo" "-v" "/home/cm/workspace/Mine/Rust-
Cookbook/Chapter09/cross-compile:/project:ro" "-v"
"/home/cm/.rustup/toolchains/stable-x86_64-unknown-linux-
gnu:/rust:ro" "-v" "/home/cm/workspace/Mine/Rust-
Cookbook/Chapter09/cross-compile/target:/target" "-w" "/project" "-
it" "japaric/armv7-unknown-linux-gnueabihf:v0.1.14" "sh" "-c"
"PATH=$PATH:/rust/bin \"cargo\" \"build\" \"--target\" \"armv7-
unknown-linux-gnueabihf\" \"-v\""
    Compiling cross-compile v0.1.0 (/project)
       Running `rustc --edition=2018 --crate-name cross_compile
src/main.rs --color always --crate-type bin --emit=dep-info,link -C
debuginfo=2 -C metadata=a41129d8970184cc -C extra-filename=-
a41129d8970184cc --out-dir /target/armv7-unknown-linux-
gnueabihf/debug/deps --target armv7-unknown-linux-gnueabihf -C
linker=arm-linux-gnueabihf-gcc -C incremental=/target/armv7-
unknown-linux-gnueabihf/debug/incremental -L
dependency=/target/armv7-unknown-linux-gnueabihf/debug/deps -L
dependency=/target/debug/deps`
     Finished dev [unoptimized + debuginfo] target(s) in 0.25s
```

6. If you have a Raspberry Pi 2 (or later), you can then run the binary there:

```
$ scp target/armv7-unknown-linux-gnueabihf/debug/cross-compile
alarm@10.0.0.171:~
cross-compile 100% 2410KB 10.5MB/s 00:00
$ ssh alarm@10.0.0.171
Welcome to Arch Linux ARM

        Website: http://archlinuxarm.org
          Forum: http://archlinuxarm.org/forum
            IRC: #archlinux-arm on irc.Freenode.net
Last login: Sun Jul 28 09:07:57 2019 from 10.0.0.46
$ ./cross-compile
Hello, world!
Compiled for ARM
```

So, how does `rust-cross` compile the code? Why use Docker? Let's look at how it works.

How it works...

In this recipe, we are creating a simple binary (*step 1* and *step 2*) with a conditional compilation that matches the target architecture in order to see if it worked. *Step 3* should show your architecture (typically `x64` or `x86_64`); we install the cross-compilation toolkit in *step 4* to try and get it to run on a Raspberry Pi 2 and above (*step 5*). After compiling the binary, we transfer it to the device (ARM binaries won't work on `x86_64` instruction sets) for execution (*step 6*).

QEMU, a popular virtualization framework, also supports emulating ARM instructions, so a device is not strictly required. Check out their wiki (`https://wiki.qemu.org/Documentation/Platforms/ARM`) to learn more.

Keep reading if you are interested in more details about cross-compiling an application. If not, feel free to move on to the next recipe.

There's more...

Cross-compilation is a very specific process where all of the following have to fit together:

- CPU instruction set, that is, assembler instructions
- Compatible libraries for linking (for example, the standard library)
- Binary layout
- Compatible toolchains (compiler, linker)

Thanks to LLVM's architecture and the GNU compiler collection, we do not need to worry much about the CPU instruction set since it is largely provided by default, which is also the reason why it's tricky to run on Windows. As we have seen in many recipes in Chapter 7, *Integrating Rust with Other Languages*, Windows and macOS use different toolchains, which makes compiling for other CPU instruction sets trickier. Our feeling is that it's easier to work smoothly in a virtualized environment these days instead of setting everything up locally.

> If you are using Fedora or any other SELinux-enabled distribution, the cross-build may fail with a permission error. Right now, the solution is to disable SELinux (sudo setenforce 0), but a fix is underway (https://github.com/rust-embedded/cross/issues/112).

Considering the target toolchain, rustup allows us to quickly install other targets (rustup target add armv7-unknown-linux-gnueabihf), yet some other aspects (for example, the C standard library (https://www.gnu.org/software/libc/)) still need to be natively installed. Along with the number of targets available, managing the number of native libraries is going to be a full-time job (we are disregarding the various library versions entirely here).

In an effort to contain these dependencies, versions, and more, rust-cross (https://github.com/rust-embedded/cross#usage) (and others (https://github.com/dlecan/rust-crosscompiler-arm)), use Docker containers that come prepared with a basic set of libraries. Typically, these containers can be customized (https://github.com/rust-embedded/cross#custom-docker-images) to add any certificates, configurations, libraries, and more you need for your use case.

Equipped with this knowledge, we can move on to the next recipe.

Creating I2C device drivers

Communicating with devices in Linux happens at different levels. The most basic layer of drivers is the kernel module. Among other things, these modules have unrestricted access to the operating system and, if necessary, provide access to users via interfaces such as block devices. This is where the I2C (`https://learn.sparkfun.com/tutorials/i2c/all`) driver offers the as `/dev/i2c-1` bus (for example) that you can write to and read from. Using Rust, we can use this interface to create a driver for a sensor device that is connected to that bus. Let's see how that works.

How to do it...

Device drivers can be implemented in a few steps:

1. Create a binary project: `cargo new i2cdevice-drivers`
2. Open the folder in VS Code and add some code to the `src/main.rs` file to:

```
mod sensor;

use sensor::{Bmx42Device, RawI2CDeviceMock, Thermometer};
use std::thread::sleep;
use std::time::Duration;

fn main() {
    let mut device = Bmx42Device::new(RawI2CDeviceMock::
     new("/dev/i2c-1".into(), 0x5f)).unwrap();
    let pause = Duration::from_secs(1);
    loop {
        println!("Current temperature {} °C",
         device.temp_celsius().unwrap());
        sleep(pause);
    }
}
```

3. Next, we are going to implement the actual sensor driver. Create a file named `src/sensor.rs` to implement all aspects of the sensor driver. Let's start by setting up a few basics:

```rust
use std::io;
use rand::prelude::*;

pub trait Thermometer {
    fn temp_celsius(&mut self) -> Result<f32>;
}

type Result<T> = std::result::Result<T, io::Error>;
```

4. Now, we add a mock device that represents the bus system:

```rust
#[allow(dead_code)]
pub struct RawI2CDeviceMock {
    path: String,
    device_id: u8,
}


impl RawI2CDeviceMock {
    pub fn new(path: String, device_id: u8) -> RawI2CDeviceMock {
        RawI2CDeviceMock {
            path: path,
            device_id: device_id,
        }
    }

    pub fn read(&self, register: u8) -> Result<u8> {
        let register = register as usize;
        if register == Register::Calib0 as usize {
            Ok(1_u8)
        } else { // register is the data register
            Ok(random::<u8>())
        }
    }
}
```

5. Next, we implement the actual sensor code that the user sees:

```
enum Register {
    Calib0 = 0x00,
    Data = 0x01,
}

pub struct Bmx42Device {
    raw: RawI2CDeviceMock,
    calibration: u8,
}

impl Bmx42Device {
    pub fn new(device: RawI2CDeviceMock) -> Result<Bmx42Device> {
        let calib = device.read(Register::Calib0 as u8)?;
        Ok(Bmx42Device {
            raw: device,
            calibration: calib
        })
    }
}
```

6. In order to encapsulate the behavior of the sensor into a proper function, let's implement the `Thermometer` trait we created at the top of `sensor.rs`. The way raw data is transformed into a usable temperature is typically stated in a manual or tech specification:

```
impl Thermometer for Bmx42Device {
    fn temp_celsius(&mut self) -> Result<f32> {
        let raw_temp = self.raw.read(Register::Data as u8)?;
        Ok(((raw_temp as i8) << (self.calibration as i8)) as f32 /
        10.0)
    }
}
```

7. We also need to adapt the `Cargo.toml` configuration to add the random number generator crate:

```
[dependencies]
rand = "0.5"
```

8. As usual, we want to see the program in action. Use `cargo run` to see it printing what we pretend to be the temperature (stop it by pressing *Ctrl + C*):

```
$ cargo run
    Compiling libc v0.2.60
    Compiling rand_core v0.4.0
    Compiling rand_core v0.3.1
    Compiling rand v0.5.6
    Compiling i2cdevice-drivers v0.1.0 (Rust-
    Cookbook/Chapter09/i2cdevice-drivers)
     Finished dev [unoptimized + debuginfo] target(s) in 2.95s
      Running `target/debug/i2cdevice-drivers`
Current temperature -9.4 °C
Current temperature 0.8 °C
Current temperature -1.2 °C
Current temperature 4 °C
Current temperature -3 °C
Current temperature 0.4 °C
Current temperature 5.4 °C
Current temperature 11.6 °C
Current temperature -5.8 °C
Current temperature 0.6 °C
^C
```

After implementing this, you are probably curious about why and how this works. Let's see.

How it works...

In this recipe, we showed how to implement a very simple device driver that is available on a bus such as the I2C (https://learn.sparkfun.com/tutorials/i2c/all). Since the I2C is a comparatively sophisticated bus (which makes implementing drivers simpler), a driver implements a protocol for reading and write operations to assumed registers and encapsulates them in a nice API. In this recipe, we did not actually use an I2C bus crate to provide the `struct` device, since it would impact OS compatibility.

In *step 2*, we create the main loop to read from the sensor in a very simplistic way (check the *Efficiently reading hardware sensors* recipe), using sleep to control reading speed. In a typical fashion, we instantiate the driver by creating the block device abstraction using the *nix path (`/dev/i2c-1`) and the device's hardware address (defined by the manufacturer).

In *step 3*, we add some constructs to make our lives easier and better structured: the `Thermometer` trait is good practice for bundling capabilities together if there are more devices or features on that sensor. Abstracting `Result` is a common strategy for reducing code verbosity.

Only in *step 4* do we create a mock for the bus, providing a read and write function for single bytes. Since we are not actually reading from or writing to a bus, these functions read random numbers and write to nowhere. For an idea of how this is done in real life (for example, reading several bytes at once), check out the real `i2cdev` crate (`https://github.com/rust-embedded/rust-i2cdev`). So far, we have only gotten it to work on Linux, however.

Step 5 creates the abstraction API. Whenever we implement a driver from scratch, we are communicating with the device by writing specific binary commands into predefined registers. This could be to change the power state of the device, to change the sampling rate, or to ask for a particular measurement (if the device has multiple sensors and triggers hardware processes on the actual device). After this write operation, we can then read a specified data registry (all of the addresses and values can be found in the device's specification) to transform the value into something usable (such as °C). This involves things such as shifting bits around, reading several calibration registries, and multiplying with overflows. Any such process varies from sensor to sensor. For a real-life example, check out the `bmp085` device driver (`https://github.com/celaus/rust-bmp085`), which shows a real-world driver implementation in Rust, and watch a talk on the driver at the following URL: `https://www.youtube.com/watch?v=VMaKQ8_y_6s`.

The following step then shows implementing and getting the actual temperature from the device and creating a usable number from the random number the raw device mock provides. This should be a simplification of what is typically done with raw values to get them into a usable form.

In the last step, we then see how it works and verify that the temperatures is generally spread nicely in realistic values, although with a frightening rate of change.

Let's move on and find out how we can read these sensor values more efficiently than with a pure loop.

Efficiently reading hardware sensors

Creating efficient I/O-based applications is tricky—they have to provide exclusive access to a resource as quickly as possible and as often as required. It's a resource scheduling problem. The basis of solving this type of problem is to handle and queue requests, as with reading a sensor value.

How to do it...

You can use I/O loops to read things efficiently in a few steps:

1. Create a binary project: `cargo new reading-hardware`.
2. Open the folder in VS Code and create a `src/sensor.rs` file to add the code from the *Creating I2C device drivers* recipe:

```
use std::io;
use rand::prelude::*;

type Result<T> = std::result::Result<T, io::Error>;

pub trait Thermometer {
    fn temp_celsius(&mut self) -> Result<f32>;
}

enum Register {
    Calib0 = 0x00,
    Data = 0x01,
}
```

3. Typically, a raw device abstraction is provided by the hardware protocol drivers used. In our case, we mock up such a type:

```
#[allow(dead_code)]
pub struct RawI2CDeviceMock {
    path: String,
    device_id: u8,
}

impl RawI2CDeviceMock {
    pub fn new(path: String, device_id: u8) -> RawI2CDeviceMock {
        RawI2CDeviceMock {
            path: path,
            device_id: device_id,
        }
```

```
        }

        pub fn read(&self, register: u8) -> Result<u8> {
            let register = register as usize;
            if register == Register::Calib0 as usize {
                Ok(1_u8)
            } else { // register is the data register
                Ok(random::<u8>())
            }
        }
    }
}
```

4. For proper encapsulation, it's a good idea to create a `struct` that wraps the raw device:

```
pub struct Bmx42Device {
    raw: RawI2CDeviceMock,
    calibration: u8,
}

impl Bmx42Device {
    pub fn new(device: RawI2CDeviceMock) -> Result<Bmx42Device> {
        let calib = device.read(Register::Calib0 as u8)?;
        Ok(Bmx42Device {
            raw: device,
            calibration: calib
        })
    }
}
```

5. The following is the implementation of the `Thermometer` trait:

```
impl Thermometer for Bmx42Device {
    fn temp_celsius(&mut self) -> Result<f32> {
        let raw_temp = self.raw.read(Register::Data as u8)?;
        // converts the result into something usable; from the
        // specification
        Ok(((raw_temp as i8) << (self.calibration as i8)) as f32 /
        10.0)
    }
}
```

6. Now open `src/main.rs` and replace the default with something more interesting. Let's start with imports and helper functions:

```
mod sensor;
use tokio::prelude::*;
use tokio::timer::Interval;
```

```
use sensor::{Bmx42Device, RawI2CDeviceMock, Thermometer};
use std::time::{Duration, UNIX_EPOCH, SystemTime, Instant};
use std::thread;

use std::sync::mpsc::channel;

fn current_timestamp_ms() -> u64 {
    SystemTime::now().duration_since(UNIX_EPOCH).unwrap().as_secs()
}

#[derive(Debug)]
struct Reading {
    timestamp: u64,
    value: f32
}
```

7. Next, we'll add the actual event loop and the `main` function:

```
fn main() {
    let mut device = Bmx42Device::new(RawI2CDeviceMock
     ::new("/dev/i2c-1".into(), 0x5f)).unwrap();

    let (sx, rx) = channel();

    thread::spawn(move || {
        while let Ok(reading) = rx.recv() {

            // or batch and save/send to somewhere
            println!("{:?}", reading);
        }
    });
    let task = Interval::new(Instant::now(), Duration
     ::from_secs(1))
        .take(5)
        .for_each(move |_instant| {
            let sx = sx.clone();
            let temp = device.temp_celsius().unwrap();
            let _ = sx.send(Reading {
                timestamp: current_timestamp_ms(),
                value: temp
            });
            Ok(())
        })
        .map_err(|e| panic!("interval errored; err={:?}", e));

    tokio::run(task);
}
```

8. For this to work, we should add some dependencies to `Cargo.toml`:

```
[dependencies]
tokio = "0.1"
tokio-timer = "0.2"
rand = "0.5"
```

9. In order to finish up the recipe, we also want to see it run and print out some mock readings:

```
$ cargo run
    Finished dev [unoptimized + debuginfo] target(s) in 0.04s
     Running `target/debug/reading-hardware`
Reading { timestamp: 1564762734, value: -2.6 }
Reading { timestamp: 1564762735, value: 6.6 }
Reading { timestamp: 1564762736, value: -3.8 }
Reading { timestamp: 1564762737, value: 11.2 }
Reading { timestamp: 1564762738, value: 2.4 }
```

Great! Let's see how this works.

How it works...

Instead of the naive busy waiting loop we created in the *Creating I2C device drivers* recipe, we now use a `tokio-rs` stream (effectively an asynchronous iterator) of events on which we can register a handler. Let's see how this more efficient structure is implemented.

First, in *step 2*, we recreate the sensor code from the *Creating I2C device drivers* recipe in order to have a sensor to use. In short, the code simulates an I2C-connected temperature sensor with a random number generator to show how a bus-connected device driver operates.

In *step 3*, we are preparing to use the driver to read a value and send it to a worker thread using a channel. Therefore, we create a `Reading` struct that saves a sensor reading at a certain timestamp. Only in *step 4* do we create the `tokio-rs` task runner and a stream. This stream is a construct that represents an iterator over asynchronous events that need to be handled. Each event corresponds to a timed interval every second, starting now (`Instant::now()`), and since we don't want to run forever in this recipe, we limit the number of events to five (`.take(5)`)—just as we would with any other iterator. `tokio::run()` takes this stream and starts executing the events on its event loop and thread pool, and blocks while there is something to execute.

In concurrent applications, the usage of something like `std::thread::sleep` is considered an anti-pattern. Why? Because it prevents the entire thread from doing *anything* while it is sleeping. In fact, the thread pauses and the OS's CPU scheduler context-switches to do some other stuff. Only after *at least* the specified time does the scheduler rotate the thread back into active mode to continue working. Drivers sometimes require some waiting time (several milliseconds to do the measuring), and `sleep` is typically used. Since devices can only be accessed from a single thread, `sleep()` is appropriate here.

The `for_each` closure implements the handler for each event and receives an `Instant` instance as a parameter. Inside the closure, we read from the sensor and send it through a channel (`https://doc.rust-lang.org/std/sync/mpsc/`) to a receiving thread that we created earlier—a pattern that we saw in `Chapter 4`, *Fearless Concurrency*. While we could process the data right away in the handler, pushing it into a queue for processing enables us to create batches and minimize the stream delay. This is especially important when the potential required time to finish processing is unknown, very large (that is, it comprises web requests or other moving parts), or requires extensive error handling (such as exponential backoff (`https://docs.microsoft.com/en-us/azure/architecture/patterns/retry`)). This will not only separate concerns and make maintenance easier, it also allows us to execute the reading operation more precisely. To visualize this, let's look at the big picture for *step 4*:

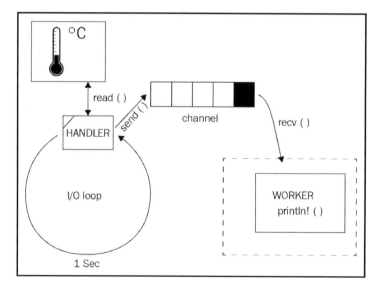

In *step 5*, we add the required dependencies, and *step 6* shows the output—take note of the timestamp to see it really does fire every second and the stream is processed in the order they appear.

This concludes our in-depth journey into device drivers; if this was your first foray into the field, you have now learned about de-coupling reading sensor data from processing it; how device drivers are built in the first place; and, once ready, how to get them onto the desired device. In the next chapter, we return to a higher level of abstraction and work on more practical recipes.

Getting Practical with Rust **10**

Even after nine chapters of Rust, we are still missing the parts that make applications pleasant to use. Many crates within Rust's ecosystem provide important functions across different domains and, depending on the application type, you might need several additional crates. In this chapter, we will look at various parts within Rust's standard library and public crate repository to make our application development faster, easier, and—in general—more productive. Although this chapter has a strong focus on command-line applications, we think that many of the recipes are just as applicable for other types, such as web servers or shared utility libraries. You can look forward to learning how to create usable Rust programs that integrate well with the OS and behave in ways that users know and expect. On top of that, we added a recipe for machine learning enthusiasts who are looking to use Rust for their work.

Here is the full list of what we will cover:

- Random number generation
- File I/O
- Dynamic JSON
- Regular expressions
- Filesystem access
- Command-line arguments
- Piping input and output
- Web requests
- Using state-of-the-art machine learning libraries
- Logging
- Starting subprocesses

Generating random numbers

Random number generation is a fundamental technology that we use daily—encryption, simulation, approximation, testing, data selection, and more. Each of these applications has its own requirements for the random number generator (https://xkcd.com/221/). While encryption needs a generator that is as close to true randomness (https://www.random.org/) as possible, simulation, testing, and data selection may need to have reproducible samples drawn from a certain distribution.

 Due to printing constraints we had to replace the original emoji with characters and numbers. Check out the GitHub repository for this book for the full version.

Since there is no random generator in Rust's standard library, the rand crate is the way to go for many projects. Let's see how we can use it.

How to do it...

We can obtain randomness in just a few steps:

1. Open a Terminal to create a new project using `cargo new random-numbers --lib`. Use VS Code to open the project directory.

2. First, we need to add the rand crate as a dependency in Cargo.toml. Open it to add the following:

```
[dependencies]
rand = {version = "0.7", features = ["small_rng"]}
rand_distr = "0.2"
rand_pcg = "0.2"
```

3. Since we are exploring how to use the rand library, we are going to add to the test module and implement three tests. Let's start by replacing the default content in src/lib.rs with some required imports:

```
#[cfg(test)]
mod tests {
    use rand::prelude::*;
    use rand::SeedableRng;
    use rand_distr::{Bernoulli, Distribution, Normal, Uniform};
}
```

4. Right underneath the imports (inside the `mod tests` scope), we are going to add the first test to check how **Random Number Generators** (**RNGs**) and **Pseudo-Random Number Generators** (**PRNGs**) work. To have predictable random numbers, we make every generator based on the first, which uses an array literal for initialization:

```
#[test]
fn test_rngs() {
    let mut rng: StdRng = SeedableRng::from_seed([42;32]);
    assert_eq!(rng.gen::<u8>(), 152);

    let mut small_rng = SmallRng::from_rng(&mut rng).unwrap();
    assert_eq!(small_rng.gen::<u8>(), 174);

    let mut pcg = rand_pcg::Pcg32::from_rng(&mut rng).unwrap();
    assert_eq!(pcg.gen::<u8>(), 135);
}
```

5. Having seen regular (P)RNGs, we can move on to something more sophisticated. How about using these RNGs to operate on sequences? Let's add this test that uses PRNGs to do a shuffle and pick results:

```
#[test]
fn test_sequences() {
    let mut rng: StdRng = SeedableRng::from_seed([42;32]);

    let emoji = "ABCDEF".chars();
    let chosen_one = emoji.clone().choose(&mut rng).unwrap();
    assert_eq!(chosen_one, 'B');

    let chosen = emoji.choose_multiple(&mut rng, 3);
    assert_eq!(chosen, ['F', 'B', 'E']);

    let mut three_wise_monkeys = vec!['1', '2', '3'];
    three_wise_monkeys.shuffle(&mut rng);
    three_wise_monkeys.shuffle(&mut rng);
    assert_eq!(three_wise_monkeys, ['1', '3', '2']);

    let mut three_wise_monkeys = vec!['1', '2', '3'];
    let partial = three_wise_monkeys.partial_shuffle(&mut rng, 2);
    assert_eq!(partial.0, ['3', '2']);
}
```

6. As we stated in this recipe's introduction, RNGs can follow a distribution. Now, let's add another test to the tests module to draw random numbers that follow a distribution using the `rand` crate:

```
const SAMPLES: usize = 10_000;

#[test]
fn test_distributions() {
    let mut rng: StdRng = SeedableRng::from_seed([42;32]);

    let uniform = Uniform::new_inclusive(1, 100);
    let total_uniform: u32 = uniform.sample_iter(&mut rng)
                                     .take(SAMPLES).sum();
    assert!((50.0 - (total_uniform as f32 / (
            SAMPLES as f32)).round()).abs() <= 2.0);

    let bernoulli = Bernoulli::new(0.8).unwrap();
    let total_bernoulli: usize = bernoulli
        .sample_iter(&mut rng)
        .take(SAMPLES)
        .filter(|s| *s)
        .count();

    assert_eq!(
        ((total_bernoulli as f32 / SAMPLES as f32) * 10.0)
            .round()
            .trunc(),
        8.0
    );

    let normal = Normal::new(2.0, 0.5).unwrap();
    let total_normal: f32 = normal.sample_iter(&mut rng)
                                   .take(SAMPLES).sum();
    assert_eq!((total_normal / (SAMPLES as f32)).round(), 2.0);
}
```

7. Lastly, we can run the tests to see whether the test outputs positive results:

```
$ cargo test
  Compiling random-numbers v0.1.0 (Rust-Cookbook/Chapter10/random-
numbers)
    Finished dev [unoptimized + debuginfo] target(s) in 0.56s
      Running target/debug/deps/random_numbers-df3e1bbb371b7353

running 3 tests
test tests::test_sequences ... ok
test tests::test_rngs ... ok
test tests::test_distributions ... ok
```

```
test result: ok. 3 passed; 0 failed; 0 ignored; 0 measured; 0
filtered out

    Doc-tests random-numbers

running 0 tests

test result: ok. 0 passed; 0 failed; 0 ignored; 0 measured; 0
filtered out
```

Let's see how it's done behind the scenes.

How it works...

The rand crate has lived through several major version revisions since 2018 and several things have changed. In particular, the crate is now organized differently (https://rust-random.github.io/book/guide-gen.html), with several companion crates that contain implementations for lesser-used parts.

This is why, in *step 2*, we don't only import a single crate, even though they all share a single GitHub repository (https://github.com/rust-random/rand). The reason for this split was presumably to be compatible with the different requirements across the field.

RNGs represent—in short—a numeric sequence that is determined on the fly based on its predecessor. What is the first number though? It's called the **seed** and can be some literal (for reproducibility in tests) or as close to true randomness as possible (when not testing).

Popular seeds include seconds since 1 Jan 1970, entropy by the OS, user input, and more. The less predictable it is, the better.

In *step 3*, we set up the remaining code with some imports that we are using right away in *step 4*. There, we get into using different types of RNGs (https://rust-random.github.io/book/guide-rngs.html). The first is rand crate's StdRng, which is an abstraction over (as of this writing) the ChaCha PRNG (https://docs.rs/rand/0.7.0/rand/rngs/struct.StdRng.html), chosen for efficiency and cryptographic security. The second algorithm is SmallRng (https://docs.rs/rand/0.7.0/rand/rngs/struct.SmallRng.html), a PRNG chosen by the rand team that has great throughput and resource efficiency. However, since it is fairly easy to predict, the use cases have to be chosen carefully. The last algorithm (Pcg32) is a pick from the list of available PRNGs (https://rust-random.github.io/book/guide-rngs.html), which comes as part of a different crate.

In *step* 5, we work with sequences and choose from or shuffle through them. Functions include partial shuffling (that is, picking a random subset) and full, in-place shuffles, as well as a random choice of one or more elements in a list. Note that the traits for these operations are implemented in a way that they are agnostic of the actual random number generator used. This provides a very flexible and easy-to-use API.

Only in *step* 6 do we get to random numbers that follow distributions. These can be very important to do more scientific work such as initializing vectors, simulation, or games.

The default of most RNGs is the uniform distribution where each number is equally likely. Actually drawing samples from the distribution requires an initialized RNG, which is provided in the form of a seeded StdRng. The assert statement (empirically) shows that it truly is a uniform distribution: after 10,000 draws, the numbers average almost exactly in the range's middle (+/-2).

The following distribution is the Bernoulli distribution (http://mathworld.wolfram.com/BernoulliDistribution.html). It can be initialized with a chance of success (0.8, in this case)—but, in general, it's easy to imagine as a series of coin flips. In fact, this distribution is used for generating Boolean values (which is why we can filter by the generated value).

Lastly, in this test, we are creating a generator for a normal distribution (http://mathworld.wolfram.com/NormalDistribution.html). This is a well-known form of distributing a random variable around a center point (mean) with a defined spread (standard deviation). The closer the values are to the center, the more likely their occurrence. In this case, we are initializing with a mean of 2.0 and a standard deviation of 0.5, which means that, after a significant number of draws, we should end up with exactly that mean and standard deviation we provided. assert_eq! confirms that for the mean.

Step 7 then shows the test output—and it works (at the time of this writing).

 The code in the accompanying repository may fail for this recipe if some implementation details of the rand crate change (for example, a minor version update).

To read more about the rand crate, read more in this book (https://rust-random.github.io/book/). However, if you are interested in how to implement a PRNG and find out more about them, check out *Hands-On Data Structures and Algorithms with Rust*, published by Packt (https://www.packtpub.com/application-development/hands-data-structures-and-algorithms-rust), where we go deeper. However, as we have successfully learned to use the rand crate, we can move on to the next recipe.

Writing to and reading from files

Processing files is a daily task and sometimes—depending on the programming language—unreasonably hard. The Rust project teams have taken care of that problem and provide an easy-to-use API to access files. Let's dive right in.

Getting ready

First, create a new project using `cargo new file-stuff`. Now, to work with files, we need a text file to read and process. Lorem Ipsum (`https://www.lipsum.com/`) is a popular dummy text that can be generated on a large scale, so to proceed with the recipe, generate a few (200) paragraphs with this generator and save the text in a file called `lorem.txt` in the root directory.

Finish your preparations by opening the project directory in VS Code.

How to do it...

We can read files from disk in just a few steps:

1. Since the Rust standard library comes with all of the basics we need, let's dive directly into `src/main.rs` to add the imports there:

```
use std::fs::{self, File};
use std::io::{self, BufRead, BufReader, BufWriter, Read, Seek,
Write};
use std::path::Path;

const TEST_FILE_NAME: &str = "lorem.txt";
```

2. First, let's take care of reading from files. For that, we create a function called `read()` that reads and extracts the contents from the prepared file, `lorem.txt`, underneath the imports:

```
fn read() -> io::Result<()> {
    let path = Path::new(TEST_FILE_NAME);

    let input = File::open(path)?;
    let buffered = BufReader::new(input);

    let words: Vec<usize> = buffered
        .lines()
```

```
        .map(|line| line.unwrap().split_ascii_whitespace().count())
        .collect();
    let avg_word_count = words.iter().sum::<usize>() as f32 /
     words.len() as f32;
    println!(
        "{}: Average words per line: {:.2}",
        path.to_string_lossy(),
        avg_word_count
    );

    let mut input = File::open(path)?;
    let mut input_buffer = String::new();
    input.read_to_string(&mut input_buffer)?;

    // ... or ...

    let lorem = fs::read_to_string(path)?;
    println!(
        "{}: Length in characters : {}",
        path.to_string_lossy(),
        lorem.len()
    );
    // reset file pointer to the beginning
    input.seek(io::SeekFrom::Start(0))?;
    println!(
        "{}: Length in bytes: {}",
        path.to_string_lossy(),
        input.bytes().count()
    );
    Ok(())
}
```

3. Writing is going to be the next part we are taking care of. In this case, we are creating a dummy file and writing to it in a variety of ways. You can add the following to `src/main.rs`:

```
fn write() -> io::Result<()> {
    let mut path = Path::new(".").to_path_buf();

    path.push("hello.txt");

    let mut file = File::create(path)?;
    println!("Opened {:?}", file.metadata()?);

    file.write_all(b"Hello")?;

    let mut buffered = BufWriter::new(file);
    write!(buffered, " World!")?;
```

```
        write!(buffered, "\n{: >width$}", width=0x5ff)?;
        Ok(())
    }
```

4. In the last step, we should tie the functions together in the `main` function:

```
fn main() -> io::Result<()> {
    println!("===== READ =====");
    read()?;
    println!();
    println!("===== WRITE ====");
    write()?;
    Ok(())
}
```

5. With `cargo run`, we can now read from and write to disk to perform various tasks. Here, we can observe some general statistics about the `lorem.txt` file and the file metadata for where we write to:

```
$ cargo run
    Compiling file-stuff v0.1.0 (Rust-Cookbook/Chapter10/file-stuff)
     Finished dev [unoptimized + debuginfo] target(s) in 0.84s
      Running `target/debug/file-stuff`
===== READ =====
lorem.txt: Average words per line: 42.33
lorem.txt: Length in characters : 57076
lorem.txt: Length in bytes: 57076

===== WRITE ====
Opened Metadata { file_type: FileType(FileType { mode: 33188 }),
is_dir: false, is_file: true, permissions:
Permissions(FilePermissions { mode: 33188 }), modified:
Ok(SystemTime { tv_sec: 1567003873, tv_nsec: 941523976 }),
accessed: Ok(SystemTime { tv_sec: 1566569294, tv_nsec: 260780071
}), created: Err(Custom { kind: Other, error: "creation time is not
available on this platform currently" }) }
```

Let's get behind how we were working with files here.

How it works...

After setting up the project, we dive right in with *step 1* and provide the imports required to work with the file APIs. Note that working with and reading/writing files are in two different modules: `std::fs` for access and `std::io` for read and write. In addition to that, the `std::path` module provides powerful and easy ways to work with paths in a platform-agnostic way.

Step 2 provides a function that shows several ways to read data from the test file we created in preparation. First, we open the file and pass the reference to `BufReader` (https://doc. rust-lang.org/std/io/struct.BufReader.html), a buffered reader. While the initial reference allows reading data as well, `BufReader` reads the file contents in bulk and serves them from memory. This reduces disk access while improving performance considerably (compared to byte-to-byte reading). Additionally, this allows iterating over lines using the `lines()` function.

With that, we can iterate over each line, splitting it on whitespace and counting the resulting iterator (`.split_ascii_whitespace().count()`). Summing these numbers up and dividing them by the number of lines found, we can determine the average number of words per line. This shows how everything boils down to iterators in Rust and allows powerful things to be created within just a couple of lines of code.

Instead of reading in an iterator, the Rust standard library supports reading into one large string directly as well. For this common task, `fs::read_to_string()` provides a convenient shortcut. However, if you want to retain the file pointer for later use, the `File` struct provides a `read_to_string()` function as well.

Since the file pointer is set to where it stopped reading in the file (which is the end, in this case), we have to reset the file pointer using the `seek()` function before further use. For example, if we want to read bytes instead of characters, the API provides an iterator for that as well (but there are better ways to get the file size in bytes).

Step 3 goes deeper into writing files. We start off by creating a `Path` instance (which cannot be changed), so we translate it to a mutable `PathBuf` instance and add a filename. By calling `File::create()`, we create (overwrite) and obtain a file pointer quickly. The `metadata()` function provides some meta-information about the file (formatted for readability):

```
Metadata {
    file_type: FileType(FileType {
        mode: 33188
    }),
    is_dir: false,
```

```
  is_file: true,
  permissions: Permissions(FilePermissions {
    mode: 33188
  }),
  modified: Ok(SystemTime {
    tv_sec: 1567003873,
    tv_nsec: 941523976
  }),
  accessed: Ok(SystemTime {
    tv_sec: 1566569294,
    tv_nsec: 260780071
  }),
  created: Err(Custom {
    kind: Other,
    error: "creation time is not available on this platform currently"
  })
}
```

Writing to a file is the same as writing to the console (for example, using the `write!()` macro) and can include any data, as long as it can be serialized to bytes. The `b"Hello"` byte literal works just as well as an `&str` slice. Akin to buffered reading, buffered writing also offers improved performance by only writing large blocks at once.

Steps 4 and 5 tie everything together in the `main` function and by running to see the result.

Nothing is surprising when working with files: the API is expectedly straightforward and profits from its integration in common iterators and by using standardized traits. We can happily move on to the next recipe.

Parsing unstructured formats like JSON

Before we start, let's define what we are talking about when we say structured and unstructured data. The former, structured data, follows a schema of some sorts—like a table schema in an SQL database. Unstructured data, on the other hand, is unpredictable in what it will contain. In the most extreme example, a body of prose text is the least structured thing we could probably come up with—each sentence may follow different rules depending on its content.

JSON is a bit more readable, but unstructured, nevertheless. An object can have properties of various data types and no two objects have to be the same. In this chapter, we are going to explore some of the ways JSON (and other formats) can be handled when it doesn't follow a schema that we can declare in a struct.

Getting ready

This project requires Python to run a small script. For the Python part of the project, install Python (3.6 or 3.7 from `https://www.python.org/`), following the instructions on the website. The `python3` command should be available in a Terminal/PowerShell.

Once available, create a new project using `cargo new dynamic-data --lib`. Use VS Code to open the project directory.

How to do it...

Parsing is a multi-step process (but it's easy to do):

1. First, let's add `serde` and its sub-crates to `Cargo.toml`. Open the file and add the following:

```
[dependencies]
serde = "1"
serde_json ="1"
toml = "0.5"
serde-pickle = "0.5"
serde_derive = "1"
```

2. Now, let's use the crates and see what they can do. We do this by creating tests that parse the same data from various formats, starting with JSON. In `src/lib.rs`, we replace the default tests module with the following:

```
#[macro_use]
extern crate serde_json;

#[cfg(test)]
mod tests {
    use serde_json::Value;
    use serde_pickle as pickle;
    use std::fs::File;
    use toml;

    #[test]
    fn test_dynamic_json() {
        let j = r#"{
            "userid": 103609,
            "verified": true,
            "friendly_name": "Jason",
            "access_privileges": [
                "user",
```

```
                    "admin"
                ]
        }"#;

        let parsed: Value = serde_json::from_str(j).unwrap();
        let expected = json!({
          "userid": 103609,
          "verified": true,
          "friendly_name": "Jason",
          "access_privileges": [
            "user",
            "admin"
          ]
        });
        assert_eq!(parsed, expected);

        assert_eq!(parsed["userid"], 103609);
        assert_eq!(parsed["verified"], true);
        assert_eq!(parsed["friendly_name"], "Jason");
        assert_eq!(parsed["access_privileges"][0], "user");
        assert_eq!(parsed["access_privileges"][1], "admin");
        assert_eq!(parsed["access_privileges"][2], Value::Null);
        assert_eq!(parsed["not-available"], Value::Null);
    }
}
```

3. TOML is a text-based format rivaling JSON and YAML for configuration files. Let's create the same test as preceding, but with TOML instead of JSON, and add the following code to the `tests` module:

```
#[test]
fn test_dynamic_toml() {
    let t = r#"
        [[user]]
        userid = 103609
        verified = true
        friendly_name = "Jason"
        access_privileges = [ "user", "admin" ]
    "#;

    let parsed: Value = toml::de::from_str(t).unwrap();

    let expected = json!({
        "user": [
            {
                "userid": 103609,
                "verified": true,
                "friendly_name": "Jason",
```

```
                    "access_privileges": [
                        "user",
                        "admin"
                    ]
                }

            ]
        });
        assert_eq!(parsed, expected);
        let first_user = &parsed["user"][0];
        assert_eq!(first_user["userid"], 103609);
        assert_eq!(first_user["verified"], true);
        assert_eq!(first_user["friendly_name"], "Jason");
        assert_eq!(first_user["access_privileges"][0], "user");
        assert_eq!(first_user["access_privileges"][1], "admin");
        assert_eq!(first_user["access_privileges"][2], Value::Null);
        assert_eq!(first_user["not-available"], Value::Null);
}
```

4. Since the last two were text-based formats, let's look at a binary format as well. Python's pickle format is often used to serialize data as well as machine learning models. However, before we can use Rust to read it, let's create the file in a small Python script called `create_pickle.py` in the project's root directory:

```python
import pickle
import json

def main():
    val = json.loads("""{
            "userid": 103609,
            "verified": true,
            "friendly_name": "Jason",
            "access_privileges": [
                "user",
                "admin"
            ]
        }""") # load the json string as dictionary

    # open "user.pkl" to write binary data (= wb)
    with open("user.pkl", "wb") as out:
        pickle.dump(val, out) # write the dictionary

if __name__ == '__main__':
    main()
```

5. Run `python3 create_pickle.py` to create a `user.pkl` file in the project's root directory (the script should exit silently).

6. Add the last test to the `tests` module in `src/lib.rs,` which parses and compares the contents of the pickle file with what's expected:

```
#[test]
fn test_dynamic_pickle() {
    let parsed: Value = {
        let data = File::open("user.pkl")
                    .expect("Did you run create_pickle.py?");
        pickle::from_reader(&data).unwrap()
    };

    let expected = json!({
      "userid": 103609,
      "verified": true,
      "friendly_name": "Jason",
      "access_privileges": [
        "user",
        "admin"
      ]
    });
    assert_eq!(parsed, expected);

    assert_eq!(parsed["userid"], 103609);
    assert_eq!(parsed["verified"], true);
    assert_eq!(parsed["friendly_name"], "Jason");
    assert_eq!(parsed["access_privileges"][0], "user");
    assert_eq!(parsed["access_privileges"][1], "admin");
    assert_eq!(parsed["access_privileges"][2], Value::Null);
    assert_eq!(parsed["not-available"], Value::Null);
}
```

7. Lastly, we want to see the tests run (successfully). Let's execute `cargo test` to see the test results and how we were able to read binary and text data of various origins:

```
$ cargo test
  Compiling dynamic-json v0.1.0 (Rust-Cookbook/Chapter10/dynamic-
data)
warning: unused `#[macro_use]` import
 --> src/lib.rs:1:1
  |
1 | #[macro_use]
  | ^^^^^^^^^^^^
  |
  = note: #[warn(unused_imports)] on by default

  Finished dev [unoptimized + debuginfo] target(s) in 1.40s
```

```
         Running target/debug/deps/dynamic_json-cf635db43dafddb0

running 3 tests
test tests::test_dynamic_json ... ok
test tests::test_dynamic_pickle ... ok
test tests::test_dynamic_toml ... ok

test result: ok. 3 passed; 0 failed; 0 ignored; 0 measured; 0
filtered out

 Doc-tests dynamic-json

running 0 tests

test result: ok. 0 passed; 0 failed; 0 ignored; 0 measured; 0
filtered out
```

Let's see how that works.

How it works...

Statically typed languages like Rust make programming a lot more comfortable once types
are established. However, in a world with ever-changing web service APIs, a simple
additional property can lead to a parser error, making it impossible to continue.
Therefore, serde does not only support fully automated parsing but also dynamically
extracting data from its Value type, complete with type parsing.

In *step 1*, we add the various dependencies, all of which comply with the serde interfaces
(which are located in the serde crate)—although they come from different sources. Using
them is demonstrated in *step 2* and later.

We begin with creating a raw string that contains a JSON string for serde_json to parse.
Once the Value variable is created, we can use the json! macro to create an equivalent
object to compare. After that, we call the Value API to retrieve individual properties and
check for their type and content. Value is an enum (https://docs.serde.rs/serde_json/
value/enum.Value.html) that implements a range of automated conversions and retrieval
functions, which enable these seamless assert_eq! statements. In case a property or list
index doesn't exist, the Null variant of Value is returned.

Step 3 parses the TOML (`https://github.com/toml-lang/toml`) format and compares it to the JSON output—thanks to the unified `Value` enum, it's very similar to *step 2*. The main difference is that the user property is a list in TOML to demonstrate the other list syntax (`[[this-way-to-declare-a-list-item]]`).

In *steps 4* and *5*, we prepare a Python pickle file containing a dictionary object—parsed from the same JSON object as in *step 2*. Pickle is a binary format, which means we tell Python's file API to write raw bytes instead of encoded text. In contrast, when we read the file, Rust reads bytes by default and requires the programmer to provide the interpretation (codec) if they care to. The `File` API (`https://doc.rust-lang.org/std/fs/struct.File.html`) automatically returns an (unbuffered) `Read` object to fetch the contents, which we can directly pass into the appropriate pickle function. The remaining portion of the code verifies whether the contents read from the pickle file are the same as for the other objects.

We showed reading three types here, but `serde` supports many more. Check out their documentation to learn more, but now let's move on to the next recipe.

Extract text using regular expressions

Regular expressions have been a part of programming for a long time and, in the context of Rust, found popularity in the form of `ripgrep` (`https://github.com/BurntSushi/ripgrep`). `ripgrep` is a grep variation that searches files for a particular regular expression—and it has been adopted as a major part of VS Code, where it powers the search engine. The reason for this is simple: speed (`https://github.com/BurntSushi/ripgrep#quick-examples-comparing-tools`).

Rust's regular expression library has been re-implemented, which may be why it outperforms earlier implementations (and because Rust is fast). Let's see how we can leverage regular expressions in our Rust projects.

How to do it...

Let's follow a few steps to explore regular expressions in Rust:

1. Open a Terminal to create a new project using `cargo new regex --lib`. Use VS Code to open the project directory.

2. First, we are going to add the regex crate to our dependencies in `Cargo.toml`:

```
[dependencies]
regex = "1"
```

3. Next, let's open `src/lib.rs` to create some tests that we can run. To start, we create a tests module, replacing any existing code:

```
#[cfg(test)]
mod tests {

    use regex::Regex;
    use std::cell::RefCell;
    use std::collections::HashMap;

}
```

4. Regular expressions are typically used to parse data or validate that the data conforms to the expression's rules. Let's add a test inside the tests module for some simple parsing:

```
#[test]
fn simple_parsing() {
    let re = Regex::new(r"(?P<y>\d{4})-(
                    ?P<m>\d{2})-(?P<d>\d{2})").unwrap();

    assert!(re.is_match("1999-12-01"));
    let date = re.captures("2019-02-27").unwrap();

    assert_eq!("2019", &date["y"]);
    assert_eq!("02", &date["m"]);
    assert_eq!("27", &date["d"]);

    let fun_dates: Vec<(i32, i32, i32)> = (1..12)
                .map(|i| (2000 + i, i, i * 2)).collect();

    let multiple_dates: String = fun_dates
        .iter()
        .map(|d| format!("{}-{:02}-{:02} ", d.0, d.1, d.2))
        .collect();

    for (match_, expected) in re.captures_iter(
        &multiple_dates).zip(fun_dates.iter()) {
        assert_eq!(match_.get(1).unwrap().as_str(),
                expected.0.to_string());
        assert_eq!(
            match_.get(2).unwrap().as_str(),
            format!("{:02}", expected.1)
        );
```

```
            assert_eq!(
                match_.get(3).unwrap().as_str(),
                format!("{:02}", expected.2)
            );
        }
    }
```

5. However, regular expressions can do much more with their pattern matching. Another task could be to replace data:

```
#[test]
fn reshuffle_groups() {
    let re = Regex::new(r"(?P<y>\d{4})-(
            ?P<m>\d{2})-(?P<d>\d{2})").unwrap();

    let fun_dates: Vec<(i32, i32, i32)> = (1..12)
        .map(|i| (2000 + i, i, i * 2)).collect();

    let multiple_dates: String = fun_dates
        .iter()
        .map(|d| format!("{}-{:02}-{:02} ", d.0, d.1, d.2))
        .collect();

    let european_format = re.replace_all(
                        &multiple_dates, "$d.$m.$y");

    assert_eq!(european_format.trim(), "02.01.2001 04.02.2002
            06.03.2003 08.04.2004 10.05.2005
            12.06.2006 14.07.2007 16.08.2008
            18.09.2009 20.10.2010 22.11.2011");
}
```

6. As a last test, we can have some more fun analyzing data using regular expressions, for example, counting the prefixes on telephone numbers:

```
#[test]
fn count_groups() {
    let counter: HashMap<String, i32> = HashMap::new();

    let phone_numbers = "+49 (1234) 45665
+43(0)1234/45665 43
+1 314-CALL-ME
+44 1234 45665
+49 (1234) 44444
+44 12344 55538";

    let re = Regex::new(r"(\+[\d]{1,4})").unwrap();
```

```
        let prefixes = re
            .captures_iter(&phone_numbers)
            .map(|match_| match_.get(1))
            .filter(|m| m.is_some())
            .fold(RefCell::new(counter), |c, prefix| {
                {
                    let mut counter_dict = c.borrow_mut();
                    let prefix = prefix.unwrap().as_str().to_string();
                    let count = counter_dict.get(&prefix)
                            .unwrap_or(&0) + 1;
                    counter_dict.insert(prefix, count);
                }
                c
            });

        let prefixes = prefixes.into_inner();
        assert_eq!(prefixes.get("+49"), Some(&2));
        assert_eq!(prefixes.get("+1"), Some(&1));
        assert_eq!(prefixes.get("+44"), Some(&2));
        assert_eq!(prefixes.get("+43"), Some(&1));
    }
```

7. Now, let's run the tests using `cargo test` and we can see that the regular expressions perform well:

```
$ cargo test
 Finished dev [unoptimized + debuginfo] target(s) in 0.02s
 Running target/debug/deps/regex-46c0a096a2a4a140

running 3 tests
test tests::count_groups ... ok
test tests::simple_parsing ... ok
test tests::reshuffle_groups ... ok

test result: ok. 3 passed; 0 failed; 0 ignored; 0 measured; 0
filtered out

 Doc-tests regex

running 0 tests

test result: ok. 0 passed; 0 failed; 0 ignored; 0 measured; 0
filtered out
```

Now that we know how to use regular expressions, let's find out how they work.

How it works...

After the initial setup in *steps 1* and *2*, we start by creating a tests module in *step 3* along with the required dependencies. *Step 4* then contains the first test that shows how the regex crate (`https://docs.rs/regex/1.2.1/regex/`) handles simple parsing of data.

By using the raw string literal syntax, `r"I am a raw string"`, we compile a new `Regex` instance that we match to date strings. The included character classes are what is commonly used across OSes and languages, which includes support for whitespaces as well as (alpha) numerical characters and raw bytes. Additionally, flags can be placed directly in the expression using a `(?flag)` notation.

The regular expression in *step 4* is composed of three parts: `(?P<y>\d{4})-` `(?P<m>\d{2})-(?P<d>\d{2})`.

The first part is named `y` (`?P<name>` declares a name) and looks for exactly four (`{4}`) digits `\d` that it can match. Parts two and three look for two digits each and are named `m` and `d` respectively. This naming is going to be important later on when we want to retrieve the matches. In between those patterns, we see a `-`, which means that the final pattern has to look like `yyyy-mm-dd` (or `1234-12-12` to be precise) to match.

Going down the test, this is what we do. By preparing a few positive examples, we can validate a date (`1999-12-01`), as well as extract the individual parts by name (`2019-02-27`). If a string has multiple matches, we can also iterate over these captures to remain efficient. In the case of the test, we also check whether the extracted content matches the expected values while iterating.

Compiling a regular expression takes a fair amount of time, especially when the expression is very large. Consequently, pre-compile and reuse as much as possible and avoid compiling in loops!

Step 5 creates a similar regular expression and replicates the `fun_dates` variable from the *step 4* test. However, instead of just extracting the content, we want to replace the pattern, which—in this case—transforms the ISO - notation into a European-style . notation. Since we named the groups in the regex, we can now also refer to those names in the replacement string.

In *step 6*, we return to matching, but instead of simply validating, we extract and work with the extracted data to create information. Assuming that a task is to count country codes in phone numbers, we can apply the regular expression and use `HashMap` for keeping track of each number's occurrence. The regular expression matches anything starting with +, followed by one to four digits: `(\+[\d]{1,4})`.

Using Rust's iterator powers, we extract the match and filter out any non-matches before folding the results into common `HashMap`. `RefCell` helps with managing mutability and, since the fold function has to return the accumulated result, we have to scope off the mutable borrowing to ensure memory safety (the compiler will tell you). Once we extract the inner value of the cell, we can see what the numbers were.

This only touches on a few common subjects inside the realm of possible tasks with regular expressions. We highly recommend reading the documentation to find out more!

However, now that we have had a taste of some regular expressions, we can move on to the next recipe.

Recursively searching the filesystem

ripgrep—as we mentioned in the previous recipe (*Extracting text using regular expressions*)—is a popular grep engine that walks through files to find anything that matches the provided regular expression rules. For that, it's not only necessary to compile and match a regular expression to massive amounts of text, but also to find these texts. To get to and open these files, we need to walk the directory trees of the filesystem. Let's find out how to do that in Rust.

How to do it...

We can understand recursive search by following a few steps:

1. Open a Terminal to create a new project using `cargo new filesystem`. Use VS Code to open the project directory.
2. Edit `Cargo.toml` to add a dependency to a crate called `glob` for walking the filesystem:

```
[dependencies]
glob = "0.3.0"
```

3. In `src/main.rs`, we can then start implementing functions to walk the filesystem tree, but first, let's set up the imports and a type alias for boxed errors:

```
use glob;
use std::error::Error;
use std::io;
use std::path::{Path, PathBuf};

type GenericError = Box<dyn Error + Send + Sync + 'static>;
```

4. Next, we are going to add a recursive `walk` function that is only using the Rust standard library. Add the following:

```
fn walk(dir: &Path, cb: &dyn Fn(&PathBuf), recurse: bool) ->
io::Result<()> {
    for entry in dir.read_dir()? {
        let entry = entry?;
        let path = entry.path();
        if recurse && path.is_dir() {
            walk(&path, cb, true)?;
        }
        cb(&path);
    }
    Ok(())
}
```

5. `glob` is also the name of a style of wildcards for filesystems (for example, `*.txt` or `Cargo*`), working on both Windows and Linux/Unix. In some implementations, globs can be recursive as well, which is why we can use the crate of the same name to implement another `walk` function:

```
fn walk_glob(pattern: &str, cb: &dyn Fn(&PathBuf)) -> Result<(),
GenericError> {
    for entry in glob::glob(pattern)? {
        cb(&entry?);
    }
    Ok(())
}
```

6. What's missing now is the `main` function to tie it all together and call the functions accordingly. Add the following:

```
fn main() -> Result<(), GenericError> {
    let path = Path::new("./src");
    println!("Listing '{}'", path.display());
    println!("===");
    walk(path, &|d| println!(" {}", d.display()), true)?;
```

```
            println!();

            let glob_pattern = "../**/*.rs";
            println!("Listing by glob filter: {}", glob_pattern);
            println!("===");
            walk_glob(glob_pattern, &|d| println!(" {}", d.display()))?;
            println!();

            let glob_pattern = "Cargo.*";
            println!("Listing by glob filter: {}", glob_pattern);
            println!("===");
            walk_glob(glob_pattern, &|d| println!(" {}", d.display()))?;
            Ok(())
        }
```

7. As usual, we want to see it running—use `cargo run` to recursively list files from your filesystem using the filters we defined in *step 6*. We also encourage you to change the paths to something that fits your system:

```
$ cargo run
    Compiling filesystem v0.1.0 (Rust-Cookbook/Chapter10/filesystem)
     Finished dev [unoptimized + debuginfo] target(s) in 0.25s
      Running `target/debug/filesystem`
Listing './src'
===
  ./src/main.rs

Listing by glob filter: ../**/*.rs
===
  ../command-line-args/src/main.rs
  ../dynamic-data/src/lib.rs
  ../file-stuff/src/main.rs
  ../filesystem/src/main.rs
  ../logging/src/main.rs
  ../pipes/src/main.rs
  ../random-numbers/src/lib.rs
  ../regex/src/lib.rs
  ../rusty-ml/src/main.rs
  ../sub-processes/src/main.rs
  ../web-requests/src/main.rs

Listing by glob filter: Cargo.*
===
  Cargo.lock
  Cargo.toml
```

Let's get into the inner workings of walking through the filesystem with a filter.

How it works...

Walking a filesystem tree is not a particularly complicated task. However, just like any other tree walks, it is much easier to be done recursively, even though there is always a risk of running into stack overflow problems if the directory nesting is too deep. While an iterative approach is possible, it is much longer and more complicated to implement.

In this recipe, we start off with setting everything up in *step 1*, adding the glob crate (https://docs.rs/glob/0.3.0/glob/) as a dependency in *step 2*, and finally importing the required modules in *step 3*. In *step 4*, we write the first walk function, a recursive in-order walk. This means that we recursively descend as far as possible into the first (by some order) directory before we start executing the provided callback on that path—we are therefore processing the nodes in the order they came up.

Rust's DirEntry struct is powerful in that it allows access to its contents via a property (instead of calling a different function). The io::Result<()> return type also allows for using the ? operator and would end early in cases of errors.

Step 5 offers a similar function using the glob iterator. Since the input is a pattern (both recursive and non-recursive), this pattern is parsed and—if it's valid—returns an iterator over matching file and folder paths. We can then call the callback with these entries.

In *step 6*, we call the functions using a range of paths. The first descends into the src directory, listing all of the files there using the recursive approach. The second pattern first goes up into the project directory's parent and then recursively matches all of the *.rs files it finds there (and below). In the case of this book's chapter, you should see all of the code files we have written (and will write).

Lastly, the filter can also be something simple and match the two Cargo.* files, as shown in the last call of walk_glob().

Now that we know how to go through the filesystem, let's move on to another recipe.

Custom command-line arguments

Working with command-line arguments is a great way to configure a program to run specific tasks, use a particular set of input data, or simply to output more information. However, looking at the help text output of a Linux program these days, it offers an impressive amount of information on all of the flags and arguments it can work with. In addition to that, the text is printed in a somewhat standardized format, which is why this is usually done with strong library support.

Rust's most popular crate for working with command-line arguments is called `clap` (`https://clap.rs/`), and, in this recipe, we are looking at how we can leverage its strengths to create a useful command-line interface.

How to do it...

A simple program that uses command-line arguments to print directories/files only requires a few steps:

1. Open a Terminal to create a new project using `cargo new command-line-args` . Use VS Code to open the project directory.

2. First, let's adapt `Cargo.toml` to download `clap` and to have a better binary output name:

```
[package]
name = "list"
version = "1.0.0"
authors = ["Claus Matzinger <claus.matzinger+kb@gmail.com>"]
edition = "2018"

# See more keys and their definitions at
https://doc.rust-lang.org/cargo/reference/manifest.html

[dependencies]
clap = {version= "2.33", features = ["suggestions", "color"]}
```

3. In `src/main.rs`, we are going to start with imports:

```
use clap::{App, Arg, SubCommand};
use std::fs::DirEntry;
use std::path::Path;

use std::io;
```

4. Then, we define a `walk` function that recursively walks through the filesystem to execute a callback on each entry. The function supports excluding certain paths, which we implement using its own type:

```
struct Exclusion(String);

impl Exclusion {
    pub fn is_excluded(&self, path: &Path) -> bool {
        path.file_name()
            .map_or(false, |f|
    f.to_string_lossy().find(&self.0).is_some())
    }
}
```

With that available, we can define the `walk` function:

```
fn walk(
    dir: &Path,
    exclusion: &Option<Exclusion>,
    cb: &dyn Fn(&DirEntry),
    recurse: bool,
) -> io::Result<()> {
    for entry in dir.read_dir()? {
        let entry = entry?;
        let path = entry.path();
        if !exclusion.as_ref().map_or(false,
                |e| e.is_excluded(&path)) {
            if recurse && path.is_dir() {
                walk(&path, exclusion, cb, true)?;
            }
            cb(&entry);
        }
    }
    Ok(())
}
```

5. Next, a few helper functions make our life easier for printing:

```
fn print_if_file(entry: &DirEntry) {
    let path = entry.path();
    if !path.is_dir() {
        println!("{}", path.to_string_lossy())
    }
}
fn print_if_dir(entry: &DirEntry) {
    let path = entry.path();
    if path.is_dir() {
        println!("{}", path.to_string_lossy())
```

```
        }
    }
```

6. In the `main` function, we are using the `clap` API for the first time. Here, we are creating the argument/subcommand structure of the application:

```rust
fn main() -> io::Result<()> {
    let matches = App::new("list")
        .version("1.0")
        .author("Claus M - claus.matzinger+kb@gmail.com")
        .about("")
        .arg(
            Arg::with_name("exclude")
                .short("e")
                .long("exclude")
                .value_name("NAME")
                .help("Exclude directories/files with this name")
                .takes_value(true),
        )
        .arg(
            Arg::with_name("recursive")
                .short("r")
                .long("recursive")
                .help("Recursively descend into subdirectories"),
        )
```

After the arguments, we add subcommands in the same way—following the builder pattern:

```rust
        .subcommand(
            SubCommand::with_name("files")
                .about("Lists files only")
                .arg(
                    Arg::with_name("PATH")
                        .help("The path to start looking")
                        .required(true)
                        .index(1),
                ),
        )
        .subcommand(
            SubCommand::with_name("dirs")
                .about("Lists directories only")
                .arg(
                    Arg::with_name("PATH")
                        .help("The path to start looking")
                        .required(true)
                        .index(1),
                ),
```

```
)
.get_matches();
```

Once we retrieve the matches, we have to get the actual values that have been passed into the program:

```
let recurse = matches.is_present("recursive");
let exclusions = matches.value_of("exclude")
                   .map(|e| Exclusion(e.into()));
```

However, with subcommands, we can match on their specific flags and other arguments too, which is best extracted with Rust's pattern matching:

```
match matches.subcommand() {
    ("files", Some(subcmd)) => {
        let path = Path::new(subcmd.value_of("PATH").unwrap());
        walk(path, &exclusions, &print_if_file, recurse)?;
    }
    ("dirs", Some(subcmd)) => {
        let path = Path::new(subcmd.value_of("PATH").unwrap());
        walk(path, &exclusions, &print_if_dir, recurse)?;
    }
    _ => {}
}
Ok(())
}
```

7. Let's see what that did. Run `cargo run` to see the initial output:

```
$ cargo run
   Compiling list v1.0.0 (Rust-Cookbook/Chapter10/command-line-
args)
    Finished dev [unoptimized + debuginfo] target(s) in 0.68s
     Running `target/debug/list`
```

Nothing! Indeed, we did not specify any required commands or parameters. Let's run `cargo run -- help` (since we named the program list, calling the compiled executable directly would be `list help`) to see the help text showing us which options we could try:

```
$ cargo run -- help
    Finished dev [unoptimized + debuginfo] target(s) in 0.03s
     Running `target/debug/list help`
list 1.0
Claus M - claus.matzinger+kb@gmail.com

USAGE:
```

```
list [FLAGS] [OPTIONS] [SUBCOMMAND]

FLAGS:
    -h, --help Prints help information
    -r, --recursive Recursively descend into subdirectories
    -V, --version Prints version information

OPTIONS:
    -e, --exclude <NAME> Exclude directories/files with this name

SUBCOMMANDS:
    dirs Lists directories only
    files Lists files only
    help Prints this message or the help of the given subcommand(s)
```

We should look at the `dirs` subcommand first, so let's run `cargo run -- dirs` to see whether it recognizes the required PATH argument:

```
$ cargo run -- dirs
 Finished dev [unoptimized + debuginfo] target(s) in 0.02s
 Running `target/debug/list dirs`
error: The following required arguments were not provided:
 <PATH>

USAGE:
 list dirs <PATH>

For more information try --help
```

Let's also try a fully parameterized run where we list all subfolders of the project directory excluding anything called `src` (and their subdirectories):

```
$ cargo run -- -e "src" -r dirs "."
    Finished dev [unoptimized + debuginfo] target(s) in 0.03s
     Running `target/debug/list -e src -r dirs .`
./target/debug/native
./target/debug/deps
./target/debug/examples
./target/debug/build/libc-f4756c111c76f0ce/out
./target/debug/build/libc-f4756c111c76f0ce
./target/debug/build/libc-dd900fc422222982
./target/debug/build/bitflags-92aba5107334e3f1
./target/debug/build/bitflags-cc659c8d16362a89/out
./target/debug/build/bitflags-cc659c8d16362a89
./target/debug/build
./target/debug/.fingerprint/textwrap-a949503c1b2651be
./target/debug/.fingerprint/vec_map-bffb157312ad2f55
./target/debug/.fingerprint/bitflags-20c9ba1238fdf359
```

```
./target/debug/.fingerprint/strsim-13cb32b0738f6106
./target/debug/.fingerprint/libc-63efda3965f75b56
./target/debug/.fingerprint/clap-062d4c7aff8b8ade
./target/debug/.fingerprint/unicode-width-62c92f6253cf0187
./target/debug/.fingerprint/libc-f4756c111c76f0ce
./target/debug/.fingerprint/libc-dd900fc422222982
./target/debug/.fingerprint/list-701fd8634a8008ef
./target/debug/.fingerprint/ansi_term-bceb12a766693d6c
./target/debug/.fingerprint/bitflags-92aba5107334e3f1
./target/debug/.fingerprint/bitflags-cc659c8d16362a89
./target/debug/.fingerprint/command-line-args-0ef71f7e17d44dc7
./target/debug/.fingerprint/atty-585c8c7510af9f9a
./target/debug/.fingerprint
./target/debug/incremental/command_line_args-1s3xsytlc6x5x/s-
ffbsjpqyuz-19aig85-4az1dq8f8e3e
./target/debug/incremental/command_line_args-1s3xsytlc6x5x
./target/debug/incremental/list-oieloyeggsml/s-
ffjle2dbdm-1w5ez6c-13wi8atbsq2wt
./target/debug/incremental/list-oieloyeggsml
./target/debug/incremental
./target/debug
./target
```

Try it yourself: several combinations show the power of `clap`. Let's see how it works.

How it works...

`clap` (`https://clap.rs/`) prides itself on being a simple-to-use crate for working with command-line arguments in Rust—and they are right. In the initial two steps, we set up the application config and dependencies. We also renamed the binary since `list` is a more to-the-point name than `command-line-args`.

In *step 3*, we start by importing the necessary structs (`https://docs.rs/clap/2.33.0/clap/struct.App.html`)—App, Arg, SubCommand for `clap`, and, in *step 4*, we are creating the function that we are going to parameterize using command line arguments. The function itself is a simple directory tree walk with the ability to execute a callback on each entry and a way to exclude certain paths as an exclusion.

 This is similar to what we did in the *Recursively searching the filesystem* recipe earlier in this chapter.

Some additional helper callbacks for printing directories and files only are defined in *step 5*. Closures could have worked as well but wouldn't achieve the same readability.

Step 6 is where we work with the `clap` API. This particular case is using the Rust API only; however, `clap` supports using external files for configuring the parameters as well. Read more at `https://docs.rs/clap/2.33.0/clap/index.html`. Regardless of how you are going to define the parameters, the structure is very similar: the `App` struct has several meta-parameters for informing the user about the author, version, and others as well as the arguments it can have.

An argument can be a flag (that is, setting something to `true`/`false`) or a value (such as an input path), which is why we use the `Arg` struct to configure each individually. Typical command-line flags have a shorthand for a longer name (`ls -a` versus `ls --all` on Linux/Unix), as well as a short help text explaining the usage. The last setting concerns whether the flag has a more complex type than a Boolean, which we set to `true` for `exclude` and leave at `false` for the `recursive` flag. These names will later be used to retrieve these values.

Many command-line applications nowadays have a subcommand structure that allows for better structuring and readability. A subcommand can be nested and have its own arguments—just like the `App` struct. The arguments we define here are positional, so they are not referred to by their name but rather have to be present at that particular position. Since the argument is required, the argument parser takes in whatever value comes in.

With a call to `get_matches()`, we execute the parsing (which also triggers help texts and early exits if necessary) and retrieve an `ArgMatches` instance. This type manages the key-value pairs (argument name and the value it got), using the `Option` and `Result` types, which allow us to use Rust code for defaults.

Subcommands behave like sub-applications in a way. They come with their own `ArgMatches` instance, for accessing their flags and more directly.

Step 6 shows a few possible calls to run the program. We use two dashes, `--`, to pass any arguments through to the application (rather than `cargo` interpreting them), and by running the default help subcommand, we can see a nice and standardized help output with all of the texts and names we supplied.

These help texts are also provided in case parsing does not work out (for example, when a flag is misspelled) and for each subcommand. However, the last part of *step 6* shows what happens when it works out, listing all of the build directories in `target/` (since we excluded `src`). Since we don't want to bore you with various parameter combinations, we encourage you to try out the other arguments we configured and see different results!

Now that we know how to work with command-line arguments, let's move on to the next recipe.

Working with piped input data

Reading data from files is a very common task that we described in another recipe in this chapter (*Writing to and reading from files*). However, that's not always the best option. In fact, many Linux/Unix programs can be chained together using a pipe (|) to process an incoming stream. This allows for several things to be done:

- Flexibility on the input source, static text, files, and networking streams—no need to change the programs
- Run several processes, writing only the end result back to disk
- Lazy evaluation of the stream
- Flexible processing up-/downstream (for example, gzipping the output before writing to disk)

If you are not familiar with how this works, the pipe syntax may look cryptic. However, it actually stems from a functional programming paradigm (`https://www.geeksforgeeks.org/functional-programming-paradigm/`), where pipes and stream processing are quite common—not unlike Rust's iterators. Let's build a CSV to a line-based JSON (each line is an object) converter to see how we can work with pipes!

Getting ready

Open a Terminal to create a new project using `cargo new pipes`. Use VS Code to open the project directory and create a simple CSV file called `cars.csv` with the following content:

```
year,make,model
1997,Ford,E350
1926,Bugatti,Type 35
1971,Volkswagen,Beetle
1992,Gurgel,Supermini
```

We are now going to parse this file and create a series of JSON objects from it.

How to do it...

Follow the steps to implement `csv` to the JSON converter:

1. Open `Cargo.toml` to add a few dependencies we need for parsing CSV and creating JSON:

   ```
   [dependencies]
   csv = "1.1"
   serde_json = "1"
   ```

2. Now, let's add some code. As usual, we are going to import a few things in `src/main.rs`, so we can use them in the code:

   ```
   use csv;
   use serde_json as json;
   use std::io;
   ```

3. The next thing to do is add a function that converts the input data into JSON. We can do this elegantly using the `Iterator` trait that each `csv::StringRecord` instance implements:

   ```
   fn to_json(headers: &csv::StringRecord, current_row:
   csv::StringRecord) -> io::Result<json::Value> {
       let row: json::Map<String, json::Value> = headers
           .into_iter()
           .zip(current_row.into_iter())
           .map(|(key, value)| (key.to_string(),
   json::Value::String(value.into())))
           .collect();
       Ok(json::Value::Object(row))
   }
   ```

4. How do we get these `csv::StringRecords` instances? By reading from the console! As a last piece of code, we replace the default `main` function with the following:

   ```
   fn main() -> io::Result<()> {
       let mut rdr = csv::ReaderBuilder::new()
           .trim(csv::Trim::All)
           .has_headers(false)
           .delimiter(b',')
           .from_reader(io::stdin());
   ```

```
let header_rec = rdr
    .records()
    .take(1)
    .next()
    .expect("The first line does not seem to be a valid CSV")?;
for result in rdr.records() {
    if let Ok(json_rec) = to_json(&header_rec, result?) {
        println!("{}", json_rec.to_string());
    }
}
Ok(())
}
```

5. Lastly, use PowerShell (on Windows) or your favorite Terminal (Linux/macOS) to run the binary with piped input data:

```
$ cat cars.csv | cargo run
    Compiling pipes v0.1.0 (Rust-Cookbook/Chapter10/pipes)
     Finished dev [unoptimized + debuginfo] target(s) in 1.46s
      Running `target/debug/pipes`
{"make":"Ford","model":"E350","year":"1997"}
{"make":"Bugatti","model":"Type 35","year":"1926"}
{"make":"Volkswagen","model":"Beetle","year":"1971"}
{"make":"Gurgel","model":"Supermini","year":"1992"}
```

Let's dive into how we streamed data through multiple programs.

How it works...

The Linux OS is largely file-based; many important interfaces to the kernel can be found in virtual filesystems pretending to be a file or folder structure. The best example is the /proc/ filesystem, which allows user-access to hardware and other current information of the kernel/system. In the same spirit, the console inputs and outputs are treated; they are actually reserved file handles with the numbers 0 (standard input), 1 (standard output), and 2 (standard error). In fact, these link back to the /proc/ filesystem, where /proc/<process id>/fd/1 is the standard output of that particular process ID.

Keeping this concept in mind, these file descriptors can be read just like any other file—which is what we are doing in this recipe. After setting up the basic dependencies in *step 1* and importing the modules in *step 2*, we create a processing function in *step 3*. The function takes in two of the csv crate's (https://docs.rs/csv/1.1.1/) generic StringRecord—which holds a row's worth of data each—for the header row and the current row. The zip() (https://doc.rust-lang.org/std/iter/trait.Iterator. html#method.zip) function on the iterator allows us to align the indices efficiently, the result of which we can then transform into a tuple of String and serde_json::Value::String. This allows us to collect these tuples into a serde_json::Map type, which gets converted into serde_json::Value::Object (representing a JSON object).

> The iterator's collect() function relies on implementing the FromIterator trait for the particular types. serde_json::Map implements this for (String, serde_json::Value).

Step 4 then calls this to_json() function—but only after it builds a custom Reader object! By default csv::Reader expects the incoming rows to conform to a Deserialize struct—something that is impossible in a generic tool. Therefore, we resort to creating an instance using ReaderBuilder by specifying the options we need:

- trim(csv::Trim::All): This makes sanitation easier.
- has_headers(false): This allows us to read the headers first; otherwise, they would be ignored.
- delimiter(b','): This hardcodes the delimiter to be a comma.
- from_reader(io::stdin()): This attaches to the Read interface of standard input.

Upon creation, we read the first row and assume it is the CSV's header. Hence, we save it separately to borrow it to the to_json() function as needed. Following that, the for loop takes care of evaluating the (unlimited) iterator over the Read interface of standard input (typically until the EOF signal is received, with *Ctrl + D* on Linux/UNIX OSes). Each iteration prints the result to standard output again for other programs to read via a pipe.

That's it! We highly recommend checking out the repository of the csv crate to learn more about the functions it offers (as well as serde_json (https://docs.serde.rs/serde_json/)), before moving on to the next recipe.

Sending web requests

Over recent years, web requests have become an important part of many applications. Almost anything integrates with some kind of web service, even if it's only diagnostics and usage statistics. HTTP's versatility has proven to be a great asset in a more centralized computing world.

 One of the libraries in this recipe (surf) is cutting edge and depends on an unstable (at the time of writing this) async/await feature of Rust. Depending on when you read this, the library or async/await in Rust may have changed—in that case, please open an issue on the accompanying GitHub repository so we can provide a working example for other readers.

Making these web requests has not always been straightforward in any language, especially with regard to sending and receiving data types, variables, and more. Since Rust does not come with web request modules available out of the box, there are a few libraries we can use to connect to remote HTTP services. Let's see how.

How to do it...

We can make web requests in just a few steps:

1. Open a Terminal to create a new project using `cargo new web-requests`. Use VS Code to open the project directory.
2. First, let's edit `Cargo.toml` to add the dependencies we are going to use later:

```
[dependencies]
surf = "1.0"
reqwest = "0.9"
serde = "1"
serde_json = "1"
runtime = "0.3.0-alpha.6"
```

3. Let's start importing these external dependencies and setting up some data structs in `src/main.rs`:

```
#[macro_use]
extern crate serde_json;

use surf::Exception;
use serde::Serialize;
```

```
#[derive(Serialize)]
struct MyGetParams {
    a: u64,
    b: String,
}
```

4. surf (https://github.com/rustasync/surf) is a recent crate developed fully
   async. Let's create a test function to see it in action. First, we create the client and
   issue a simple GET request:

```
async fn test_surf() -> Result<(), Exception> {
    println!("> surf ...");

    let client = surf::Client::new();
    let mut res = client
        .get("https://blog.x5ff.xyz/other/cookbook2018")
        .await?;

    assert_eq!(200, res.status());
    assert_eq!("Rust is awesome\n", res.body_string().await?);
```

Then, we upgrade to something more complex, form data, which we also confirm
was received well:

```
let form_values = vec![
    ("custname", "Rusty Crabbington"),
    ("comments", "Thank you"),
    ("custemail", "rusty@nope.com"),
    ("custtel", "+1 234 33456"),
    ("delivery", "25th floor below ground, no elevator. sorry"),
];

let res_forms: serde_json::Value = client
    .post("https://httpbin.org/post")
    .body_form(&form_values)?
    .recv_json()
    .await?;

for (name, value) in form_values.iter() {
    assert_eq!(res_forms["form"][name], *value);
}
```

Next, the same procedure is repeated for JSON payloads:

```
let json_payload = json!({
    "book": "Rust 2018 Cookbook",
    "blog": "https://blog.x5ff.xyz",
});
```

```
let res_json: serde_json::Value = client
    .put("https://httpbin.org/anything")
    .body_json(&json_payload)?
    .recv_json()
    .await?;

assert_eq!(res_json["json"], json_payload);
```

And finally, we query parameters in GET requests:

```
let query_params = MyGetParams {
    a: 0x5ff,
    b: "https://blog.x5ff.xyz".into(),
};
let res_query: serde_json::Value = client
    .get("https://httpbin.org/get")
    .set_query(&query_params)?
    .recv_json()
    .await?;

assert_eq!(res_query["args"]["a"], query_params.a.to_string());
assert_eq!(res_query["args"]["b"], query_params.b);
println!("> surf successful!");
Ok(())
}
```

5. Since surf is very new, let's also test a more mature (and not async)
   crate, reqwest (https://github.com/seanmonstar/reqwest/). Just like the
   previous function, it will go through several ways to do different types of web
   tasks, starting with a simple GET request:

```
fn test_reqwest() -> Result<(), Exception> {
    println!("> reqwest ...");

    let client = reqwest::Client::new();

    let mut res = client
        .get("https://blog.x5ff.xyz/other/cookbook2018")
        .send()?;

    assert_eq!(200, res.status());
    assert_eq!("Rust is awesome\n", res.text()?);
```

The next request features an HTML form request body:

```
let form_values = vec![
    ("custname", "Rusty Crabbington"),
    ("comments", "Thank you"),
    ("custemail", "rusty@nope.com"),
    ("custtel", "+1 234 33456"),
    ("delivery", "25th floor below ground, no elevator. sorry"),
];

let res_forms: serde_json::Value = client
    .post("https://httpbin.org/post")
    .form(&form_values)
    .send()?
    .json()?;

for (name, value) in form_values.iter() {
    assert_eq!(res_forms["form"][name], *value);
}
```

This is followed by a JSON PUT request:

```
let json_payload = json!({
    "book": "Rust 2018 Cookbook",
    "blog": "https://blog.x5ff.xyz",
});

let res_json: serde_json::Value = client
    .put("https://httpbin.org/anything")
    .json(&json_payload)
    .send()?
    .json()?;

assert_eq!(res_json["json"], json_payload);
```

The final request features query parameters, automatically serialized by `serde`:

```
let query_params = MyGetParams {
    a: 0x5ff,
    b: "https://blog.x5ff.xyz".into(),
};

let res_query: serde_json::Value = client
    .get("https://httpbin.org/get")
    .query(&query_params)
    .send()?
    .json()?;
```

```
assert_eq!(res_query["args"]["a"], query_params.a.to_string());
assert_eq!(res_query["args"]["b"], query_params.b);

println!("> reqwest successful!");
Ok(())
}
```

6. One major function is still required: `main()`. Here, we are going to call the preceding tests:

```
#[runtime::main]
async fn main() -> Result<(), Exception> {
    println!("Running some tests");
    test_reqwest()?;
    test_surf().await?;
    Ok(())
}
```

7. The most important command is `cargo +nightly run`, so we can see that making requests works for both crates:

```
$ cargo +nightly run
 Finished dev [unoptimized + debuginfo] target(s) in 0.10s
 Running `target/debug/web-requests`
Running some tests
> reqwest ...
> reqwest successful!
> surf ...
> surf successful!
```

Let's check behind the scenes to see what's up.

How it works...

The Rust community's web frameworks are great examples of how the lessons learned from other languages influence the design of a more recent technology. Both crates discussed in this chapter follow a similar pattern that can be observed in a range of libraries and frameworks across various languages (for example, Python's requests), which evolved to this stage themselves.

The way these frameworks operate is often called the builder pattern together with the decorator pattern (both described in *Design Patterns*, Gamma et al, 1994). For C# programmers, the pattern is explained at https://airbrake.io/blog/design-patterns/structural-design-patterns-decorator.

In this recipe, we look at two frameworks: `reqwest` and `surf`. After setting up the dependencies in `Cargo.toml` (*step 2*), we import some structs to create a serializable data type (to pass into `serde_urlencoded` (`https://github.com/nox/serde_urlencoded`)) for `GET` parameters in *step 3*.

In *step 4*, we create a function that covers `surf`. `surf` is fully `async`, which means that—to use `await`—we need to declare the function to be `async` as well. Then, we can create reusable `surf::Client`, which issues a `GET` request (to `https://blog.x5ff.xyz/other/cookbook2018`) right away. As with all of the other calls in this function, we use `await` to wait for the request to complete and the `?` operator to fail in case an error occurs.

 In this recipe, we are using the incredibly useful `https://httpbin.org/`. This website reflects many properties of the request back to the sender, allowing us to see what the server received in a JSON-formatted output (among other things).

The next request is a `POST` request with form data, which can be represented as a vector of tuples (key-value pairs). Using the same client as before (unlike other frameworks, it's not bound to a specific domain), we can simply pass the vector as the form-body of the `POST` request. Since we already know what the endpoint will return (JSON), we can ask the framework to parse the results into `serde_json::Value` (see also the *Parsing unstructured formats such as JSON* recipe in this chapter) right away. Again, any parsing errors, timeouts, and more are handled by the `?` operator, which would return an error at this point.

The returned JSON contains the form values in the request, confirming that the request contained the data in the expected encoding and format. Similarly, if we send JSON data in a `PUT` request, the returned JSON is expected to be equal to what we sent.

In the last request, we send HTTP `GET` with automatically constructed query parameters from the previously defined `struct`. After sending off the request, the reflected JSON contains the data found in the query parameters, which is what we sent off—if we (and the library) did everything correctly.

Step 5 repeats the same ideas for `reqwest`, with only a few API differences (features aside):

- Instead of `futures` and `await`, `reqwest` uses `send()` to execute the request.
- Declaring the format for receiving data (JSON, plaintext, and so on) is done on the response instance (that is, on the `send()` return type).

Step 6 shows that each of the test functions works and no panics or errors are reported.

Both libraries provide excellent ways to connect to remote web services, with `surf` having more features on the portability side (for example, various backends and WASM support), while `reqwest` is great for stable applications without `async` support and in need of cookies and proxies. For more information, read their respective documentations to match it to your project and use case. For now, let's move on to the next recipe.

Running machine learning models

Machine learning and especially deep learning has been a rising topic ever since AlexNet's triumph in 2012 (`https://papers.nips.cc/paper/4824-imagenet-classification-with-deep-convolutional-neural-networks.pdf`), with the language of choice being mostly Python for its easy-to-use syntax and flexibility. However, the underlying frameworks (TensorFlow, PyTorch, and more) are commonly built using C++, not only for performance reasons but also because accessing hardware (such as a GPU) is a lot easier. Rust has—so far—not been the language of choice to implement lower-level frameworks. Even outside the area of deep learning, Rust lacks library support in several areas including data preparation, classical machine learning, and optimization (progress is tracked here: `http://www.arewelearningyet.com/`)—so, why bother using Rust in any machine learning task?

The Rust community provides bindings to popular deep learning frameworks to a Rust API, allowing users to do some (limited) experimentation as well as using weights of known architectures for inference. While all of this is highly experimental, it represents a push in the right direction and it's fascinating to work with.

In the long run, we see Rust—as a low-level language—utilizing its low overhead and high performance to benefit the *deploying* of machine learning models (that is, model inference), targeting IoT-type devices with limited resources (for example, `https://github.com/snipsco/tract`). Until then, we can have some fun getting Rust's torch bindings to work. One example of using Rust in an efficient way for non-neural networks can be found at `https://blog.x5ff.xyz/blog/azure-functions-wasm-rust-ai/`.

Getting ready

This recipe cannot cover the details of how and why neural networks work, so we assume that you already have an idea what training and test datasets are, what a convolutional network does, and how loss functions together with an optimizer achieve model convergence. If that sentence didn't make sense to you, we recommend taking one of the many online courses such as the `https://www.fast.ai/` MOOC (`http://course.fast.ai/`), the Coursera machine learning course (`https://www.coursera.org/learn/machine-learning`), or Microsoft AI school (`https://aischool.microsoft.com/en-us/machine-learning/learning-paths`) before implementing this recipe. If you are ready to start, use a command-line Terminal to create a new Rust project by running `cargo new rusty-ml` and change into the `rusty-ml` directory to create a new directory, `models`.

To obtain the data, change into the `rusty-ml` directory and clone (or download and extract) Zalando Research's fashion MNIST (`https://research.zalando.com/welcome/mission/research-projects/fashion-mnist/`) repository from `https://github.com/zalandoresearch/fashion-mnist`. Ultimately, you should end up with three directories, namely, `models`, `fashion-mnist`, and `src` within the `rusty-ml` project directory.

 In the GitHub repository accompanying this book, the `fashion-mnist` repository is liked as a Git submodule (`https://git-scm.com/book/en/v2/Git-Tools-Submodules`). If you run `git submodule update --init` from within your local copy of the repository, it will download the `fashion-mnist` repository.

Before we can continue, we need to unzip the data files, which are located in `fashion-mnist/data/fashion`. On Linux/macOS, you can use `gunzip *.gz` from within this directory to extract all; on Windows, use your preferred tool to do the same.

The end result should look like this:

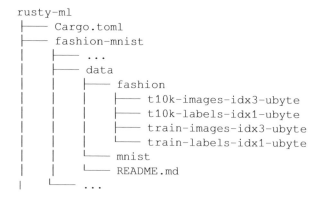

```
rusty-ml
├── Cargo.toml
├── fashion-mnist
│   ├── ...
│   ├── data
│   │   ├── fashion
│   │   │   ├── t10k-images-idx3-ubyte
│   │   │   ├── t10k-labels-idx1-ubyte
│   │   │   ├── train-images-idx3-ubyte
│   │   │   └── train-labels-idx1-ubyte
│   │   └── mnist
│   │   └── README.md
│   │
│   └── ...
```

```
├──── models
└──── src
      └──── main.rs
```

The original MNIST (`http://yann.lecun.com/exdb/mnist/`) is a dataset comprised of small images (28 x 28 pixels, grayscale) that show handwritten digits, and the goal was to classify them into classes from 0 to 9—that is, recognize the number. After 20 years, modern algorithms solve this task with exceedingly high accuracy, so it needed an upgrade—which is what Zalando, a fashion company located in Berlin, Germany, took on. The `fashion-mnist` dataset is a drop-in replacement for the original showing small clothing items instead of digits. The classification of these items is much harder, thanks to their intricate details that make up each item in the ten classes. The task is to correctly classify which class (out of ten) a clothing item belongs to. The classes include boots, sneakers, pants, t-shirts, and others.

In this recipe, we are going to train a very accurate (~90%) model to identify these items using Rust's PyTorch bindings, `tch-rs`.

How to do it...

Only a few steps are needed to train and use a neural network in Rust:

1. Open `Cargo.toml` to add the dependency for `tch-rs`:

   ```
   [dependencies]
   tch = "0.1"
   failure ="0.1"
   ```

2. Let's add some code for the imports to `src/main.rs` before diving deep:

   ```
   use std::io::{Error, ErrorKind};
   use std::path::Path;
   use std::time::Instant;
   use tch::{nn, nn::ModuleT, nn::OptimizerConfig, Device, Tensor};
   ```

3. PyTorch (and thereby, `tch-rs`) architectures typically store their layers individually, so we can store them in individual properties in `struct`:

```rust
#[derive(Debug)]
struct ConvNet {
    conv1: nn::Conv2D,
    conv2: nn::Conv2D,
    fc1: nn::Linear,
    fc2: nn::Linear,
}

impl ConvNet {
    fn new(vs: &nn::Path, labels: i64) -> ConvNet {
        ConvNet {
            conv1: nn::conv2d(vs, 1, 32, 5, Default::default()),
            conv2: nn::conv2d(vs, 32, 64, 5, Default::default()),
            fc1: nn::linear(vs, 1024, 512, Default::default()),
            fc2: nn::linear(vs, 512, labels, Default::default()),
        }
    }
}
```

4. For these layers to work together as a neural network, it requires a forward pass. The `nn` module of `tch` provides two traits (`Module` and `ModuleT`) that we can implement to do that. We decided on implementing `ModuleT`:

```rust
impl nn::ModuleT for ConvNet {
    fn forward_t(&self, xs: &Tensor, train: bool) -> Tensor {
        xs.view([-1, 1, 28, 28])
            .apply(&self.conv1)
            .relu()
            .max_pool2d_default(2)
            .apply(&self.conv2)
            .relu()
            .max_pool2d_default(2)
            .view([-1, 1024]) // flatten
            .apply(&self.fc1)
            .relu()
            .dropout_(0.5, train)
            .apply(&self.fc2)
    }
}
```

5. Next, we are going to implement the training loop. Other deep learning frameworks hide these bits from the user, but PyTorch allows us to understand the individual steps better by writing them from scratch. Add the following function to `src/main.rs`, starting with some data loading:

```
fn train_from_scratch(learning_rate: f64, batch_size: i64, epochs:
usize) -> failure::Fallible<()> {
    let data_path = Path::new("fashion-mnist/data/fashion");
    let model_path = Path::new("models/best.ot");

    if !data_path.exists() {
        println!(
            "Data not found at '{}'. Did you run '
            git submodule update --init'?",
            data_path.to_string_lossy()
        );
        return Err(Error::from(ErrorKind::NotFound).into());
    }

    println!("Loading data from '{}'",
data_path.to_string_lossy());
    let m = tch::vision::mnist::load_dir(data_path)?;
```

Then, we instantiate two important things: `VarStore` where everything gets saved in `tch`, and `ConvNet`, which we declared earlier:

```
let vs = nn::VarStore::new(Device::cuda_if_available());
let net = ConvNet::new(&vs.root(), 10);
let opt = nn::Adam::default().build(&vs, learning_rate)?;

println!(
    "Starting training, saving model to '{}'",
    model_path.to_string_lossy()
);
```

Once we have that, we can use a loop to iterate over the training data in (random) batches, feeding them into the network, computing the loss, and running the back propagation:

```
let mut min_loss = ::std::f32::INFINITY;
for epoch in 1..=epochs {
    let start = Instant::now();

    let mut losses = vec![];

    // Batched training, otherwise we would run out of memory
    for (image_batch, label_batch) in m.train_iter(
```

```
        batch_size).shuffle().to_device(vs.device())
    {
        let loss = net
            .forward_t(&image_batch, true)
            .cross_entropy_for_logits(&label_batch);
        opt.backward_step(&loss);

        losses.push(f32::from(loss));
    }
    let total_loss = losses.iter().sum::<f32>() /
                    (losses.len() as f32);
```

After going through the entire training set, we then test the model on the entire test set. Since this should not influence the model performance, we skip the backpropagation this time:

```
// Predict the test set without using batches
let test_accuracy = net
    .forward_t(&m.test_images, false)
    .accuracy_for_logits(&m.test_labels);
```

Finally, we print some statistics so we know whether we are on the right track, but only after we save the current best model weights (that is, where the loss is the lowest):

```
// Checkpoint
if total_loss <= min_loss {
    vs.save(model_path)?;
    min_loss = total_loss;
}

// Output for the user
println!(
    "{:4} | train loss: {:7.4} | test acc: {:5.2}%
    | duration: {}s",
    epoch,
    &total_loss,
    100. * f64::from(&test_accuracy),
    start.elapsed().as_secs()
    );
    }
    println!(
        "Done! The best model was saved to '{}'",
        model_path.to_string_lossy()
    );
    Ok(())
}
```

6. After having a trained model, you typically also want to run inference on other images (that is, predict stuff). The next function takes the best model's weights and applies it to the `ConvNet` architecture:

```
fn predict_from_best() -> failure::Fallible<()> {
    let data_path = Path::new("fashion-mnist/data/fashion");
    let model_weights_path = Path::new("models/best.ot");

    let m = tch::vision::mnist::load_dir(data_path)?;
    let mut vs = nn::VarStore::new(Device::cuda_if_available());
    let net = ConvNet::new(&vs.root(), 10);

    // restore weights
    println!(
        "Loading model weights from '{}'",
        model_weights_path.to_string_lossy()
    );
    vs.load(model_weights_path)?;
```

With this model in place, we can then take a random subset of the training data and run inference:

```
println!("Probabilities and predictions
        for 10 random images in the test set");
for (image_batch, label_batch) in m.test_iter(1)
    .shuffle().to_device(vs.device()).take(10) {
    let raw_tensor = net
        .forward_t(&image_batch, false)
        .softmax(-1)
        .view(m.labels);
    let predicted_index: Vec<i64> =
        raw_tensor.argmax(0, false).into();
    let probabilities: Vec<f64> = raw_tensor.into();

    print!("[ ");
    for p in probabilities {
        print!("{:.4} ", p);
    }
    let label: Vec<i64> = label_batch.into();
    println!("] predicted {}, was {}",
            predicted_index[0], label[0]);
}
Ok(())
}
```

7. The `main` function ties it all together and trains a model before calling the inference function:

```
fn main() -> failure::Fallible<()> {
    train_from_scratch(1e-2, 1024, 5)?;
    predict_from_best()?;
    Ok(())
}
```

8. That's exciting! Let's train a model for a few epochs to see decreasing loss and increasing test accuracy scores:

```
$ cargo run
    Finished dev [unoptimized + debuginfo] target(s) in 0.19s
     Running `target/debug/rusty-ml`
Loading data from 'fashion-mnist/data/fashion'
Starting training, saving model to 'models/best.ot'
    1 | train loss: 1.1559 | test acc: 82.87% | duration: 29s
    2 | train loss: 0.4132 | test acc: 86.70% | duration: 32s
    3 | train loss: 0.3383 | test acc: 88.41% | duration: 32s
    4 | train loss: 0.3072 | test acc: 89.16% | duration: 29s
    5 | train loss: 0.2869 | test acc: 89.36% | duration: 28s
Done! The best model was saved to 'models/best.ot'
Loading model weights from 'models/best.ot'
Probabilities and predictions for 10 random images in the test set
[ 0.0000 1.0000 0.0000 0.0000 0.0000 0.0000 0.0000 0.0000 0.0000
0.0000 ] predicted 1, was 1
[ 0.5659 0.0001 0.0254 0.0013 0.0005 0.0000 0.4062 0.0000 0.0005
0.0000 ] predicted 0, was 0
[ 0.0003 0.0000 0.9699 0.0000 0.0005 0.0000 0.0292 0.0000 0.0000
0.0000 ] predicted 2, was 2
[ 0.0000 1.0000 0.0000 0.0000 0.0000 0.0000 0.0000 0.0000 0.0000
0.0000 ] predicted 1, was 1
[ 0.6974 0.0000 0.0008 0.0001 0.0000 0.0000 0.3017 0.0000 0.0000
0.0000 ] predicted 0, was 0
[ 0.0333 0.0028 0.1053 0.7098 0.0420 0.0002 0.1021 0.0007 0.0038
0.0001 ] predicted 3, was 2
[ 0.0110 0.0146 0.0014 0.9669 0.0006 0.0000 0.0038 0.0003 0.0012
0.0000 ] predicted 3, was 3
[ 0.0003 0.0001 0.0355 0.0014 0.9487 0.0001 0.0136 0.0001 0.0004
0.0000 ] predicted 4, was 4
[ 0.0000 0.0000 0.0000 0.0000 0.0000 0.0000 0.0000 1.0000 0.0000
0.0000 ] predicted 7, was 7
[ 0.0104 0.0091 0.0037 0.8320 0.0915 0.0001 0.0505 0.0002 0.0026
0.0000 ] predicted 3, was 3
```

This was a very interesting detour into the world of machine learning. Let's find out more about it.

How it works...

Deep learning in Rust works—however, it comes with many strings attached. `tch-rs` (`https://github.com/LaurentMazare/tch-rs`) is a great framework if you already know some PyTorch and it lets you get into it right away. However, anyone who is new to the idea of machine learning should look at Python (and PyTorch) to get comfortable with the type of thinking that is required. `tch-rs` uses the C++ foundation of the Python version and provides a thin wrapper around the bindings it created. This means two things:

- Most ideas of the Python version should apply to `tch-rs`.
- The extensive C++ usage is likely *very* unsafe.

By using bindings, wrapped code is much more likely to leave some kind of memory unfreed thanks to the added layer of abstraction and the changed programming paradigms in the host language. For applications such as machine learning, where tens (or even hundreds) of gigabytes of memory usage is not uncommon, a memory leak has a much larger impact. However, it's great to see it working so well already and we expect that this project will go much further.

 We made a few simplifications to the model training process for brevity. It's recommended to do some research into how to properly evaluate a model and rule out overfitting before going any further with it.

In *step 1*, we set up the `tch` dependency to resolve the imports we use in *step 2*. *Step 3* is where things get interesting (model architecture). Deep learning is a set of matrix multiplications, where—technically speaking—the input and output dimensions have to match for it to work. Since PyTorch (`https://pytorch.org/`) is famously low-level, we have to set the individual layers up and match their dimensions by hand. In this case, we use two layers of 2-dimensional convolutions with two dense layers at the end to make sense of what the convolutions found. When we initialize the network in the `new()` function, we assign the input size, number of neurons/filters, and output/layers to the instantiation (`nn::conv2d` and `nn::linear`) functions. As you can see, the numbers match between the layers for it to be able to concatenate them, while the last layer outputs exactly the number of classes we are looking for (10).

Tensors are a generalized version of vectors in mathematics. They can be anything from a single number (scalar) to a multi-dimensional vector of vectors. Read more at http://mathworld.wolfram.com/Tensor.html (warning: lots of math).

In *step 4*, we implement the forward process provided by the nn::ModuleT trait. The difference to nn::Module is the train parameter, which indicates whether this run is intended for training in the forward_t() function. The other parameter in that function is the actual data represented as an nn::Tensor reference. Before we can use it, we have to assign a structure to it, and, since we are dealing with (grayscale) images, the choice is straightforward: it's a 4-dimensional tensor. The dimensions are assigned as follows:

- The first dimension is the batch, so there are zero to batchsize number of images in there.
- The second dimension represents the number of channels in the image, which is one for grayscale but three for RGB.
- In the last two dimensions, we are storing the actual image, so they are the image's width and height.

So, as we call the .view() function on the tensor instance, we are changing the interpretation to these dimensions, with -1 meaning whatever fits (typical for batch size). From there on, we are dealing with a bunch of 28 x 28 x 1 images that we feed into the first convolutional layer and apply the **Rectified Linear Unit (ReLU)** (https://machinelearningmastery.com/rectified-linear-activation-function-for-deep-learning-neural-networks/) function on the outcome. That follows a 2-dimensional max pooling layer, after which the pattern is repeated for the second convolutional layer. This is common to control the output sizes of a convolutional layer. After the second max pooling, we flatten the output vector (1,024 is a calculated value: https://medium.com/@iamvarman/how-to-calculate-the-number-of-parameters-in-the-cnn-5bd55364d7ca) and apply the fully connected layers one after the other with a ReLU function in between. The raw output of the last layer is then returned as a tensor.

In the training loop in *step 5*, we start off by reading the data from disk, using a predefined dataset function. We are taking advantage of this since the MNIST data is very common in machine learning examples. Ultimately, this is an iterator over the data (in this case, images) that comes with a few handy functions attached. In fact, there are multiple iterators since the data is already split into training and test sets.

Once loaded, we create an `nn::VarStore`, which is a `tch-rs` concept to store the model weights. This `VarStore` instance is passed into our model architecture struct, `ConvNet`, and the optimizer, so that it can do the backpropagation (Adam (`https://arxiv.org/abs/1412.6980`) is a stochastic optimizer and, as of early 2019, considered state of the art). Since PyTorch allows moving data between devices (that is CPU versus GPU), we always have to assign a device to weights and data so the framework knows which memory to write to.

The `learning_rate` parameter represents a step size of how far the optimizer jumps toward the best solution. This parameter is almost always very small (for example, `1e-2`) because choosing a larger value might overshoot its goal and worsen the solution, and a too-small value could mean it never gets there. Read more at `https://www.jeremyjordan.me/nn-learning-rate/`.

Next in the training loop, we have to implement the actual loop. This loop runs for several epochs and, generally, a higher number means more convergence (for example, overfitting: `https://machinelearningmastery.com/overfitting-and-underfitting-with-machine-learning-algorithms/`), but the number we chose (5) in this recipe is definitely too low and chosen for the training to finish quickly with tangible results. Try a higher number and see how (whether) the model improves! Within each epoch, we can then run through the shuffled batches (a convenience function provided by the dataset implementation), run the forward pass and compute the loss for each batch. The loss function—cross entropy (`https://pytorch.org/docs/stable/nn.html#crossentropyloss`)—comes back with a number that lets us know how far off we were with the prediction, which is important for running the backpropagation. In this example, we chose a large batch size of 1,024 images in one go, meaning that it has to run the loop 59 times for each epoch. This speeds up the process without too much of an impact on the training quality—if you can fit everything into memory.

Think of a loss function as a function to determine how wrong the model was. Typically, we choose a predefined loss function based on the type of problem (regression, binary classification, or multi-class classification). Cross entropy is the default for multi-class classification.

As we are walking through the batches, we also want to know how we are doing, which is why we created a simple vector to store the average loss per batch. Plotting the losses per epoch, we get a typical shape where the loss levels off toward zero:

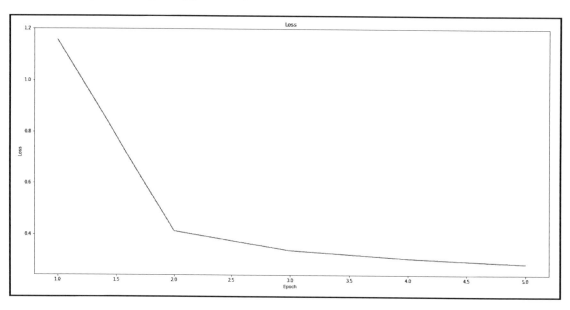

Since the algorithm has seen the training data, we need some test data to see whether it actually improved or whether it just learned to recognize the training data really well. This is why the test set is done without backpropagation and calculates the accuracy directly.

It is generally recommended to have a three-way split of your data (https://machinelearningmastery.com/difference-test-validation-datasets/). A training set that the model learns on should make up the majority, a test set that should show progress and overfitting after every epoch, and, finally, another set of data that the network has never seen before. The last one is to make sure that it performs as expected on real-world data and it must not be used to change any parameter in training. Confusingly, the naming of these three is sometimes training, validation, test (respectively) as well as training, test, validation.

In a strategy known as checkpointing, we then save the best model to disk as soon as the loss it produces is lower than what we had before. When training 200 epochs, the loss function likely shows several spikes as the model learns wrong features and we don't want to lose the best model so far. Once done with the training for one epoch, we want to print out something to see if the model converges as expected.

In *step 6*, we repeat some of the setup processes for loading the data, but, instead of training the architecture, we simply load the weights of the network from disk. The weights are the parts that we trained in the previous step and, in an inference-only scenario, we would train somewhere else and simply transfer the weights to where we classify real-world data (or load the entire model with something like ONNX: `https://onnx.ai/`).

To illustrate the prediction process, we are using the test set (again)—something that should be avoided in practice, since the model has to work on unseen data just as well as the data used in training. We take 10 random images (in 10 batches of size 1), run the forward pass, and then use a function called softmax to derive probabilities from the raw network output. After an application of `.view()` to align the data to the labels, we print the probabilities to the command line for us to see. Since these are probabilities, taking the index with the highest probability is the network's prediction. Since we used a dataset implementation, we can trust that these indices align with the input labels.

Step 7 calls the functions in order and we get to see some training and predictions in the *step 8* output. As described in the *step 5* explanation, we print the loss (for this machine, each line took about 30 seconds to appear) and training accuracy. After the training is done, we know where the best model weights are located and use those to run the inference and print out the probability matrix.

Each line in that matrix represents the possible outcomes with probabilities assigned to each class—and, while it is 100% certain in the first line, the second line is a closer call (57% for class 0 and 40% for class 6). The sixth example has been wrongly predicted, and unfortunately, the model was fairly confident as well (71% for class 3 and 11% for class 2), which leads us to believe that more training is required.

We encourage you to play around a little bit with the parameters to see how the outcomes can change quickly (for better or worse), or if you are more experienced, to build a better architecture. Regardless of what you are doing, `tch-rs` is an interesting way of using deep learning in Rust and we hope that it develops further so we can use it for a range of tasks in machine learning.

Now that we know more about machine learning in Rust, let's move on to more tangible things in the next recipe.

Configuring and using logging

While sending debug and other information out to the console is popular and easy, chances are that it becomes confusing and chaotic beyond a certain complexity. This includes the lack of a standardized date/time or origin class or inconsistent formatting, making it hard to trace an execution path through the system. Moreover, recent systems focus on logs as an additional source for information: how many users did we serve each hour of the day? Where did they come from? What was the 95th percentile response time?

 Due to printing constraints we had to replace the original emoji with their names. Check out the GitHub repository for this book for the full version.

These questions can be answered with diligent logging using a framework that provides consistent and configurable output that can be easily parsed and shipped to a log analytics service. Let's create a simple Rust application that logs data in a variety of ways.

How to do it...

Follow the steps to create and use a custom logger:

1. Open a Terminal to create a new project using `cargo new logging`. Use VS Code to open the project directory.

2. As a first step, we adapt `Cargo.toml` to include our new dependencies:

```
[dependencies]
log = "0.4"
log4rs = "0.8.3"
time = "0.1"
```

3. Then, in `src/main.rs`, we can import the required macros:

```
use log::{debug, error, info, trace, warn};
```

4. Before getting into more complex things, let's add a function that shows us how to use the macros we just imported:

```
fn log_some_stuff() {
    let a = 100;

    trace!("TRACE: Called log_some_stuff()");
    debug!("DEBUG: a = {} ", a);
```

```
    info!("INFO: The weather is fine");
    warn!("WARNING, stuff is breaking down");
    warn!(target: "special-target", "WARNING, stuff is breaking
down");
    error!("ERROR: stopping ...");
}
```

5. These macros work because they are pre-configured by the logging framework. Consequently, if we are configuring the logging, it has to be done globally—for example, in the `main` function:

```
const USE_CUSTOM: bool = false;

fn main() {
    if USE_CUSTOM {
    log::set_logger(&LOGGER)
        .map(|()| log::set_max_level(log::LevelFilter::Trace))
        .unwrap();
    } else {
        log4rs::init_file("log4rs.yml",
Default::default()).unwrap();
    }
    log_some_stuff();
}
```

6. By using `log4rs::init_file()`, we use a YAML configuration that can be changed without recompiling the program. Before continuing in `src/main.rs`, we should create `log4rs.yml` like this (the YAML format is picky about indentations):

```
refresh_rate: 30 seconds

appenders:
  stdout:
    kind: console

  outfile:
    kind: file
    path: "outfile.log"
    encoder:
      pattern: "{d} - {m}{n}"

root:
  level: trace
  appenders:
    - stdout
```

```
loggers:
  special-target:
    level: info
    appenders:
      - outfile
```

7. Back to `src/main.rs`: we saw an ability to create and use a fully custom logger. For that, we create a nested module in `src/main.rs` and implement our logger there:

```
mod custom {
    pub use log::Level;
    use log::{Metadata, Record};

    pub struct EmojiLogger {
        pub level: Level,
    }
```

Once we have defined the imports and basic `struct`, we can implement the `log::Log` trait for our new `EmojiLogger` type:

```
impl log::Log for EmojiLogger {

    fn flush(&self) {}

    fn enabled(&self, metadata: &Metadata) -> bool {
        metadata.level() <= self.level
    }

    fn log(&self, record: &Record) {
        if self.enabled(record.metadata()) {
            let level = match record.level() {
                Level::Warn => "WARNING-SIGN",
                Level::Info => "INFO-SIGN",
                Level::Debug => "CATERPILLAR",
                Level::Trace => "LIGHTBULB",
                Level::Error => "NUCLEAR",
            };
            let utc = time::now_utc();
            println!("{} | [{}] | {:<5}",
                    utc.rfc3339(), record.target(), level);
            println!("{:21} {}", "", record.args());
        }
    }
}
```

8. To avoid any lifetime conflicts, we want the logger to have a static lifetime (`https://doc.rust-lang.org/reference/items/static-items.html`), so let's instantiate and declare the variable using Rust's `static` keyword:

```
static LOGGER: custom::EmojiLogger = custom::EmojiLogger {
    level: log::Level::Trace,
};
```

9. Let's execute `cargo run`, first with the `USE_CUSTOM` constant (created in *step 5*) set to `false`, which tells the program to read and use the `log4rs.yaml` configuration, instead of the custom module:

```
$ cargo run
 Finished dev [unoptimized + debuginfo] target(s) in 0.04s
    Running `target/debug/logging`
2019-09-01T12:42:18.056681073+02:00 TRACE logging - TRACE: Called
log_some_stuff()
2019-09-01T12:42:18.056764247+02:00 DEBUG logging - DEBUG: a = 100
2019-09-01T12:42:18.056791639+02:00 INFO logging - INFO: The
weather is fine
2019-09-01T12:42:18.056816420+02:00 WARN logging - WARNING, stuff
is breaking down
2019-09-01T12:42:18.056881011+02:00 ERROR logging - ERROR: stopping
...
```

In addition to that, we configured it so that, if something gets logged to `special-target`, we append it to a file called `outfile.log`. Let's see what's in there as well:

```
2019-09-01T12:45:25.256922311+02:00 - WARNING, stuff is breaking
down
```

10. Now that we have used the `log4rs` default logger, let's see what our own logging class does. Set `USE_CUSTOM` (from *step 5*) to `true` and use `cargo run` to create the following output:

```
$ cargo run
   Compiling logging v0.1.0 (Rust-Cookbook/Chapter10/logging)
    Finished dev [unoptimized + debuginfo] target(s) in 0.94s
     Running `target/debug/logging`
2019-09-01T10:46:43Z | [logging] | LIGHTBULB
                       TRACE: Called log_some_stuff()
2019-09-01T10:46:43Z | [logging] | CATERPILLAR
                       DEBUG: a = 100
2019-09-01T10:46:43Z | [logging] | INFO-SIGN
                       INFO: The weather is fine
2019-09-01T10:46:43Z | [logging] | WARNING-SIGN
```

```
                                    WARNING, stuff is breaking down
            2019-09-01T10:46:43Z | [special-target] | WARNING-SIGN
                                    WARNING, stuff is breaking down
            2019-09-01T10:46:43Z | [logging] | NUCLEAR
                                    ERROR: stopping ...
```

Now that we have seen it at work, let's dive into why this is the case.

How it works...

In this more complex example, we are using Rust's logging infrastructure, which consists of two main parts:

- The log crate (https://github.com/rust-lang-nursery/log), which provides the facade (interface) to the logging macros
- A logging implementor such as log4rs (https://github.com/sfackler/log4rs), env_logger (https://github.com/sebasmagri/env_logger/), or similar (https://docs.rs/log/0.4.8/log/#available-logging-implementations)

After the initial setup in *steps 1* and *2*, we simply have to import the macros provided by the log crate in *step 3*—nothing more. As we create a function to write to all available log levels (think of the levels as tags to filter by) and an additional target in this line in *step 4* (as shown in the following), we cover most of the use cases for logging:

```
warn!(target: "special-target", "WARNING, stuff is breaking down");
```

Step 5 sets up the logging framework, log4rs, a crate that is modeled after the de-facto standard in the Java world: log4j (https://logging.apache.org/log4j/2.x/). The crate provides excellent flexibility when it comes to where to write which log levels and using what format, and it can be changed at runtime. Check the *step 6* configuration file to see an example. There we define refresh_rate (when to rescan the file for changes) of 30 seconds, which enables us to change the file without having to restart the application. Next, we define two appenders, which means output targets. The first one, stdout, is a simple console output, whereas outfile produces outfile.log, which we show in *step 10*. Its encoder property also hints toward how we can change the formatting.

Next, we defined a `root` logger, which represents the default. Having `trace` as the default level leads to excessive logging in many cases; having `warn` is often enough, especially in production settings. Additional loggers are created in the loggers property, where each child (`special-target`) represents a target we can use in the log macro (as seen in the preceding). These targets come with a configurable log level (`info`, in this case) and can use a range of appenders to write to. There are many more options that you can use here—just check out the documentation on how to set up more complex scenarios.

In *step 7*, we return to Rust code and create our own logger. This logger implements the log crate's `Log` trait directly and translates any incoming `log::Record` into an emoji-backed console output for our visual entertainment. By implementing `enabled()`, we can filter whether any calls to `log()` are made and therefore base our decisions on more than just simple log levels as well. We instantiate the `EmojiLogger` struct in *step 8* as a static variable (`https://doc.rust-lang.org/reference/items/static-items.html`), which is passed into the `log::set_logger()` function whenever we set the `USE_CUSTOM` constant (*step 5*) to `true`. *Step 9* and *step 10* show these two outcomes:

- The `log4rs` default format includes the module, log level, timestamp, and message, and it creates the `outfile.log` file we configured it to.
- Our custom logger creates unusual formatting along with an emoji showing the log levels—just as we wanted.

The `log` crate is particularly useful in Rust since it allows you to attach your own loggers to third-party crates as well. The crates for issuing web requests in this chapter (in the *Sending web requests* recipe) provide infrastructure (`https://docs.rs/surf/1.0.2/surf/middleware/logger/index.html`) to do that, just like many other crates do (for example, `actix-web` in an earlier chapter). This means that, just by adding a dependency and a few lines of code, you can already create an application completely with logging.

This concludes our detour into logging, so let's move on to another recipe.

Starting subprocesses

Pipelines, container orchestration, and command-line tools all share a common task: they all have to start and monitor other programs. These system calls are done in a variety of ways in other technologies, so let's call a few standard programs with Rust's `Command` interface.

How to do it...

Follow these quick steps to call on external programs:

1. Open a Terminal to create a new project using `cargo new sub-processes`. Use VS Code to open the project directory.

2. Open `src/main.rs`. Rust's standard library comes with an external command interface built-in, but first, let's import it:

```
use std::error::Error;
use std::io::Write;
use std::process::{Command, Stdio};
```

3. Once imported, we can do the rest in the `main` function. We'll start off by calling `ls` with some arguments in two different directories:

```
fn main() -> Result<(), Box<dyn Error + Send + Sync + 'static>> {
    let mut ls_child = Command::new("ls");
    if !cfg!(target_os = "windows") {
        ls_child.args(&["-alh"]);
    }
    println!("{}", ls_child.status()?);
    ls_child.current_dir("src/");
    println!("{}", ls_child.status()?);
```

In the next step, we are setting environment variables in the subprocess and, by grabbing the standard output of the env program, we can check whether it worked:

```
let env_child = Command::new("env")
    .env("CANARY", "0x5ff")
    .stdout(Stdio::piped())
    .spawn()?;
let env_output = &env_child.wait_with_output()?;
let canary = String::from_utf8_lossy(&env_output.stdout)
.split_ascii_whitespace()
.filter(|line| *line == "CANARY=0x5ff")
.count();

// found it!
assert_eq!(canary, 1);
```

`rev` is a program that reverses anything that comes in via standard input and it's available on Windows and Linux/Unix. Let's call it with some text and capture the output:

```
let mut rev_child = Command::new("rev")
    .stdin(Stdio::piped())
    .stdout(Stdio::piped())
    .spawn()?;


{
    rev_child
        .stdin
        .as_mut()
        .expect("Could not open stdin")
        .write_all(b"0x5ff")?;
}

let output = rev_child.wait_with_output()?;
assert_eq!(String::from_utf8_lossy(&output.stdout), "ff5x0");

Ok(())
}
```

4. Use `cargo run` to see the program print the `ls` output (your output will look a little different):

```
$ cargo run
    Compiling sub-processes v0.1.0 (Rust-Cookbook/Chapter10/sub-
processes)
    Finished dev [unoptimized + debuginfo] target(s) in 0.44s
     Running `target/debug/sub-processes`
total 24K
drwxr-xr-x. 4 cm cm 4.0K Aug 26 09:21 .
drwxr-xr-x. 13 cm cm 4.0K Aug 11 23:27 ..
-rw-r--r--. 1 cm cm 145 Aug 26 09:21 Cargo.lock
-rw-r--r--. 1 cm cm 243 Jul 26 10:23 Cargo.toml
drwxr-xr-x. 2 cm cm 4.0K Jul 26 10:23 src
drwxr-xr-x. 3 cm cm 4.0K Aug 26 09:21 target
exit code: 0
total 12K
drwxr-xr-x. 2 cm cm 4.0K Jul 26 10:23 .
drwxr-xr-x. 4 cm cm 4.0K Aug 26 09:21 ..
-rw-r--r--. 1 cm cm 1.1K Aug 31 11:49 main.rs
exit code: 0
```

Windows users have to run this program in PowerShell, where `ls` is available.

Let's see how it works behind the scenes.

How it works...

This recipe quickly covers some abilities of the Rust `std::process::Command` struct. After setting everything up in *steps 1* and *2*, we create the `main` function in *step 3*. Using `Result<(), Box<dyn Error + ...>>` with a boxed `dyn` trait (https://doc.rust-lang.org/edition-guide/rust-2018/trait-system/dyn-trait-for-trait-objects.html) as the return type for the main function allows us to use the `?` operator instead of `unwrap()`, `expect()`, or other constructs—regardless of the actual error type.

We start off by using the `ls` command, which lists the directory contents. Except for Windows, the program takes arguments to expand the output:

- `-l` adds additional information such as permissions, date, and size (also called a long listing).
- `-a` includes hidden files as well (a stands for all).
- `-h` uses human-friendly sizes (for example, KiB after 1,000 bytes).

For `ls`, we can pass these flags as one large flag, `-alh`, (the order doesn't matter) and the `args()` function allows us to do that as a string slice. The actual execution of the process child is only done when we check the `status()` function of the instance and, here, we are also printing the results. The status code (on Linux) represents the success or failure of a particular program when it's `zero` or `non-zero` respectively.

The next part catches the standard output of the program and sets an environment variable for it. Environment variables can be a great way to transfer data or settings to the subprogram as well (for example, compiler flags for builds and keys for command-line APIs). `env` (https://linux.die.net/man/1/env) is a program on Linux (with a PowerShell equivalent) that prints available environment variables, so when we capture standard output, we can try to find the variable and its value.

The next part passes data to the `rev` program through the standard input while catching standard output. `rev` simply reverses the input data, so we expect the output to be the reverse of the input. There are two interesting things to note:

- Getting a handle for standard input is scoped to avoid violating borrowing rules.
- Writing and reading from the pipes is done in bytes, which requires parsing to convert from/into a string. The `String::from_utf8_lossy()` function does that while ignoring invalid data.

After that, the `main` function returns with a positive empty result (`Ok(())`).

In the last step, as usual, we run the code to see whether it works and, although we only have two `println!()` statements with only the exit code of the `ls` command in our source file, there is a lot of output. This is due to the default setting of passing a subprocess's standard output through the console. What we see here is, therefore, the output of the `ls -alh` command on Linux, which will be a little different on your machine.

Having successfully created and run several commands using Rust, we can now go out and create our own applications. We hope that this book helped you with that.

Other Books You May Enjoy

If you enjoyed this book, you may be interested in these other books by Packt:

Hands-On Data Structures and Algorithms with Rust
Claus Matzinger

ISBN: 978-1-78899-552-8

- Design and implement complex data structures in Rust
- Analyze, implement, and improve searching and sorting algorithms in Rust
- Create and use well-tested and reusable components with Rust
- Understand the basics of multithreaded programming and advanced algorithm design
- Become familiar with application profiling based on benchmarking and testing
- Explore the borrowing complexity of implementing algorithms

Mastering Rust - Second Edition
Rahul Sharma, Vesa Kaihlavirta

ISBN: 978-1-78934-657-2

- Write generic and type-safe code by using Rust's powerful type system
- How memory safety works without garbage collection
- Know the different strategies in error handling and when to use them
- Learn how to use concurrency primitives such as threads and channels
- Use advanced macros to reduce boilerplate code
- Create efficient web applications with the Actix-web framework
- Use Diesel for type-safe database interactions in your web application

Leave a review - let other readers know what you think

Please share your thoughts on this book with others by leaving a review on the site that you bought it from. If you purchased the book from Amazon, please leave us an honest review on this book's Amazon page. This is vital so that other potential readers can see and use your unbiased opinion to make purchasing decisions, we can understand what our customers think about our products, and our authors can see your feedback on the title that they have worked with Packt to create. It will only take a few minutes of your time, but is valuable to other potential customers, our authors, and Packt. Thank you!

Index

Made in the USA
San Bernardino, CA
27 November 2019